30 RIGHTS OF MUSLIM WOMEN

30 RIGHTS *of* MUSLIM WOMEN

A TRUSTED GUIDE

• • • • • • • • •

DAISY KHAN

PREFACE BY
AFRA JALABI, PhD

Monkfish Book Publishing Company
Rhinebeck, New York

30 Rights of Muslim Women: A Trusted Guide Copyright © 2024 by Daisy Khan

All rights reserved. No part of this book may be used or reproduced in any manner without the consent of the publisher except in critical articles or reviews. Contact the publisher for information.

"The Clear Quran® is translated by Dr. Mustafa Khattab" and is a registered trademark of Al-Furqaan Foundation.® "The Clear Quran® translation used in this book is printed with permission from Al-Furqaan Foundation and its publishing divisions. No part of this translation can be reproduced without the explicit written consent of Al-Furqaan Foundation. Direct all licensing of The Clear Quran® to www.theclearquran.org."

Following a common custom, all verses quoted from the Holy Quran are presented in this book in italics.

Paperback ISBN 978-1-958972-33-5
eBook ISBN 978-1-958972-34-2

Library of Congress Cataloging-in-Publication Data

Names: Khan, Daisy, author. | Jalabi, Afra, writer of introduction.
Title: 30 rights of Muslim women : the definitive guide / Daisy Khan ; preface by Afra Jalabi, PhD.
Other titles: Thirty rights of Muslim women
Description: Rhinebeck : Monkfish Book Publishing Company, 2024. | Includes bibliographical references.
Identifiers: LCCN 2023051297 (print) | LCCN 2023051298 (ebook) | ISBN 9781958972335 (paperback) | ISBN 9781958972342 (ebook)
Subjects: LCSH: Women's rights--Religious aspects--Islam. | Muslim women--Legal status, laws, etc.
Classification: LCC HQ1170 .K4387 2024 (print) | LCC HQ1170 (ebook) | DDC 297.5/7082--dc23/eng/20231106
LC record available at https://lccn.loc.gov/2023051297
LC ebook record available at https://lccn.loc.gov/2023051298

Front cover graphic by Feyza Oytan
Book design by Colin Rolfe

Monkfish Book Publishing Company
22 East Market Street, Suite 304
Rhinebeck, New York 12572
(845) 876-4861
monkfishpublishing.com

CONTENTS

Preface: Divine Dialogue with Women, by Afra Jalabi, PhD   vii
Introduction   xi
    How to Use This Book   xii
    Quranic Basis for Women's Equality   xiv
    At a Glance: 30 Rights of Muslim Women   xvi

PART I: THE RIGHT TO PROTECTION AND PROMOTION OF MIND   1
    #1. To Civic/Political Leadership   3
    #2. To Secular Education   12
    #3. To Career Pursuit   25
    #4. To Freedom of Speech and Expression   33
    #5. To Testimony and Witness   42

PART II: THE RIGHT TO YOUR RELIGION   51
    #6. To Religious and Spiritual Leadership   53
    #7. To Be Jurists and Interpreters of Islamic Texts   68
    #8. To Gain Spiritual Knowledge   76
    #9. To Access Religious Spaces   86

PART III: THE RIGHT TO YOUR FAMILY   99
    #10. To Marriage   101
    #11. To Be Free of Forced Marriage   114
    #12. To Maturely Choose Marriage   122
    #13. To Accept or Refuse a Polygamous Marriage   132
    #14. To Divorce   143
    #15. To Family Planning and Reproductive Justice   153
    #16. To Care for Orphans through Adoption   163
    #17. To Motherhood and Womanhood   171

PART IV: THE RIGHT TO YOUR WEALTH   181
    #18. To Inheritance   183

#19. To Financial Independence and Equal Pay	192
#20. To Own Property	201

PART V: THE RIGHT TO YOUR LIFE — 209

#21. To Freedom of Movement	211
#22. To Expression of Modesty	222
#23. To Freedom from Domestic Violence	234
#24. To Safeguard against FGM	243
#25. To Protection from Rape, Sexual Assault, and Adultery	252
#26. To Safeguard against Child and Human Trafficking	262
#27. To Health and Hygiene	270

PART VI: THE RIGHT TO YOUR DIGNITY — 279

#28. To Fulfill Being a Trustee of God on Earth	281
#29. To Freedom from Gossip, Slander, Libel, Defamation, and to Privacy	287
#30. To Safeguard Honor	297

Resources: Toolkit and Public Awareness	304
Acknowledgments	307
Notes	309

PREFACE | DIVINE DIALOGUE WITH WOMEN

The Quran celebrates the feminine voice and gives it power to argue, discuss, and contest in a chapter titled *Al Mujadalah* that invites back the female voice to the conversation. But before we get into the story of *Al Mujadalah*, let's ask a few questions that will direct this conversation.

How do women navigate their historical archaeologies and use their voices to enhance the journey of justice? Can we walk these values in our own lives and create new forms of thought and Islamic *fiqh*, to serve justice better in our present moment?

These questions are not new. Women have been contesting, arguing, and questioning male authority and injustices for centuries, more so in a focused and articulated manner in the last few decades, but also going perhaps far into the past if we get to hop on a time machine and travel through time.

The Quran takes us on such a trip, to a moment in which this happens, during Prophet Muhammad's time, and turns it into sacred scripture, devoting a whole chapter (*surah*) to the subject, titled Al Mujadalah (The Argument). The verse deals with the story of a woman named Khawlah bint Thalaba who comes to Prophet Muhammad to discuss how her husband, Aws bin al-Samit abandoned her using a pre-Islamic custom, declaring her a "mother" to him, and therefore terminating the relationship. The Quranic narrative unfolds in a manner that requires reflection.

"[G]od has heard the word of that who is arguing with you concerning her husband, raising her complaint to God. And God hears your dialogue; For God is ever listening and constantly the seer." (Quran 58:1)

The passage deals with word, argument, and complaint, but from the divine perspective the conversation is heard as dialogue (*hiwar*) elevating the woman's argument, the problem she raises, and the whole dynamic into a form in which justice is being sought, and hence the

Quran re-casts it as a vehicle that reaches the divine. The verse is about the power of our arguments, proportionally measured in relation to their ethical content. Imagine Khawla, an Arabian woman 1,400 years ago is arguing about men's injustices but is heard by God as dialogue.

The Quran invites us to live with an ethical stance that accepts nothing less than justice, *and* to strive to rise up to a higher level of compassion. Anything less violates our ethical commitments as Muslims. Therefore, critical thinking (*ijtihad*), and creativity are not luxuries but necessities if one wants to respond to the divine command of justice and compassion. This is why it is important to think, reflect, and be accountable to justice in whichever contexts we find ourselves in. As Muslim women, it is not only a right to think, contest, and contribute, but rather a duty before God, because only with *juhd* (effort) could *ijtihad* (legal thinking) take form and serve justice.

Accepting the invitation to connect to the Divine, to reach out, to ask, and to question is a serious matter. A couple of years before the event of Khawlah, the wife of Prophet Muhammad, Um Salamah, had a daring question. She asked the Prophet, "Why is the Quran addressing only men and mentioning only men?" Her question marks a significant moment in the orientation of the Quranic revelations and in the history of Islam, if we are to reflect upon its implications. Within a short time, one of the most beautiful verses was revealed to Prophet Muhammad as a response to her question, introducing for the first time, perhaps in all of human history, a gender inclusive language, after which most of the verses begin to make references to women. The sublime verse, the divine response to Um Salamah, reads as follows:

> *Surely, for Muslim men and women*
> *believing men and women,*
> *devout men and women*
> *truthful men and women*
> *patient men and women*
> *humble men and women*
> *charitable men and women*
> *fasting men and women*
> *men and women who guard their chastity, and*
> *men and women who remember God often—*

For all of them God has prepared Forgiveness and a great reward. (Q 33:35)

This divine dialogue is a gift. The revelation came as a response to a question, showing us that we are constantly in an interactive universe, in touch with the divine that is inviting us to the conversation. God has placed us as the divine stewards on the planet. The way we respond to God is also through our interaction with each other and the movement of meaning between us.

Our women scholars in recent years have done exactly this. Through their enlightening words and scholastic works, they have continued to revive the path that Khawla and Um Salamah began in the founding years of Islam. But if women scholars, activists, and women of faith argue for justice and compassion, for solving the problems of discord, poverty, and violence, then God will hear us! God is listening when we dialogue with goodwill and with the aim to open ourselves to truth and mercy. Our conversations are sacred when they are oriented toward understanding and finding solutions beyond the desire to win. We can't unsee the creativity that happens in the encounter between different ideas and the birth of new ones. This is the blessing of diversity, creativity and the unfolding of divine wisdom and mercy through our voices.

Afra Jalabi, PhD

To God
who inspires and guides.

INTRODUCTION

If you are an educated Muslim woman, a woman of faith, or an activist ally, you may share the frustration and fury that many of us feel. In the West, Muslim women's suffering is attributed to Islam itself. Meanwhile, in Muslim-majority nations, women are essential to preserving tradition—thereby keeping Islam alive. Their struggle for emancipation is linked to their fight for justice. Muslim women—about one-eighth of all people living today—have been deeply impacted by the deliberate omission of the significant contributions women made to Islamic civilization.

As a Muslim woman myself, witnessing the subjugation of my sisters is something I cannot accept in silence. I feel a need to speak out against these injustices. However, it is essential to recognize that this mistreatment is not inherent to Islam but is the product of misguided male leaders who are oblivious to the future women need and want. They conflate cultural norms with religion, prioritizing their narrow interests over societal good by issuing decrees that deviate from the original intent of the Quran.

The pressing question is, how can we dismantle the mountains of mistrust, dispel the cloud of suspicion, and address the cruelty of injustice? In our pursuit of women's rights, we cannot disregard the significance of Islam. It must be an integral part of our overall strategy; ignoring it is counterproductive.

As Muslims, we are encountering upheavals and heightened divisions as our youth are pulled to the lure of the internet, leading to an increase in cynicism about Islam and its sacred texts. Our mission today is to eradicate stifling ideas and foster an environment conducive to change. A promising path forward is creating an environment open to healthy dialogue and disagreements.

For centuries, Islam has been a source of inspiration for positive social change. By highlighting its authentic teachings, we can combat injustices committed in the name of our religion. The research in this book and our shared history have greatly inspired me. As you read, you too will realize that what is offered here is not a new interpretation of the Quran but is as genuine to Islam as the sun is to the sky.

I invite Muslim men and scholars to reflect upon the content presented in '30 Rights." If you encounter anything objectionable, I would greatly appreciate your feedback. Since the Quran states, *[S]how me your proof of what you say is true. (Q 2:111)* and truth does not mind being questioned; I respectfully request that you present a better argument that encourages dialogue instead of silencing it. Upholding the true essence of Islam is a strategy we can all endorse. This moral imperative can lead to the transformation of Muslim thought and women's emancipation, a promise deeply rooted in the Quran.

HOW TO USE THIS BOOK

A proverb from a Sufi sage hangs on my wall: "If you truly want to change your bad habits, change your friends; if you want to be a good person, seek out good people."

In these tumultuous times, when the world needs moral guides to navigate the labyrinth of transformation, it is obvious that the Muslim community is suffering from a lack of visionary leadership. In my search for enlightenment, I instinctively turned to the Quran, a source of divine guidance, and to Prophet Muhammad for his enduring wisdom. However, I did not embark on this journey by myself. My traveling companions were the writings of extraordinary women scholars, luminaries, and enlightened male jurists whose lives were devoted to informing and imbuing our consciousness with the light of knowledge. Their writings, like stars in the night sky, led me to a deeper understanding of the truths that lie in the Quran.

This book will clarify how the Islamic faith empowers women to express or interpret their faith. You will read many poignant anecdotes of women who uplifted their communities and shaped our destiny—luminous historical figures whose impact continues to reverberate. Some of them rescued prophets; they were martyrs, they acted, taught, issued decrees, advised leaders, debated as equals, cured the ill, and fought in battles. Today our spirit merges with their theirs, gaining strength from the legacy they left behind.

INTRODUCTION

I hope this book will convince you that change is possible because it has been for the past 1,400 years. The arguments put forward in this book should persuade you that women's rights are firmly established by the Quran, Sunnah, and Shariah. I grouped the 30 Rights under the six objectives of Shariah, which represent divine intent, and which apply to everyone, regardless of gender or religious beliefs. Among the goals are promoting and protecting the principles of religion (*al-deen*) mind (*al-'aql*). Wealth (*al-mal*), Family (*al-nasl*) Life (*al-nafs*) and Dignity (*al-'ird*). It is noteworthy that the objectives are not fixed but rather sophisticated. They are classified into three. 1) most crucial is called Essentials (*daruriyyat*), 2) most significant is Necessities (*hajiyyat*), and 3) least critical is Complementary (*tahsiniyyat*). The need of the hour is to recognize, assert, and share this truth as an essential first step in unfolding divine wisdom via the voices of women. That's exactly what this book aims to do.

While writing, I observed a distinct pattern in the Quran. God does not always choose the best and most experienced individuals to serve his mission; rather, God favors the unexpected, the insecure, the defective, the skeptic, or the underdog—including single, widowed, separated, or childless women. Everyone, regardless of our circumstances, can make a difference, particularly those who have the will. Therefore, this book is tailored for spiritual seekers, novices, professionals, people of faith, or anyone seeking a deeper understanding of God's master plan for people like you.

As a reading approach, I suggest you become acquainted with the table of contents, which functions as a roadmap, and utilize it to rapidly locate the topics that interest you. You may review the "30 Rights at a Glance," which provides a snapshot of all the chapters and rights. Each chapter stands alone. You can read them sequentially or skip to those that most interest you.

All Quranic translations are from *The Clear Quran* with some exceptions when authors have cited verses in their works. When the first letter of a verse is enclosed in square brackets like this [G]od, it indicates that the verse is a continuation of a longer verse. For content clarity, I paraphrased some insights and ideas of authors. To acknowledge these scholars' intellectual contributions, I kept their citations in the endnotes. If any author has issues with how their ideas were rephrased, or believes their work was not properly credited, please bring this to my attention. In addition, if there are any mistakes or omissions, this is a human error for which I apologize in advance.

It is essential to me that my writing respects varied spiritual traditions from which you may come. I wish to explain that in Islam, we do not assign a gender to God because God is beyond gender, and I would like to clarify why I have chosen to use the pronoun He when referring to God in this book, which may be confusing or uncomfortable for some readers. This is a limitation of the English language, where we use gendered pronouns such as he and she to refer to God. English lacks a singular gender-neutral pronoun, and using *It* for God the Almighty is viewed as disrespectful.

I wrote *30 Rights of Muslim Women* so that every Muslim woman might speak with confidence and moral authority and be at the forefront of debates regarding her rights, responsibilities, and status. I hope this book will prompt you to delve into the Quran with an open heart, and explore ways to adopt viewpoints based on a thorough dive into sacred sources.

Finally, let me speak to fellow Muslim women directly: What started out as a booklet soon evolved into a full-fledged book, and I found myself venturing into uncharted territory. Despite not being a native Arabic speaker, I explored the world of jurisprudence, commentaries, exegesis, and narratives unheard of before. The path was not simple, and my research took years. But this journey has been a rewarding experience and has given me the opportunity to share it with you. I am delighted to finally release this work, like a treasured gift that I have been preparing for years.

Now, let us embark on this soul-searching journey that weaves the strands of our past into the tapestry of our future. By exercising our inner strength, we can play an active role in reclaiming our rightful place, no longer oppressed by tradition and injustice, but rather standing on equal footing as a human being and a gift of God.

QURANIC BASIS FOR WOMEN'S EQUALITY

In academic and religious circles, the distinction between equity and equality has generated heated debates. My involvement in this issue dates to 2005, when I founded the WISE organization. At that time, some Muslims told me to change "equality" to "equity" in our name to increase acceptability. After careful consideration, I agreed. As a consequence, our first conference tote bags displayed: "Women's Islamic Initiative in Spirituality and Equity," or WISE.

From 2006 to 2008, I collaborated with numerous eminent female scholars to investigate these semantics. And by the time the 2009 conference rolled around, a decision had been made to revert back to "equality," a change I hoped would go unnoticed. On the first day of our conference that year, my hopes were dashed when Professor Margot Badran, a renowned scholar, approached me clutching one of the original tote bags. She stared at me with a raised eyebrow and asked quizzically, "So, you thought you could get away with this?"

What exactly is the basis of equality in Islam? The Quran describes that all humans are created with a common nature, *fitra*, (original disposition, natural constitution, or innate nature): *"the natural Way of God, which He has instilled in 'all' people" (Q 30:30)*, which gives them the ability to choose or reject God's guidance with which they are uniquely endowed. The commonality of human nature does not mean that every person must have the same personality traits, professional obligations, or technical talents; it means that underneath all these differing appearances and behaviors, each person has a soul that is equally autonomous with the same moral dignity that is equally precious as any other person's. In fact, it is that very autonomy and preciousness that allows for the legal freedom of each person to grow into the unique individual they wish to be.

God created these unique differences among people to better highlight their underlying commonality in a way that allows them to come together in integration, not in opposition (Q 49:13). Islamic law is founded on the principle that all human beings are to be judged by an equal standard of righteousness because they are all morally equal (Q 3:195). This doctrine of human equality includes gender equality, which negates all inequalities due to race, sex, color, ethnicity, tribe, or nationality and declares in clear terms that all humans are on equal footing because they spring from the same source (Q 4:1).

The Quran acknowledges sexual distinctions without assigning gender symbolism to them. It scorns, for instance, pre-Islamic Arabs for their attitude toward baby girls (Q 16:58-59). It dispels notions that women were inferior to men, and boys had preference over girls, and instead shows them as protectors of one another (Q 9:71).

The Quran confirms that regarding moral and spiritual development, men and women stand in perfect equality; both must fulfill their religious obligations and promote the good and prohibit evil (Q 4:124). They are measured based on virtues that God says everyone should possess to be accepted by Him. These include faith in God, devotion to the Creator, truthfulness, patience, humility, charity, fasting, chastity, and prayer (Q 33:35).

During his lifetime, the Prophet increased women's agency and autonomy. In his book, *The Status of Women in Islam*, Mehmet AKGUL cites a profound statement of the Prophet that eloquently characterizes human equality transcending race, ethnicity, and gender: "All people are equal, as the teeth of the comb. There is no claim of merit of an Arab over a non-Arab, or of a white over a black person, or male over a female. Only God-fearing people merit a preference with God."

The Quran's message is clear, explains Muhammad Abdul Rauf in *The Islamic View of Women and the Family*: A woman is a moral being, worthy of dignity, a legal individual, spiritual being, social person, responsible agent, free citizen, and servant of God, allowing her to exercise her abilities and talents in all areas of human activity.[1]

AT A GLANCE: 30 RIGHTS OF MUSLIM WOMEN

In an effort to provide a concise overview, I've prepared the brief paragraphs that follow, providing a glimpse of what lies ahead. Under each right I have included a hint of what's essential, highlighting some key insights, casting light on their significance and historical value.

#1. To Civic/Political Leadership: The Quran supports merit-based leadership, citing the Queen of Sheba as a wise ruler. Women are obligated to promote peace and justice in their communities and can assume civic and political leadership for the benefit of their nation and humankind. Essential: Queen of Sheba pitted against Prophet Solomon, and five medieval women wielding political power.

#2. To Secular Education: The Quran stresses the importance of knowledge for all Muslims, and the Prophet-supported literacy initiatives.

Women/girls must have equal access to education for the advancement of society and transferring knowledge to future generations. Essential: The Prophet began teaching in a home, which served as a clandestine hub for spiritual enlightenment. Aisha propagated religious doctrines by using the transformative power of knowledge.

#3. To Career Pursuit: The Quran gives women the right to work and receive equal pay. The Prophet encouraged women to use their talents to earn a living. Khadijah contributed her wealth to the prosperity of their family and the Prophet's mission. Essential: Businesswoman Khadijah hires the Prophet, proposes marriage to him, and supports his mission.

#4. To Freedom of Speech and Expression: The Quran directs speaking the truth and fighting injustice and grants all freedoms. The Prophet told women to communicate freely, voice their concerns, grievances, opinions, and debate with leaders for constructing a resilient society. Essential: Seven freedoms of the: soul, belief, expression, speech, opinion, criticism, association.

#5. To Testimony and Witness: A woman can be witness in all legal and commercial cases. Two women's testimonies are not equivalent to one man. The first witness provides the testimony, and the second woman is a validator to prevent retraction through coercion. Essential: Two women are not equal to one man. Aisha's lost necklace and the adultery charge is disproven by God who demands four witnesses.

#6. To Religious and Spiritual Leadership: An imam is a guide. A woman can guide her faith community in many ways, as a *sheikha* (spiritual guide), *imama* (prayer leader), *ustadha* (teacher), *Qari* (Quranic reciter), marriage officiant, and blesser of life cycle celebrations. Essential: You'll meet Um Waraqa, the first woman imam/female spiritual guide.

#7. To Be Jurists and Interpreters of Islamic Texts: Women can interpret holy text and uphold justice as muftis, jurists, and magistrates. Aisha's religious knowledge surpassed many men. She alone transmitted 2,200 hadith which are the basis for Islam's jurisprudence. Essential: 9,000 women jurists; early women jurists issued decrees and taught and enlightened male scholars.

#8. To Gain Spiritual Knowledge: To gain understanding of the creator and attain spiritual maturity, the Quran commands pursuit of spiritual knowledge as a religious duty. The Prophet held classes for women to encourage and teach them about their religion. Essential: The influence of Rabri Basri's concept of divine love and why Quranic arts contributed towards the golden age of Islam.

#9. To Access Religious Spaces: The Quran requires women to completely partake in religious life. It is forbidden to prevent women from fulfilling their religious obligation by denying access to sacred spaces, mosque management, and cradle-to-grave religious rituals. Essential: The first mosque designed by the Prophet as a spiritual hub for community had no barriers separating wives, men, women, and children.

#10. To Marriage: The purpose of marriage is to unite two souls, to build a family based on mutual respect and compassion, to create harmonious kinship ties. Marriage is permitted between believers but forbidden as an exchange marriage (*shighar*) or a secret marriage (*mut'ah*). Essential: The marriage between the Prophet and Khadijah—a model marriage based on love.

#11. To Be Free of Forced Marriage: Forcing a girl into marriage to improve family, social, or financial connections invalidates the contract. A woman can choose her husband and decline an unsuitable man. A guardian (*wali*) is not required to represent the bride. Essential: Arranged marriage and the oversized role of the guardian.

#12. To Maturely Choose Marriage: A girl must be physically, mentally, and spiritually mature to assume the duties of a spouse. She must have the mental and legal capacity to understand a marriage contract and comprehend the terms to which she is agreeing. Essential: The myth that Aisha was a nine-year-old child bride. She was around eighteen years old when she married.

INTRODUCTION   xix

#13. To Accept or Refuse a Polygamous Marriage: Monogamy is the norm, with polygamy as an exception. Polygamy is allowed if the wife consents to ensure equity and comfort for her and her children and if she is treated justly with other wives. Essential: The Prophet's marriages, their significance and the insights into the identities of the wives.

#14. To Divorce: Women have a right to get out of a marriage for any reason (*khul*), or seek a divorce if her spouse abandons the family, engages in criminal behavior, deceit, or fails to provide for the children. The Quran recommends reconciliation before divorce. Essential: Triple Talak forbidden, and Mubarat, an egalitarian divorce for contemporary women.

#15. To Family Planning and Reproductive Justice: Couples have the right to family planning. When considering abortion, priority is given to the mother's mental and physical health over the unborn fetus. Pregnancy termination is permitted only within the first 120 days. Essential: Discussion regarding whether life begins at conception and is abortion a legal or moral issue.

#16. To Care for Orphans through Adoption: Orphan care is a form of worship. A childless couple or single women can add joy to their family through adoption. Only open adoption is permitted, where a child's biological identity is maintained and adopted children are treated equally to biological children. Essential: The Prophet was an orphan, and Asiya, mother of Moses, was the first woman adopter.

#17. To Motherhood and Womanhood: The Quran reveres motherhood, as her womb plays a key role in human creation. The Quran lauds women as role models for humanity for achieving spiritual and social freedoms by divine decree, setting a precedent for future generations. Essential: Hagar, matriarch of monotheism, founder of Mecca; Mary, Mother of Jesus, the embodiment of perfection; and need to monetize motherhood.

#18. To Inheritance: Inheritance is a birthright that guarantees economic independence. Women inherit as mothers, daughters, wives, and sisters. Men get double share because they maintain the family, while women can use their inheritance, fortune, and gifts however they please. Essential: Ways to end the 2:1 ratio of gender disparity in inheritance for today's woman.

#19. To Financial Independence and Equal Pay: The Quran mandates equal pay for women and men and prohibits workers' exploitation. A woman has a right to maintain a standard of living by investing, managing, and donating her wealth for public welfare, independent of her spouse. Essential: Pursuit of fair compensation includes equal pay for women. As many as half of *Waqf* founders were women and even more beneficiaries were female.

#20. To Own Property: Women can acquire, own, manage, and dispose of their property, and the Quran forbids interfering with their use. There should be no limits on how a woman utilizes her property for her personal well-being, the good of her children, and the broader good of society. Essential: Medieval women show how benefits of property ownership go well beyond monetary gain.

#21. To Freedom of Movement: The Quran enables women to engage in social, religious, commercial, and political activities without a guardian, *mahram*. In the past, concern for safety prevented women from traveling alone, but today governments maintain public safety, allowing women to travel alone. Essential: The seventy-five-kilometer hadith, a faulty basis for banning Afghan women's movement in public.

#22. To Expression of Modesty: Modesty (*haya*) signifies a virtuous way of being, respecting the self by not revealing oneself to arouse desire. Women are free to express modesty through inner qualities and culturally appropriate external expressions without societal or legal coercion. Essential: Hijab verse descends on a wedding night, and hijab as protection, protest, legislation, and choice.

#23. To Freedom from Domestic Violence: Violence against women is prohibited. The Prophet never abused any woman. For a relationship to be harmonious, women must be protected from emotional and verbal abuse, and they require personal financial control to ensure their safety and their family's well-being. Essential: Lost in interpretation, domestic violence has no sanction—don't ever beat, just leave or walk away.

#24. To Safeguard against FGM: No Islamic justification exists for this. It is a harmful cultural practice. The Quran affirms sexual satisfaction for men and women. FGM removes a vital organ that generates pleasure and denies them the right to sexual gratification and marital fulfillment. Essential: Sunnah circumcision for women is false, and a related discussion on tattoos.

#25. To Protection from Rape, Sexual Assault, and Adultery: The Quran forbids forced, coerced, or involuntary sexual behavior. Women cannot be exchanged, raped, silenced, or made to marry the rapist. In marital rape, the wife's consent is ignored, leading to pain, resentment, and marital discord. Essential: Story of Zuelykha sexually assaulting Prophet Joseph. Muslim leaders and Muslim #MeToo.

#26. To Safeguard against Child and Human Trafficking: Trafficking women is prohibited, as it violates their autonomy and dignity and wreaks havoc on the moral fiber of society. Trafficking is a form of slavery that denies people the right to life, family, intellect, dignity, and wealth. Essential: Khadijah and the Prophet emancipated slaves, set a high bar for human equality by freeing enslaved Bilal and appointing him as *muezzin*.

#27. To Health and Hygiene: Women must maintain a healthy balance between physical, mental, and spiritual life. Biological, physiological, and social factors differentiate women's health needs. Their reproductive needs as child bearers are unique, they need pre- and postnatal care. Essential: Muslim medical heritage in light of ancient medicine women, Mary's birth in the woods, and C-sections.

#28. To Fulfill Being a Trustee of God on Earth: As trustees of God and autonomous spiritual beings, women must fulfill religious duties, promote the good and reject the bad, preserve the planet, defend the weak, and promote righteousness. Essential: "Earth" is a "she"—a feminine form. As stewards we are commanded to protect her from exploitation.

#29. To Freedom from Gossip, Slander, Libel, Defamation, and to Privacy: The Quran prohibits defaming and falsely accusing women. Gossip, slander, privacy invasion, and character defamation are rigorously prohibited. Women have the right to contest any offense that diminishes their dignity or degrades their community and its religious significance. Essential: Cyber-attacks, Muslims slandering other Muslims, and Islamophobia.

#30. To Safeguard Honor: Killing in the name of honor is a crime. Killing to settle a score or a tribal dispute is a crime. Murders must be punished, and women must be allowed to live in peace and tranquility and be afforded humane treatment. Essential: Honor vs. passion killings have colonial roots, apostates of the past and now.

PART I
THE RIGHT TO PROTECTION AND PROMOTION OF MIND

• • • • • • • • •

The Quran urges all humans to pursue comprehension and knowledge and to assume the responsibility of discovering the splendor of God's creation. A woman must attain a basic or advanced education and have access to institutions, libraries, and scholarships to realize her intellectual potential and advance human knowledge. In the service of her faith, she can exercise her leadership skills in political and civic positions promoting justice and harmony. Through productive employment, she can pursue a career and opportunities to utilize her talents and abilities. She must feel safe expressing her ideas, beliefs, and opinions to reach her full moral, ethical, spiritual, and intellectual self. She can serve as a legal witness to serve community justice by relying on her sound judgment, moral faculties, and honesty.

These objectives aim to protect the intellect and actualize the potential of the mind:

- The right to basic education, mental health, and sobriety are considered essential, or *daruriyyat*.
- The development of intellect and rationality, critical thinking and creativity, freedom of thought, and the freedom to interpret, access, and express information are deemed necessary, or (*hajiyyat*).
- Cultivation of the arts and intellectual vibrancy that utilize leadership abilities and competencies to develop a vision for society are complementary, or (*tahsiniyyat*).

#1 | TO CIVIC/POLITICAL LEADERSHIP

Sophia Abdi Noor is an example of what it takes to be an effective political leader, and she serves as an inspiration to women everywhere. She recounted to those of us attending the WISE conference in Istanbul in 2019 her arduous journey to the Kenyan Parliament.

Sophia Abdi Noor had to deal with the long-term effects of a child marriage followed by a divorce after being born to Somalian pastoralists in northern Kenya. But she felt undeterred by her circumstances and was determined to control her destiny. She soon became the first woman from her region to run for political office after earning a Bachelor of Arts in development studies from Arusha, Tanzania.

However, Abdi Noor's nomination was canceled due to cultural and religious arguments that a woman cannot lead a Muslim community. Nevertheless, Noor revived her run for parliament in 2017 and this time she won. In Kenya's 10th Parliament, she made history by being elected as the first female parliamentarian. Sophia's work as a constitutional draftsperson was essential for Kenyan women. She rallied the Ijara women to work in agropastoralist professions. As a result of her initiative, the community-led irrigation system is entirely led by women of Ijara.

The Quran establishes a high standard for political leadership. The Mighty Queen of Sheba, Al-Malikah Balqis, is described as an archetype of a political leader who is politically and intellectually astute and wise. The intricate plot in the Quran is brimming with tension as the pagan Queen is pitted against Prophet Solomon in an encounter.

Solomon is presented as a king blessed with unrivaled spiritual gifts, bestowed by God for him to carry out his duty. He possesses extraordinary abilities; he understands the languages of birds and *jinn*. A hoopoe bird warns Solomon that a prosperous kingdom is controlled by a powerful queen who has no knowledge of God. This queen worships the sun, according to the hoopoe. Solomon wants to confirm this claim, so he sends her a letter via the hoopoe bird. The letter's wording instructs her to, *"Do not be arrogant with me, but come to me, fully submitting to God" (Q 27:31)*. She is warned not to be arrogant. The queen is unsure whether she is being told to obey Solomon or to surrender to his God. She does not act rashly; instead, she draws on her feminine insight to prevent a potential calamity for her kingdom. She considers his letter "noble" and ponders her next action. Using a consultative decision-making process, she solicits counsel from her subjects: *"She said, 'O chiefs! Advise me in this matter of mine, for I would never make any decision without you.' They responded, 'We are a people of strength and great military might, but the decision is yours, so decide what you will command'" (Q 27:32)*. Her deft political maneuvering and diplomatic manner solidifies her people's faith in her, not out of fear but conviction.

The Queen of Sheba was curious about the king's personality and what was behind his message extorting her to bow to his God. She was wondering as to whether he was a "pious prophet" or a "worldly one." She concluded that a diplomatic gesture would be more effective: *"But I will certainly send him a gift and see what response my envoys will return with" (Q 27:35)*. She sent him gold, silver, pearls, onyx, and horses as gifts.

When Solomon welcomed Sheba's envoy, he was angered by her extravagant gift-giving and said, *"[D]o you offer me wealth? What God has granted me is far greater than what He has granted you. No! It is you who rejoice in receiving gifts" (Q 27:36)*. He returned the messengers and gifts to Sheba with a message that said, *"visit me or face the consequences."* Despite his threats and hostility, she showed generosity, respect, and bravery, *"Indeed when kings invade a land, they ruin it and debase its nobles. They really do so!" (Q 27:34)*. She accepted Solomon's offer.

Solomon had planned a series of experiments to put Sheba to the test before she arrived. He summoned a *jinn* to bring Sheba's great throne to his court. The throne was put in the palace and camouflaged before her arrival so she would not recognize it. When she stepped in front of Solomon, he inquired whether she recognized the disguised throne. She felt she was being tested, and after scanning its shape and scale, she responded, *"It looks to be the same" (Q 27:42)*. When she saw her throne was magically transferred from her kingdom to Solomon's, she realized Solomon's power was greater, more significant than any kingdom. Despite her lack of religious practice, she impressed Solomon with her smart intuition and perception.

Solomon staged another test. He wanted to check if she could be rightly guided and if she was prepared to accept God's purpose for her life: He instructs her to walk down a palatial hall with a thin glass floor under which there is water and fish swimming. As she starts walking, she mistakes the floor for a lake and raises her skirt to not wet her clothes. King Solomon informs her that the surface is not water, rather it is slabs of polished glass. The radiance of the glass floor and the marvel of its construction, the likes of which she had never witnessed before, prompt her to confess that she had previously harmed her own soul, preventing her from experiencing the fullness of her faith. Thus, the queen gracefully abdicated her throne to King Solomon, submitted to the greater truth, acknowledged the One God, and led her people to monotheism. *"[M]y Lord! I have certainly wronged my soul. Now I 'fully' submit myself along with Solomon to God, the Lord of all worlds" (Q 27:44).*

Barbara Freyer Stowasser, author of *Women in the Qu'ran, Traditions, and Interpretation*, explains that Sheba's submission to God made her Solomon's spiritual equal, because in Islam the vanquished and victor are equal brothers or sisters, as are the "called" and the "caller," the "follower," and the "leader."[2]

The Quran depicts another political leader, Pharaoh, who refuses to recognize Moses' extraordinary powers. This tyrant's egotistical wrath is focused on his subjects, who are mostly women and children. The Pharaoh decreed, *"Kill the sons, of those who believe with them [Moses] and keep their women" (Q 40:25)*. This comparison shows that gender is not a determining factor for effective leadership; rather, meritocracy is. And that an effective leader is someone who can exert influence in achieving goals, rather than someone who manipulates to lead.

Today, Sheba's leadership must be hailed from east to west, especially in nations stricken by war. The Quran describes her governance as one of transparency, public consultation, and prioritizing the welfare of her people. She disregarded her council's advice to use her military might; instead, she tapped into her confidence and inner power to choose peace over war and conflict. She prevented her people from being mired in a political conflict, saving them from the devastating consequences of war. Through her decisive actions, she triumphed both politically and spiritually. The Queen's refusal to continue the paradigm of coercion is not due to a lack of power; her female intuition drives her to negotiate with her adversary. She acts deliberately, engages in dialogue to prevent conflict, and resolves the struggle by recognizing her opponent's superior powers.

In contrast, the Pharaoh's ego-driven personality is coercive and autocratic, and his governance style detrimental to his people and nation.

MUSLIM WOMEN SUCCEED WITH THE PROPHET'S GUIDANCE

In Mecca, near the kingdom of Sheba, the Prophet Muhammad received his Revelation in the year 632 CE. His wife Khadijah was his first follower; she was joined by women who pledged loyalty to the Prophet, supporting the validity of the new religion. *"God was pleased with the believers when they pledged allegiance to you 'O Prophet' under the tree" (Q 48:18).* These women who challenged the status quo demonstrated the virtues of bravery and faith in the face of hardship. Some were tortured, beaten, sanctioned economically, and even murdered.

The Prophet met with his companion in *shura* (council) to *"consult with them in 'conducting' matters" (Q 3:159)*, and sought advice from female followers. Muslims, according to scholar Asma Afsaruddin, must emulate the recorded behavior of the female companions since they are our moral and spiritual foremothers. Their example acts as a model for devout Muslims seeking to live a righteous life.[3]

LEADING THE WAY: MEDIEVAL MUSLIM WOMEN

There were extraordinary women political leaders in medieval Muslim civilizations, and their political power had a tremendous influence on society. They considered political authority as a sacred trust with inordinate responsibility, bound by their obedience to God. *"[A]nd raised some of them in rank above others so that some may employ others in service" (Q 43:32).* These women demonstrated remarkable skills in governance, diplomacy, decision-making, and cultural reform.

For example, in the splendor of the Fatimid dynasty, Sitt al-Mulk (970–1023 CE) emerged as the de facto ruler for her nephew during his reign. She reversed her late brother's decisions and restored order to the government while prioritizing the state's finances. Her reforms allowed women to leave the house and lifted the prohibition on music.

She prioritized the rights of non-Muslim subjects, fostering an inclusivity and allowing their return to Egypt.[4]

In the arid lands of Yemen, Sayyida Hurra Arwa bint Ahmad al-Sulayhiyya (d. 1138 CE) stood as a shining example of political and spiritual leadership. For an astounding seventy years she ruled the Sulayhid dynasty. She held the prestigious title of *hujja* (spiritual leader). She had the *khutba* (special Friday prayer) recited in her name, solidifying her authority. Recognizing the sacrosanct responsibility entrusted to her, she governed her domain effectively, earning the admiration of her people.[5]

In the bustling courts of the Delhi Sultanate in India, Raziyyat-Ud-Dunya Wa Ud-Din, (1205–1240 CE) defied societal norms by assuming the power of ruler. Appointed by her father, Iltutmish, over her brothers she demonstrated wisdom, patronage of scholarship, and military prowess. Her pursuit of power was marked by adopting a masculine appearance. She rode a horse; wore a turban, trousers, and coat; and carried a sword in plain view. Contrary to custom, she appeared unveiled in public. Her tenure was marked by the construction of schools, academic centers, and libraries, demonstrating her dedication to education and enlightenment.[6]

Years later, another influential woman emerged, Ismat al-Din, also known as Shajarat al-Durr (1249–1257 CE). She ascended the throne in her own right. During the Crusader invasion of Egypt, she exhibited strategic ingenuity by skillfully concealing her husband, King Salah-al-Din's death to maintain the morale of her forces. She captured King Louis IX of France, effectively halting the Seventh Crusade. She was the first woman in Islam to assume a throne and was praised during Friday prayers, and coins were minted in her name. Her leadership abilities were demonstrated by judicious decision-making, consultation with advisors, and the successful negotiation of a ransom treaty for the king's release.[7]

In her book, *Ottoman Women: Myth and Reality*, Asli Sancar mentions that the Valid Sultan, (mother of the Ottoman Empire's monarch) played a pivotal role in political life. In addition to being a mother, she was her son's teacher, mentor, confidante, strongest ally—and, if need be, regent. Her stipend, which was frequently greater than the sultan's, reflected her prestigious position and emphasized her importance to the empire's affairs.[8]

All these Muslim women leaders challenged societal norms and made a significant contribution to their societies. Their achievements paved the way for advancement and as an inspiration for future female leaders. But despite their successes, many women political leaders were demonized for their positions of authority. Amira Abou-Taleb in "Constructing the Image of the Model Muslim Woman" in *Islamic Interpretive Tradition and Gender Justice* explains that patriarchal societies view women as the "other" and justify their oppression as necessary for maintaining social equilibrium.[9]

OBLITERATION OF WOMEN'S POLITICAL LEADERSHIP

Prejudice against women began when the need for women's labor was reduced and male children's ability to earn a livelihood was accorded greater importance. Worse prejudices took root when man began to construct kingdoms and vast empires based on military conquest, which required the promotion of ferocious masculine qualities, decrying femininity as timid and their compassionate tendencies as shameful and weak. Partially due to cultural biases in patriarchal empires where female subordination to male authority and exclusion from civic participation persisted, women became helpless and gradually assumed their humiliating role as receptacles of human reproduction and servants to male masters.[10]

In her book, *Women and Gender in Islam*, Leila Ahmed explains how during Muslim dynastic rule men from the upper classes who had assimilated these new norms and values of women's subservient status exercised control over religious interpretation and authority, molding it to suit their skewed requirements. Many powerful men owned tens, hundreds, or even thousands of slave women (concubines), which influenced their interaction with and perception of women as "master-slave" or "woman as property" relationships. These relationships affected common society, as powerful males influenced the interpretations of early Islamic texts to rationalize the subordination of women and exclusion of them from public life. These principles were then codified into law.[11]

The argument against women assuming a political and civic role is most often based on a misinterpretation of the verse: *"Men are the caretakers of women, as men have been provisioned by God over women and tasked with supporting them financially"* (Q 4:34). In her book, Quran *and Women: Rereading the Sacred Text from a Woman's Perspective*, Amina Wadud, explains how various translations render this as "in charge of," "in charge of the affairs of," and "managers of the affairs of." The assumption is that men have authority over women because they provide for them financially, and if a woman cannot be above a man, she has no authority to rule over him. The verse deals solely with family affairs and does not address public life. It addresses the man's responsibility to ensure that a woman is not overburdened with additional responsibilities while she is fulfilling her childbearing function, thereby equalizing their responsibility to the family. It does not indicate that men are superior to women in terms of intelligence, piety, or any other attribute.[12]

UNRELIABLE TESTIMONY

The Quran, which praises the Queen of Sheba as a wise leader, directly conflicts with one saying that is often falsely attributed to the Prophet: "Never will a people prosper who delegate their affairs to women."[13] Amira Abou-Taleb explains that the narrator is Abu Bakra (al Thaqafi) (d. 672 CE), who was convicted of slander, and slanderers lack the moral integrity required to be accepted as Hadith narrators. He claims he heard this in the battle of al Jamal, where scores of people were involved, yet he is the only person to have heard it. It is incomprehensible that a decision as far-reaching as prohibiting women from leadership could be derived from a single report of contested validity and still be considered reasonable.

Muhammad al-Ghazali (1917–1996), an Egyptian scholar, questioned the veracity of this hadith, which he claimed only applied to the turmoil within the Persian state at the time, stating, "Prophet Muhammad meant only that the Persian state was doomed to fall, not that these Muslim women were unfit for political office."[14] A second dubious hadith which is not a direct quote of the Prophet and which contradicts the Quran states, "[W]omen are deficient in religion and intelligence."[15]

This is unintelligible. It contradicts all evidence of Prophet Muhammad's counsel-seeking interactions with intelligent women. Upon closer inspection it appears to point to women's biological disposition (menstruation) as a natural deficiency for women. Due to their menstrual cycle, they are assumed to be emotionally imbalanced and too weak to be political leaders. Again, the Prophet did not see it this way; he regularly met with menstruating women face-to-face, educating them and seeking their input on business and political matters.

The exclusion of women from public life is also justified by the fact that women are a source of sexual temptation for men: their presence will cause *fitna* (chaos) among men. This contradicts the well-documented fact that women have ruled over male subjects and the behavior of the Prophet's female companions, who supported men in battle, fought alongside men and sought an education.

Amira Abou-Taleb relates a story about a woman named Umm Sinan who requested the Prophet's permission to join a battle to which he replied that many women had already asked and he had already granted permission. She was permitted to either join his troop or remain with her tribe. His approval reflects his lenient attitude toward the presence of women on the battlefield, who, by participating in military operations, were exposed to a potentially hazardous public space involving foreign men. (193)

WHEN TODAY'S MUSLIM WOMEN LEAD

A better understanding of the Queen of Sheba, a competent sovereign monarch, exposes a crucial lesson in modern discourse: Islam is surrender not to a leader, not even to a Prophet, but to God—the God in whose eyes all genuine believers are the same. Her faith in Solomon's superior might and his regard for her wisdom are metaphors of might, incorruptibility, and the persuasive force of righteousness—values and characteristics that are gender-neutral and eternal.

Today's Muslim women are motivated by the great legacy of their foremothers in scripture and history who were rulers and leaders. It is hardly surprising that women leaders throughout the world are discreetly leading a drive to change Muslim cultures. Following in the footsteps of their predecessors, at least fifteen female heads of state have headed Muslim-majority countries. Among them are Indonesian Prime Minister Megawati Sukarnoputri, Prime Minister Benazir Bhutto (Pakistan), Prime Ministers Khaleda Zia and Sheikh Hasina (Bangladesh), President Atifete Jahjaga (Kosovo), President Roza Otunbayeva (Kyrgyzstan), Prime Minister Tansu Ciller (Turkey), Prime Minister Mame Madior Boye (Senegal), President Ameenah Gurib-Fakim (Mauritius), Vice President Fatoumata Tambajang (Gambia),

President Samia Suluhu Hassan (Tanzania), Prime Minister Najla Bouden Romdhane (Tunisia), President Halimah Yacob (Singapore), Prime Minister Sibel Siber (northern Cyprus), and Prime Minister Cissé Mariam Kaïdama Sidibé (Mali).

Women hold the positions of foreign ministers and ambassadors in Saudi Arabia, Jordan, United Arab Emirates, and Morocco. More than a dozen Muslim women are elected to serve in congresses, parliaments, city councils, and municipal governments as mayors in North America and Europe. Preventing women from taking on leadership roles denies the Muslim *ummah* (community) opportunities for growth and development. In Muslim nations, there is a dearth of leadership, and Muslim cultures need visionary role models that prioritize peace and prosperity above war and strife. Women leaders not only consult with others, but have heightened emotional intelligence, masterful social skills, and a profound concern for the welfare of those they lead. The Queen of Sheba is exemplified by these characteristics in the Quran.

THE LONGEST REIGNING CONTEMPORARY MUSLIM WOMAN LEADER

Sheikh Hasina Wazed, who has led Bangladesh for two separate, lengthy terms as prime minister, is an example of a leader who has changed a country's trajectory. Her combined time in office since 1996 makes her the world's longest-serving female head of government. Hasina blended her philosophy of capitalistic and socialistic virtues. She dissolved monopolies; sparked fierce rivalry among businesses; and opened hitherto off-limits areas of the economy to private investment, including: healthcare, banking, universities, the media, export processing, and economic zones. Hasina has shown how women in leadership can help everyone of their country's 60 million working people, including 18.6 million who are women. By increasing funding for welfare, she helped lift her country's poorest and most marginalized citizens out of poverty. The single most decisive factor behind Bangladesh's astonishing success is that Prime Minister Hasina has infused a sense of confidence in the national psyche of her people, especially among women and youth. Her legacy reflects a simple yet profound truth: When women lead, nations prosper, societies thrive, and a better tomorrow becomes an undeniable reality.

#2 | TO SECULAR EDUCATION

Parveen was a typical Pakistani girl who lived in London. She had hopes and aspirations of finishing school and working. One day, on her thirteenth birthday Parveen's parents told her that she would no longer attend school. They said, "It's not like you're going to be a teacher." When her absence from school was noticed, a representative came to the house to inquire about her absence, her parents lied that Parveen had left for Pakistan and wouldn't be coming back. Her parents then planned her marriage at age sixteen to a distant relative. By denying her the opportunity to receive an education, they stole everything from Parveen—her hopes, aspirations, and dreams of becoming a teacher.

Stories such as Parveen's are still too common throughout the world, even though, since its inception, Islam has placed a major emphasis on education. Over 800 references to secular and spiritual knowledge in the Quran demonstrate the significance of knowledge in Islam. The idea of *aql*, which can mean intellect, reason, or logic, is mentioned more than forty times, including in the verse, *"And they will lament, "If only we had listened and reasoned, we would not be among the residents of the Blaze!" (Q 67:10)*.

God created humanity with the awareness and inclination to discover the world's intricacies and contemplate the magnificence of his creation *(Q 88:17-21)*. The goal of acquiring knowledge is to comprehend, value, and decipher universal mysteries: *"There are countless signs in the Earth for those with sure faith as they are within yourself. Can you not, see?" (Q 51:20-21)*. Muslims are guided to search for signs of God in nature, human creation, and other life forms on earth and beyond. These include the study of natural phenomena such as cyclones, tornadoes, earthquakes, and the intricate movement of the sun and other stars.

THE FIRST TEACHER AND SCHOOL

Without a doubt, the Quran was the first Arabic literary work discovered in Arabia. During the Prophet's life, God revealed many verses concerning knowledge and its importance to humankind; some examples of these are, *"And Say: My Lord, increase me in knowledge,"* and *"You have only been given a little knowledge."* These verses may appear to be contradictory, but they are complementary. They encapsulate Muslims' need to increase their knowledge via study, reading, and writing, while fully believing that all knowledge belongs to God and even with ongoing discoveries the mysteries of God's creations are boundless and his knowledge is inexhaustible: *"If all the trees on earth were pens and the ocean 'were ink' refilled by seven other oceans, the Words of God would not be exhausted" (Q 31:27).*

Mohamad Jebara, author of *Muhammad, the World Changer,* describes how the first Islamic learning center, dedicated to pursuit of knowledge, started in the home of Arqam ibn Abu Arqam. At the first meeting, the Prophet arranged the group to sit in a circle, just like the elder's council—only here the enslaved and women sat alongside elite male merchants. Mecca had never seen this before. What united the unlikely cross-section of people was intellectual curiosity. They were intrigued by the Prophet's bold call to action despite the risk of being ostracized socially (or, for the enslaved, subjected to physical punishment).

This education was conducted in secret. The Prophet, who had never taught before, recited his Revelations so the group could memorize the verses, then led a discussion, encouraging all participants to share their ideas. The goal was to help the group train their minds to think outside tradition, restrictions, and conformity. Omar bin Khattab may have been one of the last persons to accept Islam within the walls of Dar ul-Arqam. The school was used for three years until Banu Hashim's notorious boycott of Muslims, when it was eventually abandoned.

Two women were instrumental in leading educational efforts. Baraka, who raised the Prophet, emigrated to Abyssinia, at the Prophet's request, where she organized the small Muslim group. She led efforts to construct the second mosque and an educational institution, where the first Muslims would flourish. In Medina the Prophet designated

Ash-Shifa bint 'Abdullah, a scholar, healer, and a tradeswoman, as head educator.[16]

Amjad Hussain, author of *A Social History of Education in the Muslim World*, characterizes the Prophet's era as the foundational stage of Islamic education. The Prophet personally instructed people in the Quran, as well as decorum and etiquette in a variety of situations, food and physical training, among other topics pertaining to daily life. Over the course of twenty-three years, from 610 to 632 CE, he oversaw education in both Mecca and Medina.

The first thirteen years in Mecca were instructive and enlightening for Muslims who focused on memorization and comprehension of the Quran and on living in accordance with revelation. Even though this education consisted of basic reading and writing, it was essential because it dealt with creedal ideas of Islam. Hussain describes how revelation transferred its emphasis in Medina to law, ethics, and community. Here, the first Muslim state (*dawlah*) was established, the parameters of Islam's social structures were disclosed, and Muslims were exhorted to support community efforts.[17]

VERANDA AHL AS-SUFFAH

Hussain describes how in the Prophet's mosque there was a place for poorer followers to sleep and shelter on a bench. These people were the *Ahl as-Suffah* (People of the Veranda). They led a contemplative and saintly life at the Prophet's mosque. In fact, it became a blueprint for later dormitories in Islamic education. Some seventy people of *suffah* would sometimes go to a teacher at night and engage in study until daylight. A group of teachers in the *suffah* taught students the Quran, Sunna, literacy, and poetry. The *suffah* was a place of learning for all who had a desire to learn and were able to attend the place of teaching, learning, and not only scholarship, which would figure to a greater degree later in the history of Islamic education. (10)

The Prophet, who had to fight many battles, received a verse that underlines the need of education, noting that it should continue even during times of war: "[T]he believers don't need to march forth all at once. Only a party from each group should march forth, leaving the rest to gain religious knowledge and then enlighten their people when they return to them, so that they 'too' may be aware of evil" (Q 9:122). This is why the Prophet exempted some people to join battles and told them to continue to teach and meet their religious obligations, such as when Um-Waraqa was urged to stay behind to perform her religious duties.

According to Amjad Hussain, the early community's philosophy was the use of *taalim, taadib,* and *tarbiyah*—mastering all the sciences that were available to them, which were about being ethical and moral in all situations and acting on God's rules. Scholars with insight show that both the Quran and Hadith use these main concepts to describe Islamic education: *taalim*: imparting knowledge; *taadib*: nurturing and fostering the growth of the student; and *tarbiyah*: disciplining and helping pupils to acquire courtesy, *adab*. Throughout the Prophet's time in Medina, *taalim, taadib,* and *tarbiyah* were incorporated in action and practice but were not defined as a written educational philosophy. (6)

Study circles, *halaka*, were the original approach where all subjects including writing were taught. Here, the students formed a semi-circle around the teacher, who sat against a wall or pillar. The Prophet ordered Medina's nine mosques to establish study circles, *halaqas*, to avoid overcrowding the main mosque and allow young students to easily attend school in a mosque nearby. He would teach at a suitable time so people would not become bored, and he taught that a good teacher is the one who begins by teaching simple subjects of knowledge before touching difficult ones. (10)

As the Prophet passed on, his companions proceeded to implement his strategy. Omar bin Khattab wanted children to be taught subjects such as poetry, history, and social sciences, which ensured the success of his community. Since the Quran warns that blind faith is insufficient, *"[O] Prophet, Are those who know equal to those who do not know? None will be mindful of this except people of reason" (Q 39:9)*—the companions recognized the necessity to continue the Prophet's work without stifling the educational system through blind imitation.

As the Prophet had done, he emphasized the significance of physical education for children, including horsemanship, archery, and swimming. Abdullah Abbas copied the Prophet's idea of a suitable time to study and teach. He said that once a pupil begins to divert their eyes away from you, their attention has strayed. Ibn Abbas also introduced the notion of giving pupils free time between each lecture to do whatever they liked. Ali, the fourth Caliph, emphasized the importance of discussion and review to ensure that students did not forget or make mistakes. He underscored the value of asking questions. He used to say that knowledge is a treasure, and its keys are the questions asked; therefore, ask questions, because the question is rewarded by its answers, and so is the person who asked, his teacher, the listener, and the bystander.[18]

Travel was another method of education in Medina, called *rihlah*. According to Ibn Abbas, an envoy from nearly every tribe in Arabia visited the Prophet to learn about Islam and Islamic sciences from him. The Prophet would say, go back to your family, stay with them, and teach and encourage them to do good. Even though travel for knowledge existed outside the Arabian Peninsula, the Prophet encouraged it for the specific purpose of acquiring knowledge. Because the Quran says those with knowledge are a degree above others, the Prophet dispatched select Muslims to teach those who had recently converted to Islam about their religion. Thus, during the first century of Islam, Muslims in various regions of the world held numerous scholarly men and women in high regard. The Prophet said, "The wise saying is the lost property of the believer, so wherever he finds it then he has a right to it."[19] Those who desired *rihlah* had the opportunity to travel to numerous centers of learning, including Kufa, Basra, Damascus, and Jerusalem. Many others, including Aisha, remained in Medina, and almost all the companions were seen teaching in the mosque in *halaka*.

The simple structure of the Prophet's educational approaches evolved over time into a comprehensive and coherent educational system that was thoroughly incorporated into the social and economic way of life. This distinct educational experience was a constant throughout Muslim societies, regardless of whether it occurred in a mosque, *kuttab*, *maktab*, or *madrasa*. Thus, the seeds planted by the early Muslims continue to transform individuals and societies to this day, as evidenced by *halaqas* in which Muslims learn various subjects from teachers and *rihlah*, in which a teacher travels to people or seekers travel to study under masters.

The Prophet placed an emphasis on eradicating illiteracy by employing tutors for his wife, Hafsa, teaching women alongside men, and prioritizing education for the lowest-ranking members of society, enslaved women. He designated specific periods for women to receive instruction from him. His actions and words demonstrate his commitment to women's education, and the "best of you is the one who gives his offspring a decent education."[20]

PARENTS AS GUIDES

Imam al-Ghazali, an Islamic philosopher, jurist, and theologian (d. 1111 CE) noted that education enables individuals to discern between truth and falsehood, good and bad, right conduct and wrongdoing. Because of the importance of education to individual and societal development, real education should encourage gratefulness, humility, and altruism. He emphasized that Muslims should study a balance of secular and religious fields, including theology, law, and ethics as well as secular subjects like astronomy, mathematics, and medicine. Education, he said, should be about more than just acquiring knowledge; it should also foster the growth of moral character. Because knowledge without moral principles may lead to hubris and the misuse of authority, he said that moral values and qualities should be ingrained in people via education. He argued in favor of people thinking critically and questioning and considering what they have learned. He advocated for teaching pupils to think critically, distinguish between fact and fiction, and participate in reasoned debate.

He emphasizes the importance of parents in a child's early education, as their daily interactions have the greatest impact on the child. This influence includes language, cultural traditions, and moral and religious beliefs. Parents are commended if their child demonstrates good character and held accountable if the child develops undesirable characteristics.[21] As parents are responsible for teaching their children religion, language, culture, and social norms, an illiterate woman cannot fulfill her obligation to educate her children.

As the Quran forewarns, *"Lost indeed are those who have murdered their own children foolishly out of ignorance and have forbidden what God has provided for them—falsely attributing lies to God" (Q 6:140)*. Keeping a woman uneducated "slays" children because a teacher is integral to the social development of a child, and the mother is the earliest transmitter of knowledge and the soul's continuous trainer.

Haifaa Jawad, author of *The Rights of Women in Islam*, asserts that a woman must learn from all disciplines of knowledge, particularly in areas where she bears the most responsibility, such as her child's education, health, finances, and the instruction of parenting skills. How can she fulfill these responsibilities if she lacks the intellectual capacity to do so?[22]

PIONEERS OF KNOWLEDGE

Muslims set the stage for the Renaissance, and they did so with men and women studying alongside each other—including numerous women who attended an eleven-lecture course with more than 500 students of both genders in the Umar Mosque at Damascus (1288 CE). There are also records of female attendance at a course of six lectures delivered by Ibn al-Sayrafi to a class of more than 200 students in Aleppo (1336 CE).

Medieval women proved their ability to master many subjects and achieved a high reputation among their contemporaries. Women obtained distinguished positions in the fields of hadith sciences, the science of interpretation, jurisprudence, medical science, and calligraphy. Al-Mahmali did not specialize in just one subject but excelled in many fields, such as Arabic literature, hadith, jurisprudence, and mathematics. She was an expert in *hisab* (arithmetic) and *fara'idh* (inheritance calculations), both being practical branches of mathematics, already well-developed in her time. She invented solutions to equations cited by other mathematicians, denoting algebra aptitude. Al-Mahmali's calculation skills outperformed the abilities of her peers.[23]

Asli Sancar describes how during the Ottoman Empire women attended coeducational schools funded by *waqfs* (religious endowments). The schools were usually attached to a mosque. Although girls were trained for their roles as wives and mothers at an early age, they attended a primary school where they learned basic subjects, such as writing, arithmetic, geography, and history. They also learned Islamic studies, including the Arabic alphabet, Quran memorization, and recitation. These schools existed for centuries and were so widespread that a Western traveler said, "there was no village too small to have a primary school."[24]

THE ROOTS OF ENDING WOMEN'S EDUCATION

Despite this impressive history of women as educators, regressive sociocultural attitudes infiltrated newer Islamic cultures, undermining women's participation in education. Some contend that education diverts women's attention away from their primary roles as wives and mothers, while others believe it will lead to dissatisfaction and instability in the household and society at large.

The jurists who codified laws restricting girls' and women's access to education cited three reasons: 1) restrictions on travel and the need for male accompaniment, 2) distinct and unequal facilities due to gender segregation, and 3) inadequate teacher quality.

The misuse of the mahram concept limits women's freedom by imposing restrictions on their movement. A *mahram* is usually a close male relative who travels with a woman to keep her safe (described in detail in chapter 22). Therefore, it is erroneous to assert that Islamic law requires a *mahram* in all circumstances, particularly when it violates the divinely endowed right of women and girls to pursue an education.

Separate and unequal educational facilities for male and female pupils posed the greatest impediment to the education of women. In certain nations, this was the consequence of enforcing *purdah*, which literally translates "to screen" women from interacting with males outside of their immediate family. In pre-Islamic Arabia, Persia, and India only aristocratic women observed *purdah*. As Islam spread across cultures, these customary practices were incorporated with the Quran's emphasis on modesty, and by the eleventh century, *purdah* had become a common practice in many Muslim communities. This resulted in women being confined to the household, diminishing their access to education.

Another barrier is that women received lower-quality education than males, even when they attended the same institution, resulting in fewer job and career opportunities after graduation. Families that want their girls to observe *purdah* forbid them from attending school because they do not want them to learn from unknown males. These challenges drive Muslim women to self-study, correspondence courses, and *halaqa*. While such efforts are commendable, they lack the prestige and recognition afforded by eleventh-century institutional education and the career opportunities provided to those with official degrees. As a result, the Islamic ideal of women's education and intellectual development was distorted, confused, and actively opposed. For these reasons, women's illiteracy became a widespread phenomenon in the world of Islam.

TRAVEL FAR AND WIDE TO SEEK KNOWLEDGE

Yet, the Quran emphasis on literacy became a powerful motivator for Muslim intellectuals to pursue a love of study. The Prophet stated that only learners will inherit his legacy and serve as earth trustees. And he highlighted the importance of traveling to seek knowledge, saying, "whoever goes in search of knowledge is in the path of God till he returns."[25] This, coupled with the Quranic passages, prompted medieval scholars and scientists to make significant contributions to science, medicine, philosophy, architecture, mathematics, and astronomy during Islam's Golden Age, which lasted from the seventh through the fifteenth century.

Basheer Ahmed, in *The Rise and Fall of Muslim Civilization*, describes how the House of Wisdom, or *Bayt al-Hikmah*, was the world's first scientific and educational institution, bringing together scientists, intellectuals, and translators to study, research, and publish. It became a model for all Caliphs, and many replicated libraries followed. Ahmed highlights many Muslim women who were credited with establishing more than 35 percent of the libraries and academic institutions in the Islamic world from 800 CE to 1100 CE. During that period, Zubaidah (ninth century) was the driving force and key supporter behind famed Bayt al-Hikmah. And there are many other examples.[26]

In addition, Lubna of Cordoba (d. 984 CE), born into slavery, rose to prominence as a master librarian and acquisitions expert. She founded the library in Madinat al-Zahra, where she worked with the Jewish scholar Hasdai ibn-Shaprut to amass a valuable collection of 500,000 books. Lubna was praised by the twelfth-century historian Ibn Bashkuwal as an educated author, grammarian, poet, erudite in arithmetic and comprehensive learning; none in the citadel was as noble as she. A street in Cordoba, Spain was even named after her in 2019, Avenida Escriba Lubna, commemorating her work as a copyist. (49)

Fatima al-Madrid (tenth to eleventh century) worked with her father in Cordoba on astronomical and mathematical treatises, including the astronomical tables of al-Khwarizmi. Her most famous work, *Corrections from Fatima*, was included in astronomical and mathematical treatises. She also coauthored with her father a treatise on the Astrolabe. In 1924, her name appeared in a Spanish encyclopedia for the first time. In 2016, Juan Nuez quoted from the Espasa encyclopedia the details of Fatima's corrections and how she had done original work in mathematics, astronomy, and astrolabe. She also corrected *The Almagest* of Ptolemy and found mistakes in the eclipse calculations. (48)

The most notable is Fatima al-Fihri (d. 880 CE), who left a grand legacy for education as the founder of the world's oldest running university. Al-Fihri was a devout Muslim who believed in the importance of education. She studied Islamic law, *fiqh*, and Hadith and fled from her native Tunisia to Fez, Morocco. After her father passed away in 859 CE, she constructed a *madrasa*, a place of learning, which she named Al-Qarawiyyin, after her birthplace. Initially, only the Quran and religious teachings were taught, but many other subjects were subsequently introduced, including mathematics, medicine, Arabic grammar, history, geography, astronomy, chemistry, music, and logic.

Fatima attended the university with her students and awarded them diplomas carved into wooden plaques that are now on exhibit in the library. She also regularly convened discussions and symposiums for her students, resulting in politically aware individuals. The university produced many notable intellectuals and historians, such as philosopher Ibn Rushd (Averroes), Andalusian geographer Hassan al-Wazzan (Leo Africanus), and historian Ibn Khaldun, as well as Jewish philosopher Maimonides.

Fatima was unaware at the time that the *madrasa* she built in 859 would become the world's first university more than two centuries before Bologna (1088 CE) and Oxford (1096 CE). She pioneered the concept of bestowing diplomas, oral defenses, and graduation ceremonies, which early Muslim universities imitated and to which they added the tasseled fezzes and cloaks (*burdah*), which are common features of today's commencement ceremonies.

UNESCO and the *Guinness Book of World Records* recognize Fatima al-Fihri as the founder of the world's oldest degree-awarding and continuously operating institution. Today, the esteemed university of al-Qarawiyyin is still in operation, with students seated in a *halaqah*, a semicircle around their instructors. It currently offers undergraduate, graduate, and doctoral degrees, in addition to publishing numerous journals annually.[27]

ADVANCING WOMEN FOR A FLOURISHING FUTURE

As seen from history, the scores of remarkable women who accomplished significant successes were literate or had access to education. They produced ground-breaking discoveries, created new hypotheses, and spearheaded institutions. They inspired numerous women to pursue their own potential by exemplifying what is possible. Their works were so influential that they shaped and influenced society. Their efforts impact the present and lay the foundation for a better future.

To empower women to perform larger roles in their families and communities, as did our ancestors, it is crucial to provide them with educational opportunities. The purpose of education is to equip students with the knowledge, skills, and values they need to contribute positively to their families, communities, and countries. Education will aid women to close the gender gap and achieve economic equality, as women with a higher level of education are likely to have better economic prospects. Additionally, it enables women to make informed decisions about their life and health, resulting in happier and healthier families.

AFGHAN GIRLS' EDUCATION HELD HOSTAGE TODAY

Education in modern Muslim nation-states has been marked by a conflict between secular and religious education, between which early Muslims did not differentiate. The strong focus of madrasas on Islamic studies led to discontent among religious people. They felt indignation that their children were limited to a narrow educational curriculum. This animosity resulted in growing tensions between religious and secular groups, fostering harmful competition, and causing lasting divisions in society. These fissures persist and impact society to this day.

In Afghanistan, where girls and women are currently prohibited from receiving an education, the dichotomy between the secular and the spiritual is on full display, the Islamic Emirate of Afghanistan (IEA), formerly known as the Taliban, is vehemently opposed to secular education, which they mistakenly perceive as a western attack on their deeply held Pashtunwali norms.

In 2022, I traveled to Afghanistan as part of an American Women Peace and Education Delegation to meet with the Taliban and enquire about the reopening of Girls Public High School. At the education ministry, I had the opportunity to speak briefly to the deputy minister about the importance of education in Islam. Here's what I remember saying to him.

Ghulam Hassan Khan, my grandfather, was a man of modest means but great aspirations. He was awarded a scholarship to Harvard

University. During his studies in engineering, he encountered a vast library containing numerous volumes on Islam. This prompted his interest in learning about Islam. Upon his return, our home was adorned with a motto, a Quranic verse: *"My Lord! Increase me in knowledge" (Q 20:114)*. During the day, as an engineer in Kashmir, he constructed roads, bridges, and hospitals. During the night, he manually transcribed the Quran and published volumes on Islam.

Since neither the Quran nor the Prophet made any distinction between the education of boys and girls, my grandfather sent me to America to pursue an education and actualize my potential. After graduating, I worked as a designer until September 11, 2001. In 2004, when I witnessed the Taliban striking mothers with canes, I knew I had to act. I quit my corporate job to focus on finding a solution. I decided to focus my efforts on my community's advancement. I was able to switch careers and study Islam because of my education.

I am here today because my grandfather, a self-taught *alim* (scholar), bestowed upon me the greatest gift imaginable. He instilled in me the confidence to pursue my own study of Islam. Now I can share the truth of Islam and dispel the falsehood. I can do this because my family instilled in me the *aql* and vested me with *ilm*, which serves my community in America and elsewhere.

After the victory of Badr in Medina, the Prophet instructed literate captives of war to teach ten Muslims how to read and write in exchange for their release. He made no distinction between men and women. His actions and words demonstrate his commitment to women's education: the seeking of knowledge is obligatory for every Muslim.[28]

The deputy minister surprised me when he said, "People in our rural areas have no knowledge of this information. Why don't you go to the provinces and teach this to the women?" I responded that I did not want to impose myself, as this was not my jurisdiction, but then he added, "You are welcome to come back!" Months later, he was fired.

A PAKISTANI EDUCATOR TEACHES THOUSANDS OF CHILDREN

In contrast to what is happening in Afghanistan, Fiza Shah, a Pakistani woman, has followed her heart and ambition to improve the lives of disadvantaged children through education. She understood she had to provide accessible, high-quality education because she was driven by the principle that every kid should be given the chance to succeed. So, in 1998 she established Developments in Literacy (DIL), an organization that places children at its center.

Fiza was able to open hundreds of schools in all four regions of Pakistan, providing access to education for thousands of underprivileged kids and females. She employs methods such as technology-based instruction, intensive instructor preparation, individualized lesson plans, and hands-on projects. Learning on such a broad and deep scale equips students to not only use their knowledge in practical ways but also to push the boundaries of their own creativity.

#3 | TO CAREER PURSUIT

I was once invited to speak at an English class in Brooklyn. The audience was made up of Arab Muslim women, many of whom had suffered domestic violence and had financial difficulties. They were learning English as part of their efforts to begin new lives for their young children. While I was speaking to them about women's rights in Islam, an Egyptian woman inquired if it was okay for a Muslim woman to work for herself. The ladies would have no future for themselves or their children if they were not financially independent.

Yes, I confirmed that in Islam women have every right to hold a job to earn a living and this is their duty as the primary caregivers of their children. I advised them to develop any skills they feel they have and use them to earn money. Months after that talk, I received handcrafted greeting cards with thank you messages from many of the women in attendance. We soon formed a cooperative, learned how to create greeting cards, sold them, and used the proceeds to purchase metro cards that enabled us to travel easily.

The Quran urges both men and women to contribute to the advancement of society by doing good deeds in the world (*duniya*) and for their religion (*deen*). It recognizes men's and women's rights to actively engage in God's service, saying, *"[I] will never deny any of you—male or female—the reward of your deeds. Both are equal in reward"* (Q 3:195). It also says, *"Men will be rewarded according to their deeds and women equally according to theirs"* (Q 4:32). This financially fair and equal pay revelation demonstrates that God makes no distinction between what women and men reap in terms of rewards in the afterlife or financial justice in this life.

Before Islam, certain Arab women had more flexibility to earn a living; the most well-known example is Khadijah bint Khuwaylid, a successful businesswoman with a trading business greater than all Quraysh traders combined. This capable tradeswoman required a new caravan manager, and she directed her scouting team to locate someone who could be trusted with her assets and livelihood. In the local market, they discovered an active twenty-five-year-old male. Muhammad was his name. As part of the due diligence process, the scouts inquired about Muhammad's business acumen and personal attributes from his buyers and peers and discovered that he was dubbed "Al-Amin"—the trustworthy one—and had an established track record of trading products with his uncle, Abu Talib. Khadijah instantly assigned this smart young man with her caravan after hearing accounts of his exceptional business ability, and character attributes of honesty and trustworthiness. If profitable, she promised him an impressive salary and bonus. Upon his return from Damascus, he shared the good news that he had sold everything and had taken liberties to purchase goods (fine jewelry and silk) on her behalf, which he knew he could sell for a hefty profit. Because she was so impressed with his character and his foresight, she decided to marry him.

Mohamad Jebara describes how the couple formed a working partnership in which both offered their unique talents to make the business profitable. Khadijah provided the investment funds, and Muhammad managed all business operations. Their symbiotic relationship yielded striking success, elevating them among Mecca's most affluent and influential couples.[29]

While married, their purpose revolved around their worldly affairs, caring for their children, and contributing to the welfare of their society. But despite the success in his personal life, Muhammad's hollowness harried him. He wondered why he was here, the purpose of his life, where his life was going, and why he wasn't there? As he chose to disengage from the world and reach his inner transcendental self, Khadijah's affluence liberated him from the need to earn a living, affording him the opportunity to immerse himself in a contemplative life, ultimately paving the way for him becoming a prophet.

Her trust in her spouse was essential to his mission. His opponents, the Quraysh, demanded that he cease preaching, but he refused. Khadijah continued to feed, clothe, and nurture his nascent community of followers. The Quraysh imposed sanctions on her clan, ceased trading with the Banu Hashim clan, ostracized, exiled, and relegated its members to a desolate region. Khadijah was convinced that God had a mission for her husband, which she intended to spend her entire life accomplishing. She ensured the survival of her clan by supporting them with her dwindling wealth, but the sanctions took their toll and the clan fell into impoverishment.[30] In 619 CE, when Khadijah passed away, followed by his uncle, the Prophet fell into "the year of sorrow," agonizing over the loss of his beloved wife and confidante, and Abu Talib, his uncle and protector.

PROPHET MUHAMMAD'S ENLIGHTENED PATH FOR WOMEN

The Prophet's working relationship with his wife influenced his views on women's earning potential and self-worth. He urged women, especially those who were divorced, widowed, or unmarried, to make their own living and not rely on men for financial support: "If one of you were to carry a bundle of firewood on your back and sell it, that would be better than asking a man who may or may not give something."[31] And he fostered self-reliance when he said, "The most blessed wealth is what a person gains from his own earning," then he continued to say that "your children are your earning."[32]

He gave an example of a woman who labored with her hands and contributed to charity. "Zainab [bint Jahsh] had the longest, (most generous) hand among us because she worked with her hands and gave charity."[33]

The Prophet nurtured women's potential by urging them to identify their talent, and skilled women were soon seen engaged in business activities all over the town. As a trader he was intimately familiar with the marketplace and aware of Arab women, including Khaula, Lakhmia, Thaqaa, and bint Makhramah, who made and sold fragrances for profit. Rasta, the wife of a companion (Abdullah ibn Mas'ud), made a living by making and selling handicrafts. He respected Al-Shifaa, as she was literate, experienced in trading, and adept at treating illness. He instructed her to teach his wife Hafsah how to treat common skin ailments. Al-Shifaa's home was located between the mosque and the marketplace, and the Prophet would consult with her regarding market best practices. Caliph Umar ibn al-Khattab also held Al-Shifaa in high regard. As both merchants and shoppers in the marketplace were female, he appointed her as the market supervisor in Madina to certify that all transactions were conducted fairly and with integrity. If she discovered someone to be dishonest or unethical, she could administer the appropriate punishment, which Umar could not reverse. Samra' bint Nuhayk was appointed market controller by the Prophet Muhammad, and both women were known to discharge their duties without encountering any obstacles.

THE WOMEN OF THE WELL

God sent a woman to assist Moses in a time of need, the Quran states. This demonstrates how the Divine employs working women to assist and serve His Prophet. The narrative focuses on two sisters whom Moses discovered laboring in Madyan. They attempted to carry water from the well because their ailing father was unable to care for their flock. Able-bodied Moses assisted the sisters. When their father met Moses, he offered Moses eight years of employment and gave his daughter in marriage to Moses. Since Moses was evading Pharaoh, he accepted both. After ten years of living with a loving family and financial stability, he decided to return to Egypt and meet with the Pharaoh to settle his unresolved family business.

EMBRACE A PURPOSE-FILLED LIFE

The Quran provides Muslims with guidance on the true meaning of life. Humans are "conceived in the finest of creation," it says, and God's service is the ultimate station of human dignity. God has endowed every person with unique abilities. These abilities may be innate or acquired later in life. Each person must recognize where their talents lie and then use them to fulfill the role that God has chosen for them. By recognizing our life's purpose, we assume our proper place in God's pattern of creation; failing to do so, we find ourselves at odds not only with ourselves but also with the whole of creation.[34] As demonstrated by Khadijah, Al Shifaa, and the Madyan sisters, every woman must identify her skills and use them to benefit herself, as well as be willing to be a channel for the Divine to operate through. By doing so, both she and the cause to which she is devoted will benefit.

As a role model for Muslims, the Prophet encouraged his wife, daughters, and companions to engage in all aspects of society. Women were involved in all elements of trade and other walks of life throughout the Prophet's lifetime. Asma, Caliph Abu-Bakr's daughter, assisted her husband in his fieldwork.[35] The Prophet's wives seem to have depended on their own skills and private means to support their children. Sawda, for example, made a living from her beautiful leatherwork. Maymuna, the Prophet's wife, was adept at boosting morale. She accompanied the Muslim army when they needed help. She is credited for organizing the first female group to accompany men in battle and offer medical treatment and emotional support to the injured.[36]

The Prophet enjoyed activities like swimming, horseback riding, and archery and encouraged others to do the same. Men and women were encouraged to participate in sports to develop abilities and be physically prepared for any eventuality. Aisha, Prophet Muhammad's wife, would occasionally join him in sports like racing: "I had a race with the Prophet, and I outstripped him. When I got meaty (again), I raced him, and he beat me."[37]

After his passing the Prophet's wives inherited nothing because he had meant for his modest assets to go to charity. Because of the immense revenue were produced by Arab expansion, the next caliph, Umar bin Khattab, created state pensions in 641 CE, and put the wives at the top of the list, awarding them generous sums.[38]

JURISTS AND SCHOLARS FOR WORKING WOMEN

The Quran emphasizes the rights of both men and women to earn a living and be fairly paid for their efforts. "Since all Muslims are equally required to enjoin virtue and prevent vice *(Q 4:58)*, without gender distinction, men and women are both capable of taking up work duties," theologian Ibn Hazm (d. 1064 CE) said. Islam does not forbid women from working and having a job outside the home if her external work does not interfere with her home obligations or lower her dignity, says Haifaa Jawad. (23) Azizah al-Hibri, in *Windows of Faith*, states that some traditional jurists suggested that the wife was entitled to monetary compensation for her volunteer housework activity.[39]

In "Fiqh Rulings and Gendering the Public Space," Hoda El-Saadi states that while prominent theologian Muhammad al-Ghazali said that a good wife should remain in the inner sanctum of her our home and tend to her spinning, Andalusian philosopher Ibn Rushd rejected the idea that a woman is only suitable for sewing and childbirth. He argued that confining women to procreation, spinning, and weaving resulted in female poverty and dependency on men.[40] Many jurists worried about male-female interaction, but Hoda El-Saadi stated that most did not feel that segregating women and excluding them from public spaces was the solution, since protection and seclusion were unattainable and unrealistic for the majority, and because many women needed to work to support themselves and their children. Also, women's work was integral to the economy. Their wages, no matter how modest, were part of the capital circulating in the economy. (271)

ENDURING CONTRIBUTION OF WOMEN AS WORKFORCE

Many communities confine women to motherhood and homemaking since childbearing is exclusive to women. The Quran emphasizes and reveres motherhood, yet it does not limit women exclusively to this role, which is explained in detail in #17: To Motherhood and Womanhood.

Women in some societies today are taught that becoming a teacher or a doctor are the only two noble professions for them. Yet, it is important to remind them that in seventh-century Arabia, women were fully engaged in warfare, farming, issuing *fatwas* as jurists, trading goods, engaging in politics, policing, supervising the marketplace, educating people, healing the wounded, reciting the Quran, and inspiring the masses through their knowledge.

The notion that men are preferable to women because they are the sole breadwinner is not based on reality. Since many women lack the financial support of men, they must work to survive. Women's desire to contribute to their personal growth, the welfare of their community, and the wellbeing of their family require women to pursue employment. Any attempt to confine them to the household and restrict their presence in the marketplace causes irreparable harm to the economy.

Some women choose to live a meaningful life by focusing their efforts on a higher calling that combines their skill, talents, and spiritual aspirations. Countless women have founded organizations that advance the cause of Islam and promote the social good, such as the organization I founded, Women's Islamic Initiative in Spirituality and Equality, to spread the truth about Islam, dispel myths about Muslim women, and elevate women's status.

Amany Killawi, an American Muslim who cofounded LaunchGood with her husband to energize and fund the creative potential of Muslim ingenuity, is one such woman who has had a significant effect. Her business combines social services with an entrepreneurial twist, using modern technology to raise funds for social justice projects via contemporary technologies. This high-performing pair has raised more than

$280 million to finance programs and projects, including the book *30 Rights of Muslim Women*.

Despite cultural constraints, women continue to work in all professional disciplines, and some have broken the conventional glass barrier. They work in the military, business, law, trade, education, religion, farming, politics, healing, engineering, and the fine arts, similar to seventh-century women. Some are Nobel laureates, while others are astronauts on space exploration missions, many draw strength and inspiration from the Quran, Sunnah, and the impressive history of extraordinary women.

A well-documented list of excellent Muslim women, both past and present, demonstrates that obstacles to women's job choices are not Islamic, but rather the result of customary behaviors that attempt to override Quranic injunctions. For example, Shahnaz Laghari was the first Pakistani woman to fly an airplane while wearing a headscarf, earning her a place in the *Guinness Book of World Records*. Her drive to fly while adhering to her religion inspires Muslim women everywhere. The late Zaha Hadid revolutionized modern architecture by pushing space boundaries with curves, for which she was the first woman and Muslim to earn the coveted Pritzker architectural prize. She stated that her designs are not meant to leave a personal imprint on the world or to be self-indulgent but to address twenty-first century challenges and opportunities.

A CONTEMPORARY OCCUPATIONAL SISTER OF KHADIJAH

I offer you one final example: Saira Malik, a Pakistani American, who defies the common stereotype that women are not adept at finance. Even though her career counselor advised her to attend a community college, she chose her own path. She rejected this advice and pursued her passion and earned a master's degree in finance from the University of Wisconsin-Madison. She is now the chief investment officer of Nuveen, which manages $1.2 trillion in real estate and private assets. "It's important to resist and reject bad advice," Saira remarks, recalling how her grandmother also defied the odds by being among the first class of women admitted to medical school in pre-Partition India. The diploma was written for a man, and the administrators had to cross out the male pronouns to hand-write female ones in their place. Saira said that the diploma hangs in her home as an inspirational emblem. Saira's story, coupled with her grandmother's groundbreaking achievement in a male-dominated field, serves as a testament to the strength of women who boldly challenge limitations, making their mark on history and inspiring generations to come.

#4 | TO FREEDOM OF SPEECH AND EXPRESSION

Tawakkol Karman, renowned as the "Iron Woman" of 2011 for her nonviolent methods of achieving peace, hails from the country of her famous predecessor, the Queen of Sheba. As a journalist, Karman pushed for free speech and suffered several arrests and death threats. During the 2011 Yemeni Revolution, popularly known as the "Mother of the Revolution," Karman spearheaded rallies for free speech, raising awareness for imprisoned journalists for expressing their thoughts. She received the Nobel Peace Prize for her work with Women Journalists Without Chains, an organization she cofounded. Karman, as a Nobel Laureate, continues to promote human rights by speaking out against violence and injustice on a global scale.

THE QURAN ADDRESSES OUTSPOKEN WOMEN

The Quran encourages free speech so long as the speaker is truthful and motivated by good intentions. Muslims are required to speak openly about the truth and denounce injustice. *"O believers! Be mindful of God and say what is right"* (Q 33:70). A persecuted individual has the right to speak out against oppression. *"God does not like negative thoughts to be voiced- except by those who have been wronged"* (Q 4:148).

The ability to freely communicate one's thoughts, beliefs, and opinions without fear of injury or censure is known as free speech. During the Prophet's time, women used their free speech to seek clarity and to assert their views. Um Salamah, the Prophet's assertive wife, questioned the Prophet on why God's revelation did not address women. Her concern over God's inattention to women was so sincere that her question reached the Divine throne. In response, God revealed verse 33:35, which Afra Jalabi skillfully frames in her preface. The verse masterfully underscores the importance of recognizing women's voices in spiritual matters, and also demonstrates a more inclusive perspective of faith, setting a gold standard for gender equality. More importantly, it is a testament to how important women are in God's eyes, and how God listens to and addresses their queries and concerns.

Another woman, called Barira, approached the Prophet to obtain a divorce from her husband, Mughith. Because her husband did not desire a divorce, the Prophet advised her to rethink. Barira asked the Prophet if he was "ordering her to return to her husband." He replied that she was not under such direction. She subsequently stated her intention to divorce Mughith, which was allowed by the Prophet.[41]

As mentioned in the preface of this book, Khawlah bint Tha'laba openly argued with the Prophet about an ancestral custom of *zihar*, an ancient Arabian declaration of divorce in which husbands compare their wives to the "back of their mothers," thus making the wife forbidden to her husband and preventing her from obtaining a divorce and remarrying. Khawlah's concerns were satisfied by the revelation of verses. Afra Jalabi eloquently points out how a woman's argument and the issue she raises is elevated to the heavenly realm, and as a result, the entire dynamic is transformed into a search for justice. The Quran portrays it as a method of communicating with the Almighty.

When Caliph Umar advised his people to keep dowries small, Khawlah spoke out again and publicly corrected Umar, quoting the scripture, *"If you desire to replace a wife with another, and you have given the former 'even' a stack of gold as a dowry, do not take any of it back. Would you 'still' take it unjustly and very sinfully?" (Q 4:20)*. Umar listened to her carefully and patiently until she finished. One of Umar's male companions was taken aback that a Caliph would waste his time listening to a strange elderly woman on the street. Umar is reported to have corrected the man, saying, "Woe to you, do you not know that this woman is none other than Khawlah, whose complaint was heeded by God from the heights of his seven heavens. How could I not listen to her when the creator did?"

Khawlah publicly shared her knowledge and proclaimed the truth, and Caliph Umar, a man of immense authority and respect, agreed that she was accurate. If Umar had not allowed Khawlah the freedom to speak and dispute, Muslims would have been misled and left ill-informed by their leader Umar. According to Asma Lamrabet, author of *Women in the Qur'an: An Emancipatory Reading*, Khawlah, a woman whose personality was bolstered by a verse revealed specifically for her, felt confident enough to educate Caliph Umar ibn al-Khattab years later.[42]

Mojha Kahf also makes an interesting observation. She explains that Khawlah's critique of male religion-legal rulings links her to another position, best known of Aisha, of the women who dispute men's interpretation of the faith. She depicts Khawlah's challenge as a woman accosting an authoritative person, but states that women could get away with saying more because, as women, they were not viewed as a genuine threat to the authorities.[43]

THE LEGACY OF WOMEN'S VOICES

The Prophet created a spiritually engaging environment for his followers so that all women may openly express their concerns and spread religious information. According to Leila Ahmed, the Prophet's value of women's concerns and giving weight to their ideas became a characteristic of the Muslim community after his death, as seen by the acceptance of women's contributions to hadith.[44] Many of the instructions that Muslims rely on today would not exist if Aisha had not consistently questioned the veracity of hadith from other narrators, therefore strengthening the community's religious understanding.

When the Prophet's granddaughter, Zaynab bint Jahsh, was captured in Damascus by the tyrant Yazid after the Battle of Karbala, she was accompanied by children and women from Husain's army. A man in Yazid's court asked that he be given Fatimah bint Husayn, the Prophet's young descendant. Zaynab defiantly told the man he was unworthy and did not have that type of authority. When Yazid claimed that he had the authority to decide, Zaynab recalled the Prophet's words, "the best jihad through God's path is to speak a word of justice to an oppressive ruler." She proclaimed, "You, a commander with authority, are vilifying unjustly and oppressing with your authority," she said firmly.[45]

In seventh-century Arabia, poets were highly prized, and one of the finest was a woman, Al-Khansa (d. 630 CE). Her poetry was praised by Prophet Muhammad, who described it as "unsurpassed."[46] According to one narrative, the poet Al-Nabighah informed Al-Khansa that she was the best poet among women, to which Khansa replied that she was the greatest poet among men too.[47]

Lalla Ded, another poetess and spiritual rebel of Kashmir's medieval period, had no possessions but plenty of revolutionary ideas in the fourteenth century. She questioned women's oppression and relegation to subordinate roles in rituals. As a result, she shed light on women's marginalization and objectification. She produced over two hundred poems expressing her soul's desire for the Divine: "There is no light like the knowledge of ultimate TRUTH, no pilgrimage like the love of the Supreme, no relative like the Lord himself." Lalla claimed that strength and power will come through unity. She penned poetic words that still ring true today: "The person who has no ideals and cherishes no purpose in life, the one who is engrossed in self-love and blinded by selfishness, does not exist in reality; he is dead, though living."[48]

Leila Ahmed states that by the late nineteenth century Muslim women were publishing opinions and concerns. Aisha Taymour (d. 1874) published the poem *Mi'rat al-ta'amul* (Mirror of Contemplation in the Situation), which criticized the behavior of upper-class men toward their wives. In Egypt, the first magazine for women, *Al-Fatal* (The Young Girl), was published in 1892. In the 1890s, women authors began to appear in magazines edited and published by men. In 1892, Zeinab Fawwaz published articles in *Bint al-Nil* (Daughters of the Nile) in which she urged the British to provide educational opportunities and employment for all Egyptians. Salma Quaatli, of Syrian descent, published an article advocating for the education of women in a more forceful way. She declared that women attended schools and decided to leave behind "their role of insignificance ... and give up the necessity of directing their thoughts and efforts solely to household tasks." (140–41)

MEN CENSORING FREE SPEECH

Even though early women openly expressed their ideas, a minority segment of Muslims believe that a woman's voice is *awrah* (a private part) that should not be heard publicly, citing the verse, *"O wives of Prophet! You are not like any other women: if you are mindful 'of God' then do not be overly effeminate in speech 'with men' or those with sickness in their hearts may be tempted but speak in a moderate tone" (Q 33:32)*.

In his book, *Speaking in God's Name: Islamic Law, Authority, and Women*, Khaled Abou El Fadl says this verse addresses wives and does not decree that a woman's voice is to be concealed (*awrah*). It distinguishes between two types of speech: *khudu* (gentle, alluring, seductive, enticing), and everyday speech. He argues that the verse discourages submissive speech and encourages principled and just speech.[49]

The majority of schools and jurists oppose the idea that a woman's voice is *awrah* and must be hidden to prevent men from being tempted. A small faction reject the Quranic assertion that women can speak publicly. They mistakenly believe men are easily aroused by a woman's voice, which might lead to temptation and chaos.

When I first recited the call to prayer, *adhan*, my late father-in-law told me how beautiful he thought it sounded. He explained, however, that I was not allowed to recite it in public. When I inquired as to why, he stated that my voice was *awrah*. I asked him to clarify the distinction between women publicly reciting the Quran and calling the *adhan*. The query caught him off guard and he was unable to provide me with a satisfactory answer.

Today thousands of Muslim women are utilizing their voices to serve their communities and demonstrate the power of their voices. Al-Zahraa Layek Helmee, an Egyptian, publicly recites the Quran, a job traditionally occupied by men in her nation. Helmee has almost a million Facebook fans, and many of them support her. Others—men and women—reprimand her in messages, urging her to "fear God" or arguing that her voice can tempt men, an idea she rejects.[50]

Dilshad Ali describes how Ustadha Maryam Amir, a skilled reciter, developed a smartphone application, "Qariah: The Women Quran Reciters," in 2022. This app is "women's recitations, for women, by women, for the sake of God." According to Professor Zahra Ayubi, the controversy surrounding women reciters is a matter of convention rather than law. Women reciting the Quran, she says, is an incredibly powerful response to the idea that their voices are *awrah*—because they speak the most honorable truth for Muslims and keep true to God's command to speak honorably.[51]

SEVEN ISLAMIC PRINCIPLES OF LIBERATION

As evidenced by God's discussion with Khawlah, Muslims have an inviolable right to free expression. Silencing women in public is a type of subjugation that can result in fear, harassment, persecution, and intimidation. When a woman is not allowed to speak, she loses her authority and is rendered powerless. She cannot lead a life of dignity, fulfill her purpose, redress grievances, prevent injustice, or serve her faith, community, or society.

FREEDOM OF THE SOUL

Every human being has an innate desire for freedom. The ultimate freedom is the freedom of the soul, which is a natural connection to a higher power that transcends the self and ego. According to Kabir Helminski, the material world will never satiate us completely or bring us closer to existence itself. We must not deny the material world but acknowledge what it cannot offer and concentrate on inner realization and God-consciousness.

According to the Quran, the soul is the essence of God within us, as it says: *"So, when I have fashioned him, and had a spirit of my own 'creation' breathed into him" (Q 15:28)*. Identifying the origin of the soul as a ray of light; the life force of God himself, enables a person to discern God, perceive his actions, commune with God, and recognize inspirations and insights from the soul as our source of guidance.

FREEDOM OF RELIGION/BELIEF

The Quran addresses freedom of belief explicitly: *"Had your Lord so willed, 'O Prophet,' all 'people' on earth would have certainly believed, every single one of them! Would you then force people to become believers?" (Q 10:99)*. God says in another verse that cannot be interpreted in any other way, *"Let there be no compulsion in religion, for the truth stands out clearly from falsehood" (Q 2:256)*.

Aisha Musa states that this is an absolute negation, which means it is an emphatic denial of the subject of the negation—in this case compulsion in religion. She describes the circumstances in which the verse was revealed. The verse was a command to the Prophet's followers in Medina who had raised their children as Christians or Jews and now wanted to force them to convert to Islam. When they expressed this desire to the Prophet, the declaration, "there is not compulsion in religion" was revealed.[52]

The author of *Freedom of Expression in Islam*, Mohammad Hashim Kamali, characterizes Abu Zahrah, an influential Hanafi jurist, as relating the story of an elderly Christian widow who petitioned Caliph Umar bin Khattab. She was granted her request. He then invited her to embrace Islam, but she declined. At this point, the Caliph became anxious, fearing that his invitation may have amounted to coercion, and he expressed regret. "O, my Lord, I did not mean to compel her, as I know there must be no compulsion in religion." Thus, Caliph Umar stated that only God has the power to influence the souls and minds of individuals in matters of faith.[53]

FREEDOM OF EXPRESSION

According to Kamali, a key Quranic principle states *"The believers, both men, and women, are guardians of one another. They encourage good and forbid evil" (Q 9:71)*, and this is known as *hisbah*, roughly translated as "accountability," which is the root of many Islamic laws and institutions. This includes freedom of religion, opinion, speech, assembly, and criticism. Every human being, regardless of gender or religion, is granted these freedoms, so long as they are used for a good cause or to disapprove and criticize a bad one. Without freedom of speech and expression, it would be inconceivable to carry out this obligation. (28) He points to the Quran's prolific use of expressions such as "those who exercise their intellect" (*ya-qilan*); "those who think" (*yatafakkarun*); "those who know" (*ya lamun*); "those who ponder" (*yatadabbarun*); and "those who understand" (*yafqahun*) to show how much the Quran encourages enquiry and investigation. Thought, judgment, opinion, and knowledge, the Quran suggests, must be expressed and communicated, and only when they are, can faith in God be promoted to benefit humankind. (14)

FREEDOM OF SPEECH

Kamali states that freedom of speech is also a powerful instrument when used to combat injustice, as it allows errors and malpractice in public affairs to be discovered and rectified. *"[H]ave We not given them two eyes, a tongue, and two lips and shown them the two ways of right and wrong?" (Q 90:4)*. Thus, free speech plays a distinctive role in nurturing a well-informed and vigilant society—one that is likely to exercise good judgment in matters which concern it. (13) As the spoken word carries considerable weight and meaning, it must be used with wisdom, consideration, and etiquette.

The Quran instructs individuals not to transgress speech or indulge in hearsay and to verify information *(Q 24:15)*. The Prophet wanted to make *hisbah* accessible to all people, so he instructed men and women to perform *hisbah* according to their own abilities and suggested three methods to do so. He said, "If any of you see something evil, set it right it with your hands; if you're unable to do so, then with your tongue, and if you're unable to do even that, then denounce it in your heart, but this is the weakest form of faith."[54]

FREEDOM TO CRITICIZE

The Quran indicates in fewer than twenty-five instances that people, as rational beings, are prone to arguing, as shown by Khawlah, "she who disputes, she complains," implying that she expressed herself forcefully.

The Quran also foresees a conflict between rulers and their subjects: "[S]hould you disagree on anything..." (Q 4:59)—thus, fealty to the sovereign does not supersede citizens' freedom to disagree with their leaders. Caliph Abu Bakr led by example, and set a high standard for future generations of Muslim leaders: "Oh, people, I have been entrusted with authority over you, but if I am not the best of you," he declared in his inaugural address: "Help me if I am right and correct me when I am wrong." (50)

As exemplified by Umar bin Khattab, who publicly disagreed with the Prophet's decision to accept the terms of the Hudaybiyyah Peace Treaty, Hashim Kamali explains how the freedom to criticize should be aimed at redressing transgression and wickedness and be constructive or sincere advice. The Prophet was cognizant of Umar's concern but prioritized the greater welfare of his people, which demanded peace above all else.

The Prophet then consulted his wife, Um Salamah, for advice. She was a politically astute woman who understood the advantages of peace. She spoke out and supported his peace treaty, which put an end to Muslim persecution.

FREEDOM OF ASSOCIATION

Freedom of speech and expression cannot exist without the right to nonviolent assembly. Some forms of association are permitted by the Quran, such as promoting charitable work and securing welfare, but transgression and sin are forbidden. In matters of public concern, associations must be transparent and not be clandestine. *"There is no good in most of their secret talks- except those encouraging charity, kindness, or reconciliation between people"* (Q 4:114).

Demonstrations and street gatherings are documented in the annals of Islam. During the reign of the third Caliph, Uthman bin Affan, some of his critics objected to land ownership and staged demonstrations to overthrow his government. He acted wisely in resolving their grievances and preventing the problem from escalating.[55]

FREEDOM OF OPINION

Freedom of opinion is regarded as the most important aspect of freedom of speech, according to Hashim Kamali as the latter may include other forms of expression, such as factual narration, satire, or fiction. Expressing an opinion on a topic implies a level of involvement, commitment, and competence that may or may not be the case in a factual narration of an event. Numerous times, the Quran invites people to contemplate or ponder: *"This is how God makes his revelations clear to you, so perhaps you will reflect"* (Q 2:266). The Quranic concept of *Shura*, which encourages Muslims to share their perspectives and reach consensus through consultation for the benefit of the community or society, best exemplifies the freedom of opinion. *"[A]nd consult with them in 'conducting matters.' Once you make a decision, put your trust in God"* (Q 3:159). While the Quran encourages rational inquiry, it must be accompanied by sincerity in the pursuit of truth and justice. (61)

EXAMPLE OF A JORDANIAN AMERICAN WOMAN

Amani Al-Khatahtbeh, an Arab American, was looking for a network of young Muslims online while seeking her Muslim identity. When she couldn't locate one, she decided to build her own, and in 2009, at the age of seventeen, she launched MuslimGirl.com, an online newspaper, which evolved into *Muslim Girl Magazine*, the most prominent online magazine for American Muslim women. Amani created an annual Muslim Women's Day, to establish a new standard for Muslim women's portrayal in the media and to increase their global prominence. On this day, Muslim women are honored, their experiences are shared, and their fresh, varied, and uplifting stories deluge the web. *Forbes* included Amani Al-Khatahtbeh in its list of the "Top 30 Under 30" in media due to her work and influence. Her journey is a testament to the strength of women defining themselves and weaving their stories into the rich tapestry of the global discourse at a time where their representation is shaped by external voices.

#5 | TO TESTIMONY AND WITNESS

In 2002 a divorced woman accused of adultery in Nigeria was sentenced to death by stoning. The man who fathered Amina Lawal's child had vowed to marry her, but then abandoned her with child. Amina's community charged her with adultery and the court used her newborn child as evidence and witness against her. In court, the judge demanded her to prove her innocence. She did not have counsel, was not permitted to present witnesses, and did not comprehend the trial proceedings, which were conducted in a language she did not know.

Hauwa Ibrahim, the first Muslim woman lawyer in Nigeria, heard Lawal's account after her testimony was denied, and decided to defend her. In the initial proceedings, Ibrahim's testimony was thrown out, and Lawal's appeal was denied. However, Ibrahim, a pioneer in the protection of women in Shariah courts, established a fundamental legal principle: the right to a defense and the liberty to be presumed innocent until proven guilty. Ibrahim argued the adultery case based on Islamic law, which requires four eyewitnesses to establish adultery. Since there were no witnesses, Amina was absolved, and her death sentences were overturned by the Sharia Appeal Court of Katsina.

TRUTH AND JUSTICE ARE A GENDERLESS PATH

The declaration of the Faith (*shahada*) is at the heart of Islam, which means "to witness" the truth that there is no God but God, and Muhammad is God's messenger. The testimony admits that God is neither male nor female, and the qualities of God reflected in the creation are both of feminine and masculine nature. *Shahadah*—besides its main meaning—also encompasses presence, inspection, oath, and acknowledgment. Jurists term *shahadah* as testimony of an individual who has the right to provide evidence to prove an allegation or inform the judge about what they have witnessed.

In pre-Islamic Arabia, women could only seek recourse through their tribal affiliation. Several seminal verses equated justice with faith, including: *"God commands justice, grace, and courtesy to close relatives" (Q 16:90)*, and *"O believers! Stand firm for God and bear true testimony. Do not let the hatred of people lead you to injustice. Be just!" (Q 5:8)*. These grant women the right to testify on their own behalf and allow them to file complaints, press charges, and seek compensation according to the same rules and standards as men.

Prophet Muhammad set the criterion for a witness to testify to the truth: "O My Servants, I have forbidden injustice upon myself and have made it forbidden amongst you, so do not commit injustice."[56] He obligated Muslims to provide testimony and be a witness in familial disputes, criminal activities, financial contracts, marriage, and divorce—as well as in the relationship between humans and nature.

THE DIVINE ULTIMATUM: FOUR WITNESSES

The Quran demanded four witnesses to a crime of slander when the Prophet was confronted with a terrible dilemma: his wife Aisha was accused of adultery when, after losing her necklace, she had been separated from her caravan and left behind. A man named Safwan discovered her in the desert and brought her to the Prophet. Soon, accusations circulated that she had committed adultery, but she claimed innocence. Out of intense pressure, the Prophet sent for two notable witnesses to testify for her: Usama bin Zayd and his cousin, Ali ibn Abu Talib. Usama advised that Aisha be presumed innocent. Ali's relationship with Aisha was strained, so he recommended asking Aisha's slave girl, "who would tell the truth." She had nothing to report.

Eventually Aisha was absolved by God who revealed verse 2:23-25, chastising men who unjustly accuse women without presenting witnesses, and reminding those who knew her that they should have acted in the face of such lies. The slanderers are told that they do themselves a grave injury by providing false testimony because they lose both their right to be a witness forever and to marry a righteous spouse: *"Bad, wicked, malicious women are for bad men, and bad men are for bad women. And good women are for good men, and good men are for good women" (Q 24:24-26)*. This story is elaborated further in #29, To Freedom from Gossip, Slander, Libel, Defamation, and to Privacy.

EQUALITY UNVEILED IN ESTABLISHING THE TRUTH

The requirements for being a witness are determined by the number of witnesses needed to establish the truth: *"[A]nd call two of your reliable men to witness either way- and let the witnesses bear true testimony for the sake of God"* (Q 65:2). Two witnesses are required in situations involving the requests of a dying person, or four witnesses if the defendant is away from home. *"When death approaches any of you, call upon two just Muslim men to witness as you make a bequest; otherwise, two non-Muslims if you are afflicted with death while on a journey"* (Q 5:106). In situations of infidelity, the testimony of both a man and a woman are equally weighted as per the Quran: *"And a fifth oath that God may condemn him if he is lying. For her to be spared the punishment, she must swear four times by God that he is telling a lie"* (Q 24:7-8).

Because of the frequent, incorrect reading of verse 2:282, known as the "Loaning Verse," Muslim women suffer from the misconception that one man's testimony is equivalent to that of two women: *"Call upon two of your men to witness. If two men cannot be found, then one man and two women of your choice will witness- so if one of the women forgets, the other may remind her"* (Q 2:282).

According to Amina Wadud this verse does not imply that women are innately less capable, reliable, or intelligent than men. Rather, it enhances women into a position of social responsibility by involving them in financial matters with which they are typically less familiar. This verse also recognizes that women have the right to be witnesses. Even though two women are named, and both are summoned as witnesses simultaneously, they have different functions. The first woman testifies, while the second woman is present to "re-enforce" her evidence. The main witness can be protected by her presence from being forced to recant or coerced by the accuser to drop her charges. (85-86)

Even if two women were there at the time the contract was signed, according to Mustafa Khattab, the primary witness may not remember the specifics of the contract or may not be able to attend in court due to extenuating circumstances like pregnancy or delivery. The second woman would serve as a backup in any of these scenarios.[57]

Mohammad Fadel shares an interesting perspective, that there is a likelihood that the losing party, assumed to be male, will not respect the court's decision. So, two women were required in order to lessen the blow to the losing party's already wounded male pride, thereby increasing the chance that he would voluntarily comply with the court's decision.[58]

Asma Barlas, author of *Believing Women in Islam*, mentions a historical fact that Naila bint al-Farafsa's sole witness testimony founded the campaign by Aisha and other companions to avenge the assassination of her husband, Caliph Uthman. She also explains that women during the time of revelation were rarely literate and thus unable to recognize the inscription of their names. Even more rarely were women involved in commerce. The word of God recognizes and privileges women acting as witnesses with the right to seek advice from another woman who, jointly with them, witnessed a document.[59]

Furthermore, because the verse makes a distinction between testifying in court and witnessing a debt contract, it cannot be applied broadly and is not a general rule. According to Asma Lamrabet, strictly speaking, it refers to affidavit or attestation (*ishhad*), rather than testimony (*shahada*). The verse in question refers to attestation established between two people in the case of financial debt. (145)

According to Egyptian online platform Dar Al-Ifta, jurists like Ibn Taymiyah (1263-1328 CE) and Sheikh Muhammad 'Abdu (1865-1905 CE) presented a thorough explanation of how this verse refers to the *ishhad* in which the debtor confirms his debt. It addresses the debtor, not the judges, and does not refer to the type of testimony in which the judge rules between litigants. The affidavit requires the judge to get confirmation from a witness, which does not depend on sex or the number of witnesses, but rather on the judge's assurance of the veracity of the testimony. Once the validity of the evidence has been established, the judge accepts the testimony of two men, two women, a man and a woman, a man and two women, a woman and two men, or a single man or a single woman.

The gender of the witnesses upon whom the judge bases his decision has no bearing on his decision. *"O believers! When you contract a loan for a fixed period, commit it to writing. Let the scribe maintain justice between the parties. The scribe should not refuse to write as God has taught them to write. They will write what the debtor dictates, bearing God in mind and not defrauding the debt. If the debtor is incompetent, weak, or unable to dictate, let their guardian dictate for them with justice"* (Q 2:282).

Muhammad 'Abdu clarified that, under the social context of the period, women normally did not attend meetings relating to financial transactions or business. "The reason for this is that women did not participate in financial dealings like men; not due to their nature of forgetfulness, but rather that they did not have experience dealing with commutative contracts."[60]

THE MYTH OF MEMORY LAPSE

Muhammad 'Abdu's explanation on the Dar Al-Ifta platform is that a woman's memory is not inherently weak but is related to her daily experience and may be viewed as more efficacious than a man's memory in certain domestic matters in which she typically has more expertise. Asifa Quraishi, in *Windows of Faith*, explains that assumptions such as the lack of memory, incompetence, and general weak character of women stem from a patriarchal viewpoint in a male-dominated intellectual community. The Quran does not bear this attitude because it establishes the equality of men and women before God and the responsibility of both equally as stewards of God on earth. She argues that denying women the right to testify in *zina* or *zina-bil-jabr* (rape) cases "prevents women from fulfilling the Islamic obligation to bear witness to the truth," which is repeatedly emphasized in the Quran.[61]

Jurist Ma'ruf Ad-Dawalibi on the Dar Al-Ifta platform explains that Shariah emphasizes how the testimony of a single man is not accepted in financial claims. These allegations require two men as witnesses. Adding a second man to the first will confirm his testimony and remove any doubt. No one considers this degrading to men if it protects the rights of others. Moreover, the testimony of a single male is never accepted in even the most trivial financial matters, whereas women excel men when it comes to providing sole testimony in more serious matters. Ibn Al-Qayyim remarked that the Prophet never rejected any statement from a reliable person, whether in narration or as a testimony, but he accepted the witness of a just person in all matters.

ANTIQUATED CUSTOMS DEEM WOMEN HALF A PERSON

But despite Quranic commands requiring a woman to be her own witness and testify on her behalf, there are countries and regions where patriarchal customs are still so entrenched that a woman is either prevented from testifying on her own or her case is dismissed if she is not supported by another woman. In this instance, she is deemed half a person and when her testimony is not heard (in cases such as adultery, libel, larceny, or sodomy), she has no recourse for the injustice she has endured.

Asli Sancar describes how Ottoman women were aware of their legal rights, commonly used the courts to settle disputes, and received the courts' support in their pursuit of justice. Because of this faith in the legal system, the court was considered their protector. They took any kind of problem to courts that they could not resolve by other means and were able to obtain justice. Courts were used to settle marital and divorce issues, secure financial maintenance, settle property disputes, and protest about physical violence. According to court records from the seventeenth and eighteenth centuries, women won 77 percent of legal cases involving women against men. (138)

ONE WOMAN'S TESTIMONY WILL SUFFICE

In the case of Uqbah Ibn Al-Harith, who approached the Prophet with a marital difficulty, Prophet Muhammad accepted the evidence of one woman against one man. A female slave testified that she had nursed both him and his wife, rendering their marriage null and void because they shared a milk mother. The Prophet accepted her testimony and ordered Uqbah to separate from his wife, who was surprised that an enslaved woman was on equal footing on the scales of justice, saying, "This means that the testimony of 'one woman' is accepted, even though she is a female slave."[62] The Prophet thus set a precedent for women's legal participation and emphasized the importance of justice and equality regardless of social status.

According to Khattab, many times the testimony of one woman is accepted, for example the beginning of Ramadan is confirmed when the new moon is sighted by any person. (26) The testimony of a man and a woman is equal in the case of the Oath of Lian, in which a husband "curses" or "condemns" his wife by accusing her of adultery without producing four credible eyewitnesses. *Verse 24:8-9* describes that in situations of infidelity, the testimony of both a man and a woman are equally weighted. It says, *"For her to be spared the punishment, she must swear four times by God that he is telling a lie. And a fifth oath that God may be displeased with her if he is telling the truth."*

As it pertains to lineage and inheritance, the Dar Al-Ifta platform shows there are areas in which women excel over men in terms of giving sole testimonies that are more serious. Sometimes, in fact, the testimony of a woman is preferred to that of a man. For instance, both husband and wife have the option to terminate a marriage contract if they discover an undisclosed defect in the other. If their views differ in defining the defect, then the dispute can be resolved by the testimony of a reliable female witness whose testimony must be acceptable to both parties.

Ibn Qudamah (1147–1223 CE) explains five areas in which a woman can testify alone: childbirth, the cry of a newborn infant, nursing, conditions concealed under clothing (such as virginity and leprosy), and the end of *Iddah* (the waiting period). This does not imply, by the way, that all women should be confined to the home. But a person's expertise and credibility in legal matters is based on their daily experience, not their gender.

WOMEN AS SHAPERS AND ARCHITECTS OF ISLAMIC TENETS

It is remarkable that in Islam, women's narrations are accepted without the need for corroboration, unlike their testimony. Mustafa Khattab says the highest form of witness is for someone to testify they heard a hadith (a narration) from the Prophet. (26) Many hadiths have been narrated by women and have the same authenticity as men and their narrations are accepted in every matter. Furthermore, hadiths concerning religious issues are more important than testimony in a trial. Moreover, Ash-Shawkany said on the Dar Al-Ifta platform, "There is no precedent for a scholar to reject a woman's narration just because she was a female. No scholar can deny the many narrations from women about the Prophet."

Jennifer Heath, author of *The Scimitar and the Veil: Extraordinary Women of Islam*, explains that from the very beginning a strong feminine sensibility illuminated the spirit of Islam. Women transmitted and thus shaped a great deal of Islam's tenets. The following sayings of the Prophet, which Aisha bint Abu Bakr and her pupil Asma bint Abu Bakr heard firsthand, are regarded as part of mainstream Islamic thought. Aisha's account of ablution: "God's messenger hesitated to give such instruction to men, so he directed the women to tell their husbands to use water to clean their private parts and tell them that the Prophet used to clean his private parts with water." Asma's hadith regarding charitable giving: "Do not shut your money bag. Otherwise, God, too, will withhold his blessings from you. Spend in God's cause as much as you can do."[63]

A CALL FOR EQUITY AND JUSTICE

As reflected in the Prophet's farewell sermon, delivered near the end of his life in front of a large audience on Mount Arafat, the Quran gave women equal protection against injustice and ill-treatment. When he spoke, he addressed the entire human race and instructed his disciples to be just and equitable. "[H]urt no one so that no one may hurt you, [D]o not, therefore, do injustice to yourselves. It is true that you have certain rights with regard to your women, but they also have rights over you, [T]reat your women well and be kind to them because they are your partners and committed helpers."[64]

From the Prophet's example and divine revelation, the Quran describes a community composed of men and women for whom justice is obligatory and injustice is forbidden. Today, scores of women are defending victims by prosecuting criminals, testifying on behalf of plaintiffs, and serving as barristers, attorneys, judges, and expert witnesses. Reforms have taken place in countries like Algeria and Tunisia, where laws clearly recognize the reliability of women's testimony in all cases including divorce, child custody, and damages.

EXAMPLE OF AN IRANIAN CHAMPION OF JUSTICE

Shirin Ebadi was born in Tehran with a strong passion for justice and an ardent desire to make a positive impact in the world. Shirin accomplished an extraordinary feat by becoming the first female judge in the Iranian justice system at the age of twenty-three. After the Iranian Revolution in 1979, Ebadi was removed from her post and given clerical work in the same courtroom in which she presided. Unable to pursue her career, she retired early, published books and articles, and received a lawyer's license. She then defended women, children, political dissidents, and refugees through her private legal practice.

The world took notice of Shirin's tireless efforts and unwavering dedication to human rights. In 2003, she received the prestigious Nobel Peace Prize for her work upholding women's and children's rights, supporting nonviolence, and seeing no conflict between Islam and fundamental human rights. She is the first Muslim woman to be a Nobel Laureate of Iranian heritage, who through her unwavering commitment revealed the true essence of her faith, which was founded on compassion, justice, and regard for all.

PART II

THE RIGHT TO YOUR RELIGION

• • • • • • • • •

In Islam, a woman is an autonomous member of the community endowed with an equal spiritual status, individual responsibility, and unique capacity to act in accordance with God's directives to care for his creation. She must have access to religious spaces, including its management, to fully participate in religious life, which spiritually nourishes her as an individual and strengthens her community (*ummah*). Through religious education, she can increase her understanding of faith and promote her and others' spiritual development. She can teach Islam to lead her community in faith in devotion to God for the greater good of her community. She can use her intellectual authority and scholarly credentials to interpret and disseminate religious scholarship and to achieve social and judicial justice.

The objectives of promoting and protecting religion are clear:

- The freedom to practice the Five Pillars (faith, prayer, alms, fasting, and pilgrimage) is essential, or *daruriyyat*.
- The freedom of human beings to make decisions regarding life and religion (Q 2:256) and the existence of interfaith harmony is necessary, or *hajiyyat*.
- Access to the highest quality religious institutions is complementary, or *tahsiniyyat*.

#6 | TO RELIGIOUS AND SPIRITUAL LEADERSHIP

My grandma Moji was fortunate to have a father who passed on his spiritual and intellectual knowledge to her. Despite being well-versed in the Quran, she married as a teenager. Again, fortune smiled on her; her husband supported her spiritual journey, allowing her to guide countless men and women. During my trips to visit Grandma Moji, I saw a room full of people sitting in her presence seeking spiritual direction; she would pray for them, heal their wounds, resolve conflicts, bless infants, and interpret dreams.

She was the most pious member of the family and our most revered religious figure, but she was known simply as *Buod Mojh*, "Mother of all mothers," and had no formal position or honorific title, such as *sheikha*. Moji illustrated how Muslim women have contributed to the spiritual life of Muslims for generations without ever putting anything on paper or receiving official recognition.

The Quran acknowledges role models and holds them in high esteem as they dedicate their lives to imparting knowledge and guiding others. According to the Quran, every man and woman has an opportunity to model righteousness. *"[O]ur Lord! Bless us with pious spouses, and offspring who will be the joy of our hearts and make us models for the righteous"* (Q 25:74). To become an imam for the devout and to set an example for others demonstrates a high level of commitment. In this paradigm, some view the imam as a role model. The philosopher Al-Razi (d. 925 CE) concludes, based on Prophet Abraham's words in Q 26:84, *"Bless me with honorable mention among later generations,"* that some people prioritize obtaining a position of reverence in religious matters as a positive thing since such leadership comes through true knowledge and virtuous action.[65]

Prophets and Messengers are the most exemplary role models. In *verses 32:23-24* God says, *"We made among them leaders, guiding by* our command" and Moses and Abraham are described as guides for the Children of Israel. The Quran also says, *"I will certainly make you into a role model for the people"* (Q 2:124). God describes Prophet Muhammad as one who *"has come to you as a messenger from among yourselves, concerned for peoples for their suffering, anxious for their wellbeing, and gracious and merciful to the believers"* (Q 9:128). Maryam (Mary) is cited as a virtuous example whom Ibn Arabi characterizes as the ideal *imama*, a prototypical mystic whom God exalts above all else so that she may attain spiritual purity.[66]

WHO IS AN IMAM?

The word *imam* is derived from the Arabic root *A-M-M*, which means "to be bound for," and can be translated as "leader" in English. German theologian Halima Krausan asserts that the word *imam* derives from the root *amma*—move forward, lead, be in front—and is related to *umm* (mother). Imam appears approximately ten times in the Quran and refers to much more than a person designated to conduct religious rituals. A more accurate definition is "one who guides," in both the political and religious senses. In the west, imam has become synonymous with religious leader, specifically "one who leads prayer in a mosque," and is incorrectly compared to ordained Christian clergy.

The Quran does not specify how a religious leader is chosen, but the two main sects (Sunni and Shia) concur that knowledge and moral characteristics of fairness and justice are the most important qualities in an imam. The Shia believe that God selects imams to lead humanity in all aspects, and they cite this verse as the basis for choosing a Shia imam. *"It is solely Our responsibility to demonstrate the way to guidance"* (Q 92:11). Sunnis assert that the Quran does not specify a specific process for selecting an imam.

EXAMINATION OF THE QURAN'S ABSENCE OF FEMALE IMAMS

The Quran does not mandate that an imam's position be restricted to men only, or a less-educated man over better-qualified women. Imams are responsible for leading prayers—during the day, in Ramadan, *tarawih* prayers, and on Fridays, congregational prayer. Friday prayer involves delivering a sermon, or *khutba*. As a religious functionary, an imam officiates at weddings, presides over burials, blesses newborns, provides religious education, and offers advice to community members on spiritual matters.

Some Muslims contend that the practice of appointing only men as imams stems from the Prophet's alleged exclusive appointment of men to this position, while other proponents refer to Islam's gender-specific roles and responsibilities. Women can instruct and guide other women and contribute to society, but they should not conduct mixed-gender prayers, according to these views. This stems from a desire to uphold modesty, maintain appropriate gender segregation, and minimize potential distractions during worship.

The Prophet stated, "When there are three people, one of them should be in charge. The one among them who is best educated in the Qur'an is the most qualified to serve as imam."[67] So, it is incorrect to assume that a mediocre man is more capable of conducting prayer than the most exceptional woman. The qualification for the role of imam is contingent on a candidate's religious knowledge, rather than their position, community standing, or gender. This is reiterated in another hadith, which states that if all individuals are equally versed in reciting the Quran, then the individual with the most knowledge in the Sunna should lead the prayer.[68]

EVIDENCE OF WOMEN LEADING PRAYER AND BEING IMAMA

During the early period of Islam, women fulfilled a variety of religious duties, including Quranic reciters, religious teachers, spiritual advisers, ritual leaders, and text interpreters. They led women in congregational prayers, as did the Prophet's wives for other women. Jasser Auda, author of *Reclaiming the Mosque* describes how Umm Salamah led other women in prayer while standing among them in the same row, and Aisha used to call the *adhan* and *iqamah* and lead women in prayer standing in the same row during Ramadan.[69]

Umm Waraqa Al-Ansarriyah, a companion of the Prophet, memorized and transmitted the Quran before it was recorded in history. Umm Waraqah once asked the Prophet, as he prepared for battle, if she could accompany him and tend to the wounded, and if she died, she would become a martyr. The Prophet denied her request and "commanded" her to stay home. He placed a high value on the religious service she provided in leading the people of her *dar* (area) in prayer. He designated an old man as a *mu'adhdhin* (one who calls people to prayer), indicating that the group she led was larger than just her immediate family. (116) Her refusal to be relieved from her religious obligations over joining a battle accentuates the importance the Prophet placed on the religious service she provided for her community.

Scholars who dispute this precedent assert that she did not conduct a public prayer but did so privately. According to them, *dar* (translated as "area" above) alludes to her residence, not a public location. *Dar* in Arabic can refer to anything from a single residence to the entirety of Islamic territory. For instance, *Dar al-Islam* is also known as the House of Islam. If *dar* signified Um Waraqa's residence, it would contradict the requirement for a *mu'adhdhin*. Why would she need the *mu'adhdhin* to call three individuals to prayer? Since there is evidence that a *mu'adhdhin* was appointed for her, it is fair to conclude that *dar* is not her residence but rather a larger geographical area.

Since Umm Waraqah requested permission from the Prophet, some scholars assert that women must do the same today. In her paper, "The Islamic Basis for Female-Led Prayer," Nevin Reda states that individuals did not seek permission individually to accompany the Prophet into combat. Umm Waraqah's peculiar request was explained by the fact that they sought individual permission to be absolved of their duty. Since the Prophet's death, those who conduct congregational prayers or recite the call to prayer do so without his permission. His permission is neither possible nor required, regardless of gender.[70]

Reda asserts that prohibiting women's religious leadership is not prohibited universally. Prominent scholars including Tabari (d. 923 CE) supported female ritual leadership and believed that women could lead men in prayer. Among his followers were Abu Isma'il ibn Yahya al-Muzani and Abu Thawr Ibrahim ibn Khalid ibn Abi al-Yaman al-Kalbi, who developed their own school of law. Prior to the fourth century, al-Thawri permitted women to lead males in prayer if they were the most knowledgeable. A subgroup of Kharijites acknowledged women as religious leaders. For example, Ghazala al-Haruriyya (d. 696 CE), the wife of the city's founder, Shabib ibn Yazid, entered the city mosque after seizing possession of Kufa, Iraq, to lead her warriors in prayer. During the Friday sermon, she allegedly recited the two longest surahs in the Quran. Another woman, Qatam ibnat al-Shinja, attended a religious retreat in the Great Mosque of Kufa around the same time. The actions of Ghazala and al-Shinja were typical of Muslim women at that time.

According to Khaled Abou El Fadl, Ibn Arabi states that some individuals permit the *imamate* (leadership) of a woman before both men and women, and then he endorses this idea. He objects to those who oppose female imams, arguing that there is no evidence or text prohibiting women from performing combined prayers. He asserts that the *imama* represents spiritual perfection and the Prophet has attested that some women, like some men, have attained this perfection. (111)

In his article, "Story of Female Scholars, Teachers and Leaders in Islam," Mohamed Jebara states that even the strict Ibn Taymiyyah declared, "I say, for men to be led by a woman who is an expert in the Quran during taraweeh is permissible, based on the widely known [traditions] from the opinion of Ahmed [founder of the Hanbali school]."[71]

FEMALE IMAMS TODAY

The most striking contemporary example of Muslim women's religious leaders is the Nu Ahong, or female imams, that have led Chinese Muslim communities for centuries. The Nu Ahong serve as role models for Muslim women, offering advice, counseling, spiritual guidance, and prayer leadership.[72] One female imam named Du Ahong explains that Aisha and Fatima are the most popular role models for Chinese Muslim women, further explaining that since these two holy women are leaders in heaven, it is only right that Muslim women follow their example on earth.[73]

Since women serving as *imamas* in mosques is still a rarity worldwide, women have created their own spaces where *imamas* are in charge of all facets of Islamic life, from birth to death, and conducting Friday *Jummah* prayers.

Amina Wadud was an American *imama* who made headlines in New York in 2005. I recollect a young African American woman's impassioned description of an impending prayer gathering. She stated that it was being organized by progressive Muslims in New York, whose members I was familiar with. When she told me that Amina Wadud would conduct a mixed-gender *Jummah* prayer, I was not surprised, as I am familiar with Sufi women who lead both men and women in prayer. However, something about the affair was unsettling. I was puzzled that a respected scholar and author who had devoted her academic career to furthering an egalitarian understanding of Islam was propelled into a prominent religious role with such mystery and abruptness.

As soon as I discovered that journalist Asra Nomani was behind the affair, my anxiety grew. I was aware of her media savvy, efforts to break down mosque barriers, and the "Muslim women's liberation tour" to publicize her new book. By invoking Rosa Parks, who moved to the front of the bus, she contrasted an African American *imama* leading a mixed gender *Jummah* prayer to the Civil Rights movement. I was concerned that the world's focus would be on the woman imam, a sentiment I shared with the person who broke the news to me.

While I was attending *Jummah* at my mosque in lower Manhattan, Amina Wadud performed the first public Friday prayer attended by men and women without a mosque or minbar to stand on. *Time* magazine reported that she led sixty women and forty men on a prayer rug in a sanctuary of St. John the Divine Cathedral.[74] This was March 2005.

Many of the well-meaning Muslims who prayed behind her were individuals I knew. They sought to create an American Muslim identity while asserting that gender equality is integral to the Islamic faith. They prayed behind an *imama* in the hopes that the event would spark a spiritual revolution. However, many Muslim New Yorkers were taken off guard and unprepared to cope with the controversy, as it was still the aftermath of 9/11; they saw Nomani, a well-known provocateur, behind the initiative, and they perceived it as provoking controversy. Not the substance of her arguments, but her combative approach, was the issue for many would-be supporters.

Muslims protesting the *Jummah* prayer created, as anticipated, a media spectacle. Demonstrators carried signs reading, "Mixed-gender prayer today, hellfire tomorrow." One conservative woman stated restrictions on women are for their protection and are manifestations of respect. The event was discredited on religious grounds by Salafi men who did not know any of the people in attendance. They claimed that the prayer was an innovation, *bida*, and insult to Islam. With BBC, CNN, and *Time* providing extensive coverage, the event sparked a worldwide controversy. Although this was a one-time Friday prayer, Muslims around the world believed Wadud led weekly mixed-gender *Jummah* prayers.

Those who endorsed Wadud cited Umm Waraqa's precedent of leading a mixed-gender congregation. However, this hadith was virtually unknown, so its historical significance fell on deaf ears. Victims of institutionalized patriarchy inwardly yearned for Wadud's success. For them, she was a trailblazer and a revivalist. For religious women and social activists, it was distressing to see a woman theologian with mastery of the Quran suffer the fury of Muslims on a global scale. She was vilified by the majority and hailed by a silent minority.

The raging fires were thankfully extinguished by the diverse responses of Islamic scholars. The validity of women leading non-*mahram* men was criticized (not condemned) by scholars such as Yusuf Qardawi and Sheikh Tantawi. Gamal al-Banna, an Egyptian scholar, disagreed, arguing that Islamic sources validated her actions. Leila Ahmed believed the event would draw attention to women's issues. Both Ebrahim Moosa and Khaled Abou El Fadl supported the decision. Even though Wadud faced insults and threats, Muslim communities around the globe continued inviting her to lead prayers, even when their members resisted.

After years of enduring verbal assault, Wadud has graciously moved on; she has returned to writing books and teaching. As do many male preachers, she utilizes online platforms to reach global audiences. She routinely teaches classes and imparts her vast knowledge to those who wish to learn. This *imama* has adopted a public identity that is quintessentially American. The Lady Imam!

THE DEBATE CONTINUES

According to scholars, the legal evidence supporting the exclusion of women from conducting prayer is limited and based more on customary practice than textual evidence. The following hadiths are cited to reject women conducting males in prayer: "Verily! The woman is not an Imam over men." This hadith has been refuted by scholars because its chain of transmission includes 'Abdullah ibn Muhammad al-Tamimi, a known hadith forger.

In Nevin Reda's paper she explains the hadith by Abu Hurayrah: "The best rows of men are the front rows, and the worst [rows of men] are the back, while the best rows of women are the back rows, and the worst [rows of women] are the front rows." The Arabic word for "rows" used is *saff*. This term is not associated with prayer in the Quran, but rather with battle rows. *"Surely, God loves those who fight in his cause in solid ranks, as if they were a concrete structure" (Q 61:4)*. This is a metaphor for the community, which is bound together like bricks of a house masonry with no gaps. Nothing in the text of that hadith connects the above arrangement with prayers. It's possible that a rule which originated while praying in battle was later applied to prayer.

Numerous scholars prohibit women's religious leadership because of female biology. They cite menstruation, *fitnah* (temptation), and *awrah* (female private parts) as their justification. Using menstruation is illogical, as women are not perpetually menstruating and it does not explain why postmenopausal women, like Wadud, who no longer menstruate are prohibited from leading prayer. The second assertion is that a woman, regardless of her age, marital status, spiritual stature, or accomplishments, is the source of *fitnah*.

This is contrary to the Quran, which defines *fitnah* as the prohibition of illicit sexual relations and not sexual advances. The *fitnah* argument is profoundly distressing because it prioritizes sexuality over spirituality. It implies that men and women are unable to distinguish between the sacred and the sexual. It perpetuates a stereotype about men, suggesting that all men are susceptible to temptation and unable to control their natural desires in the presence of women.

Most men approach sacred spaces with the same reverence for God as do women. They place their shoes and sexuality on the same rack, recognizing that the sacredness of the moment trumps the desire for want and distraction.

The *awrah* of a woman is the third cited reason why an imam's role is unsuitable for women. There are body movements involved in the supplication, such as bending, kneeling, and prostrating. According to some men, prayer requires focus, humility, and submission to God. A female imam standing in front of males may divert their attention or arouse their sexual desires.[75] Thus, prohibiting women from serving as imams is to prevent men from giving in to their sexual inclinations. This is implausible, as morally upright men attending a prayer service are likely to focus on their spirituality than on the gender of the imam, who is not only covered but whose spiritual stature would transcend worries about her gender.

SPIRITUALITY OVER BIOLOGY

Centuries ago, Sufis affirmed the superiority of the spiritual over the biological and encouraged women to freely pursue their spiritual calling. Despite their primary role in the family as wife, mother, and sister, Sufi women were able to overcome society's limitations and play a significant role by participating in Sufi *dhikr* sessions, assisting the shaykh, commenting on men's behavior, and even opposing their views.

Marcia Hermansen explains that exemplary religious figures can be found in Sufi practice throughout Islamic history. Numerous early sheikhas had a significant impact on the men they taught. Their proximity to men allowed numerous sheikhas and Sufi devotees to profoundly influence them. This effect was reciprocal, as men also influenced women.

In her book, *Women of Sufism: A Hidden Treasure*, Camille Helminski describes the writings of Ibn al-Arabi (1165-1240 CE) on women as egalitarian because he was instructed by female Sufi mentors named Shams, Mother of the Poor, and Nunah Fatima bint al-Muthanna. He stated about Shams, "in her spiritual activities and communications, she was among the greatest." Friends and confidants of Rabia Al Basri included Sufyan al-Thawri and Malik Dinar. She is rumored to have lectured some of her friends on the dangers of indulging in worldly pleasures. Her affection for her friends was stoic and unbending. Sufi biographers hold Rabia in the universal highest esteem and extol her single-minded devotion to God and uncompromising stoicism. They also often grant her a much higher spiritual status than her distinguished male contemporaries.[76]

To spread the virtues of generosity, hospitality, love, and peace, Sufi women practice *futuwwah*, a time-honored code of spiritual chivalry. A sheikha is required to help others reach spiritual perfection once she has been initiated by her spiritual master. She molds followers who embody ideals of harmony, justice, and spiritual and material satisfaction, and who can, in turn, fashion a world centered around these same ideals.

Sufi circles led by women continue to be popular among spiritual aspirants because of the emphasis on personal transformation, inclusion of women, community, and where one's gender is not an inhibitor to their spiritual leadership potential. Many find these contemplative gatherings appealing as they equally honor the wisdom of Rumi and the spirit of Rabia.

A TURKISH SUFI GUIDE INFLUENCES MILLIONS

Cemalnur Sargut, a Turkish Sufi Sheikha, is one such example. At the age of twenty-four, she felt driven to share with young people her experience of a spiritual awakening after learning about Rumi. Her spiritual discourses had such a powerful effect that she amassed millions of followers. She believes that the way to a peaceful society is to let go of the need to change those who are different from us. Sufi scholar, Sadk Yalszucanlar, calls Cemalnur the modern Rabia, as she has attained spiritual maturity through remembrance of God (dhikr), and devotion to the Prophetic path."[77]

Sheikha Maryam is an American who was born into a liberal Jewish family in Hollywood, California. She was in search of the liberating truth, and was guided to embrace Islam at the hands of an ancient Sufi master a few minutes from the tomb of the Prophet Abraham in Jerusalem. She received permission to teach in the Muridiyyah and Mustafawiyyah *tariqahs*, to which she says, the permission to teach *(ijaza)* is, in reality, the responsibility to serve and to share the ever-deepening experience of *ibadat*: love, worship, and service to God. She describes how entering the core of Islam liberated, elevated, empowered, and guided her to discover the true purpose of her existence.

CONTINUING THE TRADITION OF WOMEN'S LEADERSHIP

According to Leila Ahmed, the debate over female religious leadership is vital to the prosperity of *ummah*. Even though many women are discouraged, marginalized, or refused permission to perform religious roles, they continue to be inspired to be a part of a lineage of women in Islam who have held leadership positions. These unprecedented and ever-increasing numbers have carved out a space for themselves in religious life and are part of a vibrant intellectual and spiritual community; creating an awareness of religious issues for women; encouraging debate about women's role; and reclaiming the right to serve as various religious functionaries. (101)

Halima Krausen engages in interreligious dialogue in Germany. She became Muslim as a teenager. When there were few German-speaking Muslims, Krausen sought theological training at the Imam Ali Mosque in Hamburg. She continued her theological studies in several Islamic nations. She worked on translating the Quran into German. In 1996, she succeeded Imam Mehdi Razvi as the leader of the German-speaking Muslim community in Hamburg, where she held the office of *imamim* until 2014, when she was granted *sheikha* status.

To prevent fragmentation of the community, she led by consensus.

Due to the controversy surrounding women preaching, she realized that her community would benefit tremendously from her words and insight. Therefore, she composed the sermons, or *khutbah*, which were delivered every Friday by a male imam. By doing so, she quietly shaped the spiritual narrative of her community without upsetting established norms.

Meanwhile, the Moroccan government sought to dispel the traditional notion that mosques are exclusively male spaces for preaching and guidance. They appointed *murshidat*, Arabic for "guides," as female religious preachers so that they could attract large numbers of women, particularly in rural areas. The initiative is a resounding success because the *murshidat* have been able to combat illiteracy among women and teenagers and have asserted themselves in a traditionally male-dominated field.

In Turkiye, the Ministry of Religion appointed *vaize*, women religious authorities, to accompany pilgrims to Mecca for Hajj. The mosques employ more than 450 female clerics (*wa'iz*). Mehmet Gormez, then-deputy director of the Ministry of Religion, stated that according to Islamic doctrine, men and women are equal, and this should also be applied in practice. The objective of a *vaize* is to advocate for women's issues in mosques, making them welcoming for women. Instead of leading prayers or sermons in mosques, *vaizes* conduct religious seminars and courses for women. One *vaize* states, "In the past, women believed whatever their older brother, father or teacher told them. However, as they become more educated, they are asking more questions." She explains: "We need new answers for new questions."[78]

OTHER EXAMPLES

MARRIAGE OFFICIANTS (MA'ZOUNA)

Amal Soliman earned a master's degree in law in 2007. When the town's wedding officiant passed away in 2009, she applied for the position, which had been held exclusively by males for centuries. Soliman obtained her license and became the first woman in Egypt to become a *ma'zouna* following a lengthy legal procedure lasting over a year and a half. She explains that just because it had never occurred before, everyone presumed it was impossible. Nonetheless, the law is unclear and does not specify a particular gender for the position. People were divided. Some were supportive, others ridiculed her, and a few outright rejected the concept. She explains that Egyptians grew up with a preconceived notion of a *ma'zoun* dressed in imam attire. She questioned how that would work for a woman who could not wear a robe, *galabiya*, like imams do. After she began officiating weddings, public opinion began to shift in her favor. With diligence and a strong work ethic, she gradually became a trusted religious figure.[79]

Today, Muslim women serve as marriage officiants all over the globe, including in the United Arab Emirates, Turkiye, the United States, and Canada.

RECITERS OF QURAN (QARIAS)

Women *qarias* demonstrate their devotion to God and religiosity through public Quran recitations. This strong tradition of *qarias* in Malaysia and Indonesia is exemplified by Hajjah Maria Ulfah, the internationally renowned *qaria*. She began learning the Quran at the age of six. Her father instilled in her the importance of her Quranic education, and to immerse his daughters in this experience, he organized Quran competitions in their community. As a result, Maria Ulfa won multiple competitions growing up. She is now one of the most renowned *qaria* in the world and a lecturer at Indonesia's Institute for the Study of the Quran and National Islamic University.

THE PROPHET'S TEACHING

"Each one of you is a shepherd for his flock," is a teaching often attributed to the Prophet.[80] In other words, we are all guides for those we are responsible for. Everyone must develop their sight, hearing, and critical thinking and tap into our wisdom to become effective guides. Leadership is based on merit and determined by both subject mastery and the acceptance of those we serve. Therefore, it is incumbent on Muslims to avoid ancestor and scholar veneration and to remain faithful to God. In the realm of spiritual leadership, hierarchy does matter, and at its core are spiritually committed souls, male and female, answering a call: "Here I am your Lord, at your service." Those who rise to this stage are beyond gender; they are guided by a higher power, by God himself, to fulfill a purpose or play a vital role. Their initiation is proven not by their claims but by their works.

Numerous women I know have accepted this obligation to promote and preserve divine revelation through service. The manner in which they exhibit, impart, and demonstrate their spiritual insight and knowledge determines their stature and renown. Some devote their time and talent to teaching in Sunday schools, developing youth activities, conducting halaqas, arranging lecture series, speaking in public, organizing interfaith programs, and even training young men to serve as *khateeb*'s for Friday prayers. As with my grandmother, their goal is to inspire personal transformation while seeing themselves as God's servants, rather than leaders.

MY OWN EXPERIENCE

Early Islamic communities flourished because of men and women adhering to the Quran's description of being mutual friends and allies (*awliyâ'*) who provide each other good and deny each other evil *(Q 9:71)*. As an extension of his work, I assisted in providing spiritual mentoring and marriage counseling when I was married to an imam. I had never heard of a woman officiating a Muslim marriage, so, in 2006, when I was asked to perform a ceremony, I thought this was a definite breach of tradition.

I learned that women's exclusion from religious leadership stems primarily from normative practices and social conventions, not from the Quran itself. I learned that woman officiating a marriage was not prohibited, yet I felt conflicted. On the one hand, I knew that people would say it's a man's role, but on the other hand, I felt that women needed to excel in areas that are rarely explored by women in our culture. I had to be prepared for criticism, particularly the first time; but I knew from previous experiences that once people become accustomed to it, other women would follow suit.

The uncle of the groom was not persuaded that a woman could officiate, so I had to obtain a digital *fatwa* from Al Azhar's hotline stating, "We already have *mazoonas* [woman officiators] in Egypt."

I am at ease with my relationship with God, and serving God through community service is an integral aspect of my devotion. I must confess, however, that every time I am thrust into a role that has traditionally been reserved for men, I barrage God with questions. Why am I placed in this predicament? I ask. What else have you planned for me? And the response is always the same: because a void in your community needs to be filled.

What began as private counseling sessions with women has now evolved into a more visible role. I have been asked to provide premarital counseling on how to raise children in an interfaith marriage, mediate disagreements around who initiates the marriage proposal, intervene when tensions flare up between families, speak at funerals, organize burials, lead prayers, provide *duas* (petition prayers) at sicknesses, call the *adhan*, interpret dreams, suggest baby names and children's books, and give my opinion on egg freezing.

But I was completely unprepared when the women's mosque in Los Angeles asked me to lead their *Jummah* prayer and give a *khutbah*. I told the mosque's founder right away that this would be my first time. "We will train you and provide you with all the help you need," she wrote back. My *khutbah* was prepared the day before, but I wasn't well-versed in the Arabic language enough to give the second half of the *khutbah*. Arabic is not my mother tongue, and the *khutbah* is somewhat challenging. Even though I could have done it in English, I choose to make this a more genuine experience by reciting it in Arabic.

Seemi Ghazi, a great reciter, was the first person I phoned. She emailed me the pronunciation over WhatsApp a few hours beforehand, and I practiced it in my hotel room until I perfected it. After the *khutbah* and the Friday prayer, I returned to my room, fell to my knees, and told God, "I hope this was pleasing to you! As a humble servant of God, my strength derives from my unwavering devotion to God and a yearning to sow seeds of spirituality, and share them with open hearts and carry them into fertile grounds.

Given that the Quran is silent on the issue of women's spiritual leadership, should a woman's religious knowledge and achievements not be mirrored in her opportunities to serve as a religious leader in her community? By contributing my knowledge, skill, and talent to my community I was able to restore gender balance and promote greater well-being for all.

It is in the best interests of Muslims, especially in the west, for women to play a larger role in public, even during Friday prayers when communities gather. Khaled Abou El Fadl suggests that priority should be given to what is in the best interests of the community, and that knowledge is the highest benefit. If a female possesses greater knowledge than a male—for example, if a female is more capable of setting a good example in how she recites the Quran and also teaches the community more about the Islamic faith—then, according to him, she should not be excluded from leading *Jummah* solely on the basis of her gender.[81]

In certain circumstances, it may be impractical for women religious leaders to perform rituals. Inasmuch as male scholars are slow to accept women as imams, an equitable division of labor in which women serve as co-*khateebs* is an essential steppingstone. According to *verse 33:35*, women and males are each other's co-stewards. To restore gender imbalance, the male imam can deliver the required Arabic *khutbah*, lead the prayer, and the women *khateebah* can deliver the *bayan*, the advice to the community. Once a qualified *imama* has earned her place in a religious setting and the community has grown accustomed to seeing her in that role, she will invariably assume a larger role, which may include leading the prayers if the members of her congregation authorize her to do so.

It is a woman's prerogative to pursue, achieve, and occupy the roles she chooses to express and share her faith. Instead of endorsing a list of religious leadership roles that others deem appropriate, a woman should consider, identify, and pursue the roles that enable her to express her devotion to God while also responding to the needs and sensitivities of her community.

#7 | TO BE JURISTS AND INTERPRETERS OF ISLAMIC TEXTS

I invited Judge Kholoud Al-Faqih to a WISE conference in Malaysia in 2009. The first Muslim woman nominated to a Shariah court in Palestine had the two hundred women in the room on the edge of their chairs. Prior to being chosen as a judge, she worked for groups that supported and offered legal help to battered women, where she obtained substantial litigation expertise. She did exceptionally well when studying Islamic law and decided to pursue a career as a jurist.

Al-Faqih was selected to serve as a judge at the Ramallah Shariah Court, where she quickly realized that female defendants did not take her seriously and preferred male judges. All that changed when a growing number of female victims confided in Judge Al-Faqih the private details about their cases that they were embarrassed to share with the men. Judge Al-Faqih's popularity also grew as women defendants saw even-handed justice applied to their cases.

Early Islamic history distinguishes itself from other world religions by producing an abundance of extraordinary female scholars.[82] Their contribution to the Quran's preservation, hadith transmission, and the development of religious disciplines was significant. "Those who listen to the words of God and follow the best of it," says the Quran in 39:18. "They are the ones God has guided, and it is they who possess intellect." This passage most likely spurred early-Islam women to spread Islam through interpretation of the Quran, which in turn contributed to the development of the Islamic legal system.

Prophet Muhammad underscored the importance of upholding justice, saying, "Those who act justly will be seated upon pulpits of light before God. They will be those who do justice in their decisions, in matters relating to their families, and in everything entrusted to them."[83] Female companions, particularly the wives of the Prophet, were among the Sunnah's foremost authorities. Aisha bint Abu Bakr spent eight years close to the Prophet. She had such an intimate knowledge of the Prophet's teachings and the Quran's emphasis on justice that she issued numerous legal opinions that were cited by later jurists to bolster their arguments.

According to Fatima Marnissi author of *The Veil and the Male Elite*, Imam Zarkashi (b. 745 CE), a scholar of the Shafi school, bequeathed thirty compendiums, one of which was entitled "Collection of Aisha's Corrections to the Statements of the Companions," where he recorded in writing all of Aisha's objections. It underscores her disagreements with the religious scholars and how she provided additional information. In 1939, Al-Afghani discovered Zarakashi's manuscript dedicated to the Judge of Judges (*qadi al-qudat*), which recognized Aisha's importance by citing the Prophet: "draw part of your religion from the little Humera"—Aisha's moniker. Aisha refuted a number of Abu Hurayra's hadith, stating to anyone who would listen, "He is not a good listener, and when he is asked a question, he gives wrong answers." Aisha criticized him because of her exceptional memory.[84]

Leila Ahmed asserts that Aisha and her female companions contributed significantly to the oral texts of Islam, transcribed later into written form by men. These texts became part of Islam's official history and the literature that established Islamic society's normative practices. Their contribution to major literature demonstrates that, at the very least, the early generations of Muslims and their immediate ancestors had no problem acknowledging women as jurists. (47)

Amrah bint Abd al Rahman, a student of Aisha, excelled among male scholars as a jurist. In a case involving a Christian thief from Syria, the Judge of Madinah, Imam Malik, ordered the thief's hand severed. Amrah sent her student to notify Imam Malik that the crime did not warrant this punishment because the offender had stolen an item worth less than one dinar (one gold coin). As soon as Imam Malik heard Amrah's opinion, he released the man without injury, never questioning her authority or requesting the opinion of another scholar. This incident was recorded by Imam Malik in his *Al-Muwatta*, and this ruling characterized his ruling in similar cases.

WOMEN JURISTS ENLIGHTEN MALE MINDS

Jasser Auda explains that after the Prophet's death, many hadith transmitted by women were readily accepted, and Islam was enriched because male scholars learned about hadith from their female companions. This was true during the Islamic Golden Age, from the eighth to fourteenth centuries, when women played a crucial role in educating their followers. He describes the book by Amal Qurdash, *Women's Role in Serving Hadith during the First Three Decades*, which lists many female companions who influenced male scholars. They are Fatima, daughter of Imam Malik ibn Anas; Khadijah Umm Muhammad; Zainab bint Sulaiman al-Hashimiyah; Zainab bint Sulaiman ibn Abu Jafar al-Mansur; Umm Omar al-thaqafiyah; Asma bint Asad ibn al-Furat; Sulaiha bint Abu Naim; Samah bint Hamdan al-Anbaiyah; and Abdah Abdulrahman ibn Musab. (109)

Auda cites Hadith scholars who reference female hadith narrators. Al-Bukhari attributes Hadith to thirty-one women in his encyclopedia, and Muslim cites thirty-six; Abu Dawud cites seventy-five; Al-Tirmidhi cites forty-six; Al-Nasa'i cites sixty-five; and ibn Majah cites sixty. Al-Hattab, a sixteenth century jurist, describes how his teachers and their teachers trace their works back to books he read by two women: Zeynab bint al-Kamal al-Maqdisiyya al-Musnada, a transmitter of hadith; and Al-Kinani, who developed the theory of intention and intentionality in law to Al-Qarafi, a Maliki jurist. (110)

Aisha Geissinger mentions the compilation Sifat al-Safwa, in which male scholars compiled the names and stories of female teachers and jurists who provided counsel to relatives or others, held *dhikr* circles, addressed audiences, preached, or taught.[85]

Another remarkable example is Amat al-Wahid (987 CE). This renowned Quran scholar issued *fatwas* (legal judgments) which other scholars emulated and transmitted based solely on her authority. Leila Ahmed highlights others like Hajar (b. 1388 CE), the most renowned Hadith scholar of her time, who carried on this tradition but without a veil. Al-Sakhawi, who believed women should veil themselves, did not study under her, even though students flocked to her lectures. However, he studied under female teachers, including Al-Suyuti; As-Qalani; and Khadia bint Ali (d. 1468 CE), a Quran and Hadith scholar. On rare occasions, patrons like Princess Tadhklaray of Cairo encouraged female scholarship. She founded a convent in 1285 CE for Zeinab bint Abu'l-Barakat and her female students. (113–114)

A HIDDEN LEGACY

In *If the Oceans Were Ink*, Carla Power describes how Professor Mohammad

Akram Nadwi uncovered a radically different version of Islamic tradition. In his publication, *Al-Muhaddithat: The Women Scholars in Islam*, he discovered women luminaries such as Umm al-Darda, a jurist from the seventh century who taught law in the mosques of Damascus and Jerusalem. Her students were men, women, and even the caliph. Fatima al-Bataihiyyah, a fourteenth-century Syrian scholar who taught both men and women in the Prophet's mosque in Medina, drew students from as far as Fez. She taught while leaning against the Prophet's tomb, according to one of her male students who couldn't resist adding that she leaned on the most revered location, directly next to the Prophet's head.

Akram discovered evidence in medieval Mauritania suggesting that hundreds of girls could recite *Al-Mudawwana*, a famous *fiqh* book, by heart. Students in Egypt during the twelfth century lauded a female scholar for her mastery of a "camel load" of religious texts. In medieval times, Fatma al-Samarqandiyyah was trained in both Hadith and *fiqh* (juridical theology) by her father. She judged court cases and issued *fatwas*, and advised her famous husband on how to issue his. Fatima bint Yahya's husband was also a jurist and used to consult her on his more challenging legal cases. "This is not from you," his classmates exclaimed anytime he used her *fatwas*. "This is coming from behind the curtain."

Powers is rightfully baffled that, from eras when many women were forbidden from entering mosques, let alone teaching in them, reading about female scholars enjoying such freedoms is inspiring. These women taught judges and imams, issued *fatwas*, and rode horseback or camels to faraway places to study with male masters. As another example, in *Al-Muhaddithat*, for example, the biography of a notable Hadith scholar from the eleventh century, Umm al-Kiraam Karimah bint Ahmad ibn Muhammad ibn Hatim al-Marwazziyah, is sketched out in tantalizing brief details. She was a well-known narrator of the famous book, *Hadith Sahih al-Bukhari*, and lived in Mecca, where she died at the age of 100. Great imams and the well-known historian al-Khatib al-Baghdadi were among her students. She traveled in the "path of knowledge" to Iranian cities of Sarakhs, Isfahan, and Jerusalem.

"If I found 9,000 of them, there are many, many more," Akram believes of all the female scholars he discovered. Many of the women described in the *Al-Muhaddithat*, for example, were not named as sources. Despite this, they were only described in heart-rending descriptions as "sister," "wife," or "daughter." He adds that "In the history of Islamic scholarship, no woman has ever been accused of fabrication or inaccurate reporting of the Hadith." They didn't need to make up hadith since it wasn't a source of money for them, and they didn't do it to become famous. They resolved to learn for the sole purpose of learning. A scholarship was a spiritual vocation rather than a career for women.[86]

Biba al-Harthamiah, an eminent female scholar from medieval Kabul, was also an anomaly, according to Mohamad Jebara's article "The (downplayed) Story of Female Scholars, Teachers and Leaders in Islam." It is ironic that in a country where women have lost all their autonomy, thousands of Afghans centuries earlier braved the frost as they followed the bier of Biba al-Harthamiah, an eminent region's mufti, in 1099 CE. Biba is among the hundreds of Muslim jurists who once occupied positions of prestige and influence in the Muslim world yet who are now all but forgotten.

EROSION OF WOMEN SCHOLARS

Women's education was first primarily obtained within the family, but later on, they could have access to male scholars and teachers. Scholarship entailed learning by rote memorizing. They would study Hadith, *fiqh*, and *tafsir* (Quran interpretation). They were awarded certificates attesting to their ability to teach. Umm Hani (d. 1466 CE) was educated by her grandfather; when she accompanied him to Mecca, she was "heard" reciting hadith and obtained "certification" from several male scholars. She knew Hadith and *fiqh* so well that she was one of the distinguished scholars of her day.[87]

As Islam spread into the Persian and Byzantine empires, cultural norms fused with the faith, causing female scholars to decline. In studying Islamic law, women were the biggest casualty of customary norms, regressive state policies, and discriminatory practices. The emphasis on custom created a schism between divine revelation and societal standards. While Islamic law originated from revelation, it gradually shifted and became influenced by jurisprudence, resulting in more men than women studying theology.

In Powers' book, Akram Nadawi describes that the erasure of women was complex in Muslim societies that emphasized female modesty. Traditionally, many Muslim families did not want their daughters' names to be publicized, and the parents protected those names—assigning a broad interpretation to the concept of *hijab*. For this reason, given the tradition of the unnamed women, Nadawi's 9,000 names were most likely a fraction of female Islam scholarship throughout history. (132)

THE QURANIC BASIS FOR FEMALE MUFTIS

Although male guardianship and testimony were cited by some as justification for preventing women from serving as interpreters of the law, many scholars agreed that women could serve as *muftis* (jurists) and *qadis* (judges). Hadith specialist Ibn Salah (1169–1225 CE) says in *Adab Ul Mufti Wa Al Mustafti*, "Maleness and freedom are not required of the mufti, just as they are not required of the narrator (of hadith)."[88]

Dr. Ahmed al Haddad, the chairman of the UAE's Islamic Affairs and Charitable Activities Department, issued a *fatwa* in 2009 that legalized women's roles as *muftis*. He encouraged competent Emirati women to enroll in the program, which would train women in Shariah law and legal reasoning. This sparked controversy among the other religious establishments, such as Egypt's Al Azhar University, which opposed the notion of women becoming grand *muftis*. Dr. al Haddad points to the Prophet's female contemporaries and women jurists who came after them, stating that a learned woman, trained in issuing *fatwas*, is not limited to issuing for women's issues only; she is also qualified to issue *fatwas* about worship, jurisprudence, morality, and behavior. He cites the Quran *(4:85* and *9:71)* to explain why women can serve as *muftis* in all aspects of society: *"Let there be a group among you who call 'others' to goodness, encourage what is good, and forbid what is evil—it is they who will be successful" (Q 3:104).* "Evidence suggests that women, like men, can promote acts of virtue and prohibit acts of vice," he stated, referring to the basic tenement of a mufti's position.[89]

Similarly, Mohamed Hamed al-Gemel, former head of the Egyptian Fatwa Council, stated that there is no specific provision in the Quran or Sunnah prohibiting the appointment of female judges.[90] The Chairman of the High Council of Islamic Law for Palestine also stated that the Hanafi School of Islamic jurisprudence legitimizes the candidacy and appointment of women as judges. In addition to Judge Khalood al-Faqih, Judge Asmahan al-Wahidi was appointed to serve on Islamic Shariah courts in the West Bank cities of Hebron and Ramallah.[91]

FEMALE JURISTS AND ISLAMIC TEXT INTERPRETERS

The widespread illiteracy of Islam hindered women's ability to assert or defend their rights, as well as their intellectual advancement, and Muslim women could not match the intellectual gravitas of the early women in Islam.[92] Despite these historical setbacks, women with expertise in Hadith and jurisprudence are regarded as authorities in their fields, with many developing refined *fiqh* approaches that emphasize the ethical aspects of jurisprudence by employing reason, justice, and consensus. For example, American scholar Asifa Quraishi-Landes, with expertise in Shariah, has published many seminal opinions and papers. Among her works are "Five Myths about Sharia" and "How to Create an Islamic Government—Not an Islamic State."

On the other side of the world, Uganda's Association of Muslim Women increased the number of Ugandan Muslim women educated in *fiqh*,[93] and scores of women there who are often the top-performing students are pursuing careers in Islamic law—from judges and lawyers to court mediators.

Today, women contribute immense value to preserving and propagating the divine law of Islam. For example, Zohreh Sefati, from Iran, achieved the highest jurisprudence degree (*ijtihad*), an accomplishment made by only a small number of women. Her *ijtihad* was approved unanimously by prominent Ayatollahs, including Ali Yari Gharavi, Safi Gulpaygani, Fazel Lankarani, and Mohammad Ahmadi-Faqih. Sefati is a *mujtahida* (an *ayatollah*) and a representative of the Supreme Council of Cultural Reforms.

Some male jurists, including Yousef Saanei, believe a female *mujtahid* can become a source of *marja* (emulation) and that both men and women can perform *taqlid* (emulation) of a woman *mujtahid*. Sefati cofounded a theology school for women in Qom, Maktab-e Tawhid. Many female scholars complain that reaching the degree of *ijtihad* is no use if they cannot be a "source of emulation" and be respected as Islamic scholars. She replied in her works that the responsibilities of a jurist are not only limited to those of a Source of Emulation, and that female jurists can also serve society by helping Muslims interpret Islamic principles.

#7: TO BE JURISTS AND INTERPRETERS OF ISLAMIC TEXTS

EXAMPLE OF ONE MALAYSIAN SHARIAH COURT JUDGE

Nenney Shushaidah bint Shamsuddin, a forty-two-year-old mother of three, made history in Malaysia when she was appointed as a female Shariah High Court judge in 2010. Currently, twenty-seven of the 160 Islamic court judges in the nation are female.

When Mohd Na'im Mokhtar, a former top judge, appointed Judge Nenney, he asserted that it was not an issue of gender. They were looking for the finest individuals to administer justice. Under Malaysia's two-tier court system, Judge Shamsuddin may, on a given day, allow a man to have a second wife or convict him to be caned for violating Islamic law. "When I'm sitting on the bench, I'm neither a man nor a woman," says Shamsuddin. "I am a judge. I need to deal with the case fairly and firmly, to follow the law, and not be biased."

Judge Nenney's opponents have suggested that female judges may favor women, which she disputes: "We can put our emotions aside, I empathize with them; I can put myself in their shoes, not sympathize with them. I need to play my role as a judge, then decide how they present their case." The increasing number of female judges, according to Nenney, could create a balance and dispel the myth that Shariah courts do not treat women equitably. "After this, I hope the women who appear before me will understand there is no difference between a man and a female judge," she says.[94]

#8 TO GAIN SPIRITUAL KNOWLEDGE

When two well-known Afghan religious scholars urged the Taliban to reconsider their ban on girls' education, it prompted a harsh rebuke from the minister who warned clerics not to rebel against the government on a contentious issue. One scholar, Abdul Rahman Abid, who understands that knowledge is obligatory for both boys and girls, laments, "My daughter is absent from school; I am ashamed, and I have no answer for my daughter." He explained: "My daughter wonders why girls are not permitted to attend school in the Islamic system. I don't know what to say to her."[95]

When I received a call from a private girl's school in Afghanistan saying that the girls wanted to learn about Islam, I immediately started a weekly online class for them. In one class, a young student expressed her sadness with being cooped up in the house. I told her that the Prophet's wives were instructed to stay at home and spread the message of Islam from there. "What is stopping you from turning your house into a school?" I asked. A few weeks later, the principal informed me that this student had converted her room into a classroom: "She simply shares what you have taught her with her mother, father, brother, cousins, and aunts, eagerly awaiting the next lesson!" This reminded me of the Prophet's adage, "The best of charity is when a Muslim man gains knowledge, then teaches it to other Muslims."[96]

The first verse revealed to Prophet Muhammad instructs him to read, understand, and spread divine truth: *"Read, 'O Prophet,' in the Name of your Lord Who created—created humans from a clinging clot. Read! And your Lord is the Most Generous, Who taught by the pen—taught Humanity what they knew not"* (Q 96:1-5). The Quran is the primary source of knowledge, serving as a comprehensive blueprint for Muslim individuals and society; its main goal is guidance (*hidayah*), which Muslims should strive for.

The Quran describes learning as an ongoing process in which Muslims must adhere to the truth rather than limiting concepts of ancestral habits and beliefs. In *verse 2:44*, the Quran speaks of the error of approaching the Quran in the wrong way: *"You forget while you recount the Book? Will you not then be reasonable?"* Thus, Muslims must examine divine revelation critically—utilizing God-given reason, grasping its meaning—and reflect on its significance. To access guidance and apply knowledge to the self and for the betterment of society we must use our discernment (*furqan*) to reflect on the questions. *"This is a blessed Book which We have revealed to you 'O Prophet' so that they may contemplate its verses, and people of reason may be mindful" (Q 38:29)*.

KNOWLEDGE: PERFECTION OF FAITH

The aim of education in Islam as specified in the First World Conference on Muslim Education held in Jeddah, Mecca (1393-1977 CE): "Education should cater to the growth of people in all aspects: spiritual, intellectual, imaginative, physical, scientific, linguistic, both individually and collectively and motivate all aspects towards goodness and the attainment of perfection. The aim of Muslim education lies in the realization of complete submission to God on the level of the individual, the community and humanity at large." The goal of Islamic education is certainty that knowledge without the origin in faith and religion is merely partial education.[97]

Knowledge contributes to the growth and perfection of one's faith. There can be faith without perfection, but no perfection without faith, as demonstrated by the often quoted but unverified prayer of the Prophet: "God, grant me knowledge of the ultimate nature of things."

According to Imam Ghazali, seeking knowledge is a process that involves the whole individual, including rational, spiritual, and social aspects. Knowledge is gained to actualize and perfect all dimensions of the human being and Prophet Muhammad is the model of perfection.

The Quran defines education as having two components: acquiring intellectual knowledge (via reason and logic) and developing spiritual knowledge (by divine revelation and spiritual experience). As previously mentioned in #2, *talim* means "to know, to be aware, to perceive, to learn." It refers to learning by instruction and teaching. *Tarbiyah* means "to increase, to grow, to rear," implying spiritual and ethical growth following God's plan. *Taadib* means to be "cultured, refined, well-mannered," implying good, sound social behavior.

Ghazali differentiates between two types of knowledge. Profitable knowledge what increases reverence for God and enables people to recognize their flaws and the best way to serve God. It decreases the desire for this world while enhancing the desire for the next. It opens the individual's senses to defects in their own work so they can avoid them.[98] Therefore, any knowledge that creates a closer relationship with God is beneficial. On the other hand, knowledge that hinders closeness to God must be avoided,[99] as it leads people to spiritual bankruptcy.

Verse 4:162 commands men and women to conduct their prayers, pay their charity tax, enjoin good, and forbid evil in all its forms, to make the pursuit of religious knowledge an inviolable tenet of Islam. Studying the Quran is fundamental to religious instruction, whether intellectual, spiritual, moral, social, or legal. To grasp its meaning Muslims must memorize, comprehend, write, and recite the Quran. Denying a person the ability to seek knowledge denies them the chance to reach the highest status as a human.

The Prophet taught that knowledge is an act of piety that leads to a deeper understanding of the Creator, and that everyone who leaves behind knowledge is rewarded if others benefit from it. These teachings led to a comprehensive and unified educational system based on moral and spiritual boundaries. This commitment to lifelong learning continued as knowledge was transmitted to students through a system of ijazah, which means "permission," "authorization," and "license." Denying someone the opportunity to pursue religious knowledge prevents them from attaining spiritual maturity, and from fulfilling a religious obligation.

EARLY LEARNED WOMEN

In *Revival of the Religious Learnings*, Al-Ghazali cites the Prophet saying, "To be present in an assembly with a learned man is better than praying one thousand *rakats*." It is well known that men and women prayed with him, listened to his spiritual discourses, learned new verses, memorized them, and recited the revelations. They attended lectures, delivered sermons, composed poetry and orations, and the acclaimed ones trained future scholars.[100] Women were so present that Aisha praised them by saying, "How good are the women of the *Ansar* [helpers] that their shyness does not prevent them from learning religion."[101] Ingrid Mattson, author of *The Story of the Quran*, states that Umm Hisham, a female companion, memorized Sura Qaf from the Prophet, which he recited every Friday in his sermons.[102]

Umm Hani Maryam (d. 871 CE) studied Islamic sciences such as theology, jurisprudence, and history before traveling to study Hadith with the greatest traditionalists of her day. She pursued a rigorous learning program in Cairo's renowned college, awarding *ijazas* to several scholars. Ibn Fahd himself studied various technical works on Hadith under her tutelage.[103]

Bai Khatun (d. 864–1459 CE) a Syrian, excelled in teaching. She studied traditions with Abu Bakr al-Mizzi and other traditionalists, and after obtaining the *ijazas* of several Hadith teachers, both men and women, she conducted lectures on the topic in Syria and Cairo.[104] Nafisa bint al-Hasan (762–823 CE) memorized the Quran and was trusted by the scholar Imam Shafi.[105]

Women continued to be driven by their longing to pursue knowledge and impart it to others. Those who could not advance their own study invested in their children's. One example is the mother of Imam Rab'iyyatu-Rai, a scholar of great repute and a teacher of Imam Malik (d. 795 CE) and Hasan Basri (d. 728 CE). Her husband gave her 30,000 *ashrafis* before leaving for a long expedition. While he was away, she spent it all on her son's instruction. When the father returned after twenty-seven years, he could not contain his joy when he saw his son, Imam Rab'iyyatu-Rai in a mosque delivering a lecture on Hadith. When he returned home, his wife asked him, "Tell me, which is better, 30,000 *ashrafis* or the blessing of our son's study?" He remarked, "The *ashrafis* are worthless."

According to the Prophet's assurance, this mother's deed benefited society and secured her place in the hereafter: "When a person dies, all his deeds come to an end except for three: an ongoing charity, beneficial knowledge, and a righteous child who prays for him."[106]

Some women even remain unmarried to demonstrate their singular commitment to lifelong learning. Karima al-Marwaziyya was born in 975 CE into a vibrant Hadith culture in eastern Iran. She was only two steps removed from Al Bukhari's discipleship. Anyone interested in Al-Bukhari's works would seek out Karima al-Marwaziyya for instruction. Her command of Al-Bukhari's book distinguished her and explains her popularity as a teacher in Mecca, where she lived and died in 1070 CE. There, she attracted scholars and scholars-to-be from as far away as Spain, with many of them attending her lectures while on pilgrimage in Mecca, where she granted *ijaza* certificates to her students.

Decades later, Nana Asma'u (1793–1864 CE), a Fula princess, poet, and teacher, established Nigeria's Yan Taru system of communal learning organizations. This school of female teachers established the practice of women serving as the first religious educators. Teachers went to remote regions to educate not only children, but also adults and women from the Sokoto Caliphate.

Syrian Dhayfa Khatun (d. 1242 CE) was a political and social activist. She supported education in Aleppo by establishing two schools: al-Firdaous School, which specialized in Islamic studies and Islamic law, and Khankah School, which specialized in Shariah and other subjects.[107]

DECLINE OF THE MADRASA: A RETURN TO IGNORANCE

According to Carla Power the growth of colonial rule in many Muslim nations led to a decline in women's scholarship, which was exacerbated by the widespread decline in intellectual confidence among Muslims. As the *madrasa* system languished, patriarchal customs filled the void. Many *ulama* abandoned scholarship in favor of politics, leaving Muslims ignorant of their own history. Consequently, "Our traditions were weakened," explained Akram Nadawi. "And when people are weak, they grow cautious. When they're cautious, they deny women their freedoms." (134)

As societies segregated the sexes in the name of modesty, women were relegated to the private sphere and sidelined from the production and consumption of religious knowledge. Even though neither the Quran nor Hadith stated such a prohibition, women weren't allowed to study with male teachers.[108]

Using the *waqf* system, the state began patronizing boys' *madrasas*, over girls', with financial resources and status. Without financial support, women's educational facilities were not built to same quality as those for men. Due to the neglect, women were unable to complete their education and there were fewer qualified female teachers available to teach. This led to lower levels of education for women, even within the same institution, and fewer career opportunities in religious affairs. As

Islamic scholarship and jurisprudence became formalized and oriented toward establishing careers in courts and mosques, after the sixteenth century the number of women scholars declined dramatically.

In addition, colonization and modernization rendered all *madrasas* obsolete. As European-style governments, bureaucracies, and legal systems were introduced, European-style education supplanted *madrasa* graduates as judges and administrators. *Madrasas* became predominantly educational institutions for the poor.[109] Again, according to Nadawi, the erosion of educational opportunities for Muslim women reflects a "decline in every aspect of Islam." (134)

BAND WAVE MADRASA

Fakhira Najiba was concerned about the Pakistani girls who were under pressure to leave school after completing their basic or secondary education due to a lack of resources for secular education. She used her imagination to respond to a request for nonreligious content from a madrasa. Her "Broad Class—Listen to Learn" radio program, which blended interactive learning with radio broadcasts, was introduced under the Power99 Foundation, which she created. The radio program consisted of three grade-level portions with radio correspondents providing instruction. Engaging activities such as puzzles were part of every thirty-minute lesson. More than 200,000 youngsters, 60% of whom are girls, have benefited from Najiba's creative program, and remain literate.

LEARNING IN THE LAP OF THE MOTHER

According to Dr. Ingrid Mattson, Ibn Khaldun (d. 1406 CE) considered the imparting of the Quran to children to be the symbol of Islam. Muslims have and continue to practice such instruction in all their communities because it instills a firm belief in Islam and its articles of faith. The Quran is the cornerstone of education, the basis for all habits acquired later. (89)

The Prophet urged parents to teach their children the Quran, saying, "The best among you are those who learn the Qur'an and teach it."[110] The education of the child must include physical, mental, moral, social, and spiritual components. If only one aspect of a child's development is addressed, his or her education will be inadequate. They must be taught self-awareness, environmental consciousness, and empathy for others. Then, as adults, they will be magnanimous and bring a spirit of generosity into the world.

It is not the same educating a child at home as it is in school. If a mother instills positive traits in her child, such as compassion, sympathy, affection and tenderness, these values will serve the child into adulthood.[111] Dr. Mattson asserts that the most influential religious authority in the lives of many Muslims is a parent, a wise elder, or even a friend who appears to have internalized the spirit of the Quran despite lacking scholarly knowledge. Many people will recognize good character and wisdom as evidence of genuine comprehension of the Quran. (250)

Aisha Gray Henry, an American, observed the difficulties Muslim parents confront in transmitting Islamic knowledge to their children. She created a home-schooling curriculum, "The Ghazali Children's Series," which incorporates the wisdom of traditional Islam into today's challenges. Children of all ages receive authentic, high-quality guidance at a time when their values are being formed. These creative, enjoyable, and spiritual supplements focus on the purification of the heart as children develop self-observation and self-correction.

HEART AWAKENS THE DIVINE WITHIN

When a companion asked the Prophet, "What action is more meritorious?" Al-Isfahani in his *History of Isfahan*, reports the Prophet saying, "Die while your tongue is moistened with the *Dhikr*, remembrance of God." In another tradition, he said "God spreads his shade upon seven people on the day when there will be no shade. And among them are people who remembered God privately and whose eyes overflowed with tears."[112]

Over the centuries, men and women spiritual seekers sat in these circles to increase their intimacy with God, the source of their being. Their focus was to purify their hearts, seek inner contentment through chanting the words of God, and experience Divine Love, *"Surely, in the remembrance of God, do hearts find comfort"* (Q 13:28). This connection between humans and their Creator is described as *dhikrullah* in the Quran, a direct communication with God that transcends language. Several individuals gained notoriety for their exceptional piety. They focused on the *qalb* (heart), as it is the locus of faith. Rabia Basri of Basra, Iraq, formulated the doctrine of Divine Love eighty-two years after the Prophet's death in 714 CE. She was the fourth of four daughters whose parents were so poor on the day she was born that there was neither oil to light a lamp nor a cloth to wrap her in. Her father, an ascetic, knew she was a blessed child, and when her parents died she became an orphan.

Camille Helminski, describes how Rabia was sold into slavery, where she spent her days doing house chores and her nights praying to draw closer to God. *"O, [b]elievers! Always remember God often and glorify Him morning and evening" (Q 33:41)*. Rabia's gratitude to God was exemplified by her pure, unconditional love for God. She was so transcendent that, even while in bondage, she requested nothing from God other than the chance to please him. "Oh God, I am a stranger," she said, "without father or mother, I have been sold in bondage, and now my wrist is broken. But despite all this, I am not distressed about anything that has befallen me. I wish you to be content so that I might know whether I have gained your satisfaction."

One night, when her owner saw the light surrounding her, he realized she was no ordinary person. He set her free out of concern for his life. Rabia then ventured into the desert outside Basra, where she prayed and lived in semi-seclusion for many years. She believed that love is the only way to God, proclaiming, "I love God: I have no time left / In which to hate the devil."

She ran through the streets of Basra with a pot of fire in one hand and a pail of water in the other, proclaiming, "I want to put out the fires of Hell and burn down the rewards of Paradise, because they are blocking the path to God. I desire to venerate God not out of fear of punishment or the promise of rewards, but out of pure love for God." The doctrine of *Ishq-e-Haqeeqi*, Divine Love, was revolutionized by her undying devotion to God, patience, and intense self-denial. As a spiritual guide for men and women, she taught that to be fully devoted to God, one must understand that the relationship between humans and God is personal and selfless, not bound by personal rigidity or ancient traditions.

Though not corroborated, it is widely reported that Hasan al-Basri acknowledged her spiritual and intellectual standing, saying, "I spent one day and night with Rabia.... It never occurred to me that I was man, and it never occurred to her that she was woman…when I looked at her, I saw myself as bankrupt [i.e., spiritually worth nothing] and Rabia as truly sincere [rich in spiritual virtue]." Hassan al-Basri became a pivotal figure in the evolution of Sufism after he preached against worldliness and materialism.

Farid al-Din Attar, who included her as a saint in his series of biographical profiles, penned, "If anyone asks, 'Why have you included Rabia in the ranks of men?' my response is that 'God does not regard your outward forms.'"[113]

Furthermore, if it is permissible to derive two-thirds of our religion from Aisha, it must be permissible to receive religious instruction from one of Aisha's servants." He stated that Rabia was not a woman but rather a hundred men over. Helminski states that Rabia lived into her eighties, exemplified ecstatic religious freedom, transcending ideas of divine punishment and teaching the spiritual art of living within Divine Love. She said, "I seek no reward for it; I do it so that the Messenger of God will take pleasure in it on the Day of Resurrection and tell the other prophets, 'Take note of what a woman from my community has achieved.'"

VISUAL ARTS AND SPIRITUAL AESTHETICS

The verse from the Quran, *"[R]emembrance of God is an ever-greater deterrent" (Q 29:45)*, implies that a person's entire existence should consist of acts of devotion and remembrance toward his Creator. This preoccupation with remembering God fostered the development of artistic expression. The artist initiated the process of translating Islamic principles into an aesthetic language, in other words, rendering them into forms and motifs that will be incorporated into structures and used as ornamentation.

When the Prophet said, "God is beautiful, and God loves beauty,"[114] it became the doctrinal basis of Islamic arts and aesthetics. In *Seven Doors to Islam: Spirituality and the Religious Life of Muslims,* John Renard asserts that the Quran is the first work of Islamic art to emphasize the superiority of God's word over humans. These were known as "Quranic arts." Rumi, the renowned mystic and poet, defined the spiritual aesthetic and its purpose: "No painter, potter, or calligrapher constructs a work of art for its own sake. One must view all forms of creation as vehicles for appreciating the God's unseen beauty."

For a Muslim, Renard says, the purpose of art is to inspire contemplation and remembrance of God. There is no more suitable agent than the poetically inspiring passages of the Holy Quran to attain this objective. The Quran says, *"[R]ecite the Quran properly, in a measured way" (Q 73:4)*, and the Prophet instructs his followers to "adorn the Quran with your voices."[115] This indicates that there is a genuine consubstantiality between the divine word and the human voice. Thus, the art of Quranic recitation was prioritized and took center stage. In God's eyes, the reciters have a privileged status, as they are known for keeping the ultimate treasure safe in their hearts.

Likewise, mosque architecture is the most sacred artform because of its role in worship. The Jerusalem Dome of the Rock built in 691 CE is a manifestation of this. The artisans celebrated the sacred message by adorning its walls with exquisite calligraphy emanating from divine revelation. Since then, artisans inlay Quranic texts onto mosques, mausoleums, and mansions and have etched inscriptions on anything imaginable—from clay vessels to lamps, furniture, chests, walls, textiles, and prayer rugs.[116]

WOMEN ARTISTS

Since the Quran is an essential literary education tool, artists used Arabic calligraphy to embellish its aesthetic appeal. *Khatt* is the Arabic term for "line" or "design" in calligraphy. These lovely letterforms, inspired by the Quran, convey the grace of the holy book's message. In Muslim societies, calligraphy remains a preeminent form of traditional art. Quran manuscripts were covered with magnificent illuminations called *tezhip*, derived from the Arabic word for gold.

Traditionally, this art form could be a family vocation with men and women working side-by-side. Boys would learn calligraphy and daughters would learn illuminations. In contemporary times, a sweeping shift has taken place whereby women artists are studying and mastering both forms. One example is Sefika Ulker, who at the age of nine, became passionate about calligraphy. She was told by her teacher: "God created you to write." After she learned the art of illumination from a master, she produced her first piece in her mid-thirties and began to gain notoriety. She talks about the difficulties women face in the art of calligraphy: "Female calligraphers were signing their works with a male pen name." She ponders whether she ought to go by a different name or use her own name. After discussion with her mentor, she now signs her work with her name and has authorized her students to follow suit.[117]

#9 | TO ACCESS RELIGIOUS SPACES

In her article, "Mosques Have Become 'Boys' Clubs,' Despite What Islam Really Says," Hafsa Lodi expresses her disdain for mosques, a sentiment shared by many Muslim women today since the prayer areas are uncomfortable. For example, running children make it hard to hear prayer or *khutbah*. She also explains that patriarchy has perversely thrived in "mosque culture" over the world. Some authoritarian religious leaders justify their male-centered approaches to mosques by quoting the Prophet, who reportedly said that the best place for a woman to pray is in the innermost part of her home.[118] However, this statement is often taken out of context, ignoring the fact that it was intended as a "concession" to women rather than a "commandment."[119]

Every Muslim has a sacred duty to worship God, and God warns wrongdoers against obstructing people from fulfilling their religious duties by preventing them from entering sacred spaces: *"Who does more wrong than those who prevent God's Name from being mentioned in His places of worship and strive to destroy them?" (Q 2:114).*

THE FIRST MOSQUE AND COMMUNITY CENTER

In 622 CE, Prophet Muhammad migrated to Yathrib (Medina) on his camel Qaswa in pursuit of a peaceful location for his expanding community. According to Fatima Mernissi, numerous locals offered their residences and land to the Prophet. He knew that accepting one or the other would open the door to accusations of favoritism. So, employing his diplomatic skills, he deferred to his camel Qaswa, who meandered through streets and alleys and led the Prophet to a house with a *mirbad*, a place for drying dates. Much to the delight of his people, the Prophet purchased the land from Abu Ayyub, its owner, to build his residences and a mosque. When he began the constructions, he lived on the site. A

#9: TO ACCESS RELIGIOUS SPACES

believer said "that it was practically impossible to stay seated while the Prophet was toiling away on the construction site." (106-107)

The Prophet's primary objective in designing the first mosque was to shape the Islamic public realm so that his community could confidently look to the future. The mosque reflected the multifaceted needs of the community by facilitating daily prayers, welcoming new Muslims, disseminating knowledge, and hosting gatherings with visitors, companions, and followers.

Despite the Prophet's limited resources, his vision was lofty. He combined public and private spaces by building the mosque compound next to nine chambers, or *hujurat*, exclusively designed for the wives. This deliberate arrangement implies that he consulted with them during the planning stage. By blending the sacred and the social, along with active presence of companions, fostered a vibrant center for religious, civic, and political exchanges.

This first mosque was a humble, utilitarian structure optimized for efficiency and flexibility, according to Jasser Auda. It was thirty-five meters long, thirty meters wide, and its ceiling was two-and-a-half meters high. It had three entrances, two entrances provided convenient access for worshippers to the open area outside the mosque. One corridor on the eastern side connected to the Prophet's chambers. The wives' dwellings were located to the left of the mosque. Aisha's room had direct access to the mosque. This allowed the Prophet to hear what was happening inside and gain easy access for ritual purification. Integral to the religious life of the first Muslims—who taught, received followers, supported community expansion, and preserved the Quran— were visual connections between the wives' living quarters and the mosque. Its design reflected Medina's inclusive culture by providing equitable access to both genders, and its interior spaces encouraged social interaction within the community, resulting in the rapid integration of converts. (63-64)

This spatial closeness between the mosque and the house gave the Prophet the confidence and strength he required. He recognized that excluding women from sacred spaces would result in a significant loss of religious guardianship within the community. Therefore, he advocated for women to have limitless access to mosques, allowing them to partake in the mosque structures as well as in open, shared areas.

He cautioned his followers, "Do not prevent the female servant of God from going to the mosque."[120]

According to Haifaa Jawad, the Prophet actively encouraged women, particularly those with a greater degree of knowledge, and who, owing to their circumstances, were able to attend regular prayers. When the Quran was recited, explained, and interpreted, the Prophet ordered men, including their wives and relatives, not to prevent women from attending dawn and night prayers. (88)

The men lined up in the front rows behind the Prophet while women filled the back rows, according to Jasser Auda. Between the men's and women's rows, children would form a queue. There were no partitions or curtains separating the rows for men and women. This design provided women with a clear view of the imam when he preached, enhancing their focus, and enabling easy conversation. (65) To highlight the presence of women in the mosque, Auda recounts the story told by Aisha of an enslaved person who was falsely accused of theft but was proven innocent: "After the family freed the young lady, she immediately came to the Prophet and embraced Islam." She then erected a tent with a low roof in the Mosque and lived in it." (100)

Jebara paints a picture of the mosque as family-friendly. He states that the Prophet's public acknowledgment of children impacted the demographics of public assemblies, leading parents to feel free to come to the *masjid* with their children. A man once attended with his son and daughter, placing his daughter on the ground besides him and the son on his lap. The Prophet admonished him, "Treat your children equally." (277)

Fatima Mernissi states that Prophet Muhammad's proximity to the people enabled him to experience the tensions, pressures, and opposition surrounding him. Yet, he discovered love, admiration, and enthusiasm, despite encountering resistance and inhibition everywhere. (111).

At the invitation of the Prophet, King Negus sent a delegation of Abyssinians to Medina. Jebara describes that during the reception at the mosque, the Abyssinians performed a traditional dance accompanied by musical instruments. A week later, a delegation of Christian clergy from Najran visited Medina. On the Sunday of their visit, the Prophet offered the *masjid* for Sunday worship services. Crucifixes, saint icons, bells, and incense filled the *masjid* for several hours. As a community center, the *masjid* welcomed all. (246)

WOMEN'S INTEGRATION IN THE MOSQUE

Due to the integration of women's residences into the mosque, Ibn Sa'd describes the spatial proximity in the early days of Islam as the most apparent triumph for Islam. He describes how Umar Ibn Abd al-Aziz, the governor of Medina between 705 and 715 CE, decided to demolish the Prophet's wife's apartments to expand the mosque. When this decision was made, the Medinan's wept because they wished that people would not spend so much money on the new construction, and that people could see with their own eyes where the Prophet, who held the keys to the universe, once lived.

A young witness showed the difference between the pompous scene and the Prophet's humble dwelling: "I was still an adolescent. When I entered the Prophet's Mosque, I could easily touch the ceiling with my hand. He stated that the simplicity of the housing, their closeness to the mosque and to one another, gave the Islamic community a democratic dimension." (110)

DEFYING BARRIERS TO CONTINUE PRAYING IN MOSQUES

Marion Holmes Katz, in *Women in the Mosque,* describes that in subsequent years, women continued to attend mosques despite the emergence of numerous legal discussions on segregation. For instance, the Spanish Umayyad caliph, Hisham I (788–96 CE), constructed prayer areas for women in the rear of the Great Mosque of Cordoba; these areas were later expanded. While the Malaki school preferred women to remain at home, they acknowledged women's right to enter the mosque. Because of this, North Africa and Spain had allocated spaces for women. According to Ibn al-Hajj (1336 CE), the Egyptian (Mamluk) Empire seemed to have a vibrant female presence in the mosque. Women enjoyed going to prayer and attending Eid celebrations. The women were granted their own prayer space, but some women disregarded the designated prayer area, entered the main mosque (with men), and prayed behind men.[121]

During the seventeenth century, ethnic Han women known as *Hui* were prohibited from entering mosques in China. These women established the first women's mosque for their community, *Qingzhen nusi*, or *nusi*. The *nusi* also had (and still have) a female religious leader comparable to an imam, known as a *nu ahong*, who oversaw prayer, education, and social/political issues. This prayer space, which was originally intended to be a facility for women's education, evolved into a distinct mosque with full facilities. The *Hui* women who founded the mosque lived in a highly segregated society based on the Confucian conception of gender, and they recognized that a mother who lacked Islamic education could not adequately serve her community.[122] The ideal Confucian woman is one who serves her male relatives in all manners. How can a Chinese Muslim woman achieve this if she is ill-informed about Islam and unable to exercise her religious rights?

Jasser Auda explains that the belief that only males should attend the mosque and women should pray at home is a common justification for women's outright exclusion. This is due to a mistranslation of the Arabic words that refer to the mosque's dwellers and visitors as "men" or "mankind," rather than "people": *"[A] mosque founded on righteousness from the first day is more worthy of your prayers. In it are 'men' who love to be purified. And God loves those who purify themselves" (Q 9:108).* (27)

He describes that in colloquial Arabic, the word *rijjal* pertains to men, whereas in Quranic Arabic (high Arabic), the term implies people—men and women—who attend the mosque. *"That light shines through houses of worship which God have ordered to be raised, and where His Name is mentioned. He is glorified there morning and evening by men [rijjal] who are not distracted—either by buying or selling—from God's remembrance, or performing prayer, or paying alms-tax" (Q 24:36-37).* He cites two verses that use the word *rijjal* to refer to both men and women: *"Among the believers are rijjal true to what they promised God" (Q 33:23),* and *"[O]n its elevations are rijjal who recognize all by their mark" (Q 7:48).*

Mohamad Jebara notes that in Quranic Arabic, the term *rijjal* refers to "experts," "reliable witnesses," or "authorities," regardless of gender. In these verses, it's a reference to both men and women who excelled at their tasks.

SENSUALITY DOES NOT UPEND SPIRITUALITY

Not every Muslim possesses the same degree of faith. While some were willing to give their lives for Islam, others couldn't resist inappropriate gazes, even within the Prophet's mosque. According to Ibn Abbas, an attractive woman used to pray in the women's section of the Prophet's mosque. To avoid seeing her, some men moved to the front row, while others remained in the back. When the men in the front row bowed, a few of the men in the back row turned around to stare at her. This conduct continued until God intervened with a verse admonishing man for their misconduct. *"We certainly know those who have gone before you and those who will come after you" (Q 15:24)*. Remarkably, the woman is not accused of being a source of temptation, a common argument used to prevent women from entering mosques.

Despite this guidance from the Quran, Marion Katz says some jurists impose a burden on women by presuming their presence may cause men to transgress due to sexual arousal. Importantly, both men and women are prohibited from engaging in sexual misconduct, but men are not banned from mosques. Women's exclusion is shaped by false hadiths rather than explicit Quranic teachings, and this is why the Maliki school permitted older women to attend the mosque while prohibiting younger women. The claim that women in the mosque would cause *fitnah* remained prevalent, resulting in an innovation *bida* that prohibits women from the mosque and other public places; but this is not good for a society that relies on women for labor in fields, healthcare, markets, and domestic work. (17-41, 111-134)

Andalusian scholar Ibn Arabi (1240 CE) according to Katz, argued the concept of *fitnah*. He believed that a man who forbids his wife from attending the mosque is not preventing men from succumbing to her alleged attractions, but rather succumbing to base sentiments of sexual possessiveness. He analyzed men's hostility to the divine decree allowing women to pray in mosques, attributing it to jealously (*ghayra*) and contending that personal animus can cause humans to be jealous of God's decision. Because he was taught by women in mosques his entire life, he provided a scathing critique of *fitnah*. To overcome this resentment, *haraj* toward God's decree, he suggested gaining intellectual and spiritual authority. (41)

Marion Katz affirms Aisha never prohibited women from entering mosques, and neither did the caliphs she advised. Some scholars attribute this hadith to her: "If the Prophet had lived today and seen what we see of women today, he would have forbidden women from entering mosques just as the Children of Israel prohibited women from entering mosques."[123] But Ibn Hazm (1064 CE), a scholar of the Zahiri sect, refuted this by contending that it has no religious significance. He argued that since the Prophet did not prohibit women from entering the mosque, neither can we! He believed that women could perform Friday prayers in a mosque because, to his knowledge, they used to attend public liturgies alongside the Prophet, referring to the hadith of the Prophet that stresses the significance of congregational prayer for both men and women. If it had been preferable for women to pray at home, he argues, the Prophet would have instructed them to do so. (39–40)

A MUSLIM NEVER BECOMES IMPURE

The Quran recommends purification after menstruation, sexual activity, and natural urges, emphasizing that uncleanliness results from specific biological functions rather than biological differences. *"O believers! Do not approach prayer while intoxicated until you are aware of what you say, nor in a state of 'full' impurity"* (Q 4:43). Nonetheless, some scholars cite menstruation as a reason for prohibiting women from entering mosques, adopting a blood taboo specific to menstruation that is not part of Islam. Asma Barlas explains that the claim that menstruating women are considered impure is dubious and simple to refute. The root meaning of *adhan* is "damage, harm, injury, trouble, and annoyance," not pollution. Even if menstrual blood is polluting, this does not imply that the woman or her body is inherently polluting, as this is not stated in the Quran. (111)

Ibn Hazm asserts that if something is not forbidden by the Prophet it is permissible. He points to menstruating women who resided in the Prophet's mosque and were permitted by him to remain there. In addition, blood was not deemed a "pollutant," as is demonstrated by Rufaydah Al-Islamia, a female physician who had her medical tent in an ancient mosque to heal the injured. (32)

This hadith is frequently used to justify the exclusion of menstruating women from certain rituals: "Neither a mensurating woman nor a person who is ritually impure should recite anything from the Quran." It is reported by Abu Dawud and others, but is deemed unreliable by all scholars of the Hadith. The Prophet did not prohibit menstruating women from reciting the Quran or making supplications; he allowed them to perform the Hajj rituals at Muzdalifah and Mina, and to recite the Takbir Hajj. As far as circumambulating the Kaaba, doing *tawaf,* he instructed women to perform this only while ritually pure, in *tahara.*

SEGREGATION DENIED BY TRADITION, NOT CREED

Jasser Auda describes how the second Caliph, Umar bin Khattab, constructed separate mosque entrances for women but not separate prayer areas.

Katz says it is unknown what led to his decision, but according to a report by Umm Subayya Khawla bint Qays, he disapproved of women using the mosque for personal benefit by engaging in activities such as spinning and weaving. (136) Others assert that, despite his disapproval of women, he did not prevent his wife Atika from worshiping at the mosque. "What prevents him from forbidding us?" she said when asked why she insisted. (18) The fact is that Umar was unable to carry out his directives due to *verse Q 2:114*, which urges people not to deny believers the duty to pray in the mosque, and the Prophet's unequivocal injunction regarding allowing women to participate.

The first gender segregation was recorded in Kufa, Iraq. Over time, the adopted practice of *purdah* came to be associated with the Quran's emphasis on modesty, and a standard practice in many Muslim communities. Yet, segregation of the sexes is neither a matter of faith nor a tenet of Islamic creed. The Quran never emphasizes any form of segregation. Instead, it suggests methods for women and men to observe modest boundaries in the presence of one another. Gender separation in the mosque also reflects gender inequality in terms of space. Amina Wadud explains: "Separation in congregational prayer usually relegates women to an inferior place, either behind the male prayer lines or rendering them invisible in the congregational setting." Also, women and men do not observe gender separation during the Hajj pilgrimage, another of Islam's most important ritual observances.[124]

Marion Katz describes Ibn Hubayya (1165 CE), a Hanbali jurist who affirmed this by using the example of Hajj, where women did not conceal their faces and prayed alongside men to refute the *fitna* criterion. He explains, "In my opinion, it is not only permissible but preferable (*masnun*) for women to attend congregational prayers and to stand in the last rows behind the men, as stated in hadith texts and as was the custom during the time of the Prophet and the first generation of

Muslims. This argument is refuted by the example of the Hajj for anyone who argues that this is objectionable due to the fear of temptation from women." (90)

THIS IS OUR HOLY SITE AS MUCH AS YOURS

This longstanding tradition of gender equality during the Hajj was about to be overturned in 2006. I recall an email sent by a Saudi woman: "There is a proposal to move the women's prayer area from the Holy Kaaba and from out of the Mataaf [circumambulation area]," she wrote. "History is being reversed. Women and men have prayed in this space called '*haram*' [sanctuary] since the seventh century, and now some clerics want to drive us to the margins. What would the Prophet have to say?!"

I promptly forwarded the email to the women in my WISE network to determine what we could do. Aisha Schwartz addressed the petition to the authorities of the Kingdom and titled it the "Grand Mosque Equal Access for Women Project." Within days, we received over 1,000 signatures and scores of comments such as "Follow the Prophet's example, there will be a mutiny" and "This is OUR holy site." I transmitted the signed petition to the Saudi woman who requested assistance, anticipating that this would be the beginning of a lengthy campaign. To my astonishment, her response was prompt: "Petition delivered to the King. He is delighted to receive signatures from women worldwide." My Saudi friend had realized that women's signatures asserting their rights would provide the king with the strongest ammunition against the proposal. Another Saudi woman, Aziza al-Manie, was quoted in *Okaz Daily* as saying, "Women are not all young beauties that rush to the mosque intending to seduce men."

The issue of relocating women from Masjid al-Haram was soon shelved as pressure mounted from all factions. We all felt privileged that our modest efforts had restored our rightful position in full view of the House of God, where our foremothers Hagar, Khadijah, Fatima, Baraka, Al Shifa, and Aisha had resided. Indeed, they must have applauded us for remaining steadfast in our courage and unwavering in our faith in God.[125]

WHEN MEN CENSURE WOMEN'S ACCESS

According to the *Quran 22:26*, Abraham constructed a house of worship as a sacred sanctuary to symbolize the unity of believers in their devotion to God: *"And remember when We designated to Abraham the site of the House, saying, 'Do not associate anything with Me in worship and purify My House for those who perform Tawaf and those who stand 'in prayer' and bow and prostrate themselves."* Despite this egalitarian message, it is remarkable that many women's accesses to mosques around the globe remain marginalized, minimized, or entirely restricted.

The primary barrier to women's free access begins during the design phase when, unlike the Prophet, male decision-makers designate a main prayer area exclusively for men and consign women worshippers to the balcony, veranda, basement, or rear entrance. Some mosques are so strictly segregated that women have no visual access to the prayer space or the imam. As a result, women's prayer spaces are devoid of the aesthetics, ornamentation, and illuminations of Quranic inscriptions that are typically associated with mosques.

As a young architectural apprentice in 1980, I was requested to evaluate the floor plans for a new mosque on Long Island, which was to be the area's first mosque. When I inquired as to where the women would pray, the architect informed me that women would be praying in the basement. I knew this would not be acceptable to the professional women members of the mosque whose funds were being used to construct it.

By relegating women to the dungeon, it was made abundantly plain that they were second-class citizens. The leadership of this mosque, however, was a member of my family. The women agreed immediately that the architect's presumption must be promptly corrected. The architect inquired, "How many rows should we allot to the women?" "Rows?" I questioned. I explained that half of the prayer space must be reserved for women! Husbands and wives would visit this mosque together, so the women require the same amount of space, not less.

The next time I viewed the floor plans, I was pleased to see that both sexes were allocated equal sections in the main prayer hall, without a visible partition. Today, the trustees of the Westbury Mosque in Long Island are women, and *HuffPost* ranked it among the top ten spiritual spaces in the United States.

To sustain the Muslim community's growth and development, every effort must be made to reintegrate women into our religious institutions. When women are marginalized and isolated, a diminished sense of belonging persists among them; hence, they are unable to meet their spiritual requirements and are deprived of the opportunity to contribute to the well-being of their community.

The impact on society is even greater. Men continue to have more authority and control over religious matters whereas; women are relegated to passive roles; and their opportunities for personal growth, leadership development, and religious identity are diminished, not to mention the divisions and rifts it creates within the community.

To promote an equitable mosque environment, Muslim men in leadership must exemplify the highest standards by following the Prophet's directives. This involves removing the visible and invisible barriers that hinder the full participation of women in mosque activities. Men should remember the incident of "the beautiful women" being ogled in the Prophet's mosque, prompting God's revelation in verse 15:24, reprimanding the onlooker. It underscores that women shouldn't bear the responsibility for men's misdeeds.

Also, in accordance with the Prophet's tradition, women must serve on committees and have complete access to the mosque through the main entrance. Men, women, and children must be protected from men's offensive and sexual advances through policies and management rules, not by prohibiting women from entering their sacred spaces. Even if such errors did occur during the Prophet's lifetime, they had no bearing on the norms he established for the interaction between men and women in the mosque, let alone the construction of the mosque.

EXAMPLE OF A DANISH, AMERICAN, AND CANADIAN CREATING SPIRITUAL SPACE

In the west, where Islamic culture is not the norm, the loss of female worshipers and female education leads practicing Muslims to decline. Some leave Islam entirely, while others are unmosqued. Despite this setback, many Muslim women in Europe and the Americas are forging a spiritual path by developing their own sacred places. They are creating new precedents, together with male scholars who support women's desires to reclaim the standing they had during Prophet Muhammad's lifetime.

Sherin Khankan said in 2014 that she intended to create Denmark's first women's mosque, with an emphasis on families. Traditionalists accused her of "diluting Islam." She countered that the mosque's objective was to bring together those who had been separated from their faith.

Her ambition came fulfilled in 2016, when she opened the doors of the Mariam Mosque in Copenhagen, named after the Arabic version of Mary. Sherin stated, "We represent a modernist, spiritual approach to Islam. We want the Mariam Mosque to be a place where everyone can come, and we can flourish together. What happens in a mosque goes way beyond the Mosque itself—it affects society."[126]

In 2015, in southern California, M. Hasna Maznavi cofounded the first women's mosque, which was inspired by a group of Muslim women's growing disillusionment with many US mosques and Maznavi's childhood dream of starting her own mosque.[127] The dream that Maznavi had since her childhood had not only materialized but has grown into a global movement. In 2017, Qal'bu Maryam Women's Mosque in San Francisco was the second mosque built where women lead the prayers, and there is no gender separation. It offers marriage, divorce, and funeral services and counsels' women on issues on domestic violence.[128] In 2019, the Women's Mosque of Canada in Toronto was established, which provides a safe space for women, helps victims of abuse, and educates women on Islam.[129]

The story of the women's mosque and the unwavering strength of women is unfolding a broader narrative of Islam, where the call to prayer is not simply echoing in the halls of mosques but in the hearts and minds of women everywhere.

PART III

THE RIGHT TO YOUR FAMILY

• • • • • • • • •

Islam gives women the right to choose their spouses and enjoy harmonious marriages in which they and their husbands share mutual love and respect while building happy, healthy families. A woman can reject a marriage partner she dislikes or considers unsuitable; enter a marital bond only with her consent; and marry only when she has attained the physical, mental, and spiritual development required to enter legally binding contracts.

A woman cannot be forced into a polygamous marriage without her explicit permission; she can terminate an unhappy marriage on her own, and she must be treated with dignity throughout the dissolution of her marriage.

She can use contraception to plan a family with her partner or terminate a pregnancy with her well-being in mind. She has the right to increase the size of her family such that she may adopt an orphaned child, maintain their lineage, and nurture their individual development. To serve society in the complementary roles of woman and mother, she can rear well-adjusted children while confronting no impediment to her individual societal contributions.

These objectives all involve protection and promotion of family lineages:

- Marriage, reproduction, divorce, inheritance, and conflict resolution are all essential, or *daruriyyat*.
- Cohesion among family members is necessary, or *hajiyyat*. Family cohesion involves economic independence; respect for children; and sufficient money for food, shelter, and clothing.
- Extended support networks made up of friends and relatives provide what is complementary, or *tahsiniyyat*.

#10 | TO MARRIAGE

One Uzbek woman I knew in New York at thirty-five was ready to marry a Christian man who was willing to convert to Islam. Her father, an imam at an Uzbek mosque, disapproved of her fiancé because he insisted that she marry an Uzbek. He feared that allowing his daughter to marry someone outside their culture would set a bad precedent. Her heart was broken, since her father's blessing was essential to her.

I pleaded with the imam, explaining that it was against Islam to disallow his daughter to marry a man based on his culture. I mentioned that she had a right to marry, and if she did not marry now, then when? I was taken aback by his unexpected appearance at the wedding, and his emotional outpouring as he blessed his daughter and welcomed his son-in-law into his tightly knit Uzbek clan.

According to the Quran, the family unit is a strong force that unites all facets of society, contributes significantly to the spread of humankind, and serves as the cornerstone of civilization. *"And He is the One Who creates human beings from a 'humble' liquid, then establishes for them bonds of kinship and marriage"* (Q 25:54). The goal of marriage is for the spouses to find kindness, love, and tranquility in one another, as these qualities are crucial for the growth and stability of the family. *"And one of His signs is that He created for you spouses from among yourselves so that you may find comfort in them, and He placed between you compassion and mercy"* (Q 30:21).

Prophet Muhammad dissuaded eligible Muslims from monasticism and celibacy, saying, "So he who does not follow my tradition in religion, is not from me."[130] He stressed that matrimonial alliances strengthen friendships more than anything else.

THE CONTRACTUAL HEART OF MARRIAGE

In Islam, marriage is known as *nikah* (originally meaning *aqd*, or uniting); it is a contractual agreement between two consenting people founded on the principles of consultation (*tashawur*) and common accord (*taradi*), which serve as the basis for a healthy and harmonious relationship. The marriage is contracted legally with an offer made by one side and accepted by the other with two witnesses present. Haifaa Jawad stresses that the woman is a subject rather than an object in the marriage contract. (35)

A mutually agreed upon nuptial gift, or *mahr*, is part of the contract, imposed solely on the groom to denote his commitment to the marriage, his admission to the wife's financial independence, and the use of the gift in the event of a divorce. Azizah al-Hibri explains that the *mahr* is not a "bride price," as some have erroneously characterized it; nor is it money that either the woman or the man pays to obtain the other. (60)

Yasmin Amin states that according to Al-Ghazali there are five purposes to marriage: bearing children, satisfying the sexual drive, establishing the household and a family, companionship, and providing for women in a humane manner. (336) A wife retains her legal independence and is not required to change her identity or surname. If the bride is assumed to have a vulnerable position in a marriage, she or her family can stipulate contract conditions to safeguard her interests. When Prophet Muhammad married Aisha, he stipulated the provisions of their marriage contract. In it, he agreed to treat her well, to provide her good life as commanded by God, and to keep their marriage in good standing or let her go in peace. He added the condition, or *sharata*, that if he took another wife, the new marriage would be at Aisha's discretion, and if she wanted, she could ask that he divorce the second wife.[131]

THE FIRST BLESSED UNION: A MODEL MUSLIM MARRIAGE

Before he was a Prophet, young Muhammad worked for Khadijah bint Khuwaylid, an accomplished businesswoman who, to his astonishment, proposed marriage to him. She was the twice-widowed mother of four children, and he was an orphan with no means.

According to common belief, Khadijah was forty years old when she proposed to the twenty-five-year-old. However, some scholars have refuted her older age by asserting that she was twenty-eight. They explain that if Khadijah married at the age of forty in 595 CE and gave birth to her last child sixteen years later in 611 CE, she would have been fifty-six. Even to a modern reader, this appears to be a miracle, but those who contend she was forty, assert that Quraysh women in Mecca bore children well into their fifties.¹³²

Whether Khadijah was forty or twenty-eight, it is indisputable that she was in her prime. She was older and more experienced than young Muhammad, who had never been with a woman. After their marriage they established a working partnership where she put her fortune under his direction, which he invested to expand her already successful trading business. Jebara describes how the Prophet respected and adored his confident and cultured wife. Their children were Al-Qasim, Zainab, Abdullah, Um Kulthum, Fatima, Ruqayya.. When Al-Qasim died in 601 CE, they raised their five children along with Zayd and the Prophet's cousin Ali, whom they supported. Both young men witnessed the transformation of their guardian into the Prophet and threw their support behind him. Ali would play a critical role in his life: many of the most revealing personal stories about the Prophet are known because he shared them with Ali. (114)

Mohamad Jebara describes the Prophet as a self-assured man unintimidated by Khadijah's wealth, stature, or possessions, even though, through his marriage, his status among Meccans was elevated. Despite his meteoric business success, he felt a profound void and questioned his life's purpose. To attain inner transcendence, he undertook an arduous journey to Mount Hira in search of answers. Ali and Zayd occasionally accompanied him for security purposes, but Khadijah supported his quest the most. With her financial backing, he was able to pursue a contemplative life, laying the groundwork for his eventual role as Prophet.

In 610 CE, fifteen years into their marriage, while on Mount Hira, God revealed himself to Muhammad through the archangel Gabriel, who imbued Muhammad with a divine message and a significant mandate that would radically alter the course of his life. Initially, he was frightened because he did not comprehend what he had experienced. Concerned that he was possessed by a *jinn* or going insane, he approached his wife, who dispelled his doubts, validated his spiritual experience and reassured him: "God would never do this to you; you help the needy and feed the poor." Guided by her unwavering belief in him, she brought him to her cousin, the reputed Christian monk Waraqa, who confirmed his prophethood and added a dire warning:

"They will drive you out of town, as they have done to other Prophets." In this moment, Khadijah made history as the first individual to embrace Islam and accept Muhammad as God's Prophet and Messenger, forever altering the course of human history.

Despite being a messenger, the Prophet "served his family" by doing household chores such as mending his clothes, milking his goats, and fixing his sandals. Imam Malik, al-Shafi', and Abu Hanifa followed the Prophet's lead and concluded that a wife is not compelled to cook, clean, wash, sew, or do other domestic duties for her husband. Nevertheless, if she is willing to do so, she must be compensated.

CONFLICT BETWEEN RELATIVES

Jennifer Heath in her book reports that when the Prophet began his public preaching, his eldest daughter Zaynab was married to her non-Muslim cousin. When she became Muslim, his family demanded that he divorce her. The Prophet was distraught, but Khadijah consoled him regarding his daughter's fate, saying, "[God] smiles on those who love totally and truly, and Abu al-As will come through when he is ready." (58) The Prophet chose not to divorce his Muslim daughter from her pagan husband because Abu al-As refused to divorce Zaynab.

When the Quraysh and their clans refused to adopt Islam, Khadijah invited forty prominent men from the Hashim clan to her home for a meal. When no one responded to the Prophet's message, in frustration Ali yelled at his relatives: "I, though the youngest, pledged my help to the Prophet of God." Hakim the nephew of Khadijah, did not accept Islam but visited his aunt often, while Khadijah's brother despised the new religion. Even though his uncle and protector, Abu Talib, was under intense pressure from the clans, he told his nephew Muhammad, "Go and say whatever you wish, nephew. I will never abandon you."

Heath recounts how Abu Lahab, his uncle, an avowed enemy, decided to teach his nephew a lesson. He sent an envoy to Khadijah to rescind his sons' marriage proposals for Ruqayyah and Umm Kulthum. The Prophet, a father of four daughters, worried that his mission was affecting his daughters' chances of getting married. But his fears were allayed when handsome, elegant, and wealthy Uthman ibn Affan from the clan of Umayya asked for Ruqayyah's hand; for he had long admired her beauty and grace. The Prophet rejoiced as he gazed upon the two, exclaiming, "God is Beautiful," and "He Loves Beauty." (63) Uthman remained the Prophet's close companion and became the third Caliph of the Ummayad dynasty.

Khadijah supported the Prophet as he preached in public. As she nourished, clothed, and nurtured her husband's nascent community, her faith in him became crucial to his efforts to propagate his message. The Quraysh demanded that he stop his preaching, and when he refused, they ceased trading with Khadijah's clan, the Banu Hashim, ostracizing and expelling them, and relegating their members to a desolate land.

Convinced that God had a specific plan for her husband, Khadijah continued to provide for the clan with her diminishing wealth. When the clan became impoverished because of the sanctions, Khadijah's nephew Hakim urged her to divorce Muhammad and marry Amr, a wealthy man. Astounded by the proposition, she responded, "So long as a breath passes through my lips, I will stand with Muhammad."

Khadijah's health suffered due to the agony of the sanctions, and she passed away in 619 CE, plunging the Prophet into a "year of sorrow." As he grieved the loss of his beloved wife, he never contemplated marrying again. His admiration for her eclipsed his subsequent marriages to other women. Years later, when his wife Aisha grew resentful of his enduring affection for Khadijah, she questioned why he cherished her so much. He replied, "She believed in me when no one else did; she accepted Islam when people rejected me, and she helped and comforted me when there was no one else to lend me a helping hand. And she is the only one from whom I have children."[133]

The Prophet's family life was characterized by heartbreaking losses. Even before he became a Prophet, he buried two infant sons. After he began his prophetic mission, the losses continued to accrue. The death of his daughter Ruqayyah was followed by those of Um Kulthum and Abdullah. Fatima, who was married to Ali and was the mother of four, passed away six months after the Prophet's death. Both her sons Hassan and Hussain were martyred. Hussain was killed at the devastating event of Karbala, a defining moment in Islamic history. Mernissi describes how Fatima's lineage has immeasurable significance in the history of Islam. Right up until today, all *sharifs* and *sayeds*, that is, those who claim to be descended from the Prophet, as I do from my mother's family, trace their genealogy to Hassan and Hussain, Fatima's two sons. (108) Jebara describes how, despite these losses, the Prophet turned his suffering into one more act of greatness; he focused on ensuring that his message would endure for all time. (278)

THE EVER-EVOLVING ROLE OF A WIFE

How does one appropriately honor a woman whose life, work, and passing have left an indelible legacy? Khadijah was revered for her ethical leadership and decision-making, in addition to her entrepreneurial qualities. She envisioned a brighter future for their community and addressed urgent social issues with her generous spirit; she overcame obstacles and adversity that affected her family. This explains why the Prophet remained faithful and monogamous to her even though, at the time, he could have married other women. Khadijah was acutely aware of her spiritual identity; she was the first cherished wife of the last Prophet and sacrificed everything for the sake of God and her husband's mission. She received a salutation from God through Gabriel, the highest-ranking angel, in which she was informed of her afterlife destination and the layout of her home in paradise.[134] She shows the extraordinary continuity of a wife's unshakeable loyalty to her husband.

When I married an imam, I instinctively drew inspiration from Khadijah. Like her, I was a working woman married to a man devoted to God's service. I imagined myself as an extension of her noble mission. In addition to celebrating his achievements I assumed the role of his confidante, creating an environment for him to assume a larger role in the community. While maintaining my essential role in our partnership, I saw his accomplishments as my own success. His mission merged seamlessly with mine.

FORBIDDEN MARRIAGES

However, with the passage of time, Muslims veered away from the first couple's model marriage. They developed marriages that contradict the true message of the Quran, and which go against the core ethical values on which the foundation of parenting, protection, and harmony of marriage is built.

Islam gave up the pre-Islamic practice of *mut'ah* because the temporary nature of marriage disregards its sanctity. *Mut'ah*, which means profiting from or enjoying a thing, devalues women by using them as a source of pleasure for men who may abandon their wives after a certain period, causing numerous problems for individuals and society. Temporary marriages are only permitted in Shia communities where a contract stipulates that the spouse is responsible for any children born from such a union. Temporary marriages in which a man could abandon his wife and children are un-Islamic and should not be practiced.

According to Mohammad Ali, author of *The Religion of Islam*, there are exchange marriages called *shighar*, where one man's daughter or sister is exchanged for another man's daughter without the bride receiving *mahr*. This cultural practice commodifies women as objects devoid of human rights. In addition to being coerced into marriage, the woman's autonomy is forfeited for the sake of her family. This type of marriage is expressly forbidden by the Prophet because it diminishes the significance of marriage and deprives the woman of her dowry.[135]

INTERFAITH MARRIAGE FOR WOMEN

Every woman has a right to marry, build a family, lead a pleasure-filled life, produce new life and raise educated children, as stated in the objectives of Shariah. However, this opportunity is not always available to Muslim women in the West as they increasingly face hurdles in finding a suitable Muslim man to marry. This situation exists in part because of Muslim men, who freely exercise their right to marry outside the faith, reducing the pool of eligible Muslim men for Muslim women to marry. I personally know many Muslim women who have poured all their efforts into developing careers and nurturing their minds, hoping for a partner who recognizes their value and worth. I sense their longing and their agony when their search is seemingly fruitless. They pray endlessly to God: *Where is he? And when will he appear on my life's horizon?*

Muslim women, according to Dr. Khaleed Mohammed, are socialized to believe that they can only marry a Muslim male or a non-Muslim who accepts Islam. This inability to choose a "believing" spouse outside of Islam weighs heavily on the emotional and psychological states of women. Unnecessarily, women's aspirations for marriage, sexual intimacy, motherhood, childcare, and raising a family remain unfulfilled.[136]

I had initially decided not to write about this topic but then realized that excluding it would be a major oversight. I am writing this to offer practical solutions to the personal dilemmas faced by many women. The arguments presented here are intended to encourage an honest discussion and exploration of our faith, so we can search for solution to the biggest challenge our women face.

For a thorough examination, we will examine three verses that instruct Muslims to marry. The first, *verse 5:5*, addresses men only: *"[P]ermissible for you in marriage are chaste believing women as well as chaste women of those given the Scripture before you."* This explicitly states that men can marry "chaste" believing woman and or "chaste" women of scripture. This means that a man may marry a woman among the "people of the book," which includes Christians, Jews, or even Zoroastrians.

Second, *verse 2:221* addresses both men and women, forbidding them from marrying polytheists or disbelievers—who do not believe in God—and instructs both to marry believers, or enslaved men and women (people with no status) who are believing: *"Do not marry polytheistic women until they believe; for a believing slave-woman is better than a free polytheist, even though she may look pleasant to you. And do not marry your women to polytheistic men until they believe, for a believing slave-man is better than a free polytheist, even though he may look pleasant to you" (Q 2:221)*. While this verse addresses both sexes. It is widely interpreted to prohibit women from marrying a polytheist or nonbeliever, which is defined here as Christians, Jews, etc.

The third verse is *24:32*: *"Marry off the free singles among you, as well as the righteous of your bondsman and bondswoman."* This grants permission to both men and women to marry a "righteous" slave, even if they are not a believer. Some who oppose women marrying non Muslims argue that only followers of Islam can be considered "believers." But this argument is flawed because the Quran describes believers, or *mumin*, in a broader way: *"They 'all' believe in God, His Angels and His Books and His messengers. [W]e make no distinction between any of His messengers" (Q 2:285)*.

God comments on the oneness of followers of Moses, Jesus, and Muhammad: *"Yet the people have divided it into different sects, each rejoicing in what they have. So, leave them 'O Prophet' in their heedlessness for a while" (Q 23:53-54)*.

In *verse 49:10*, God says, *"The believers are but one brotherhood, so make peace between your brothers,"* and *verse 9:71* says, *"The believers, both men and women are guardians of one another."* According to Aisha Musa, the Quran suggests a broader meaning of the term Islam as "submission" to the One God, as it refers to the followers of the earlier prophets, such as Moses, Jesus, and Abraham as "Muslim," and in the story of Noah, he is commanded to be among the "Muslims."[137]

Another argument advanced by some scholars is that Islam is the only true religion, so women must marry a Muslim. *"Whoever seeks a way other than Islam it will never be accepted from them, and on the hereafter, they will be among the losers" (Q 3:85)*, says the Quran. If this were true, why would God allow men to marry Christian and Jewish women, who, according to this logic, are presumably unbelievers? In *verse 5:69*, God declares: *"Indeed, the believers, Jews, and Sabaeans, and Christians—whosoever truly believes in God and the Last Day and does good, there will be no fear for them, nor will they grieve" (Q 5:69)*. Some contend that *verse 5:69* was superseded by *3:85*. However, according to both Muslim and non-Muslim chronologies of the Quran, *verse 5* was revealed after *verse 3*.[138]

ROOTS OF THE PROHIBITION

These types of juridical dilemmas have confounded jurists and scholars for centuries. They assert that when the Quran is "silent"—when it does not expressly state or prohibit something—the issue in question is subject to interpretation and the action may be permissible. According to the Quran, the issue of religion in marriage is the distinction between believers and nonbelievers, not a specific religion. If the Quran clearly permits a woman to marry a believing man, as opposed to a nonbeliever, why do scholars prohibit it? The answers lie in the two objectives of Shariah: preservation of family and religion. The objective of family emphasizes a child's spiritual lineage, and religion includes the free exercise of religion.

In Islam, a child inherits its religious lineage from the father, whereas in Judaism this is traditionally transmitted through the mother. The implications are significant for Muslim women: If a Muslim man marries a believing woman, his offspring are considered Muslim. However, if a Muslim woman marries a believing man, it is presumed that her offspring will not be Muslim because they will inherit their father's religion. Once, when I officiated a marriage between a Muslim man and a Jewish woman, both parties were certain that their offspring would be Muslim and Jewish.

The issue that a Muslim women's child would assume the religion of the father suggests that a mother has no agency, cannot stipulate her children's religiosity in her marriage contract, and has no influence over her child's religious upbringing. Within my circle of friends, women I know who marry "believing" men actively assume full responsibility for raising their children as Muslim. On the contrary, what many imams and scholars fail to recognize is that some Muslim men who marry believing women (Christians or Jews) are unable to raise Muslim children. I know a Christian mother whose husband lacks the time and inclination, and their children are Muslims in name only. I shared this issue with Sheikh Ali Gomaa of Al Azhar, at a conference, that some men who marry non-Muslim women are then unable to raise Muslim children, enforce dietary restrictions, and have unrestricted flow of pork and alcohol in their lives. Shocked and perplexed, I felt he was ready to issue a *fatwa*; he promptly responded, "We must halt men from marrying *kitabi* women"! I shook my head, fully aware that rolling back 1,400 years of freedom was an impossible feat.

The second and more dire argument against Muslim women marrying believer men, Jewish or Christian, is that such marriages may result in the forcible conversion of Muslim women. This is predicated on the remote possibility that non-Muslim in-laws could exert pressure on a Muslim woman living in a Christian or Jewish household. Their religion would dominate the household, causing her to abandon her religion. Again, these rules were developed in patriarchal societies, where the underlying belief was that all women were subservient to men. A non-Muslim husband would therefore impose his religious beliefs on his Muslim wife.

BALANCE BETWEEN EXPECTATIONS AND CULTURAL VALUES

Today the nuclear family is the predominant social unit in the West, and residing with extended families is atypical. In a nuclear family, husband and wife share equal decision-making authority, with minimal influence from extended family or in-laws. The couple divide responsibilities such as childrearing, housework, and employment more equitably. Typically, mothers organize the secular and spiritual education and extracurricular activities of their children.

I know scores of American Muslim women who have been navigating their way through this difficult terrain. Sara is a nonpracticing Muslim who met and married a Christian man in college. When their two sons were close to five years old, religion thrust itself upon the family. The boys were curious about their religion, which prompted Sara to frantically search for a Sunday school where the boys could learn about Islam and make Muslim friends. There they were taught the Quran and stories about the Prophet, which even Sara's immigrant parents did not teach her. Sara is delighted because she learns something new about Islam from her young boys. They celebrate Eid with their family and Christmas with their father's. They respect the heritage of both parents while remaining true to their Islamic identity.

The Quran states unequivocally, *"Let there be no compulsion in religion" (Q 2:256)*, indicating that no one should force religion upon another, including the wife on the husband or vice versa. In many cases, a believer man (Christian or Jew) is not willing to accept Islam in order to marry a Muslim woman. If his heart is not inclined to accept Islam willingly and lovingly; what then are the options for the family? Should he be rejected, and the daughter left with no one to marry, or should he be brought into the fold of Islam using a minimum threshold of a believer, as mentioned in the Quran?

At the center of this equitable solution and ethos is Islam's religious tolerance, which emphasizes the special covenant believers have with God, Judaism through Moses, Christianity through Jesus, and Islam through Muhammad—all of which are required for an interfaith marriage to flourish and remain harmonious.[139] The believer husband should accept a minor *shahadah* in which he affirms his faith in God and accepts the prophecy of the Prophet Muhammad. This is not conversion; rather, it is "embracing Islam" in its universality and the all-encompassing message sent by God, through various scriptures. This is also a clear way to recognize the husband and wife's shared beliefs in God, where they together acknowledge moral responsibility and accountability to their creator.

WHAT MUSLIM MEN SHOULD CONSIDER

The Prophet married Jewish and Christian women, and through these unions he forged alliances with opposing tribes, enacted social reforms, resisted growing opposition, and inspired his diverse followers. When he advised his male followers to select a suitable wife, he advised, "Seek a grateful heart, a sweet tongue, and a believing, righteous wife who would help you in your endeavor to succeed on the last day."[140]

The Prophet also taught, you must "First tie your camel, then trust in God."[141] In an interfaith marriage, it is incumbent for women to use their marriage contract to stipulate reasons that scholars cite as justification for prohibiting women from marrying believing men; namely, the fear of forced conversion and raising Muslim children. The contract should include the husband's need to univocally support the wife's lifelong commitment to her religion, and that the wife will assume sole responsibility for raising their children in the Muslim faith, which should include Islamic dietary rules by which the family will abide.

The decision to leave one's religion to fulfill the innate desire to get married should not be taken lightly by the community and its leaders. If an empowered, educated, and independent Muslim woman in the West is denied the right to marry a believer man, and is abandoned by her community, she may choose to marry whomever she pleases in a manner that complements her lifestyle. At worst, she may forsake her religion and be unlikely to raise her children as a Muslim.

Even though the role of Muslim women today is vastly different than it was in seventh-century Arabia, some values remain the same. Many women are motivated and inspired by the Prophet's marriage to Khadijah in which their love and respect for each other allowed them to work cooperatively and interdependently. These values are timeless, as they are a training ground for the vicissitudes of life; they parented children, endured loss, exhibited fortitude, bereaved loved ones, displayed forbearance in adversity, and supported family and followers.

Today's Muslim men should draw inspiration from the Prophet. Regardless of a women's age, marital status, or earning capacity, they should welcome the chance of marrying a self-confident, accomplished, and gainfully employed woman; in doing so, they will contribute to an equitable partnership. By following the *sunnah*, men can participate in domestic chores, support their wives' aspirations, and acknowledge that a higher calling is more important than material possessions.

The Prophet recognized that marriage serves as a means of uniting two souls. Verse 2:187 *"Your spouses are a garment for you as you are for them"* uses the analogy of a garment to symbolize this union, suggesting that just as clothing is closest to the human body, there should be no separation between a husband and wife: By not divorcing his daughter from her non-Muslim husband, who subsequently converted to Islam and became the Prophet's companion, he avoided separation.

Married life ought to be interwoven between partners in the same way that a garment protects, conceals, and adorns. Couples can emulate the marriage of our Prophet and his wife, Khadijah, which was characterized by enduring love, compassion, and devotion.

#11 TO BE FREE OF FORCED MARRIAGE

I received an anonymous email from a concerned person appealing for help. He wrote: "I know two exceptional yet burdened young women from Bangladesh who could make the world a better place if they could shed the layers of abuse that are slowly eroding their confidence and progress. One woman, a talented painter from Dhaka, was married against her will and remains in the relationship. The second woman, a potential world-class chef from Chittagong, has been confined in her home since 2018 with no career, business, or income allowed. She too will be married off against her will to a wealthy candidate in the name of family honor. Both women are devout, compassionate, and disciplined. What their families have done to them in the name of Islam is repulsive. Social status and conformity to age-old family traditions appear to be of more importance to these guardians than their daughters' happiness. It is solely with God's blessing that their faith is still strong enough to prevent them from committing suicide."

Prophet Muhammad opposed coerced marriage categorically, declaring, "No female, whether a widow or divorcee, will be forced to marry anyone unless her express and categorical consents have been freely taken. In the same way, a woman not previously married can never be forced to marry anyone unless her free consent and permissions are taken."[142]

Once a woman complained to the Prophet that her father had married her against her will to his nephew. She stated that he did this to improve his status through marriage. The Prophet promptly annulled her marriage. She later told him, "Now that I am free, I willingly accept this marriage. I only wanted it to be known that men have no say over women in marriages."[143]

Women's right to approve or reject a marriage proposal is unhindered in the Quran. No one, including her father, can force a woman to accept a proposal. She can reject a marriage partner if she dislikes him or deems him unsuitable, and she must be protected from the pressures of family or relatives to accept a partner she rejects. If she is coerced into marriage, she can petition the court to rectify the injustice, as was demonstrated by the Prophet in the example given above. Also, according to Haifaa Jawad, compelling a couple, or even just one of them, to enter an unsatisfactory union is detrimental to the interests of both sides because it may result in a disastrous outcome. (33)

MOVING BEYOND ARRANGED AND ASSISTED MARRIAGE

The widespread acceptance of arranged marriages in Muslim countries is predicated on the belief that a kernel of love planted in the human heart will grow into a lifelong commitment of trust, mutual respect, and loyalty. In this practice, the bride's parents take the lead in determining the character and status of the betrothed to avoid potential conflicts. A candidate whose financial standing is comparable to theirs is given preference with the belief that this will provide the couple with a comfortable lifestyle and widespread acceptance in the community. After an appropriate groom has been chosen, the proposal is offered to the intended bride for consideration. She has the right to accept (*qubul*) the proposal or reject it. For an arranged marriage to be valid, the woman must desire it without coercion, and the intended groom must either accept or deny the proposal.

Hena Zuberi in her article, "Arranged Marriage Is Not Forced Marriage," explains the process: "After the initial introduction, some families grant the prospective groom and bride a chance to meet in private, under supervision; others allow them to get to know each other on the telephone, via text, or email. Some families encourage the potential couple to go out in public, usually in a group setting. Today, women are being introduced through relatives, well-meaning community members, matchmaking services, online matrimonial sites, imams, teachers, and friends, with the preplanned goal of being married."[144]

In Islam, maintaining kinship ties is highly valued, and therefore, it is customary for the bride and groom to request their parents' approval and blessing. Zuberi says, efforts must be made to ensure that family ties and relationships are not severed in the event of a disagreement. Some parents rationalize imposing their will on their children by arguing, "This is part of our faith." However, this false claim favors man-made customs over the divinely sanctioned word of God.

A woman or girl has the right to meet her prospective spouse before entering a marriage contract, but her silence does not constitute consent, according to Zuberi. Forcing a daughter into a marriage against her will to strengthen familial bonds or business ties is tantamount to treating her as a commodity, which is prohibited by (Q. 4:19). Coercing a girl into nonconsensual marriages to alleviate financial problems is akin to selling her into a life of servitude, which is also prohibited.

Parents must show deference to their child's choice to ward off any escalation by family members who may wish to prevent the marriage. According to Zuberi, they must understand that insisting on maintaining kinships, over the desires of their children, may have calamitous results. Among the rights of parents is that their children obey them, but this obedience is not blind, deaf, and dumb. Zuberi explains that while it is important to heed our parents, it should not be at the expense of the sincerity of the bride and/or groom. A *nikah* is a spiritual contract, and it is impossible to uphold a contract if one or both parties have not pledged their body and soul to the other for the sake of God.

THE OUTSIZED ROLE OF MALE WALIS IN MARRIAGE

On my wedding day, as I made my grand entry carrying my bouquet and wearing a beautiful white *lehenga*, I was in for a seismic shock: Tradition had intervened to play a greater part in our marriage. Unbeknownst to us, the imam performing the ceremony was my future father-in-law's former student, who had convinced him to conduct our marriage by proxy. At the altar, I was told that two men—my father and my prospective father-in-law—would act as guardians (*wali*) to marry off their adult children. This made no sense to me; I was an empowered woman—my husband, an imam. I was astounded that I hadn't been asked before, and I found it even more unbelievable that my father had approved of it. A marriage by proxy makes sense only under situations where either spouse has not reached maturity when betrothed, but for an adult woman and a middle-aged man, it didn't make sense. There was simply no justification for either of us to be treated as if we were helpless children by our fathers. No reason, except tradition.

According to scholar Asma Lambrabet, in medieval times a *wali*, or guardian, was usually a family member who would protect the bride's interest by ensuring that the marriage contract is equitable. Although not prescribed by the Quran, the obligation of the guardian became an intrinsic component of the marital contract, and the tradition of *wilaya* was incorporated into Islamic law.

Over time, jurists coined the concept of *wali* into *wali jabri*, which means "compulsory guardian," endowing the *wali* with authority, the capacity to compel, and the misuse of power. However, there was no consensus among the jurists; the earliest legal texts referred to *wali* as an open and flexible notion. For example, the Maliki and Shafi schools believe that the guardian's approval is required for marriage, but the Hanafi and, to a lesser degree, the Hanbali schools believe that the guardian's permission is not required. An adult woman, according to Hanafi, can approve her marriage contract without consulting a guardian.[145]

In many cultures today, the guardian (father, grandfather, uncle, or brother) continues to play an outsized role in determining a woman's marital destiny. Instead of defending women's rights, some *walis* suppress women, preventing them from making their own decisions. When a woman's consent is ignored, it is often attributed to a guardian's abuse of authority. Although the *wali*'s intention was not to coerce women, some guardians subjugate women's autonomy to meet the goals of the family. They intimidate, repress, and silence her, resulting in forced and proxy marriages.

Ibn Rushd, a jurist who authored an encyclopedia of Islamic law, disagreed that women require a guardian, for the Quran demonstrates women's ability to contract their own marriages: *"But, if they choose to leave, you are not accountable for what they reasonably decide for themselves"* (Q 2:240). And in another verse: *"[U]ntil after she has married another man and then is divorced"* (Q 2: 230). Ibn Rushd claims that during the Prophet's lifetime, many women without family or relatives arranged their own marriages without guardians. He asserts that the Prophet did not serve as a guardian to those lone women. If the guardian were required for women to enter a marriage contract, he asserts, the Quran would have specified the guardian's type and degree of kinship in a verse. Undoubtedly, the Prophet, encircled by such women, would have left instructions regarding the responsibilities, rights, and restrictions of a guardian.

Asma Lamrabet agrees with Ibn Rushd: "This is why scholars who are against the obligation of the *wali* suggested that the woman can pact her marriage contract alone and that no one should forbid her from freely choosing her partner, provided that he has the competence and good manners."

MATRIMONY AND CONTROL OF SEXUAL AUTONOMY

Despite the Quran's mandate that women can choose their life partner—cultural, social, and financial factors lead to forced marriages. One reason for forced marriages is to preserve the family's honor (*izzah*), to cover up percieved immoral behavior. Some girls are rushed into marriage out of parental concern that their unmarried daughter may act on her sexual desires. By forcing their daughter into the marriage, the parents enable their fears to override her free will. If they perceive misbehavior on the part of the daughter, they ignore the groom's incompetence and force her to marry him. But Haifaa Jawad cautions that the prospective wife's consent is crucial to the success of the marriage contract. Any coercion or extortion on the part of the relatives would automatically render the contract invalid. (29)

Economic insecurity is another factor. Families desire to keep land, property, and fortune within the extended family. Therefore, they pressure girls to enter nonconsensual marriages with cousins or relatives. Hena Zuberi explains that family pressure tends to be the cause when parents have made promises or commitments to relatives. Sometimes, relatives will employ emotional blackmail to threaten to cut off family ties. Girls who do not comply with their parents' demands may be emotionally forced, mentally tortured, ridiculed, kidnapped from their families, or even raped by their prospective groom. Some girls are riddled with guilt: The parents feign an illness and threaten to disown or disinherit their daughters. Others are reduced to becoming mere property of men, without autonomy over their lives, and thus exploitable.

This clearly violates egalitarian teachings in the Quran that state, "Women have rights similar to those of men equitably" (Q 2:228). Many mistakenly believe that the father or spouse has complete authority over family matters. Asma Barlas adds, "Muslims who view children, or wives, as the father's or husband's property, fail to consider that the Quran delineates relationships—between parents and children, husbands and wives, and even masters and slaves—in terms that rule out the idea of ownership altogether." (209)

In numerous war-torn regions, young females are forced into marriage without ever seeing their prospective spouses; their silence is interpreted as consent. This is what happened to Halima, a young Afghan girl. A local imam, named Mohammad, had recently attended a workshop on Marriage Rights led by WISE and its local Afghan partner. The imam sent WISE a note of gratitude for facilitating the workshop, relaying this story. "A man who had heard my sermon on forced marriage told me that he had a fourteen-year-old daughter who was engaged to a cousin she had never met. The father realized he had committed a sin by not obtaining his daughter's consent prior to the engagement. Additionally, he realized she was too young to be engaged or married. After hearing my sermon, he wanted to fix his mistake, so he postponed the engagement. He promised to allow his daughter to continue her education, and he would seek her permission to marry when she reached an appropriate age. Halima's father wrote to me, saying, 'It is because of you that I was able save my daughter's future.'"

REJECTING RACIAL PURITY

Maulana Muhammad Ali explains that the Quran eliminates all distinctions of caste, race, and culture. It asserts that no individual is superior to another except through righteousness (*taqwa*), demonstrating that there is complete equality among nations, communities, and ethnicities, and that marriage should be permitted between them. (470) *"O humanity! Indeed, we created you from a male and a female and made you into peoples and tribes so that you may [get to] know one another. Surely the most noble of you in the sight of God is the most righteous among you"* (Q 49:13). Although the Quran contains no reference of marriages between like-minded or same nationalities, such as an Arab marrying an Arab or a Pashtun marrying a Pashtun, certain societies utilize the custom of likeness (*afka*) to restrict marriages within the same race, ethnicity, or tribe. Some elders intentionally discourage cross-cultural unions by pressuring their children to enter marital bonds that preserve cultural ties and fortify the family's social standing.

In recent decades, religious authorities have stepped up juridical efforts to end the scrouge of forced marriages. As an example, it was reported that half of Saudi marriages end in divorce, and the large number of forced marriages is thought to be the main reason behind the growing divorce rate. In 2005, Saudi Arabia's Grand Mufti,

Abdul Aziz ibn Abdulllah al-Sheikh, issued a statement and called for imprisoning those who force women to marry. "Forcing a woman to marry someone she does not want and preventing her from wedding someone she chooses is not permissible under Islamic law," the Grand Mufti said.[146]

In 2008, at a meeting in India attended by one hundred Islamic organizations, the Islamic Fiqh Academy (IFA) declared that girls have the full right to choose their husband. If they were forced to marry against their will, they could claim that the marriage was "null and void." Over three hundred individuals concurred unanimously.[147]

For decades, women in Afghanistan were regarded as property, as a means of exchanging blood money or settling disputes or tribal feuds. In stark contrast, the Taliban, reversed their stance in 2021, allowing widows to freely choose new husbands and remarry seventeen weeks after their husband's death. Hibatullah Akhunzada, the Taliban leader, issued a decree banning forced marriage, stating that, "Both (women and men) should be equal, no one can force women to marry by coercion or pressure forced marriages."[148]

The transformation in attitudes towards forced marriage in the United Kingdom was led by Shahien Taj founder of the Henna Foundation. She developed the Forced Marriage Knowledge Centre and Directory, a centralized online portal which provides victims and service providers with real-time information. They designed school-training initiatives and videos for police officers on forced marriage titled, "Her Choice…Your duty to protect." Shahien received an achievement award for her contribution to advancing the United Kingdom's response to forced marriage.

THE REASON FOR THIS BOOK

Sana, a young Muslim intern at WISE in 2018, shared her harrowing experience of narrowly avoiding a forced into marriage planned by her immigrant. She explained this as follows. "Since I was twelve years old, my immigrant parents have taken me annually to their native country to introduce me to potential suitors. Because my parents thought they knew what was best for me, their message was clear: I needed to choose one of the men I had been introduced to. I ignored this for years, but when I learned that they planned to force me into a marriage, to prevent me from attending college, I knew I had to act. I fled before they took me on the next trip back to their native country, where they would have forced me to sign a marriage contract. I applied to universities and got admission; worked part-time to pay for my tuition and secured a Truman scholarship!"

Her struggle moved and distressed me. What assistance could WISE offer her? I queried. When she approached the mosque, she reported that the management refused to intervene because her father was a revered elder whom they could not offend. No one she knew would assist her, and there was no information online that she could use to fight for her cause. She suggested WISE create a Muslim Women's Rights Manual. This book stands as the realization of that vision—a tool for women like Sana to advocate for their rights within the framework of Islam.

Sana perseverance paid off, and she is now an accomplished professional woman, happily married and the pride of her parents owing to her professional success. She will always be recognized for inspiring this community-led educational tool that will enable scores of girls to negotiate their rights within faith and society.

#12 | TO MATURELY CHOOSE MARRIAGE

A drug addict and habitual gambler lost his entire fortune in Afghanistan. Without any assets to place his bets with, he decided to wager on his nine-year-old daughter. According to the terms of the bet, if he won, he would marry his opponent's daughter, and if he lost, his opponent would marry the addict's daughter. Following his loss, he gave his daughter to his opponent. The winner brought the girl back to his village and introduced her as a woman he had won through a bet. The villagers and the man's first wife regarded the girl as a disgrace. She spent her entire life being mistreated by her husband's family and the villagers. She lost any opportunity for a life of dignity, and her dreams of becoming a teacher were shattered forever.

Amid such tragic circumstances, its crucial to recognize that, in Islam, marriage is intended to provide a legal and socially accepted framework for companionship, affection, and emotional support between a husband and wife. However, it is important to note that the Quran doesn't stipulate an age requirement for a marriage, instead, it emphasizes the condition of reaching puberty, known as *baligh*.

Since marriage is a legal contract between two people, some have argued that the age at which a person is considered morally responsible should replace a simple biological threshold such as puberty. This is evidenced by the Quran, which emphasizes that custodians assess the maturation (marriage age) of orphans, typically at puberty, to ensure that they have discernment and the capacity to manage property: *"Test the competence of the orphans until they reach marriageable age. Then if you feel they are capable of sound judgment, return their wealth to them"* (Q 4:6).

Sayeed Hossain Nasr defines discernment or sound judgement as the possession of a rational faculty, a healthy and upstanding character, the ability to manage property, and a sound religion—to the extent that one no longer requires custodial care. From this, other scholars have deduced that complete mental capacity (*ahliyyah*) is required, even though marriage at puberty or maturity is permitted. Two of the four major schools of law state that the minimum age for marriage should be at least seventeen years old. The Maliki school specifies eighteen years for both males and females. The Hanafi school specifies eighteen years for males and seventeen years for females, and the Shafi and Hanbali schools specify fifteen years for both sexes.[149]

According to Islamic Jurisprudence, a person entering a marriage contract must be *baligh*, have *ahliyyah*, and consent to the marriage. Even if a girl reaches puberty, she may not be mentally mature enough to consent to a marriage or negotiate the terms of a marriage contract because she lacks the necessary life experience and intellectual acumen to do so.

To reiterate, both spouses have the right to stipulate conditions in a marriage contract. Immature, non-*baligh* girls are simply incapable of comprehending a covenant and its long-term implications.[150] Based on this, a marriage is invalid if a minor girl is not physically, mentally, emotionally, and sexually prepared to undertake the responsibilities of marriage and childbearing or is cognitively unprepared to meet the demands of her spouse.[151]

PRIORITIZE CULTURE OVER CONSENT

The Quran commands, *"Let there be no compulsion in religion" (Q 2:256)*. No one should be coerced into anything, including marriage, which is a lifetime commitment. However, some prepubescent girls, whose options are limited, are compelled to take marriage as their allotted fate and are forced to consummate a marriage prior to puberty.

The Prophet established a foundational principle that if a man forces his daughter to marry against her will, the marriage is annulled.[152] Ashgar Ali Engineer explains in *The Rights of Women in Islam* that if a Muslim child is married by a guardian prior to reaching puberty, the child has the right to repudiate the marriage. This "option of puberty," known as *khiyar al-bulugh*, specifies that if a girl is given in marriage by her guardian in her childhood, she can accept or reject the marriage when she reaches adulthood. This right of hers is absolute, and no one, not even her father or any other female or male relative, can interfere with it.[153]

In many cases the consent of a child bride is done by proxy through a guardian, claiming that the virgin minor's silence constitutes consent. Consent by silence typically occurs in cultures where girls are socialized to never express their opinion in the private or public sphere. Ibn Rushd, a jurist from the twelfth century, explains that consent to marriage occurs in two ways: 1) for males and non-virgin women, consent occurs through their words; 2) for virgin women, consent occurs through their silence, but her rejection occurs through words.[154]

Unfortunately, child marriages persist despite the Quran's (Q 4:19) stern warning against the commodification of women for economic, cultural, and religious reasons. And in cultures where seeking retribution is part of maintaining family honor, minor brides are still traded among men; each man marries the sister of the other man in what they perceive as an equal exchange. In extreme circumstances, females are offered as compensation for a crime committed by an uncle or distant relative, and the guilty family resolves the claim by marrying off their five- to twelve-year-old daughter.

Some poor families offer child brides to older men for a price or send them abroad for older, wealthy men. Haifaa Jawad explains that in order to feel younger, these predatory men remarry younger girls and seek a girl who is pliable enough to be molded to fit their preconceived gender roles. (48) Through a child bride, they are assured a highly fertile wife, a moldable homemaker, a lifelong caregiver, and a person who extends their lifespan.

Reem's story unveils the suffering of millions of girls. She comes from Yemen, where girls are married at a young age because it is believed that their primary function is to be a mother, and parents fear that their daughters will have difficulty in finding a husband after what is typically considered the desirable childbearing age. Reem was eleven when her father married her to her cousin, who was twenty-one years older. The father drove his daughter 150 kilometers from home and forced her into a marriage. Three days after marrying, her husband raped his eleven-year-old wife and cousin. Razor-cutting her wrists, Reem attempted suicide. Her husband returned her to the family. Reem's divorced mother took her to court for a divorce. The judge said,

"We don't divorce little girls." Reem said, "But how come you allow little girls to get married?" It is remarkable that courts, scholars, and families have not used this precept about child marriage despite decades of wounded children.[155]

HARMING ISLAM'S REPUTATION

In verse 33:21, the Quran demonstrates that the Prophet is a shining example for Muslims to emulate. Many Muslims use Aisha as evidence and justification for child marriage, ignoring the fact that the Prophet's marital bonds were unique to him and were not meant to be imitated by other Muslims.

For over 1,400 years, Aisha's young age has remained unchallenged by Muslims. Unfortunately, this has been seized upon by critics of Islam to paint the religion as incompatible with contemporary values. They distort the religion's stance on women's equality and the Prophet's reputation, and propagate the misconception that Muslim women need rescuing from misogynistic men.

However, the controversy surrounding Aisha's age raises an important issue. The persistent depiction of Aisha as a child bride has led to a tragic reality where countless prepubescent girls, notably in Yemen, Africa, and Afghanistan are forced into marriage. Furthermore, the canonization of Aisha's marriage age has provided legal and spiritual justification for scholars, institutions, and governments to endorse child marriage. This blind adherence to traditional canon persists, with advocates rejecting any attempts to scrutinize the veracity of the hadith. They resist investigating contradictory sources that question Aisha's young age and, call into question her marriage age.

Dr. Salah al-Din bin Amad al-Idlib, a Syrian Hadith scholar, wrote a seminal paper on Aisha's marriage age, stating that while many Muslims are satisfied with the commonly accepted narrative, it remains a fact that for many non-Muslims the Prophet's marriage to a nine-year-old remains an insurmountable obstacle to them accepting Islam as a respectable doctrine. And what a waste this would be if historical evidence shows that the Prophet did not marry a nine-year-old, but rather a young woman who was almost eighteen!

Fortunately, many other scholars, academicians, and historians have re-examined all sources, analyzed historical facts, and reviewed the chain of transmissions. This sincere, passionate, and vigorous effort to resolve Aisha's age by comprehending all its dimensions must never be characterized as insecure Muslims engaging in historical revisionism.

Muslim scholars today offer a variety of evidence and explanations regarding her age. Their accumulating evidence states that Aisha's marriage age ranges from seventeen to twenty-seven. The different perspectives stem from the complexity of historical analysis of multiple data sources. To create a narrative that is both exhaustive and readable, I omitted numerous references; readers who wish to investigate the sources themselves will find them in the endnotes.

To understand Aisha's age in the context of the main historical events transpiring during the early years of Islam, I listed the major milestone dates that can help you keep track. The Prophet received his first Revelation in 610 CE; he began publicly preaching in 613 CE; Khadijah died in 619; his night journey from Mecca to Jerusalem occurred in 621; he migrated to Medina in 622, where he married Aisha in 622. He fought in three battles (Badr in 624, Uhud in 627, and Trench in 627), and then he signed a peace treaty with Meccans in 628; peacefully conquered Mecca in 630; and passed away in 632. Dr. Salah al-Din bin Amad al-Idlib concludes that Aisha was born four years before the first Revelation in 606 CE, and engaged at the age of fourteen in the tenth year of the Revelation, 619 CE. At the conclusion of the first year of the Hijrah in 622, when she was close to eighteen years old, the Prophet married her.

The hadith that states Aisha was six at her engagement and nine at her wedding has a reliable chain of narrators. Nonetheless, it contradicts these credible historical sources. Scholars of Hadith have stated that when the content (*matn*) of a hadith is contradicted by more reliable historical evidence, the hadith is rejected because it shows that an error seeped in due to the delusion of one of its narrators. Dr. al-Idlib explains that since there is only Aisha's word for it (there is no other evidence that backs up her statement), and since all the other evidence from many different sources points to her having been closer to age eighteen, it is his conclusion that even though the hadith is an authentic narration, it must be rejected in favor of alternative theories because it is contradicted by historical reality.[156]

In *Islamic Interpretative Tradition and Gender Justice*, Yasmin Amin describes that the primary narrator of this hadith was Hisham Ibn

Urwa, who spent most of his life in Medina but moved to Iraq at the age of seventy-one, where he suffered some memory loss. He was accused by numerous traditionalists (*muhaddithun*), most notably Ibn Hajar and al-Dhahabi, of distorting traditions related to Aisha's marriage, and he was seen as an untrustworthy narrator as a result. The hadith that "Aisha married at six or nine" was "not narrated in Medina," but years later only in Iraq, when his memory had started to fail him in old age. This is a significant fact to keep in mind. This hadith does not, by any means, correspond with the actual realities of the period in question. In addition, his two pupils from Medina, the most notable jurists Imam Malik and Imam Abu Hanifa, do not cite this hadith at any point in their writings.[157]

Mohamad Jebara provides an exhaustive timeline alleging that Aisha was closer to twenty-seven. He states that if Aisha married at nine it would place her birth at 615 CE, which is impossible; Ibnu Hisham's narrative (via Ibnu Ishaq) says that in 610 CE, when the Prophet received the first Revelation, nineteen people accepted Islam, including Abu Bakr's daughter Aisha. If she was nine in 615 CE, she would not have been born in 610. He explains that Um Ruman, Aisha's mother, was widowed at the age of twenty-seven in the year 592 CE; she married Abu Bakr at the end of the year (during the *Jahiliya*) and gave birth to Aisha three years later in 595, which puts Aisha's age at twenty-seven years old at the time of her marriage to the Prophet in 622. The maturity Aisha exhibits during the Meccan period and her accounts of major incidents also reveal her to be a mature woman, not a young child. (331)

According to Jasser Auda, Bukhari narrates that Aisha witnessed her father migrate to Abyssinia, around year 615 CE. This could not have happened before Aisha herself was born, as the "nine-year-old" hadith implies. He says that Aisha witnessed *verse 54* of the Quran being revealed while she was a *jariyah* (an Arabic term for a girl between six and thirteen) playing in Mecca. This chapter was revealed between years two and four after the first Revelation (612–614 CE). Which means in the first year after the Hijrah her age must be between fifteen and twenty-five. (36)

What does all of this mean? Are we to believe that the Prophet, whose morality is so exemplary that God Almighty remarked, *"And You are truly a man of outstanding character"* (Q 68:4), would marry a nine-year-old child? First, it is uncharacteristic for the Prophet, as he married mature women. Second, he refused to marry his minor daughter to his companions. Third, he married his daughters as adults: Fatima at nineteen, Ruquiyya at twenty-three. His companion Abu Bakr followed in his footsteps, marrying off his eldest daughter Asmaa at age twenty-six, and Aisha at about eighteen. Fourth, scholarship tells us that the hadith that states Aisha was married at age nine is unreliable.

As Muslims, our faith is unshakable because it is firmly anchored in our beliefs. Criticisms of past scholars' works must never shake the rock-solid foundation of our faith. Instead, let us adopt a spirit of unshakeable confidence that allows us to pursue the truth with an open mind while rejecting falsity with discernment.

MARRIAGES AIMED TO BUILD PEACE AND ALLIANCES

After Khadijah died, the Prophet was grief stricken. His companion Kawlah suggested he remarry so a new wife could comfort him and manage his home and four children. She suggested two qualified candidates: Sawda, a sixty-five-year-old widow; and Aisha, a single woman. Would Kawlah recommend a nine-year-old child who would be unable to give his children the care they needed? The Prophet knew Aisha's age; she was the daughter of his best friend Abu Bakr. If she was indeed nine, how could she reassure a fifty-year-old Prophet?

The Prophet sent Kawlah to present proposals to the two qualified candidates. Abu Bakr, Aisha's father, was unable to accept the proposal because Aisha was betrothed to another man, an indication that she was of marriageable age. Meanwhile, Sawda was honored and accepted the proposal, and the Prophet wed her. When Abu Bakr met Aisha's future in-laws, they withdrew their proposal due to Aisha's conversion to Islam. Still, Abu Bakr was worried about the Prophet's offer. He feared that marrying Aisha to his best friend would constitute an incestuous relationship, to which the Prophet responded, "You are my brother in Islam, but not my blood brother."[158] The Prophet got engaged to Aisha and married her after the Hijrah in 622 CE.

According to Yasmin Amin, the scholars rarely mention the Sunnah of the Prophet where he refused to give his daughter Fatima in marriage when she was a minor, "when Abu Bakr and Umar ibn al-Khattab request Fatima's hand in marriage, both are rejected by the Prophet Muhammad, who cites her immaturity and inability to manage marital responsibilities as a result of her youth. If the Prophet had married nine-year-old Aisha, would he have rejected his father-in-law? It is inconceivable that the Prophet, characterized by his sublime morality in the Quran, would refuse something for his daughter, then allow the same for someone else's." (331)

Another point that negates Aisha being under ten years old when she married the Prophet is the age difference between her and Fatima, who was five to ten years younger than Aisha. Fatima was nineteen when she married Ali in 624 CE. (A ten-year difference indicates that Aisha was twenty-seven in 622, while a five-year difference indicates that she was twenty-two.) According to a common belief, Fatima was born five years before, close to, or shortly after the Revelation in 610 CE. If Aisha had been born four years after the Revelation, in 614, then Fatima would be eight to four years older than her.

When the Prophet spoke his final words to Fatima before passing away, Aisha wanted to know what he said, so she asked her, "O daughter, tell me what he said."[159] Yasmin Amin states that it seems strange and unlikely that Aisha would address Fatima as, "O daughter" even if the younger was the elder's father's wife.

Amin also cites Ibn Ishaq (d. 767 CE) and Ibn Hashim (d. 833 CE), stating that Aisha and her sister Asma accepted Islam together in 610 CE, and Aisha could not be nine years of age in the second year of the Hijrah, because she would not have been born. The important observation here is that Ibn Ishaq and Ibn Hashim wrote their accounts well before the hadith written by Bukhari. Yet, later scholars simply glossed over the contradictions and made no attempts at reconciling the conflicting information.[160]

In addition, Aisha's eldest sister Asmaa was ten years older than Aisha and was twenty-eight years old at the time of the Hijrah to Medina (662 CE), when Aisha would have been eighteen. Asmaa was born twenty-seven years before the Hijrah, or fourteen years prior to the first Revelation in 610. This means Aisha was born four years before the start of the Revelation (606 CE). There is an incontrovertible historical record that Aisha participated in the Battle of Badr in 624 CE and the Battle of Uhud in 625 CE. If she married at age six or nine in 622 and participated in two battles, she would have been only eight to eleven or nine to twelve years old during those battles. The minimum age to participate in a battle was fifteen. During the Battle of Uhud, the

Prophet enacted his law to prevent boys less than fifteen years of age from joining in warfare. Aisha, at ten, would have been ineligible to join the mission. The Prophet would not breach his own laws.

Anas narrates how he saw Aisha at the battleground. "On the day (of the battle) of Uhad when (some) people retreated and left the Prophet, I saw Aisha bint Abu Bakr and Um Sulaim with their robes tucked up, so that the bangles around their ankles were visible, hurrying with their water skins." In another narration it is said, "carrying the water skins on their backs." Then they would pour the water in the mouths of the people and return to fill the water skins again and come back again to pour water in the mouths of the people.[161] There is no report indicating that Aisha participated as some sort of "cheerleader," as proponents of child marriage profess, but there is this report indicating that she was among the women fetching water.[162] Here, Aisha is described as a woman wearing robes and bangles and carrying water skins like Umme Sulaim. She was a powerful woman who lifted the dead, treated the wounded, carried water in goatskins, provided ammunition, and even took up the sword.

AISHA'S CALL: HALT THE CHAINS OF CHILD MARRIAGE

Despite being the Prophet's youngest wife, Aisha stood out among other wives and all female companions. Her acceptability was not based on her age, but because she was lively, argumentative, and intellectually stimulating. She possessed a colossal personality and exuded self-confidence in everything she did. Her exceptional wit, eloquence, and memory won her the respect of her husband and the admiration of scholars and jurists. By refuting myths about her marriage age, we take a significant step toward combating the pervasive practice of marrying prepubescent girls around the globe.

For these child brides, there exists only harm and no gain. In comparison to elder women, they hold a subordinate position within their husband's family, resulting in diminished influence. Their childhood and social interactions are taken from them, and they become financially dependent on their husband. Additionally, their lack of preparation for sexual activity and childbirth heightens the potential for complication during childbirth, underscoring the need for long term reform. While these minor brides may experience feelings of hopelessness and anxiety, it is crucial to shift the focus to sharing stories that demonstrate the potential for change.

One shining example is found in the life of Aisha, who, despite being the Prophet's youngest wife, made extraordinary contributions to Islamic civilization. In contrast to the missed opportunities faced by some young girls, Aisha's story inspires us to advocate for young girls everywhere. Let us work toward a future where they are protected, respected, and provided the opportunities to realize their full potential, just as Aisha did.

EXAMPLE OF A PAKISTANI VICTIM TURNED ADVOCATE

In our own time, Naila Amin was only eight when she found out she was engaged to Tariq while visiting Pakistan for her cousin's wedding. When she was thirteen, her family married her to her twenty-one-year-old cousin without a marriage license. Amin curled up on the floor because she was afraid of being abused or beaten during her marriage.

She explains that child weddings occur even in the United States due to poverty or cultural expectations, and that "people must abandon the notion that this is a Muslim problem, because it is not, this is an American problem." So she founded the Naila Amin Foundation to fight child marriage. Her inspiration came from not having a childhood. In the process, in 2021 she helped New Jersey become the second US state to increase the minimum marriage age to eighteen. The bill is known as "Naila's Law."[163]

She says her past has taught her resilience and survival skills. "I've been surviving for the past thirty-one years, and there's a fire inside of me that won't go out."

#13 | TO ACCEPT OR REFUSE A POLYGAMOUS MARRIAGE

Amina met her spouse in high school and fell in love with him. She claims they were a wonderful fit and intuitively knew one other. They married right after high school, much to the chagrin of his family: Amina was white and non-Muslim. She embraced Islam and began wearing a headscarf and a robe to seek favor with her husband's family. Amina's mother-in-law wanted the daughter-in-law to live with her and care for her. But Amina could not, as she worked, was independent, and did not speak Urdu.

Amina's husband was forced by his family to take a second wife, a cousin from Pakistan. He was told this was his Islamic right and that treating both spouses equally served God and his mother. Amina was promised that God would strengthen her. Amina has had to share her husband for over twenty years. She admits that it is painful, but she feels God willed it for her.

Before Islam's arrival in Arabia, males were free to marry as many spouses as they wished. Some women were forced to marry their captors because they were not required to consent to marriage or were obligated by contractual obligations. Another regrettable practice prevailed by which the wealth of an orphan was embezzled by their guardian. Some guardians were drawn to orphan girls who were wealthy and beautiful, and they would exploit the vulnerable girls by marrying them for the most minimal dowry possible, as observed by Aisha.

During the Battle of Uhud in 625 CE, seventy out of 700 men were martyred, leaving behind destitute widows and orphans. In this aftermath, a verse was revealed to promote social welfare and justice for female orphans: *"If you fear you might fail to give orphan women their due rights, if you were to marry them"* (Q 4:3). By marrying the widows and or orphans, men assumed physical, financial, and social responsibilities for their well-being, providing the tribal protection they needed. Then, the orphan had parental supervision and protection from financial exploitation and sexual predators, and the widow had the opportunity to live comfortably and satisfy her sensual desires without being forced into illicit relationships.

Before we set out to analyze *verse 4:3* in depth, it is remarkable to note that the Quran is the only sacred text that limits the number of wives, as neither the Talmud nor the Bible contain such restrictions. King Solomon, for example, had 700 wives, and David had many wives, while Prophets Jacob and Moses each had four.

The Quran permitted polygamy to ensure the welfare of vulnerable individuals—such as orphans, divorcees, and widows—by granting them legal rights. To emphasize fairness, men could marry up to four wives provided they treated them equally. If justice proved challenging, they were advised to marry just one. Lastly, by stating that monogamy is a superior standard, the Quran prioritizes society's most vulnerable over men's inclination for multiple wives.

JUSTICE AND POLYGAMY: A RESTRICTIVE PERSPECTIVE

Polygamy is not outlawed by Islam, nor is it required, encouraged, or promoted. It is permissible if certain requirements are satisfied; however, in such cases, the husband is held to a higher degree of fairness, justice, and responsibility. According to Amina Wadud, equal treatment of food, clothes, shelter, and intimacy is just as much a part of a husband exercising *adl* (justice) as is providing financial assistance, recreation, safety, and well-being. (83)

The Quran's demand for justice is clear; the consent of the first wife is required prior to the marriage of a second wife. No one can coerce her consent, and a husband may not favor one wife over the other: *"You will never be able to maintain 'emotional' justice between your wives- no matter how keen you are. So do not totally incline toward one while leaving the other in suspense"* (Q 4:129). The Quran limits polygamy by imposing a financial burden on the man who must give his new wife her dower, just as he did with his previous wife. *"Give women you wed their due dowries graciously. But if they waive some of it willingly, you may enjoy it freely with a clear conscience"* (Q 4:4). The Quran informs men that ensuring justice between wives can be challenging, and it suggests monogamy as the preferred option, underscoring the importance of contentment with a single wife. *"But if you are afraid you will fail to maintain justice, then, content yourself with one" (Q 4:3).*

THE DELICATE BALANCE OF PAIRING

Nilofar Ahmed explains that in the Quran, the Arabic word for spouse is *zawj*, which means one of a pair. Husbands are the *zawj* of their wives, and wives are the *zawj* of their husbands. As is the case with all couples, husband and wife are expected to be singular. This rule is only permitted to be violated in extraordinary circumstances. In his book, *Fiqh-ul-Quran*, Maulana Umar Ahmed Usmani asserts that verse 4:1 states that God created humanity from a single *nafs*, created its companion from it, and then produced an infinite number of men and women from them. Even when there was a need for population growth, only one man and one woman were created.

In verse *30:21* God proclaims that he has put compassion between couples, recognizing the challenges in maintaining justice among multiple wives. An additional emphasis is placed on the recognition of emotional fragility in the verse "Q 33:4," which states, "God does not place two hearts *in any person's chest.*" In addition to urging men to follow the correct follow the straight path and be honest, this verse appeals to their consciences. It serves as a reminder that the human heart is singular, unable to accommodate two loves in equal measure. The Quran asserts that emotions such as love need a unique trust and bond between two people, which is hard to attain due to the inevitable tendency of men to favor one wife over another. For the sake of maintaining the sanctity of matrimony, God recommends marriage to only one wife.

THE PROPHET'S STANCE

Although polygamy is neither obligatory (*fard*), nor prescribed (*mustahab*), it rapidly became a general rule in which men could marry four wives regardless of who they were and without regard for justice or equity. It is possible that scholars, influenced by cultural and social factors, diverged from the verse's original intent and over time their interpretations were enshrined in law, permitting a more permissive approach to polygamy by quoting verse 4:3 selectively.

These legal edicts were legitimized during the height of the Muslim empires and sanctioned reprehensible sexual exploitation practices in the name of Islam, such as the practice of keeping captive women in harems in the hopes that one of them would become the Sultan's consort or the practice of giving concubines as gifts to show favor to influential men. Thus, it is necessary to reexamine the original intent of *verse 4:3—"[T]hen marry other women of your choice, two, or three, or four"*—and consider the larger Islamic teachings, which treat all individuals fairly, promoting justice and harmonious marriages. Again, this reexamination is likely to be met with some resistance due to people's views, beliefs, and or convictions.

As with anything else, the Prophet, who is the walking Quran, serves as a good starting point. He was a father of four girls and was confronted by this dilemma. When Ali, his son-in-law, asked Fatima, his daughter, for permission to marry another woman, Fatima complained to her father, who then made this impassioned declaration from the *minbar* (pulpit): "The people of Hisham ibn Mughira have asked for my permission to marry their daughter to Ali ibn Abi Talib," he stated." "Of course, if Ali divorces my daughter and marries the daughter of Ali ibn Abi Talib, he has the right. My daughter is part of me. Whatever harms her, harms me; whatever hurts her, hurts me."[164]

As a lawgiver, the Prophet expressed his views publicly to inform his community that he does not approve of polygamy unless it is wartime or another stressful situation in which it will benefit the family especially women and their children. Yet, when the issue of multiple wives arises, the Prophet's refusal, his staunch stance, and compelling appeal are never mentioned.[165] We barely hear about his twenty-five-year monogamous marriage to Khadijah and only hear about his wives, whom he married not for personal purposes but to advance religious, political, and social programs.

MULTIFACETED EFFECTS OF TRANSLATION ERRORS

Let's return to the verse most often cited regarding polygamy, which is commonly understood to permit men to marry up to four women: *"If you fear you might fail to give orphan women their 'due rights,' if you were to marry them, then marry other women of your choice, two, or three, or four. But if you are afraid you will fail to maintain justice, then content yourself with one or those bondwomen in your possession. This way, you are less likely to commit injustice" (Q 4:3).*

Asma Barlas focuses her research on whom men may marry,

specifically in Arabic, *al nisa*: (orphans and mothers of orphans). This is commonly interpreted as "any women" or "all women," and some interpretations omit "widows or orphans" and substitute it with "other women." Men who claim it is permissible to marry up to four women (not just widows and mothers of orphans) cite these translations: "marry such women as seem good to you," or "marry those of other women who please you," or "marry women of your choice."

Such interpretations, according to Barlas, are problematic. The word "other" does not appear in the Quran, and the reading does not make sense. "Other women" who have families are not readily susceptible to "injustice." In contrast, female orphans whose fathers have been killed in battle, and their mothers, may be financially abused. She says there is no explanation for how marrying a woman or several women other than female orphans or widowed mothers of war orphans would protect orphans or widowed mothers. (194–236)

The context in which the verse was revealed, according to Maulana Muhammad Ali, indicates that "women" is meant to be "mothers of orphans." He explains that the meaning of this verse is explained by verse 4:127: *"And they ask you, O' Prophet regarding women. Say, 'It is God Who instructs you regarding them. Instruction has 'already' been revealed in the Book concerning the orphan women you deprive of their due rights but still wish to marry, also helpless children, as well as standing up for orphans' rights."* When a widow was left with orphans to bring up, she and her children would get no share of the inheritance, nor were people inclined to marry the widows who had children. God enjoined men to marry the mothers so that the men would be interested in their welfare. (474)

Nilofer Ahmed cites scholar Omer Ahmed Osmani in her article, "Polygamy and the Quran," who rejects the notion that the verse generally applies to all women. He asserts that the condition of marrying more than one wife applies only to orphan girls and widows and does not apply to other women. He further adds that the word *yatama*, meaning orphan, not only includes orphans but also widows and divorcees. This follows the logic that marrying an orphan girl will prevent her property from being misappropriated.

Ahmed demonstrates, according to Imam Abubakr Razi, how the word *yateem* is sometimes used for the child who is left fatherless and sometimes for the woman who, either because of her husband's death or due to being divorced, is left single. Even aged women who have lost their husbands are called *yateema*.

When Professor Debra Majeed was doing research for her book, she asked an African American imam from New York how he could justify verse 4:3, which is directed at the care of orphans. He replied, "Our people are orphans already," referring to structural racism. "So, when a Muslim man wants to take a second wife, he is taking responsibility for an orphan in that regard."[166]

The second part of Q 4:3 is explained as follows: *"But if you are afraid you will fail to maintain justice, then content yourself with one or those bond[s]women in your possession. This way, you are less likely to commit injustice."* The "bondswomen" are presumed to be war captives or "slaves and concubines," who were an unbroken element of seventh-century Arab society. As a motive to release people from slavery, the Quran provides recommendations to treat them fairly and marry them. Many jurists interpreted aw as "or" thus allowing men to marry such women. In *The Spirit of Islam*, Islamic scholar Syed Ameer Ali translates aw as "that," which refers to "women whom men's right hands possess" as their spouse.[167] Taking these various interpretations into account, the verse can be read as follows: *"If you fear that you will not be able to deal justly with the orphans, marry orphan girls or women [mothers of orphans] of your choice, two, three, or four; but if you fear that you will not be able to deal justly [with multiple wives], then [marry] only one, that your right hand possesses [your wife, because you are financially responsible for her]. That will be more appropriate since it will keep you from doing wrong [embezzling the orphan's fortune or committing adultery]."*

SEEKING SUNNAH—THROUGH MULTIPLE WIVES

Still, advocates of polygamy frequently cite the Prophet's Sunnah to justify the practice. The Prophet's marriages are an essential aspect of his life, and they must be presented accurately. He was able to positively influence the social, political, and religious milieu through his eleven marriages. Each wife played a crucial role by establishing alliances with their tribes and groups hostile to his message; and collectively, they strengthened their homes as a center for spiritual activity and community development.

The first marriage was to Sawda, a sixty-five-year-old widow who contributed to the household's stability by providing comfort and care for his children. A significant marriage to Aisha, the virgin, solidified a marital bond with Abu Bakr, his best friend and companion. A year after marriage, Zaynab, a war widow in her sixties, died. He married thirty-six-year-old widow Hafsa, Umar bin Khattab's daughter, and her father's conversion to Islam benefited Mecca's Muslims. Umm Salama, a widow with five children, forged an alliance with her tribe, who were the Prophet's fiercest opponents. Rayhana bint Zayd, a Jewish woman, was held captive after her tribe's defeat; upon her release, she converted to Islam and wed the Prophet. This marriage strengthened ties between Jews and Muslims.

His marriage to the thirty-eight-year-old Zaynab bint Jahsh, the wife of his adopted son Zayd, sparked controversy. This divinely sanctioned marriage was to show the importance of lineage, and its intent was to invalidate the Arab practice of assuming adopted sons as biological sons: *"[S]o when Zaid totally lost interest in 'keeping' his wife, We gave her to you in marriage, so that there will be no blame on the believers for marrying the ex-wives of their adopted sons after their divorce" (Q 33:37)*. Juwayria, whose father and ex-husband were the Prophet's sworn enemies, proposed to marry him. Following their marriage, members of her tribe were liberated. Ramla was thirty-six years old and the daughter of the fiercest enemy of the Prophet, Abu Sufyan. Her tribe eventually converted to Islam, demonstrating the power of faith. Safiyya, a Jewish widow of war who had been captured in war, wed the Prophet. Some wives questioned her loyalty. The Prophet allayed this concern by instructing Safiyya to say, "My husband is Muhammad, my father is Aaron (Haroon), and my uncle is Musa (Moses)," thereby fostering closer ties between the Jews and Muslims in Medina. Maymuna, a fifty-seven-year-old divorcee whose tribe converted to Islam, and Maria, a Coptic Christian, were gifted to the Prophet by the Christian governor of Alexandria. Maria gave birth to a son, Ibrahim, who died in infancy.[168]

Except for Aisha and Maria, all the Prophet's wives were *yateema*, women who had lost their husbands. Although the Prophet encouraged *yateema* women, widows, and divorcees to remarry, his own wives were forbidden from marrying again after his passing. They were considered "the mothers of all believers," and no believer may marry his mother. As the Prophet aged, he gave his wives the option to leave and marry other men if they wanted. All but one wife refused to leave him.

RATIONALES IN THE REALMS OF SEX, MONEY, AND PROGENY

According to Amina Wadud, those in favor of polygamy argue that it addresses societal issues such as adultery, prostitution, sexually transmitted diseases, out-of-wedlock births, and women's unmarried status. These reasons in favor of polygamy have emerged over time, reinforcing the actions of many men who believe that God permits them to have multiple wives. But often, under such circumstances, a husband neglects his first wife by marrying a younger wife, with or without her consent. (84)

Some men see polygamy as an entitlement for producing an offspring, preferably a male heir. If the woman is unable to conceive or give birth to a son, the husband will marry a second wife, defying God's instructions: *"He grants both sons and daughters, 'to whoever He wills,' and leaves whoever He wills infertile" (Q 42:50).*

There is also financial polygamy, for which there is no direct Quranic sanction. This implies that a financially capable male should support multiple wives to alleviate economic hardship. Amina Wadud rejects this argument that assumes all women are financial burdens: reproducers, but not producers. She argues that the efficacy of the marketplace is influenced by several factors, gender being only one, and that polygamy can never be a simple solution to complex economic problems.

According to Wadud, polygamy that seeks to satisfy male sexual desire contradicts Islamic teachings because it attempts to legitimize unbridled lust among men. In such cases, if a man's sexual needs cannot be met by one wife, he might have two, and if he desires more, he might have three or four. Wadud stresses the importance of moral virtues by emphasizing the Quranic principles of self-restraint and modesty. (84)

FACTORS DRIVING WOMEN TOWARD POLYGAMOUS MARRIAGES

Kecia Ali, author of *Sexual Ethics and Islam*, explains that the justification of polygamy as giving all women a chance to be wives and mothers is partially real. But when it is reinforced by a scare tactic that there are not enough eligible men to marry, it commodifies and devalues the worth of women.[169] The reality is that women choose polygamy for a variety of reasons. Depending on their individual circumstances, some seek companionship. Others are motivated by their family's financial security, as merging their resources with co-wives can be advantageous for all parties; they are willing to be co-wives, nurture sisterly relationships, divide household duties, and rear children communally.

Debra Majeed, author of *Polygyny: What It Means When African American Muslim Women Share Their Husbands,* describes how multiple wives practice polygamy in three different ways: polygamy of liberation, polygamy of coercion, and polygamy of choice.

Majeed's research found that most women who engage in the practice do so as an exercise of agency and liberation. Women who choose such marriages, unashamedly defend their partnering choices, citing a lack of marriageable black men and their desire to maintain cultural norms. For them, polygamy is not a violation of their marital rights; rather, it is a means of adhering to the communal responsibility that Muslim men and women have to care for themselves. For them, polygamy provides an assemblance of a family rather than none at all.

Despite polygamy being liberating for some, Majeed is ultimately skeptical of the practice being pro-women or pro-family. She highlights issues with children who don't understand why their father is switching between households, as well as children from the first marriage who are resentful of sharing their inheritance with their half-siblings.

Malaysian Dr. Wan Zumusni Wan Mustapha worked on a research initiative for Sisters in Islam. She interviewed over a thousand polygamous family members, including: spouses, first wives, second wives, and children. She discovered that women have multiple reasons for being second wives. Primary were women's desires to be provided for and protected. Many disadvantaged women welcomed the opportunity to live more comfortably. Some women attempted to deflect the negative attention that being single attracts. Becoming a second wife enabled them to "upgrade their status," and as married women, they would no longer be subject to sexual advances from males.

Dr. Wan explained that some first wives who are coerced or pressured into accepting their husband's decision, "voice their dissatisfaction, but others, to save the marriage or for the sake of the children, simply go along with it." In her previous research, she interviewed other first spouses who were "unhappy, miserable, and depressed." She concluded, "I cannot see how this could be in the best interests of the first wives."[170]

In many societies, women who are educated, unmarried, and economically independent are stigmatized. Being a second wife is degrading for them. In addition, the likelihood of a single woman experiencing the pleasure of motherhood and sexual satisfaction on equal terms is bleak.

The Saudi columnist Tariq Al-Maeena has written on Saudi Arabia's legalization of *misyar* ("temporary marriage with no strings attached"). The passage of this decree in 1996 made Arab women feel vindicated. As primary beneficiaries of *misyar*, they could flee spinsterhood, engage in "halal courting," have "matrimonial sex," and divorcees and widows could start over with a man of their choosing.

Misyar marriages proliferated not because women flocked to them, but because men reticent to assume the full responsibilities of polygamy opted in. The women realized that despite their legal status as wives, they were regarded no differently than mistresses or companions. In this arrangement, the woman granted her temporary spouse sexual access in exchange for gifts, legalized sexual intimacy, vacations, and limited companionship.

The purpose of marriage in Islam, however, is to promote "mutual love, protection, tranquility, and contentment." These women were not forming a family, establishing kinship ties, or bearing children. Many were burdened with remorse and humiliation; they concealed their marriages from their family; some endured more negative consequences than polygamous women who were legally protected. Some women who gave birth under *misyar* were compelled to pursue legal action against men who refused to recognize their offspring. According to official Saudi Arabian sources, many of these unions terminate in divorce within fourteen to sixty days.[171]

MALE SCHOLARS CALL FOR MARRIAGE REFORM

Some scholars believe polygamy is here to stay and that the reason it is not outright forbidden is because some people and communities experience unique challenges that make its restricted use acceptable. Yet, the reality is that societal conditions have changed significantly since 625 CE, when the safety net for orphans and widowed women rested on the shoulders of men. There are now institutions for orphans, and widows can establish their means of livelihoods, consider remarriage, and live independently. By bringing this to the attention of scholars and men, we can raise the bar to uphold polygamy as it was originally intended—to address the well-being of *yateema* (orphans), their mothers, widows, and other women whose lives are profoundly compromised. Depending on the individuals involved and their motivations, this practice must have familial and social benefits, involve consent and mutual agreement, in order to retain its original intent.

Muhammad Abdu, an Egyptian scholar, describes that polygamy was sanctioned in order to strengthen and consolidate the nascent Muslim community; this objective was attained. When this practice ceases to serve its intended purpose due to Muslim abuse, it becomes more harmful than beneficial. According to Abdu, today it is in the best interest of Muslim communities to restrict or prohibit the practice.

In some countries polygamy is unconstitutional. Turkey has abolished the practice. Tunisia has outlawed it and emphasized that its actions conform with the Quranic injunctions on the subject. Egypt, Iraq, Syria, and Pakistan have all restricted the practice. In Egypt, for instance, a man cannot contract a second marriage without the consent of his first wife; Syria and Iraq require permission from a judge, and Pakistan requires written permission from an arbitration council. In Morocco and Malaysia, polygamy is subject to a judge's authorization under strict legal conditions, whereas Singapore requires three conditions: the husband's "financial means," "fair treatment between wives," and "lawful benefit involved in the second marriage." But suppose the result of the practice is the breakup of first family units, with financial and parental burdens being distributed unfairly. In such cases, it can greatly damage the emotional wellbeing of mothers and their children, undermining the very protections that marriage was intended for.

#14 | TO DIVORCE

I received an email from the concerned sibling of an Indian woman whose husband was refusing to divorce his sister. He stated, "My sister got married last year, and for some reason she requested a *khula* from her spouse. However, he divorced her over the phone, telling her, 'Go, I've divorced you.' Then he changed his mind, stating that 'Islam grants the husband the right to divorce, and I will not divorce you, or release you, nor will I return your belongings.' The sister is in limbo and devastated because he will not set her free, nor will he return the furniture and jewelry she received as wedding gifts. She is despondent, and so is her entire family."

Although marriage in Islam is strengthened by love and affection, yet numerous factors can cause marital strife, including adultery, financial instability, and mental and physical abuse. The Quran allows a divorce if there is a "breach between the two" that prevents couples from fulfilling the purpose of their marriage. *"But if they choose to separate, God will enrich both of them from His bounties" (Q 4:130).*

Prophet Muhammad taught that God regards divorce to be "the most hated of permissible things,"[172] and that it should only be used as a last choice. When the Prophet was unable to give his wives the attention they desired, he did not stop them from leaving him. When Laila bint El-Khatim offered marriage to the Prophet, he accepted, but she had difficulties getting along with the others: "I am a woman with a sharp tongue, and I cannot bear your other wives," she said to the Prophet. "So please let me be free." He divorced her immediately, saying, "I've set you free."[173]

When Caliph Umar bin Khattab was contacted by a woman seeking a divorce, he advised her to stay with her husband. When she disobeyed his advice, Umar imprisoned her in a filthy room for three days. He questioned her about her health on the fourth day. "I had genuine peace of mind," she said, "but only for those three days." Umar responded by dissolving her marriage.

Marriage must remain a revered institution for the sake of the community, as evidenced by the Prophet's and his companion's actions. The Quran prohibits men from unfairly divorcing their wives and advises couples not to make hasty decisions. They must engage an arbiter to help them reach a mutually beneficial arrangement to resolve their issues. *"If you anticipate a split between the two, appoint a mediator from his family and another from hers. If they desire reconciliation, God will restore harmony between them" (Q 4:35).* During the reconciliation period men are commanded not to take advantage, prolong, escalate, or resort to violence: *"But do not retain them only to harm them or to take advantage of them" (Q 2:231).* To deter the husband from abruptly divorcing and reclaiming the wife at his whim, the husband may remarry his ex-wife after she has married and obtained a divorce from her new husband: *"[U]ntil after she has married another man and then is divorced" (Q 2:230).*

TYPES OF DIVORCE

The Arabic word for divorce is *talaq*, which means "untying" or "untying a knot." Either spouse may file for divorce on the grounds of maltreatment due to poor temperament, abuse, cruelty, denial of paternity, severe illness, or impotence. If the couple chooses to initiate divorce proceedings, the first pronouncement of divorce or repudiation must be followed by two waiting periods of three months each, *iddah*, to enable the couple to reconcile and to ensure that the wife is not pregnant. As God says, *"Divorced women must wait for three monthly cycles before they can remarry" (Q 2:228).*

A husband-initiated divorce is determined by an arbitrator. *"Divorce may be retracted twice, then the husband must retain [his wife] with honor or separate [from her] with grace" (Q 2:229).* The wife's indisputable right "to get out of a marriage" for any reason is known as *khul* (taking off or shedding). *"So, if you fear they will not be able to keep within the limits of God, there is no blame if the wife compensates the husband to obtain divorce" (Q 2:229).* The *khul* must be initiated via arbitration and while women can obtain a divorce easily, they must return the dower, forfeit the deferred dower, marital assets, or future support. Therefore, this divorce is typically limited to women with sufficient financial resources or those who urgently want their marriage ended. In *khul*, most jurists consider a husband's consent essential, although it is not mentioned in the Quran or the Prophet's traditions. Numerous jurists concur that the wife may be exempt from repayment of the dower if the couple separates due to the husband's ill-treatment, and such charges are proved during the legal inquiry.

Mubarat, which means "to be released from one's obligations," is an egalitarian form of divorce based on mutual consent that is favored among independent and working women. *"If a woman fears indifference or neglect from her husband, there is no blame on either of them if they seek 'fair' settlement, which is best. Humans are ever inclined to selfishness"* (Q 4:128). Either spouse can initiate divorce, but before the divorce is finalized, the *iddat* period must be observed. This divorce also does not require court intervention as it typically involves a settlement regarding finances, child custody, and other issues.

A couple may also seek to annul their marriage by initiating *faskh*, which is not mentioned in the Quran but derived from the People of the Book. This is illustrated by how the Prophet annulled the marriage of a woman who was married against her will. *Faskh* may be pursued on the grounds of cruelty, disease, life-threatening illness, desertion, irregular marriage, *fasid* (prohibited marriage), *batil* (the spouse becomes an apostate after marriage), or inability to consummate. A *faskh* calls for impartial witnesses who can attest to the evidence in front of a judge.

AN ANCIENT-PROGRESSIVE APPROACH

In early Islam, some men who wanted to bypass the staged approach of three pronouncements ignored the waiting period and pronounced *talaq, talaq,* and *talaq* in one sitting. This morally reprehensible act of disobeying the Quran was deemed sinful by Caliph Umar, who punished them.

I remember when a distraught Florida woman called me. She said her older sister was verbally divorced by her husband, who yelled, "I divorce thee" three times. Some Muslims believe that saying *talaq*, "I divorce thee," three times finalizes a divorce. The woman from Florida wanted to know if her sister was really divorced after her husband said "I divorce thee" three times. I explained to her that according to US law she was not divorced. She sounded relieved. The next day, she called again to tell me that her brother-in-law had called his imam in Gujarat; the imam told the brother-in-law that his divorce was final, and she was no longer his wife. When the brother-in-law said he'd made a mistake, the imam told him that if he wanted to remarry his wife, then she had to marry another man first, and only after she divorced her new spouse, could he remarry her.

I asked if the brother-in-law had pronounced the divorce in a fit of anger. "Oh yes," the woman said, "he went mad!" I reminded her that if a divorce is pronounced in a state of temporary insanity, it is invalid. The woman was relieved and said she accepted all I stated—and did I know a male who could communicate this information to her brother-in-law? "Because they will only believe a man," she said, embarrassingly.

Asma Barlas says there is no Quranic verse that gives this sort of easy divorce presently awarded to men in most Muslim societies. In fact, in response to Khawlah's plea to God in verse 58:1, the Quran discouraged divorce. Barlas observes that if men were to take the Quranic verses seriously, a divorce would be among the hardest situations to discern. A husband planning on divorcing his wife must maintain her the same way as himself. Both spouses must settle issues between them in a mutually agreeable manner. (230-231)

The Prophet divorced several wives. One divorce that elicited a divine response was when he divorced his wife Hafsa after she disclosed a secret to another wife which the Prophet had asked her not to share. The actual content of the secret is unknown. His intention was not to take her back until Angel Gabriel ordered him to for these reasons "she fasts, prays and is your wife in paradise." The Prophet remarried Hafsa, and shortly after God revealed this verse: *"Remember when the Prophet has once confided something to one of his wives, then when she disclosed it to another wife and God made it known to him, he presented to her part of what was disclosed and overlooked a part. When he informed her of it, she exclaimed, 'who told you this?' he replied, "I was informed by the all-knowing. It will be better if you wives turn to repentance for your hearts have certainly faltered"* (Q 66:3).

Hafsa lived with the Prophet until his death and is honored with the title, "Mother of the Believers," and she was entrusted with the folios of the Quran by the Prophet.

THE PRICE OF PARTING WAYS

Despite the Quran's insistence on maintaining justice, Azizah Al Hibri states that the way in which Islamic jurisprudence and court practices regarding *khul* became skewed in favor of men deserves close scrutiny and urgent reform (71). Hadia Mubarak demonstrates that, despite the explicit warnings in the Quran, premodern exegesis disproportionately placed the burden on the wife. Exegetes assumed that a woman's willingness to give up certain rights in exchange for marital stability signaled that she wanted to stay married and considered marriage a superior alternative to divorce.[174] This often remains true in many Muslim societies today.

For example, in Egypt, women face a series of obstacles when attempting to obtain a *khul*. The misuse of legalities is aimed at discouraging, delaying, preventing, or negotiating terms. Though the Quran gives a woman the right to free herself from her marriage, Egyptian courts define *khul* as either fault-based or no-fault-based. In divorces based on fault, courts have broad authority to grant divorces. A woman must persuade the court that she is unable to cohabitate with her spouse and must establish evidence of harm, typically through first-person testimony and mediation. When a woman discovers her husband has married a second wife, she has one year to file on the grounds of polygamy.

Also in modern Egypt, before granting divorces to women, courts frequently wait a year to determine if impotence has improved. And after a woman sues for financial neglect-related injury, a man may terminate the lawsuit by investing in the property. A woman seeking a divorce on the grounds of physical abuse must provide the court with a medical certificate from a government hospital and two witnesses (preferably unrelated to her) who witnessed the assault.

It is in the "no-fault" *khul* where she can initiate divorce for reasons that negatively impact the family, such as if he deserts the family, is imprisoned, does not provide for his children, or is addicted to substances, or is suffering illness (including impotence). Also, if he becomes a burden on the family, behaves immorally (lying, thieving), or is unable to fulfill his marital and parental responsibilities. Here, the wife is not required to find witnesses to establish she was injured. Once she files for divorce, the husband has no legal standing to appeal.

ALIMONY AND CHILD SUPPORT

After a maximum of four months of non-sexual separation, an irrevocable divorce is finalized. The husband is forbidden to lay a claim on his wife's property, including the marital gift she received at the marriage ceremony: *"It is not lawful for husbands to take back anything of the dowry given to their wives" (Q 2:229)*. In this type of divorce, the husband must continue financially supporting his wife for three months. If the wife is pregnant during this time, then divorce must be delayed until after the delivery of the child. The divorced woman and her children may not be left without legal and financial support: *"Divorced mothers will breastfeed their offspring for two whole years, [T]he child's father will provide reasonable maintenance and clothing for the mother during that period" (Q 2:233)*.

Asli Sancar shows how, during the Ottoman Empire, men were legally required to fully support their wives and children, including: food, clothing, shelter, household help, and medical expenses. This maintenance (*nafaka*) continued if the couple was married and for three months after the divorce. The husband was responsible even if he was absent or disappeared. If the husband refused to pay for her support, the wife could alert the court, and the judge would enforce payment by ordering a loan on behalf of the husband. The wife was granted a daily allowance and the husband was responsible for the loan payment. (146)

Wael B. Hallaq asserts, based on evidence from legal practice, that divorce was a costly venture for the husband, and ruinous in many cases. Upon divorce, the ex-wife was entitled to at least three months' maintenance, deferred dower, children's maintenance, any debts the husband incurred to her during the marriage (which was relatively common), and if the children were young, a nursing fee. If the husband had not consistently paid for marital obligations (also a common occurrence), he would owe the full sum due upon filing for divorce.[175]

This three-month maintenance assumes that a divorced woman would return to her family and be sustained by them. The amount of support varied between the schools. The Shafi says it is determined by the husband's lifestyle and ability to pay. Maliki and Hanafi determination is based on the wife's own status and wealth, or her previous lifestyle. But the traditional rulings have no bearing on the twenty-first century divorced women who rarely return to their parents' homes. Some scholars are attempting to establish a basis for alimony payment after divorce, citing *Quran 2:241: "Reasonable provisions must be made for divorced women- a duty on those mindful of God."* The implied benefit to women in this verse has not been thoroughly examined and codified.

Based on the work of the minority of medieval scholars who determined that the "fair provision" for divorced women was obligatory, modernists proposed that it should consist of sufficient support during a woman's lifetime, or until she remarries, and not simply during the waiting period and nothing afterwards.[176]

CHILD CUSTODY

According to Muslim custom and law, child custody is based on four principles: descent through the male bloodline, male responsibility and authority, maternal care, and the child's best interests and wishes. Children, especially female children, are believed to need maternal care in the earliest period of their life. As worldly matters such as education become more essential following the period of maternal care, the father's supervision is considered more appropriate. The best interests of the child must also be considered when determining the suitability of a guardian, visitation rights, and the decision to relinquish custody.

The Shafi, Hanbali, and Shia schools consider the child's wishes regarding which parent they want to live with. For Shafi and Hanbali, the decision of whether to reside with a mother or father is made at the age of discernment, which occurs around age seven.

When the period of maternal custody (*hadanah*) expires, the father assumes physical custody of the child as well as his legal custody, *wilaya*. The child moves in with the father or his family, unless the parents consent to extend maternal custody or the child elects to stay with the mother. A woman who remarries might not retain custody of her child due to concerns about the potential influence of an unrelated man, particularly in the case of a girl. Despite legal emphasis on the issues related to an unrelated husband lacking natural affinity for the child and monopolizing the mother's attention, Hasan Al Basri contends that remarriage, in itself, does not result in loss of custody for the women. He suggests that a remarried mother could regain custody if she later divorces her second husband. Furthermore, bargaining child custody as part of a *khul* agreement is not allowed. This is related to the child's rights, since it is in the child's best interest (*anfa*) to remain with the mother.

Unfavorable child custody laws, which are unfair to the mother, including the ban on remarriage and the automatic award of legal custody to a father, were codified into law and have spread to modern

Muslim cultures. But at least a few changes are being made, including raising the age at which custody of the children is transferred from mother to father, or considering the child's best interests—a law already present in the traditional rulings. Some judges are also inspired by the best interests of the child and have awarded custody to the more suitable parent.

BENEFITS OF AN ISLAMIC MARRIAGE CONTRACT

Some women can opt for conditional or delegated divorce, in which they write in their marriage contract that if specific criteria are met, she will be immediately divorced. When I officiate marriages in the United States, some brides, especially those who are financially secure, are less concerned with their dower and more focused on the type of relationship they want with their spouse. Legal contracts containing provisions are attached to the Islamic Nikah certificate, whose requirements are as diverse as the cultures of the couple. Some wish to maintain separate bank accounts and a joint account for the household—in other words, the right to invest and advance their careers.

Some Muslim women stipulate wanting to learn from one another, advance their spiritual pursuits, and ensure freedom from verbal or physical abuse. Some will desire consensual sexual relations, and also to agree that any decision to relocate will be mutual. A minority of women will include a form of a prenuptial agreement in a marriage contract, stipulating that the parties' individual wealth will not be subject to state laws in the event of a divorce. A small minority will include specific grounds for divorce, such as infidelity or polygamy.

MOTIVATION NOT TO DIVORCE

Divorce has—and should have—financial implications. A wife who receives a divorce retains the dower she received, or if it was divided into advanced (*muqaddam*) and deferred (*muakhar*) portions, the deferred amount is due upon divorce. For husbands as well as wives, the prospect of receiving or having to pay a large, deferred sum can serve as an incentive or deterrent for divorce.

I witnessed this at a wedding I officiated. The groom was so smitten with the bride that he listed $1 million under the deferred dower (*mahr*). I inquired as to why he included such a significant amount. "So that I will never consider divorcing her," he explained.

Some women use a substantial, deferred dower to discourage their husbands from divorcing them hastily. Nonetheless, if the wife desires a *khul*, this strategy may backfire, as the wife must return her dower, waive her deferred portion, or pay the husband another sum to obtain a divorce. Kecia Ali explains that the dower is fundamental to the legal structure of marriage and the social structure of Muslim communities, and it frequently assumes a symbolic form among American Muslims. (22)

I concur with Ali, as my dower was also intended to be symbolic; however, due to my father's intervention, it served as crucial support during my own divorce. When I married, I was a confident professional with a good salary. I marked the diamond ring that I had gotten as my advanced dower and one dollar as my deferred dower (to convey that I did not require financial aid from my husband because I worked). When my father saw this, he scratched out the one dollar and replaced it with $50,000. He angered me by going against my decision. "I'm your father, and I know what's best for you!" he murmured, shrugging his shoulders.

When I divorced twenty-two years later, I was no longer employed by a Fortune 500 company, earning a big salary. Instead, I volunteered at my nonprofit organization. At that time, I came to appreciate my father's foresight and intervention in my affairs. This time-honored custom enabled me to end my marriage with grace. If my father had not replaced the one dollar in my deferred dower, my pride in independence would have left me destitute. The dower enabled me to retain legal representation and obtain my rightful share. In accordance with the Quran, I rejected my attorney's advice to engage in a protracted legal battle and opted for an amicable settlement.

Although the prospect of a divorce initially frightened me, it eventually turned out to be the best option for both of us. The Quranic verse, *"Perhaps you dislike something which is good for you and like something which is bad for you. God knows, and you do not know" (Q 2:216)*, comes to me when I think back on closing this chapter of my life.

I've learned that making the toughest choices can result in the greatest progress. I appreciate the courage the Quran has given me as well as the support of those who stood by my side. I walked into the next chapter of my life with hope and optimism, free from the weight of resentment, knowing that God's purpose for me was greater than I could fathom. I looked forward to a future full of possibilities, love, and spiritual growth as I gracefully and gratefully entered the next phase.

EXAMPLES OF REFRESHING REFORM

But in some countries, granting a divorce with dignity remains difficult and humiliating for women. Just recently, in India, when Muslim men used triple *talaq* to divorce their wives, Muslim women demanded the practice be outlawed.

Shayara Bano, a victim of triple *talaq*, was subjected to mental and physical violence at the hands of her spouse and his family because of dowry demands. Through a triple *talaq* letter, her husband ended their fourteen-year marriage and denied her custody of their two children. Bano argued before the Supreme Court that the practice was discriminatory and violated the dignity of women. The Supreme Court ruled in her favor, declaring triple *talaq* to be arbitrarily enforced. It highlighted how her spouse had capriciously and frivolously severed their marital ties without attempting to reconcile. Then, in August 2017 the Supreme Court of India ruled that the triple *talaq* violates article fourteen of the Indian Constitution. Within one year of the act's passage, cases decreased by 82 percent.

Here's another example of reform—on the West Bank, in Palestine, Reema Shamasneh grew up in a large family. As a child, she observed her older sister's troubled marriage, and as a sixteen-year-old, she witnessed her agonizing divorce. This experience motivated Shamasneh to pursue a law degree so she could advocate for other women. As an attorney at the Women's Centre for Legal Aid and Counseling in Ramallah, now she represents women pursuing divorces from abusive husbands. While some of her legal colleagues are hesitant to support equal divorce rights for men and women, Shamasneh says, "I dream of a society governed by law and equality, where women have their own place and are given the respect they deserve. A society that values their opinions and treats women with respect and equality."

#15 TO FAMILY PLANNING AND REPRODUCTIVE JUSTICE

The Quran depicts children as treasures and blessings of this world, underlining the pleasure they bring to their parents: *"Wealth and children are the adornments of this worldly life" (Q 18:46)*. Healthy reproductive rights comprise more than just the act of fertilization; they also include sexual activity for pleasure, procreation, and childrearing: *"God...has given you through your spouses of your own kind, children, and grandchildren. And he has granted you good, lawful provisions" (Q 16:72)*.

According to the Quran, the mother is exclusively responsible for the biological process of reproduction and has the unique honor of being divinely ordained to bring forth new life. *"[H]e creates you in the wombs of your mothers [in stages], one development after another, in three layers of darkness" (Q 39:6)*. Since "womb" and "mercy" are synonymous, this signifies the intimate relationship between God and the mother. After God implants the zygote in her womb, she is entrusted with the unborn fetus and is held accountable for it. If a woman dies during pregnancy or childbirth, she is regarded as a martyr for the sake of God.[177]

BREASTFEEDING: EMPOWERING LITTLE LIVES

Once a child is born, the mother plays a crucial part in nursing the infant. Breastfeeding deepens the bond between mother and child, passes the mother's immunity to the child, and provides the neonate with naturally sterilized, optimal-temperature milk.

If a mother is unable to breastfeed, it is permissible to use a wet nurse if she is compensated fairly.[178] *"[I]f both sides decide—after mutual consultation and consent—to wean a child, then there is no blame on them" (Q 2:233)*.

As an infant, the Prophet struggled. Amina, his mother, entrusted him to Halimah, a strong Bedouin woman. This wet nurse nursed him in the desert dry air, where he spent days sitting on her knee and learning to speak. She cared for him until he was two-and-a-half years old. As he grew, he was entrusted with shepherding their vast herd of goats. The skills he gained as a child herding sheep taught him patience and responsibility, allowing him to shepherd a vast community of believers as an adult. (30)

SEXUAL RIGHTS: ISLAMIC PERSPECTIVES

Sexual relations—are viewed as a divine blessing with three functions: reproduction, health, and recreation. Put another way, sexual relations promote pleasure, gratification, and produce offspring. Kecia Ali mentions Sa'diyyah Shaikh who points out that a wife is "entitled to a full sexual pleasure" right independent of a decision to have children. She views this doctrine as evidence of priority given in Islam to mutual sexual fulfillment. (8) This freedom of sexual relations is accompanied by few conditions and prohibitions. For example, sexual activity is forbidden during the fasting period *(Q 2:187)*, the menstrual cycle *(Q 2:222)*, and the postnatal period. And incest and anal intercourse are always prohibited.[179]

Since the husband and wife are responsible for having satisfactory sexual relations, the Prophet said, "In the sexual act of each of you, there is charity (*sadaqa*) which comes with a reward."[180] According to Kecia Ali, Al-Ghazali says that it is the husband's duty to satisfy his wife, as her dissatisfaction can harm the relationship. Because women are more typically shy, a male spouse should not be preoccupied with his own pleasure. Al-Ghazali recalls that the Prophet counseled men, "not to fall upon their wives like beasts, rather to start it with stimuli for both, such as caresses and gentle sayings." (7)

The husband has the right to sexual satisfaction, which the wife should indulge in so long as she is not fatigued, sick, or menstruating. The wife has the right to get stimuli (foreplay, etc.) before sexual intercourse takes place. Kecia Ali cites the hadith in which the Prophet instructs his followers to partake in normal human activities—food, sleep, and sex: "Truly, your body has rights over you, your eyes have rights over you, and your wife has the right to you."[181] This hadith is significant because it advances beyond the issue of women's satisfaction in a particular act, which Al-Ghazali and others have addressed, to the larger question of the wife's right to sex. (12)

FAMILY PLANNING AND SPACING

Farzaneh Roudi-Fahimi, in her paper "Islam and Family Planning," explains that family planning is permissible in Islam because the Quran makes no mention of contraception. Therefore, neither birth control nor spacing pregnancies is prohibited. Legal scholars who have permitted contraception assume that the practice is only for good uses. For instance, Islam prohibits contraception to avoid female offspring.

Roudi-Fahimi explains that coitus interruptus (*Al-azl*), a method of contraception that inhibits sperm and ovum from fusing, is permitted to prevent conception. As a wife has the right to sexual enjoyment, some jurists argued that ejaculation is necessary for a woman to achieve climax; therefore, prior consent is required before withdrawing. Most theologians from the three major schools (Hanbali, Hanafi, and Maliki) agreed, whereas the Shafi School disagreed.

Those who view childbearing as a preferable outcome of sex, say that it is the best way to build a family and expand the *ummah*. They consider contraception undesirable (*makruh*), even though the Prophet allowed it as follows: "During the Prophet's lifetime, we practiced '*azl*. This information was communicated to the Prophet, but he did not prohibit us."[182] The Prophet also told couples to avoid pregnancy during the two-year period of breastfeeding. Using contraception instead of abstaining from sex for two years, to avoid pregnancy, can ease this difficulty. "[G]od intends ease for you, not hardship" (Q 2:185).[183]

Kecia Ali quotes Sa'diyya Sheikh who states that Muslim authorities accepted contraceptive measures and approved of sex with pregnant women and nursing mothers, making clear that sexual pleasure was a worthwhile aim even where pregnancy was an impossible, unlikely outcome of sex. (8)

Above all, family planning reduces hardships and regulates fertility. In certain instances, excessive fertility can result in proven health risks for mothers and children, economic hardship, and shame for the father due to his inability to provide for a family. However, some Muslims believe that this contradicts the reliance (*tawakkul*) they have on God's ability to provide (*rizq*) for them *(Q 6:151)*. According to Roudi-Fahimi,

Al-Ghazzali accepted contraceptives to alleviate the financial and psychological burdens imposed by numerous dependents. He reasoned that "a large family might compel a person to resort to illicit means to support these excessive responsibilities, and that fewer material burdens are beneficial to religion."

Roudi-Fahimi highlights the opinion of Dr. Abdel Rahim Omran, who said that spacing pregnancies and limiting the number of children does not violate the Quran or the Prophet. He explains the most common reason for adopting contraception in Islamic jurisprudence is to safeguard the health of mothers and children from risks posed by additional pregnancies. He compiled a list of justifications for the use of contraception: avoid health risks to the mother resulting from repeated pregnancies; avoid pregnancy in an already ill wife; avoid transmission of disease from parents to children; allow for the education, proper rearing, and religious training of children, which is more feasible with fewer children; avoid the risk of children being converted from Islam in enemy territory; avoid having children during periods of religious decline; allow for separate sleeping arrangements for boys and girls during adolescence, which is more practical with fewer children; and retain a wife's beauty and physical health in order to ensure a happy married life by keeping the husband faithful.

While most Muslim theologians believe that contraception is permissible, Roudi-Fahimi says they restrict the practice to temporary methods such as condoms and intrauterine devices (IUDs) as opposed to oral contraceptives, which may have more adverse effects on a woman's health, or those that intervene after fertilization. Permanent methods such as sterilization are permitted only as emergencies. For instance, if a woman delivers three babies via cesarean section, she may not survive a fourth pregnancy. To prevent pregnancy, she can undergo a procedure such as a tubectomy, and the husband can have a vasectomy to prevent further pregnancies.[184]

THE JOURNEY OF PREGNANCY

In *Abortion, Stages of the Embryo, and the Beginning of Life,* Usama Hasan describes the seven phases in the Quran which depicts the formation and development of the embryo.

"[W]e alone created humans from a drop of mixed fluids" (Q 76:2) refers to the mixing of sperm and ovum in the process of human reproduction. The mixed-fluid stage is from one to eight days, where the fertilized cell becomes sixteen cells after around four days, which settle *"in a secure place"* e.g., in the womb *(Q 23:13)*. Then, *"We developed the drop into clinging clot of blood" (Q 23:14)* is the alaqah stage, which lasts two weeks, (nine to twenty-three days), composed of a nucleus and cytoplasm sucking sustenance and oxygen inside the womb. This is followed by *"then developed the clot into a lump of flesh" (Q 23:14)*, called the "chewed up" al-mudghah stage, where the heart cavity and reproductive organs are formed ending at six weeks (forty to forty-two days), and the embryo manifests physical human features and form. After forty-two days, *"then developed the lumps into bones, then clothed the bones with flesh, then We brought into being as a new creation" (Q 23:14)*—here the embryo enters a new stage in which it is transformed into a being.[185]

The second embryonic stage, after forty days, is the beginning of *taṣwīr khafī*: even though the fetus may have subtle human features, and may show movement before forty days, most scholars consider these movements as involuntary (*harakatanzātiyatan ikhtiyāriyatan*). Rather, they are involuntary reflexes, or *harakatan 'āriḍatan*.[186] The third stage occurs around eighty days when the unaided eye can perceive the fashioning, but the development process is still incomplete. A fourth and final stage occurs at 120 days, *"then We brought it into being as a new creation* [by breathing life into it]." And then, as the Quran explains, *"when there is complete fashioning,* tamām al-taṣwīr, *the fetus is ready for ensoulment" (Q 23:14)*.

Rashid Ali states that for most Sunni scholars, life begins neither at the moment of conception nor in the first stage of development (known as the *"nutfa,"* or drop), nor with the presence of the *"alaqah"* (that which hangs), or the *"mudgha,"* which literally translates as a mass of flesh that resembles chewed skin. Rather, *"khalqan"* defines the point at which it becomes a distinct creation. This is when the Archangel Gabriel breathes a soul into the embryo by creating a connection with God and the universe that gives it life. According to the Prophet, this moment occurs 120 days into the pregnancy, or roughly four months.

Rashad Ali in "How Islam Settled Roe v. Wade" states that while Islamic scholars are known for debating scripture at length, it is widely accepted—a rare instance of near unanimity—that a cluster of cells does not become a person until the soul enters the body.[187]

A LEGAL ISSUE, NOT A MORAL ONE

Those who oppose abortion compare it to infanticide, when pre-Islamic infant girls were killed in favor of male offspring *(Q 16:58-59)*. In another verse it says, *"Do not kill your children for fear of poverty. We provide for you and for them" (Q 6:151)*. Both verses refer to the killing of children already born and not the unborn fetus, as in the case of infanticide, nor do they address ending a pregnancy.

Rashad Ali states that a terminated pregnancy, whether abortion or miscarriage, was never considered absolute religious evil (*munkar*), and those who sought it were never considered morally repugnant. As a result, discussions about abortion or miscarriage have traditionally been legal, not moral, debates. Opinions regarding whether the fetus is ensouled at forty days or at some point within the first 120 days of human development, are what determines the legality of abortion.

In addition to the Quran and Hadith, jurists' opinions center on the practicalities of pregnancy. In general, safeguarding a mother's life and mental health takes precedence over that of an unborn fetus. Others agree that abortion is allowed to protect a woman's health, yet the permissibility of abortion varies. Sa'diyya Shaikh quotes Shaykah Jad al-Haq's four distinct viewpoints on abortion before 120 days. He states that some Muslims consider abortion to be *makruh* (highly opposed) or *haram* (prohibited). Some Zaydi and Shafi schools concur with the Hanafi school that it is permissible to terminate a pregnancy without justification or fetal defect. The Hanbalis allow it through use of oral abortifacients within forty days. Most Hanafis and Hanbalis state that if there is no valid reason during this period it is disapproved but not forbidden. Some Malikis strongly disapprove of abortion, whereas other Maliki, Zahiri, Ibadiyya, and Imamiyya schools consider abortion absolutely forbidden, *haram*.[188] The Shafi, Hanbali, and prominent Shia schools restrict abortions to the first forty days after conception.

According to Rashad Ali, the reason why Hanafi scholars permitted unrestricted abortion was an inability to provide for the infant, especially when wet nurses were scared or when there were other children who relied on the mother's milk. One prominent scholar, Ahmad Raza Khan, issued a *fatwa* stating that abortion is permissible for a single mother. He suggested it might be a preferable option for her, given the social stigma of carrying a child out of wedlock. Additionally, he stated that abortion is permissible in instances of rape.

Even though Maliki prohibit abortion, it has never been compared to murder; even in the most conservative viewpoints, it is permitted to save a woman's life. Scholars such as the late Chief Cleric of Egypt at Al Azhar University, Mahmud Shaultut, and the Syrian cleric Mustafa al-Zarqa, as well as the Egyptian cleric Yusuf al-Qaradawi, justify this as the "lesser of two evils" from a theological standpoint.[189]

It is illegal to abort at the fourth trimester "unless physicians determine that continuing the pregnancy would endanger the mother's life," whose survival takes precedence because her life is established, and she is the giver of life.[190] In cases of rape or incest, the decision to terminate a pregnancy is crucial for providing justice and compassion to the victim. Compelling a woman to bear a child conceived by coercion or rape, outside the institution of marriage, is *haram*, prohibited, and it is a type of revictimization since it violates the sanctity of marriage and her physical autonomy. It is also a constant reminder of the trauma she has endured, and by unjustly imposing everlasting responsibilities on her, the well-being of both she and her child are at stake.

According to Usama Hassan, the 120-day ensoulment is corroborated by the Prophet's description of how the fetus develops into a human being as follows: "The creation of every one of you starts with collecting the material for his body within forty days and forty nights in his mother's womb. Then he becomes a clot of thick blood for a similar period (forty days), and then he becomes like a piece of flesh for a similar period. Then an angel is sent to him (by God), who breathes the soul into him."

BRIDGING PRO-LIFE AND PRO-CHOICE

Reproductive choice from the Quranic perspective prohibits aborting at whim. As the descendants of Adam and Eve, and as stewards of God, we are obligated to ensure that life is not only sacred but respected, and every birth should bring genuine joy and fulfillment. Yet, God mentions a mother's sacrifice and why she must not be considered merely an incubator; her desires and concerns must take precedence as she deliberates bringing life into the world, *"[T]heir mothers bore them in hardship and delivered them in hardship"* (Q 46:15).

Sa'diyyah Shaikh states that as we address terminating a pregnancy and the concern for the fetus, it is important to situate the issues in a broader context by considering matters related to the well-being of the mother, family, and society. While science can contribute to the description of fetal development, it is outside of the scientific method to determine the point of spiritual transition into a full human being. The ensouled fetus is referred to as "formed" and has a legal personality. Aborting a formed fetus then becomes both a criminal and religious offense, and if a formed fetus is caused to miscarry, the mother is entitled to full compensation as if the child had been born.

According to Shaikh, a *fatwa* permitting abortion in cases of rape or a defective fetus, issued by Sheikh Tantawi of Egypt, has been accepted in many Muslim majority countries. In Iran, Ayatollah Ali Khameni allowed abortion of fetuses under ten weeks that were tested with genetic disorder of thalassemia. In South Africa, abortion is permitted within the first 120 days when justified by a reasonable cause, such as the impairment of the mental capacity to shoulder the responsibility of parenthood, among others. (122)

Accordingly, Rashad Ali says it is useful to consider how this holistic approach to the intersections of faith and an unwanted—or unsafe—pregnancy could be applied to abortion everywhere, including in the US, the epicenter of this debate. There is much to learn about being both "pro-choice" and "pro-life" from Islam's discourse.

SANCTIONING WORST-CASE SCENARIOS

In Islamic law, birth control and abortion are regarded differently, according to Rashad Ali. He cites the story of Caliph Umar ibn al-Khattab, summoning a woman to his court as one of the most well-known examples. She miscarried after receiving the summons, so he was informed. Umar, overcome with remorse, consulted Ali Abu Talib, the future fourth Caliph, a man of great status and esteem in the court, whose opinion Umar valued. Ali suggested Umar pay the woman an indemnity to compensate for her miscarriage. This legal decision formed the basis for determining that, should a woman miscarry due to circumstances out of her control, it is her right as well as her husband's to be compensated for the loss of their child.

God acknowledges the desire for progeny and mentions those from whom He withheld children and their fervent supplications for righteous offspring: *"[O]ur Lord! Bless us with pious spouses, and offspring who will be the joy of our hearts and make us models for the righteous"* (Q 25:74). In her paper on reproductive issues, Fatima A. Husain argues that there are no religious objections to an infertile married couple pursuing infertility treatments including in vitro fertilization, surgical sperm retrieval, and micro-assisted conception. However, there must be strict control to ensure that the gametes belong to the husband and wife. This relationship is referred to as *halal* (permitted), whereas any union of gametes outside of a marital bond, whether by adultery or in the laboratory, is prohibited, as are pregnancies from donor sperm. Due to the advent of ovum donation and surrogacy, some Islamic scholars now allow this procedure between co-wives, thereby avoiding the forbidden relationship between sperm and egg. However, there is still debate on the definition of the mother.[191]

Many successful single women I know have frozen their eggs in anticipation of marriage and a future family. This communication was sent to me from a married woman who is eager to start a family. Because of preexisting medical condition (uterine fibroids) and her advanced age, her doctor advised that she utilize a gestational carrier. "My husband has researched and spoken to imams who all say surrogate carriers are not *halal*, primarily because it would be introducing his sperm into a third party. I don't feel that a fertilized embryo equates sperm nor are any of the reason given by imams accurate for how we contractually and legally do gestational surrogacy in this country. My husband does not feel comfortable in his heart as the Islamic jurisprudence on this is so unequivocal and adamant. I am struggling to find an Islamic argument for the acceptance of gestational carriers. None of the arguments against it (confusion on lineage, considered adultery, etc.) seem valid. I want to have a child!"

PERSONAL EXPERIENCES AND DECISIONS

I know what she is going through, I have experienced the agony of losing a child and the subsequent desolation that followed. After my second and third miscarriages, I promptly began the fertility gauntlet, a voyage familiar to women who struggle to conceive. A female physician proposed an alternative: donor egg. But the Quran mentions procreation solely within the sanctity of marriage. A donor would have to marry my husband. The realization that I could not conceive and give birth to a child, nurture and shape it into a remarkable human, became an unyielding challenge. The hadith, "Paradise lies at the feet of the mother," continued to plague me: Who would pray for me? Was I responsible for this tragedy? Was I paying for unknown transgression? I knew in my heart that I was not at fault.

As I grappled with the spiritual significance of God's plan, I came across this verse, *"[H]e leaves whoever He wills infertile" (Q 42:50)*, implying that in this divine plan, God was sparing me from the responsibilities of motherhood so that I could focus on a higher calling. I accepted that I would not be a birth mother, difficult as that might be. Instead of focusing on my narrow world, work, and personal life, I turned outward toward an entire community of young people. I would nurture them and help them grow.

#16 | TO CARE FOR ORPHANS THROUGH ADOPTION

When a tsunami struck Aceh, Indonesia on December 26, 2004, it was the most terrifying moment of Dian Alyan's life. She lost family members and friends and witnessed the destruction of her homeland. The waves and flooding claimed the lives of over 166,000 people and left behind a large number of bereaved children. The severity of the anguish compelled Alyan to take action.

Within two weeks, she created Project Noordeen to give orphans in Aceh a brighter future. Alyan's family donated 3,000 square feet of land for the construction of a permanent home for fifty orphans, including a residence, library, computer lab, and multifunctional hall with a learning and activity center. This orphanage was just a beginning. Alyan's vision would go on to alter the future of destitute children in Indonesia, Pakistan, Sri Lanka, Cambodia, Bangladesh, and Morocco, as well.

Prior to the advent of Islam, adoption was undertaken with the intention of usurping an orphan's property. Adoption was closely linked to enslavement, as captors held the power to strip captives of their birth identities and adopt them into their families, leading to a total "erasure of natal identity."[192] The Quran condemned this discriminatory practice: *"[N]or cheat them by mixing their wealth with your own. For this indeed would be a great sin" (Q 4:2)*; likewise in another verse: *"Indeed, those who unjustly consume orphans' wealth, in fact, consume nothing but fire into their bellies" (Q 4:10)*.

In Islam, caring for an orphan is an act of piety, and providing a parentless child with a nurturing, compassionate environment in which their physiological, physical, and intellectual needs are met is highly regarded. Refusing to meet the requirements of an orphan violates Islamic ethics and morality. As it is written, *"Have you seen the one* who denies the 'final' Judgment? That is the one who repulses the orphan and does not encourage feeding the poor" (Q 107:1-3).

ISLAMIC HISTORY AND ORPHANS

Asiya, the wife of Pharaoh, despite being childless, adopted Moses and raised him as her own. This remains an extraordinary example of a "woman adopter" provided by the Quran. Moses was raised in a loving family where his every need was met, and his talents were nurtured and developed. God declared Moses as a prophet for the Israelites, entrusting him with the mission of rescuing his people from the tyranny of Pharaoh, his adoptive father.

At age six, the Prophet Muhammad became an orphan. As one who grew up without parents, the Prophet paid close attention to the needs of orphans. He was very critical of those who lacked compassion for vulnerable children. He urged Muslims to care for orphans regardless of their lineage, heritage, or circumstances. He stated that those who care for orphans will receive heavenly rewards: "[O]ne who cares for an orphan will be together with me in heaven like this."[193] And in accordance with his principles, he adopted Zayd ibn Haritha, a Bedouin slave only ten years his junior, who chose to stay in the Prophet's household instead of returning to his father, who had come to claim him. As Zayd was not a minor, their agreement regarding filial rights and responsibilities were voluntary. The Prophet treated him with love, respect, and compassion, even though his situation was not comparable to a conventional adoption involving a minor child.

Regarding orphan girls, Aisha feared that they might be denied the right to bridal gifts and inheritance, in response, God revealed a verse commanding their protection: *"And they ask you, O' Prophet regarding women. Say, 'It is God Who instructs you regarding them. Instruction has 'already' been revealed in the Book concerning the orphan women you deprive of their due rights but still wish to marry, also helpless children, as well as standing up for orphans' rights"* (Q 4:127).

THE ISLAMIC OBLIGATION TO GUARD INNOCENCE

An orphan is a child who lacks parental care owing to the death or desertion of their parents, or when the parent ends the parental relationship freely or involuntarily. According to the Quran, *"Improving their condition is best (islah)"* (Q 2:220). In this passage, the word *islah* is used to signify "mend, heal, and make good." While some scholars have interpreted this phrase in a financial context, it really refers to a child's overall well-being and may be translated as "the best interests of the child." The Quranic admonition to save a life was utilized by early jurists to care for abandoned children and orphans, and classical jurists equated taking in an orphan with saving a human life: *"[A]nd whoever saves a life, it will be as if they have saved all of humanity"* (Q 5:32).

In the chapter on orphans in the Shafi *fiqh* handbook, *Minhaj*, it is stated that taking care of orphans is a communal obligation: *"[A]nd be kind to parents, relatives, orphans, the poor, near and distant neighbors, close friends, 'needy' travelers, and that 'bondspeople' in your possession"* (Q 4:36). A person is required to remove a foundling from the street if there are credible concerns that the infant would perish. In the Hanafi *fiqh* manual, *al-Hidaya*, it is both improper and prohibited for a believer to find and take a foundling before putting it back where it belonged.

Scholars also believe that all Muslims have a communal obligation to ensure that homeless and parentless children have a guardian and family to care for them. That pre-Islamic adoption, in which the child's paternal identity is absorbed into the adoptive parents, has been universally rejected. Scholars base this rejection on Q 33:4, which references Zayd ibn Haritha: *"[N]or does He regard your adopted children as your real children. These are only your baseless assertions."*

ETHICAL GUIDELINES AND NURTURING OPEN ADOPTIONS

Despite the Quran's emphasis on orphan care, it is still a common misconception that Islamic law prohibits adoption, despite above *verse's* reference to "your adopted children." This has resulted in many orphans being raised in public institutions as opposed to nurturing families, as Asiya and the Prophet did with Moses and Zayd. This misnomer is not supported by the Quran or Hadith, as Islam permits open adoption whenever fundamental ethical principles are adhered to, allowing full disclosure of the child's and the parents' identities, and facilitating respect for the child's birth culture and identity.

Adoption is the legal formation of a parent-child relationship, including rights and responsibilities, between a child and adults who are not the child's biological parents. It allows a child to be integrated into a new family regardless of genetic ties, to be cared for by a mother, and to grow up in a secure family environment where their familial needs are met. This is mutually beneficial for both orphans and society as it protects abandoned children against abuse and exploitation.

Jurists devised alternative methods to circumvent the complexities of the permissibility of "full adoption" to encourage the care of orphans. They instituted a system of guardianship *kafala*, which is a commitment to voluntarily provide for the maintenance, education, and protection of a minor, as a parent would do for a child. *Kafala* is intended to be a permanent arrangement that can lead to adoption. This system of fostering a child does not in any way disrupt biological family ties, as children reared under the *kafala* system do not inevitably inherit from their guardians.

In 2009, my host Yasmine, who had established an orphanage in Africa, declared, "We must do something about adoption!" Even though the Quran instructs Muslims to take orphans into their households and raise them as if they were their own children, the permissibility of this practice was constantly contested. "Why do sheiks make blanket statements that adoption is prohibited, if caring for orphan children is a requirement in Islam? Why are individuals discouraged from adopting?" Yasmine was asking important questions.

Then I remembered what the Prophet said regarding orphan care: "No other action will bring you closer to me than caring for an orphan." So, in 2011, WISE's Global Muslim Women's Shura Council issued a position paper on "Adoption, Care of Children." The arguments used throughout this chapter had their first form in this position paper and have helped Muslim families and single women adopt children from Muslim majority nations.[194]

Many scholars argue that the law on adoption is indifferent (*mubah*) because the Quran does not prohibit it. As a result, to facilitate adoption in accordance with Quranic injunctions, Sunni and Shi'a scholars developed principles to protect the child's biological lineage. These include: naming practices—a child has the right to know their natal identity; inheritance—a child has the right not to be excluded from inheritance of their biological and adopted parents; also, the importance of not allowing marriage to a *mahram*; and paying close attention to nursing a child and fostering ties between families. Let's look at each of these principles, now, in detail.

The most frequently cited restriction relates to the issue of dissimulation through naming. The Quranic prohibition against lying to an adoptive child is consistent with contemporary psychiatric theory: *"Let your adopted children keep their family names. That is more just in the sight of God. But if you do not know their fathers, then they are [simply] your fellow believers and close associates. There is no blame on you for what you do by mistake, but [only] for what you do intentionally" (Q 33:5)*. Adoptive parents must ensure that the child retains their birth family name so that the child's identity is not absorbed by the adoptive family.

When the adoptee's lineage is uncertain, many countries permit the transfer of the guardian's surname to the child. In Egypt, for example, "an orphan or child of unknown parentage, male or female, carries the surname of the guardian family at the end of his or her first name."[195] The emphasis on calling adoptees by their biological fathers' names obscured the legal implications of adoption by women. In fact, according to some scholars, the patriarchal nature of pre-Islamic adoption created a loophole, allowing women to adopt and give their last names to their adopted offspring.

Regarding inheritance, the Quran states that the adopted child is not entitled to the full/equal inheritance share as is a biological child. Instead of preventing orphans from receiving a reasonable portion of their adoptive parents' inheritance, the purpose of these laws was to protect them. This is because, while blood relatives are prioritized, spending on other dependents, such as "parents, relatives, and orphans," is highly regarded in Islam *(Q 2:215)*. Sunni and Shi'a law, for example, permit parents to leave more than one-third of a child's inheritance to an adopted child, if the biological heir consents to the transfer. In the absence of the heir's consent, adoptive families may also use alms *(zakat)* and charity *(sadaqah)* to transfer wealth to an adopted child. This arrangement permits an adopted child to inherit a portion of their biological inheritance in addition to any wealth, alms, or donations left to them by their adoptive parents.

The reference to segregating at puberty to prevent marriage with a *mahram* (a close male relative who travels with a woman to ensure her safety) is because adopted children are not biologically related to their adoptive families, and they may develop sexual feelings for family members at puberty which could lead to marriages between siblings. The Quran recognizes that sharing a life and intermixing are important to the establishment of family ties: *"And they ask you 'O Prophet' concerning orphans. Say, 'Improving their condition is best. And if you partner with them, they are bonded with you in faith'" (Q 2:220)*, therefore, segregating an adopted child based on his or her gender upon puberty does not qualify as treating them as brothers and sisters.

Sexual intimacy is not related to blood connections but to social ties, and it is the experience of growing up in the same household that generates ties we then perceive as biological. Adoption results in the prohibition of marriage within the adoptive family. However, if the marriage occurs despite the prohibition, the government allows the adoption to be annulled and the marriage to continue. As an example, in Turkey, an adopted person who marries an adopted sibling must relinquish all adoption rights, including the right to inherit from adoptive parents.

The Quran specifies which relatives are forbidden to marry. This is a *mahram* relationship, which occurs through one of three means: kinship, marriage, or milk-foster (*rada*—the relationship created by breastfeeding): *"[F]orbidden to you for marriage are your mothers, your daughters, your sisters, your paternal and maternal aunts, your brother's daughters, your sister's daughters, your foster mothers, you foster-sisters, your mothers-in-law, your stepdaughters under your guardianship if you have consummated a marriage with their mothers" (Q 4:23)*.

If the adopted child was not breastfed by the adoptive mother, the child is eligible for marriage to adoptive family members. Wet nursing, which has historically been used to establish legal relations between non-blood-related families, is another method to form blood ties. Halima, the wet nurse of the Prophet Muhammad, was considered his blood relative. When an adopted mother nurses the child, he/she cannot marry any adoptive relative. And the mother does not have to be a nursing woman, as breast milk can now be induced medically and technologically.[196] According to Maulana Muhammad Ali, Imam Abu-Hanifa believes that one suckling is sufficient to create blood ties; Imam Shafi contends that the infant must be suckled four times; and Shia believe that the infant must be suckled for at least twenty-four hours. (454)

VALUES OF WELL-BEING, WHOLENESS, AND PEACE

In summary, transparency, justice, the child's dignity, and compassion must take precedence over the general tenets of one's faith tradition when adopting. Since the Quran's broad recommendation regarding orphans is to "make things right for them is better," open and legal adoptions are a means to improve the condition of orphans. "Islam" literally means "making whole, sound, safe, and peaceful." Therefore, making orphans well, safe, whole, and at peace is integral to the faith.

Adoption is prohibited in most Muslim countries, except for Indonesia, Malaysia, Somalia, Tunisia, and Turkey. *Kafala* is still permitted in countries where adoption is illegal. Infertility can put a strain on marriages, leading to unjust polygamous arrangements or divorce. Therefore, adoption can strengthen marriages and advance the public interest.

There is no greater act of altruism than adopting an orphan; it is the pinnacle of selflessness. An infertile couple can be blessed with a child and experience the joy of nurturing that child into adulthood, just like Asiya did when she adopted Moses as a newborn and saved him from Pharaoh's edict. Had she not intervened, would Prophet Moses have revolted against Pharaoh? Asiya is remembered in the Quran as a devout believer *(Q 66:11)* who adopted Moses even though his family did not share her faith. Asiya's heart was filled with Truth, and she recognized that his safety and well-being as a Jewish child were crucial. She knew that, in addition to bringing her joy, her son, the prince of Egypt, might also bring much-needed change to his people.

EXAMPLE OF AN EXTRAORDINARY PAKISTANI WOMAN

Bilquis Edhi was the cofounder of the Edhi Foundation, where she gives up children for adoption to childless couples or single women. She requires the couple to sign *a'shariat-nama'* expressly stating that in the event of a separation between the parents, the foundation will reclaim the child or allow the mother to keep the child.

When Bilquis Edhi passed away in April 2022, an adopted "Edhi baby" thanked Bilquis on Facebook for giving her a chance at life:

> Twenty-eight years ago, I was abandoned in a baby carriage at the Edhi Orphanage in Karachi, Pakistan. You found me, named me after your mother Rabia Bano, forged my identity, and gave me a home. Because of you, a little Pakistani girl orphaned at birth dared to dream. You taught me the power of women, to always have an unwavering sense of self, and to be unapologetically ambitious. Thanks to you, I have two loving parents who ensured I had everything a little girl could have ever asked for. I went to a great high school, got scholarships

throughout college, did an internship in NYS Assembly, Bronx District Attorney's Office, US Congress, and US Senate, and went to law school to pursue a master's in Cybersecurity and Data Privacy Law. All. Because. Of. You. Your loss has made me feel orphaned again today.... My name is Rabia Bibi Osman, and I will forever be a proud Edhi baby.

#17 | TO MOTHERHOOD AND WOMANHOOD

Nadia is a mother of five children in Afghanistan, the youngest of whom is only two months old. She says, "We could not afford to buy anything to help my child to be born healthy. There was no available vehicle, and the road conditions were poor. At times, physicians informed us that there is no treatment available."

"My infant and I were both very frail," Nadia explained. "We only have a small amount of rice, wheat, flour, and nothing else. Pregnant women face the risk of mortality in addition to numerous other dangers. We must perform a great deal of labor because no one else is available. In the future, I expect that my children will grow up, study, and assist others. I do not wish for them to be like us."[197]

The Quran acknowledges the crucial role of mothers in the creation process and uses the term "mother" to denote the origin or essence of something. It employs various definitions of the word to describe significant individuals and objects in Islam.

The Quran refers to itself as The Master Record. Or *Umm* ("Mother of the Books") stating: *"And indeed, it is-in the (Master) Mother of the Book, with us, - highly esteemed, rich in wisdom" (Q 43:4)*. Mecca is known as the mother of cities *(Q 42:7)*: *"[W]hich we have revealed- conform what came before it- so you may warn the Mother of Cities and everyone around it" (Q 6:92)*. The Prophet's wives are described as "Mothers of the Believers": *"The Prophet has a strong affinity to the believers than they do themselves. And his wives are their mothers" (Q 33:6)*.

In 1990, this Arabic lexicon entered American politics when US President George Bush waged war against Saddam Hussain to recapture Kuwait. The mission was titled "Desert Storm" and Bush called it "The mother of all wars" to convey its enormity.

THE MOTHER OF MONOTHEISM AND THE FOUNDING OF MECCA

The Quran recounts tales of mothers who acted as autonomous agents, received divine guidance, and shaped the course of human history. Hagar, or Hajar in Arabic, is considered "The Mother of the Arabs," and is referred to in the Bible.

Hagar and her son were left behind by Abraham in the valley of Bacca, known as Mecca. As he was leaving, Hagar clung to Abraham's robes and questioned him, "For whom are you leaving us in this forsaken valley?" When Abraham was ready to leave her, she asked, "Has God commanded you to do this?" He said, "Yes." She said, "Then God will not cause us to be lost." Hagar let Abraham go peacefully with the conviction that God would ensure their survival.

When her son Ishmael was thirsty and her waterskin was empty, Hagar ran seven times between the hills of Safa and Marwa in search of water. Just as she was distraught over her son's survival, she found herself face to face with the Angel Gabriel, who scraped the earth with the tip of his wing until the "primordial water" (the well of Zamzam) gushed forth. Hagar built a dam to contain the water and birds hovered over the spring, signaling to approaching caravans that there was water there. Hagar allowed travelers to drink from the well because it was a gift from God; as a result, Mecca became renowned for its abundant water source and the valley of Becca, today's Mecca, flourished.

The holy house Kaaba, a cubical structure, was built by Abraham with his son Ishmael as a sanctuary of well-being for all people. *(Q 5:97)*. Today, all Muslims pray in the direction of Mecca, where two million pilgrims conduct the annual Hajj by circumambulating the Kaaba in unison. To symbolize human struggle, they retrace Hagar's footsteps, traversing the same path she strove between Safaa and Marwa: *"Indeed the hills of Safa and Marwa are among the symbols of God, let them walk between the two hills" (Q 2:158)*.

God choose Hagar for the dual role of mother and pioneer, as an archetype of a courageous mother whose conviction and bravery resulted in laying the foundation for the "Mother of the Holiest Sites." Although separated from her husband, Hagar used tenacious resilience to nurture, protect, and raise her son Ishmael, who later became a prophet. Had she succumbed to weakness the town of Mecca would not have been founded, Prophet Muhammad may not have been born, and Khadijah, a tradeswoman, may not have proposed marriage to young Muhammad. Bilal, who was enslaved by the Meccans, might not have been liberated to demonstrate human equality. Fatima's endurance in the face of adversity and Aisha's commitment to disseminating the Prophet's message might not have occurred.

Barbara Stowasser says Hagar is one of the pillars of Islamic consciousness. In her acceptance to stay in the desert, she symbolizes faith, reason, and resourcefulness in her ordeal—to run to save her child from death. She is an image of the submitting and active aspects of being Muslim. As a participant in Abraham's mission, she helped reestablish true monotheism on earth. She was also the ancestor of Abraham's true heirs—the Muslims—since it was her descendant, the Prophet Muhammad, who restored Abraham's religion after the world had fallen away from the true faith and proper worship of God. (47)

THE MOTHER OF ALL MOTHERS CHOSEN IN SERVICE OF GOD

The Quran lauds many women as role models for humankind who achieved social, spiritual, and public freedoms through God's will, independent of their role as mothers, setting a precedent for future generations of the Divine Will.

Mary, or Maryam in Arabic, is the most virtuous, and chapter 19 of the Quran is named in her honor. She possesses attributes of eternal perfection and prophetic dignity and is informed by Angel Gabriel that God has chosen her for a mission: *"He responded, I am only a messenger from your Lord, 'sent' to bless you with a pure son"* (Q 19:19-21). Aliah Schleifer, author of *Mary the Blessed Virgin of Islam*, states that despite her being an unmarried virgin, her womb will serve to bring the Messiah, the "Word of God" into this world. After Jesus is born, God refers to him as "Son of Mary" rather than Mary being called "Mother of Jesus." He is the Son of Mary because he has no father, and Mary is his sole parent. The infant Jesus speaks from his cradle to define his relationship with his mother, *"and to be kind to my mother. He has not made me arrogant or defiant" (Q 19:32)*. Hence, the two, mother and child, are bound together as one in their representation of the best of human virtues, among which is the reciprocation of concern and affection, which God has decreed between parent and child.[198] *"Be fair to your parents and* children, as you do not 'fully know who is more beneficial to you,'" it says in Q 4:11.

The Quran also says that God made Maryam and Jesus a sign for all people, "And remember the one who guarded her chastity, so We breathed into her though Our angel, Gabriel, making her and her son a sign for all peoples" (Q 21:91). According to Schleifer, Maryam never laments her situation, even though such behavior would be normal for a young woman who is shunned by her people and living in an alien environment. In contrast, she appears as a dutiful mother who provides for her infant son and encourages him to face life with the steadfastness of faith as he grows up. (46)

Schleifer states that, according to historians, Maryam's entire life after conception, with respect to routine and worldly concern, centers around the love, guidance, and protection of her son, dreading the hostility of her people toward her and her son, as well as Herod's wrath. She flees into unfamiliar territory, where she lives among odd people whose behavior is sometimes hostile. Then she returns with her son to his native land, fully aware of the perils inherent to his mission. She defends this mission while encouraging him to remain steadfast. Maryam suffers the greatest pain of a mother before she is made aware of the reality that her son Jesus was raised to an exalted position in heaven. (52)

Mohamad Jebara describes how Maryam's mother had pledged her child to serve the temple when she was pregnant, not realizing that her child would be a girl. So, Maryam insisted on fulfilling her mother's vow. At age six, she lived up to her name, (Maryam in Hebrew means "rebellion") by marching into the temple in Jerusalem. She strode past all the priests and went straight to the holy of holies: the sacred place where only the high priests were allowed to enter once a year, on Yom Kippur. She instilled that same commitment in her son, who also rebelled against society's elite. He delivered his greatest sermon not in a temple but on a mountain, in nature where everyone could attend. (71)

Barbara Stowasser finds a significant spiritual connection between Mary, the virgin mother, and Eve, the first mother. She says, to clarify that Jesus is fully human, the Quran compares Jesus to Adam in the sense that both are God's creation, brought into existence by the power of divine speech and decree. Mary is parallel to Adam, and Eve to Jesus.

In the same way that Eve was created from Adam without a woman, so was Jesus created from Mary without a man. (81)

MOTHERHOOD AS A LIFELINE FOR MEN IN DISTRESS

According to Celene Ibrahim, author of *Women and Gender in the Qur'an*, reproduction, pregnancy, and birthing are repeated themes in the Quran, in which women are not only aides in domestic and reproductive spheres who bear children but also provide lifelines to male family members (prophets) in distress. For instance, Miriam, Moses' biological sister, watched over him as he sailed down the Nile, where he was ultimately discovered by Asiya, Pharoah's wife, who adopted him against Pharoah's wishes *(Q 28:11-13)*. Then Miriam persuaded Asiya to allow Jacohebed, Moses' biological mother, to be his wet nurse.[199]

Khadijah, a merchant and mother of six, supported her husband during the most tumultuous time of his prophetic mission. Her unwavering belief in his mission and her sacrifices helped lay the groundwork for spreading Islam. She utilized her influence to convince Meccan elites to accept her husband as God's messenger, and her reputation and status as a noblewoman lent credibility to the followers of this fledgling faith.

Umm Salama, a mother of five, advised the Prophet to accept the Hudaybiyyah Peace Treaty, preventing the persecution of thousands of early Muslims.

Fatimah bin al-Khattab convinced her brother Umar to accept Islam, thereby preventing Umar from killing the Prophet.

Aisha, the childless wife of the Prophet, is known as the "Mother of Believers" because she relayed the majority of the hadith, on which we rely today.

Zaynab, the granddaughter of the Prophet Muhammad, flung herself on top of her nephew Ali ibn Husayn Zayn al-Abidin, who was sentenced to execution by the governor of Kufah. Her actions saved a crucial member of Ali and Fatima's bloodline. Zaynab is revered by the Shia community and is buried in the Sayyidah Zaynab Mosque in Damascus. In Iran, her birthday is recognized as Nurse's Day because she took care of the wounded during the Battle of Karbala and nursed Husain's son Ali. She is another member of Prophet Muhammad's household, Ahl-al-Bayt, who defied convention by performing multiple roles as a caring mother, a warrior, a nurse, a politician, and an erudite speaker on Islam.

Rabia Al Basri (714 CE) did not consider motherhood essential for a woman's success in life and the hereafter. Her gratitude to God was so deep that no man could ever compare to it; she refused many marriage proposals saying, "God can give me all you offer and even double it. It does not please me to be distracted from Him for a moment, so, farewell." Her life did not fit the patterns of the women of her time. Instead, she retained complete control and legal autonomy over her own life—she was neither a wife nor a mother, nor was she under any male authority.[200]

This list could go on and on.

THE MERCIFUL WOMB

One of the ninety-nine names of God is *Ar-Rahman*— the root meaning is "womb" and "mercy," indicating the closeness between God and mother (Q 39:6). In the Quran, the mother's womb is related to piety: *"[A]nd be mindful of God- in Whose name you appeal to one another- and honorary ties" (Q 4:1)*. The word comes from *rahm*, and in human beings this quality is naturally felt in relation to pregnancy. God provides human beings a womb to be born into and through which to have the realization of love that is at the very foundation of all that exists.[201]

The Study Quran commentary states that the above verse instructs men to reverence God through obedience to His command and to reverence family relations, by maintaining good relations with family members. Family relations translates *arham*; the singular is *rahim*, the primary meaning of which is womb.[202] Asma Barlas argues that the Quran elevates the status of mothers by associating them with piety (*taqwa*) and mercy (*rahma*), giving them an advantage over fathers, who are never associated with these concepts. (205)

Muslims are commanded to be grateful to their mothers as they go through hardship during pregnancy and childbirth: *"[T]heir mothers bore them through hardship upon hardship, and their weaning takes two years" (Q 31:14)*. The Prophet described mothers as an embodiment of God's mercy: "Verily, God created, on the same very day when He created the heavens and the earth, one hundred parts of mercy. Every part of mercy is coextensive with the space between the heavens and the earth, and He, out of his mercy, endowed one part to the earth, and it is because of this that the mother shows affection to her child."[203]

In another moment, the Prophet was asked by a man, who was

most deserving of his love and respect. The Prophet replied, "Your mother."[204] The man inquired again, and the Prophet reiterated, "Your mother." Only on the fourth time did the Prophet say, "Your father."[205] In another commonly cited hadith, a man conveyed to the Prophet his desire to join a battle and engage in *jihad*, a defensive war for religious freedom. In response, the Prophet asked if he had a mother, to which the man responded affirmatively. The Prophet advised him to stay with his mother because, "paradise lies at the mothers' feet."[206] Taking care of one's mother is a virtue that can help one reach paradise in the next life. It is a validation of the mother's sacrifices and a way to show appreciation for the hours of work spanning the child's life that motherhood entails.

A flourishing civilization depends on respecting mothers and nurturing the next generation, a principle deeply rooted in Islam's religious, social, and cultural values.

Even though parents have rights and responsibilities, the Quran notes that the mother plays a greater role in the early years of a child's development, inferring that she receives a greater degree of consideration. A Tunisian leader once remarked that women are one-half of society, and they raise the other half on their laps. Author Ziauddin Sardar writes in his book, "I grew up reading the Qur'an on my mother's lap, a common experience among Muslim children."[207]

My grandmother, Moji, was known as "Bodh Moj," which translates to "mother of all mothers." She influenced my soul in unfathomable ways. One day, I fell unconscious with my head on her lap, and I dreamed that a magnificent light descended from the heavens like a bright tunnel to the ground where I stood. I felt small and insignificant as a gravitational pull was exerted by this luminous approaching light. She murmured in my ear, "You dreamed of *nur*, God's light," after I exclaimed that it was unlike anything I'd ever seen.

I remember Grandma Moji preparing an offering for the poor, hoping they would make a special supplication (*dua*) for her. I looked at the poor with their tattered clothing, many of them toothless but smiling at me, and prayed to God for blessings. Their smiles are etched in my memory. They planted a seed in me that nurtured my soul, moving me to seek a higher road. I must confess, it never occurred to me that a day would come when I would be following in the footsteps of Moji, the "mother of all mothers," albeit in America.

Children observe and imitate their mothers' actions, values, and attitudes. A mother transmits cultural traditions and moral principles and imparts values that shape her child's moral compass. She teaches them self-reliance and personal responsibility, plays a crucial role in fostering a child's intellectual development and offers them emotional support during difficult times. Her unconditional love, listening, and comforting provide the child with a sense of security.

A mother is essential to the creation of a more egalitarian society because she empowers her daughters and teaches her sons to value and respect women. Due to their role in bringing up the next generation, the prosperity of a nation depends on the care provided by mothers.

WORKING WOMEN

A recent case study in Senegal found that many women appreciate their position as the family's focal point. When the father departs, she holds the family together, and when she is absent, the family disintegrates. She is the "brain of the family" and its gravitational center; she cooks, gives advice, restores, and consoles. She is the "pillar" of the family because she interacts with everyone daily, understands their requirements, and makes the majority of decisions.

The study also reveals that some husbands appreciate their wives working—bringing additional income to the family. Those mothers enjoy financial autonomy because they are not dependent on spouses to fulfill their children's needs. One husband in the study remarks that when his wife works, they share family responsibilities, and he will even take her out to dinner when she returns home tired. Other males are receptive to women working, helping with the family, using her money, and caring for the family in all of these respects.[208]

But for other Muslim working women, there is a sense of clear inequality. One woman explains, "My husband and I depart and return home together. Upon his return, he relaxes while I care for him and the children, prepare dinner, draw showers, and send the children to bed. The following day, after preparing the children for school, I go to work. My husband is not expected to do housework, even though I work the same hours. I work twenty hours without a break, whereas he unwinds after six or eight hours of labor."[209]

It is unclear, from this study, whether working outside the home strengthens a woman's authority or jeopardizes her central position in the household. She must consistently multitask, care for her spouse and children, perform well at work, and manage the household. Many contemporary women hope for the day when husband and wife can become co-breadwinners and share co-authority in everything.

MONETIZING MOTHERHOOD

In her Ted Ex talk, Muna Abu Suleyman, a single Saudi mother, speaks about creating a society in which motherhood is recognized as a major productivity wheel, part of the GDP of a nation and a tool for progress.

Motherhood is a demanding and challenging role that involves countless hours of housework and childcare. Despite the measurable value of this work, mothers at home receive no compensation for this labor, despite the fact that they are, in effect, raising future generations. They feel unsupported at home and by society. Additionally, when in the workforce outside the home, most women receive less pay than men, even when doing similar work. Women who employ nannies pay a high price for pursuing a career, whereas women unable to find care easily wind up on a "mommy track," often with a dead-end work opportunity.

Muslim women are increasingly suggesting that, similar to senior citizens, mothers should receive special motherhood deposits or discounts, such as tax breaks, low interest loans for cars and homes, discounts on airlines, and other incentives and rewards. Workplace resources should include flexible time, which a woman can opt out of, and paid parental leave, as standard workplace benefits.

To demonstrate the substantial economic contribution mothers make to their families and society, I used a twelve-hour workday and $15/hour wage to calculate that a mother's childcare is minimally worth $60,000 per year, or $1.080 million over eighteen years. But since a mother's care is unpaid labor, the message to mothers is that their contributions have no value. Possibly for this reason, the Quran stipulates a spouse must compensate his wife for nursing the child, paying for raising the children, providing for her upkeep, and contributing to the household.

The Quran does not designate reproduction as a woman's solitary duty. *Verse 4:1* acknowledges and values the important role women play in procreation, and emphasizes their unique ability to bear children, but it does not state that motherhood is her exclusive role. According to Asghar Ali Engineer, motherhood is important and should not be downgraded, but it is essential to prioritize women's individual rights because they have the right to choose whether to compromise in motherhood. (148)

Women who thrive in parenting, working, or saving the planet, are skilled at achieving some balance between their professional and personal lives and are proficient at establishing distinct boundaries. They may be adept at managing tasks, delegating responsibility, and managing time effectively. Most women succeed when they utilize a strong support system—consisting of friends, family members, acquaintances, and communities—to share the load and receive assistance when necessary. Therefore, it is no surprise that many women and many mothers are heads of state, serving their nations while discharging their parental and family obligations. Their example demonstrates that motherhood is not the only normative role for women that dominates their lives and ambitions. The fact that motherhood and womanhood are two aspects of the same coin does not compromise a mother's ability to assume multiple roles. On the other hand, if a woman is childless by divine decree, she has other options. She can assume a greater societal role like Aisha did, as a social and spiritual entrepreneur in the service of humankind.

Consider, for instance, Sally Sabry, who wears a *niqab*, and defies all prevalent maternal and female stereotypes. When she was breastfeeding her infant, she received a lactation cover as a gift from an overseas friend. It made nursing so much easier for her that she wished all Egyptian mothers had one. But when none were to be found, she felt inspired to act.

Sabry approached her friend Doaa Zaki with a business idea. In 2006, the two founded the company "Best Mums." Since then, they have sold tens of thousands of these covers and expanded their product line to include affordable, practical items designed to make motherhood simpler. Sabry and Zaki say they want to disprove the notion that *niqabi* women are subjugated and voiceless. On the contrary, they are active in their pursuits to positively impact their surroundings. Best Mums is more than a company; it stands as a declaration: Niqabi women aren't concealed, they are at the forefront, leading the conversation.[210]

PART IV

THE RIGHT TO YOUR WEALTH

• • • • • • • • •

In Islam, a woman can secure an adequate standard of living by receiving equal pay and can manage her finances without coercion from her spouse. She can amass a fortune in the form of gifts, monthly stipends, and other resources, which she can then spend as she sees fit. She receives inheritances in the form of money, property, land, and personal effects, which may ensure her biological identity and financial independence, and she can manage these as she pleases without pressure or coercion. She has the right to independent property ownership and has no restrictions on how she uses her wealth for her well-being, her progeny, and for the benefit of society. She also faces no obstacles in obtaining legal documents pertaining to an inheritance or business ventures.

This objective of protection and promotion of wealth involves the right of every human being to work and receive fair compensation for their labor. This includes:

- Rights to earn a living wage; protection from bribery, theft, and corruption; and an economic environment that enables workers to gain wealth or property in an honest and legal manner are essential, or *daruriyyat*.
- The right to maintain an adequate standard of living is necessary, or *hajiyyat*.
- The opportunity to constantly improve that standard of living as complementary, or *tahsiniyyat*.

#18 | TO INHERITANCE

After her father passed away, an Afghan woman was told by her brothers that she would not receive any inheritance. They claimed that they were responsible for her and she did not need a share of the property. Despite her efforts to fight for her rights, she was unsuccessful, and the relationship between the siblings deteriorated.

Ten years later, she attended a Friday prayer at the mosque where the imam spoke about women's rights. She informed the imam that her brothers had denied her inheritance. The imam met with her brothers and told them it was against Islam to deny a woman her inheritance. He instructed them to redistribute the property according to inheritance rules and give their sister her fair share. After receiving her inheritance, this woman's relationship with her brothers improved and family ties were restored.

Haifaa Jawad explains that, prior to Islam, inheritance in Arabia was limited to men. Women, girls, and young males were excluded from receiving an inheritance. Women were considered property that could be passed on as inheritance. For example, if a man died, his oldest son inherited his father's widow, and if she was not his mother, he would marry her or ask his brother or nephew to do so. The Quran brought about significant changes that explicitly safeguarded against these inequities. *"[I]t is not permissible for you to inherit women against their will" (Q 4:19)*. It introduced numerous rights and restrictions to inheritance practices in which women had a legal right to inheritance (61) and were no longer inherited as personal property.

Jawad explains how God, in verse 4:7, granted inheritance rights to women in response to an Ansari woman who pleaded with the Prophet because her husband had died, leaving her with five daughters. Her male relatives deprived them of their wealth, leaving them penniless. Her brother-in-law justified his action by stating, "Since women do not ride horses, put themselves in danger, or fight in battles, they could not inherit." (61-66) In response, God granted inheritance shares to women as well as men: *"For men, there is a share in what their parents and close relatives leave, and for women, there is a share in what their parents and close relatives leave—whether it is little or much. 'These are' obligatory shares"* (Q 4:7).

RULES EASILY FORGOTTEN

Even though the new inheritance laws altered the social structure of Arabian society, many Arab men disregarded the Quranic commands. This is when Kubaysa bint Ma'an informed the Prophet that men were disobeying the Quran and explained that her son-in-law denied her inheritance. "I have neither taken my share of inheritance from my husband nor been left alone to enjoy my freedom to re-marry." The Prophet chastised the son-in-law and other hypocrites and exhorted his followers to spread the knowledge of inheritance rules: "You, all of you, should learn the inheritance rules (*faraid*) and teach them to the succeeding generations. This is equivalent to merit in all areas of knowledge. The rules are easily forgotten, and they are the first area of knowledge that my nation will lose."

The *Quranic verse 4:7* prohibits from disinheriting female heirs, and *verse 4:11* provides protections for the inheritance of all direct heirs, outlining rules for distributing shares based on the heir's relationship to the deceased: *"God commands you regarding your children: the share of the male will be twice that of the female. If you leave only one or more females, their share is two-thirds of the estate, But if there is only one female, her share will be one-half. Each parent is entitled to one-sixth if you leave offspring. But if you are childless and your parents are the only heirs, then your mother will receive one-third. But if you leave siblings, then your mother will receive one-sixth—after the fulfillment of bequests and debts. Be fair to your parents and children, as you do not 'fully' know who is more beneficial to you. This is an obligation from God."*

This is irrefutable proof that women cannot be denied inheritance and that—despite their gender—mothers, daughters, and sisters are afforded the status of direct heirs. They may inherit from their deceased family members, including: parents, spouses, children, and siblings.

Typically, a daughter's share of an inheritance is half that of a son. For example, if a father dies, his daughters inherit 50 percent of what his sons inherit. A daughter with no brothers receives half the inheritance, and if there is more than one daughter with no sons, they receive two-thirds of the estate. Each parent (including a mother) receives one-sixth of the inheritance, and a wife gets one-fourth of her deceased husband's estate if he has no heir. Otherwise, she receives one-eighth; the mother gets one-third if there are no children and no surviving brothers or sisters. The grandmother receives one-sixth if there is no surviving mother and no surviving father (in the case of the father's mother).[211]

In cases when parents, spouses, or children are not surviving, their share is split up among siblings of the deceased. Children conceived but not yet born are included, as their shares are reserved for them. Even a woman waiting for divorce is considered a wife and is entitled to inheritance. The Quran says that after direct heirs' portions are granted, orphans and needy relatives' people should be provided for: *"If non-inheriting relatives, or orphans, or the needy are present at the time of distribution, offer them a 'small' provision from it and speak to them kindly" (Q 4:8).*

EXAMINING THE GENDER GAP: THE 2:1 INHERITANCE RATIO

According to *verse 4:11*, a male will receive twice the amount as a female. The interpretation of *Q 4:11* as implying that Islam regards women with less care and equity than men has caused Muslim women considerable distress. In actuality, the Quran ensures that women can inherit as daughters, mothers, and wives, and the issue of a daughter receiving one-half of an inheritance must be understood in the context of the social and economic conditions of the time.

Asma Lamrabet explains that in the Quran, gender is not always considered in the case of inheritance, except in cases where the financial responsibility is significant or entirely the responsibility of the male, such as in 4:11, where the brother inherits twice as much as the sister. Men were required to provide for the needs of their respective families, women, children, and the elderly, in accordance with Quranic principles and social customs of the time. This logic of additional financial responsibility for men did not arise with the advent of Islam; it has existed across all civilizations from the beginning of time. (150)

According to Ali Engineer, it is a well-known principle of Islamic Shariah derived from the Quran that the husband is responsible for providing for his wife, even if she is extremely wealthy. She has no obligation to expend her wealth. It is her privilege to receive maintenance from her husband; therefore, as a wife, she has no obligation to support herself or her children, in addition to the inheritance she received as a daughter. (71)

A comprehensive examination of this verse, according to Amina Wadud, reveals a variety of proportional divisions between males and females. If there is only one female child, she receives half the inheritance. In addition, numerous combinations of parents, siblings, distant relatives, and descendants are discussed. This indicates that "the proportion for the female is one-half the proportion for the male" is not the only proportional arrangement for property division, but only one of several. In the context of masculine preference over females, Wadud explains as follows: The absolute inheritance of men will not always exceed that of women. Initially, the quantity left depends on the family's wealth. The relationship between privilege and responsibility is reciprocal. Men are responsible for providing their wealth for the support of women, and as a result, they are granted a double inheritance share. (86-87)

The male is customarily responsible and accountable for all family matters, as he must provide safety, protection, and sustenance for his wife, children, and elderly parents. The wife has no obligation to contribute to the financial upkeep of the property or the family. The property a woman inherits and any earnings from her labor, except for what she may voluntarily offer to her spouse, belong solely to her.[212] Haifaa Jawad explains that the marriage gift (dowry) she receives becomes her exclusive property and remains with her even if she is subsequently divorced. In addition, the inheritance that she receives as a daughter is added to the inheritance she receives as a wife. There is no legal obligation to support her or her children. (66)

In some Muslim societies, women are subjected to social pressure to relinquish their inheritance, which is co-opted by male family members who believe their financial obligations to women grant them the right to overlook Quranic injunctions. Haifaa Jawad explains that women are led to assume they are not in dire financial straits and are therefore forced to accept the loss of their share. Women who demand their share are criticized for being ungrateful, inconsiderate, and greedy, causing other women to remain silent and allowing their husbands to keep their share. Denying women the right to inherit is tantamount to eliminating their biological identity and the guarantees it offers. (68) These practices are antithetical to the Quran, which states that inheritance is a birthright that no one has the authority to deny. According to Fariba Zarinebaf-Shahr, "Inheritance was an important source of economic power for women, and in cases of abuse, women were particularly vocal in defending their rights."[213]

EXEMPLARY USES OF INHERITED WEALTH

Over the course of history, Muslim women have played a significant part in using their inheritance for the benefit of society. In response to the Prophet's advice to educate future generations, the rules governing inheritance were codified, allowing women to receive their fair share.

The verse, *"Indeed, those men and women who give in charity and lend to God a good loan will have it multiplied for them, and they will have an honorable reward"* (Q 57:18), emphasizes the virtue of giving to charity. Muslim women driven by this command used their inheritance to help the needy and disadvantaged with the belief that such acts would be rewarded by God. For example, there are several examples of women who developed institutions for religious, medical, educational, and pious purposes—leaving an indelible mark on history through their iconic deeds.

In the ninth century, Mariam Al Fihri channeled her inherited wealth into the noblest cause. She constructed the Al-Andalus Mosque in Morocco, which acquired prominence in Fez because the city's ruler at the time, Obaidullah, designated it the location for the weekly Friday sermon. The *khutbah* had political, religious, and societal implications, and it served to bring the people together. This symbol of faith became a cherished place of worship for generations to come.

Zubaydah bin Jafar, (d. 831 CE) the wife of Abbasid Caliph Harun Al-Rashid, etched her name in the annals of history by constructing a 1,400-kilometer route known as the Zubaida Trail, which was once a necessary route for Hajj pilgrims traveling from Kufa, Iraq, to Makkah. The trail was named after Zubaydah in recognition of her charitable endeavors, which included refreshment stops to provide respite to travelers along the route.[214]

In the thirteenth century, Gevher Nesibe Sultan, a princess of the Sultanate of Rum, endowed a splendid educational and healing complex in Kayseri, Turkey, which included a mosque, a hospital, and *madrasa*. This preeminent Seljuk architectural landmark was partially constructed during her lifetime, and the adjacent *madrasa* and hospital became a beacon of hope for the sick and a sanctuary for scholars.

Moving eastward to the Mughal Empire, Princess Jahanara, (d. 1681 CE), the daughter of Shah Jehan, who built the Taj Mahal, embarked on a unique philanthropic journey. In the year 1643, her heart yearned to help those less fortunate. She owned ships that traded between the English and the Dutch. She ordered one ship, the Sahibi, to travel to Mecca and Medina, carrying 151 pounds of rice to be distributed to the destitute and needy.[215] In addition, she used her personal funds to construct a *madrasa* and the Jami Masjid in Agra, Delhi, leaving a legacy of devotion to God.

These examples illustrate the proactive participation of Muslim women in utilizing their inheritance and personal fortune for the benefit of society. Their contributions spanned religious, medical, educational, and charitable endeavors, demonstrating their commitment to public welfare.

UNLOCKING WOMEN'S FINANCIAL FUTURES

In an era when the socioeconomic context has changed, Zainab Chaudhry contends that the rationale behind a law mandating a two-to-one inheritance ratio may seem outdated. Extended family has been replaced by the nuclear family. Many unmarried and divorced women now maintain careers outside of the family and live alone. Due to this, "many governments of Muslim countries have already enacted changes into their personal status codes to reflect the realities of modern life." Countries such as Sudan, Egypt, and Iraq have enacted laws allowing a testator to leave bequests to whomever he wishes, including female heirs.[216]

The situation for women has changed, according to Asghar Ali Engineer. Myriad domestic lifestyles of Muslims cannot be accounted for by oversimplification and gendered role expectations. One may inquire, "What about the daughter who chooses not to marry for social or other reasons?" She may also need to take care of herself. Many women without male support are divorced or widowed, and some are solely responsible for their own maintenance and that of their children and parents. "Then, what happens if a daughter is unable to marry and is not properly provided for?" (74)

Asghar Ali Engineer acknowledges the common belief that the shares allocated to heirs in *verse 4:11* must be rigorously adhered to and that the testator has no authority to make any additional gifts. But this is not simply the case. (74) The Quran clarifies that a testator is entitled to leave an additional sum in favor of an heir if they make a will, or *wasiyat*: *"It is prescribed that when death approaches any of you—if they leave something of value—a will should be made in favor of parents and immediate family with fairness. This is an obligation on those who are mindful of God" (Q 2:180).*

The Prophet emphasized this by saying, "A Muslim who has something to bequeath should not let two nights pass without writing a will."[217] In accordance with the proportions specified by the Quran, heirs will inherit whatever remains after the will is executed. Parents who wish to increase their daughter's inheritance to compensate for her lack of resources may use this Quranic provision, which permits a person to leave one-third of their wealth as a gift to any beneficiary, in addition to the specified share of the inheritance. The rules they must abide by are that they consider the approval of all legal heirs, and not to give a gift that would deprive another heir of their share of inheritance.

In her book, Ingrid Mattson describes how some Muslims have questioned whether the family's wealth distribution system satisfies Quranic objectives in modern societies with vastly different economic and social structures than premodern societies. Some argue there is no clear evidence that equity is the only objective of maintaining inheritance laws. They suggest the Quran also aims to support the role of a man as primary breadwinner to free women from this burden. Thus, women can provide primary care for their offspring and other needy family members (the elderly, the ailing, etc.). Requiring women to provide equal financial support to the family would lessen their ability to provide such care.

Mattson explains that the obligation of males to provide complete support for women furthers the Shariah's primary objective, which is the preservation of the family. Thus, injustices created by new social and economic conditions should be rectified by means other than circumventing the Quran's wealth distribution rules. For example, liens can be placed on men's inheritance for maintenance past due. But because no transnational authority can compel a man in one country to support his female relatives in another, many women do not receive adequate support from their brothers, who receive a double share of inheritance, even though their sister may have a greater need.

She mentions how in the age of globalization, sons or brothers who may have migrated to a wealthier nation may return to their home country to claim a larger share of the inheritance upon the death of their father, without ever supporting their female relatives. But because the purpose of Quranic wealth distribution is to ensure equality between men and women, it makes sense in modern societies to impose the same financial obligations on men and women and provide them with the same financial benefits. (236)

Women should have the same financial opportunities as men, and when they do, they demonstrate time and again how to use their wealth for the betterment of others. Consider the example of Sheikha Moza, the wife of Qatar's former monarch, Emir Hamad bin Khalifa Al Thani. Her commitment to education and community development led her to cofound Qatar Foundation, which is dedicated to promoting education and scientific advancement.

In 2009, Sheikha Moza significantly contributed to my work, by supporting my mission for social change. During the time when the media often portrayed an inevitable divide between Muslims and Western civilization, I became concerned about the potential consequences of the next generation of Muslims feeling alienated and isolated in a world seemingly against them. I recognized that empowering them through dialogue and meaningful connections was a crucial step forward.

I devised a plan to bring together young Muslim leaders, male and female from across the globe to empower them through the creation of long-lasting connections. However, this ambitious plan would have remained a mere idea without the necessary resources. Determined to turn this vision into reality, I traveled to Qatar to discuss my concept of a global gathering known as Muslim Leaders of Tomorrow (MLT) with Sheikha Moza. After explaining that these young men and women would eventually emerge as the future leaders of our *ummah*, she immediately extended her support. Sheikha Moza played a pivotal role in facilitating a three-day gathering in Qatar bringing together 300 young leaders from diverse corners of the world. These leaders not only strategized for the future but also forged enduring friendships. Today many have ascended to prominent positions in their respective fields around the globe.

This idea would never have materialized without the resources that Sheikha Moza invested in it, in so doing, she left an indelible mark on the inheritance of intellectual and social progress for generations to come.

#19 TO FINANCIAL INDEPENDENCE AND EQUAL PAY

Gul Makai Sultanzada, a Kandahar, Afghanistan defense attorney and head of her local bar association, worked for eleven years without pay. She was informed that the position was unpaid. But when a male was appointed to replace her and perform the same duties, he was paid a full salary. The Prophet warned about the repercussions for those who perpetrate this transgression: "God said, 'On the Day of Resurrection, I will oppose three types of people: one who makes a covenant in My name but turns out to be treacherous; one who sells a free person and eats his price; and one who employs a laborer and takes full work from him but does not compensate him for his labor."[218]

God, also known as *Ar-Razzaq*, The Provider, is revered as the divine source of all provisions including wealth. God, arranges the affairs of the righteous, ensuring that sustenance can come from unexpected sources: God reinforces this assurance stating, *"Whoever is mindful of God, He will make a way out for them and provide for them from sources they could never imagine" (Q 65:2-3).*

Furthermore, God may favor individuals by increasing their provision, especially those who generously share their wealth: *"And God has favored some of you over others in provision. But those who have been much favored would not share their wealth with those 'bondspeople' in their possession, making them their equals. Do they then deny God's favors?" (Q 16:71)*

Although the Quran assures us God will provide, this does not imply we should wait for God to send sustenance. Imam Ali advised individuals to actively pursue their needs, as God's assurance is for those who actively seek it.

PIONEERING ENTREPRENEURSHIP

Khadijah, the Prophet's wife, accumulated wealth, protected it, distributed it widely, and purified it for social good. She utilized her assets to create an economic environment that enabled her workers to improve their living standards. Motivated by values and morals rather than reward, she freed her slaves and remained equitable in trade dealings. Her gender was not a factor in her business transactions or her social and philanthropic works.

The Prophet's marriage to Khadijah taught him firsthand how a woman's ability to earn a livelihood enhances her stature. "The upper hand is better than the lower hand; the upper hand is that which gives, and the lower hand is that which asks."[219] He advised people against asking others for money and directed men and women to become financially independent by earning their own money.

After the death of Khadijah, when Umm Salama married the Prophet, he was no longer a merchant. She recognized the significance of his mission and did not want to add to his financial burdens. To provide for her five children from her previous marriage, she sold handiwork in the marketplace. This allowed her to care for her children, support her husband, and live a dignified life as the Prophet's wife.

EQUAL PAY

Prior to Islam, worker abuse was pervasive, and individuals lacked safeguards against harsh economic conditions. The Quran emerged as a champion of equitable labor laws, vehemently rejecting any forms of labor exploitation. Employers were commanded to treat employees with respect, dignity, and kindness, and withholding or underpaying a worker was deemed a grave sin. This verse underscores this ethical imperative: *"Give just measure and weight and do not defraud people of their property, nor spread corruption in the land after it has been set in order" (Q 7:85).*

The Prophet compensated his employees generously and treated them with respect and dignity, stating that no employer is morally superior to their employee: "Pay the worker his wages before his sweat has dried."[220] Thus, every worker has the right to a living wage; protection from extortion, theft, and corruption; and an economic climate that allows them to acquire wealth or property in an honest and lawful manner.

In Islam, wealth entails the right of every individual to work and receive a fair wage in exchange for their labor. They have the right to earn money to maintain a sufficient standard of living. Several verses introduced the revolutionary notion of "equal pay" for men and women, proposing that wage differences should be based on skill rather than gender. Every worker, regardless of gender, is entitled to equal compensation according to these verses: *"Men will be rewarded according to their deeds and women equally according to theirs" (Q 4:32)*, and *"[I] will never deny any of you—male or female—the reward of your deeds. Both are equal in reward" (Q 3:195)*.

The Quran's insistence that men and women must be compensated equally demonstrates that both sexes can become productive human beings in terms of their service to God, themselves, and others. Economic equity can only be accomplished by collaborating with members of the larger society so that the collective wisdom and all available human capital—men and women alike—are brought to bear fruit.[221]

FULFILLING THE ZAKAT OBLIGATION

Equal emphasis must be placed in Islam on using wealth to advance spiritual goals, as well as fulfill worldly obligations. This is made clear in the Quran, which instructs that wealth be purified through charitable giving: *"[D]onate from what We have provided for them" (Q 2:3)*. The purpose of charity (*zakat*) is wealth distribution, not only accumulation. *"Take, from their wealth, 'O Prophet' charity to purify them and bless them and pray for them" (Q 9:103)*. Scholars concur unanimously that *zakat* is obligatory for anyone who can pay on his own behalf. *Zakat* is on the person, not the wealth.

Pious Muslim women committed to reaching spiritual heights utilize charitable giving to promote social welfare. They distribute wealth among the poor and enable low-income earners, the majority of whom are women, to care for their families. Also, if wealth is not distributed equitably, as evidenced by contemporary instances in which women are denied these rights, it has serious repercussions for women's afterlife, as evidenced by the Prophet, who said, "When a person dies, their good deeds come to an end, except for ongoing charity, beneficial knowledge, and a righteous child who prays for them."[222] By hindering women financially, we impact them spiritually, as they are unable to care for the needy and poor through charitable initiatives.

Haifaa Jawad explains that this privilege cannot be changed regardless of a woman's marital status. This economic independence is based on Quranic principles, particularly the *zakat* teachings, which encourage women to own, invest, save, and distribute their earnings and savings at their discretion. It also recognizes and enforces the right of a women to participate in various economic activities. (7)

DECLINE OF MEDIEVAL SYSTEM OF WEALTH DISTRIBUTION

It is important to note how early Muslim women advocated justice, fostered mutual care, and promoted the public good by utilizing religious endowments (*waqf*) to widen the circle of beneficiaries. As it encompassed religious studies, education, financing for mosques, libraries, teacher salaries, student stipends, healthcare, hospitals and expenditure on patients, and apprenticeships, *waqf* played a significant role in sustainable development. It also included walks for pilgrimages, wedding expenditures for those who could not afford them, and animal welfare.[223]

According to Asli Sancar, Ottoman women amassed wealth through *waqf*, also known as "pious funds." In 1546 CE, 36 percent of the foundations in Istanbul were established by women. Over 26,000 *awqaf* (the plural of *waqf*) were established by Ottoman Muslims in Ankara, Turkey, of which 1,400 were run by Muslim women. According to Dr. Tamara Gray, Islamic law allowed a culture of women managing and investing their own money. Ottoman women established safe houses, *ribaats* for companionship, community, and spiritual growth. They also made cash business investments and formal loans, demonstrating their financial involvement in society. (163)

Understanding *waqf* is crucial to understanding how Islamic society functioned and how its downfall adversely affected women. Sumbul Ali Karamali explains that the destruction of the *waqf* system by colonial powers led to the financial dispossession of women in Muslim lands. This resulted in the disintegration of 50 percent of the economy and the arrest of Islamic legal education and development. The fall of the *waqf* system had a detrimental effect on *madrasas*, schools, charitable donations, and hospitals, many of which were supported financially by and for women. As many as half of all *waqf* founders were women, and even more *waqf* beneficiaries were female.[224]

REIMAGINING PARENTAL DIVISION OF LABOR

God ensures that wealth is not concentrated solely among men or the rich: *"As for gains granted by God to His Messenger from the people of 'other'* lands, they are for God and the Messenger, his close relatives, orphans, the poor, and 'needy' travelers so that wealth may not merely circulate among your rich" (Q 59:7). Through inheritance, gifts, and dower, women are guaranteed financial liquidity and independence, which they can use for productive means such as investments, social welfare, or in times of financial uncertainties.

The family is an important economic force and parents have the moral and legal responsibility to support their offspring to preserve the family unit. Most parents make sacrifices to provide their children with a better existence than they had. A mother will forgo her own self-interest to maintain her household and prevent the disintegration of her family. If a mother was paid "wages for housework," or had an opportunity to earn a living, her economic influence and standing in her family and community would be enhanced. She would be able to establish a bank account, invest her money, pursue business loans, and participate in public life. The Prophet, an ardent supporter of children, said, "The best dinar a man spends is that on his children, on his camel for the sake of God, and on his friends for the sake of God."[225]

There is no doubt that the Quran established equitable labor laws and the right to fair compensation for workers. Nevertheless, as we've seen in previous chapters, the division of labor has always favored men. If a wife relies solely on her spouse for her financial security, her life is constrained, preventing her from leading a fulfilling existence.

Ibn Khaldun (d. 1406 CE) highlighted the need for division of labor by stating that it is well-known and well-established that individual human beings are not by themselves capable of satisfying all their individual economic needs. They must cooperate for this purpose. The needs that can be satisfied by a group are many times greater than what individuals can satisfy by themselves.

Asghar Ali Engineer says women must play an increasingly greater role in a modern industrial economy. They must take up jobs to ensure a comfortable family life—remember, there is nothing in the Quran that prevents women from working. On the contrary, it says that whatever she earns (*ma kasabat*) is hers and hers alone.

There have been legislative developments in places such as the Shi'a community of Afghanistan. A woman could claim that she is entitled to a portion of her ex-husband's property as pay for the domestic duties she performed during the marriage. While in Iran, the Family

Protection Act of 2013, in accordance with the civil code, permits the court to order the husband to pay the wife "wages in kind" (*ujrat al-mithl*) for housework done during the marriage, based on a monetary value determined by the court, as long as the divorce is not her fault or the result of her actions.[226]

AUTONOMY AND FINANCIAL INDEPENDENCE

When a woman brings her own wealth to a marriage, her spouse does not have access to her matrimonial gift, property, and finances unless she gives him permission. The Prophet warned that nobody has the right to take even a penny without consent. Before, during, or after marriage, any assets (land, property, livestock, cash, gifts, and personal objects such as jewelry and vehicles) acquired by a woman through her labor or inheritance are solely hers. It is inaccessible to others, such as her brother, father, and spouse.

A *fatwa* issued by the Egyptian seminary Dar Al-Ifta Misriyyah discourages spouses from combining their possessions, whether it be money, property, or shares: "[I]t is not permissible for either spouse to control the other's financial dispositions under the marriage contract."[227] The wife should be free to use her finances to improve her family's living standard, invest her money to set up a business, create an endowment for charitable purposes, or carry out public works. Merged finances in a marriage—such as savings, investments, insurance, property, vehicles, and retirement accounts—may, on the other hand, limit the freedom that comes with making decisions about how, when, where, and for what purpose a woman can use her finances.

Many women are not socialized to be financially proactive. Financial literacy is essential for financial empowerment, particularly in societies dominated by men and where sociocultural values prohibit women from engaging in finances. But the mindset of wealth creation must be taught to women, beginning with how to break the habits of not handling money, not demanding reasonable wages, and being in perpetual debt. Financial literacy is vital for all demographics, especially rural, less educated women. Training must include mothers, teachers, and especially girls who pass on these values to future generations.

They must learn that wealth enables individuals and communities to live comfortably and independently, regardless of whether the immediate beneficiaries are individuals or small groups. They must learn the fundamentals of wealth, how it can be acquired (*muktasab*), circulated (*tadawul*), earned (*takassub*), or kept (*iddikhar*); how it is protected through guarantors (*takaful*) and trusteeship; how it is distributed through fixed portions, ownership, and endowments; and how it is purified through almsgiving and spent on doing good for the sake of God (*fi Sabillah lah*) without expectation of return (Q 92:18–20).

It is essential they understand the two fundamentals of wealth creation: ownership and income. Ownership is the basis of wealth formation. It consists of exclusive possessions from which the owner can derive profits for their sustenance, needs, and safety. Earning involves exerting oneself through physical labor or mutual consent with others. This is contingent on three primary factors: land (*ard*), labor (*amal*), and financial capital (*ra's al-mal*). Financial capital enables one to continue working to increase wealth. It consists of savings that are invested in a manner that generates profit and supports the continuation of work. Without sufficient financial resources, a worker might be unable to continue working, and her earnings would cease.

I recall my mother's mantra: "Stand on your own feet," a phrase she loved to repeat. Her dowry was her security. One day a local broker informed her that he had an almond grove to sell. "You must buy it—when spring comes, the whole orchard is covered with white blossoms and almonds. It comes with a well, which irrigates the land!" She went through her treasure chest and entrusted him with her heaviest gold bangle. I knew then that this revenue-generating almond grove was ours to keep. Each year, the orchard would produce fruit along with substantial profits. Years later, when the family required financial liquidity, the orchard was sold at a hundred-fold profit.

Muhammad Yunus describes a woman in Bangladesh who made stools out of bamboo and earned only two cents per day because she had to repay so much money to her bamboo supplier. If she had a dependable source of credit, Yunus thought, she and others in similar situations could make their way out of poverty. That idea, along with his conviction that "all human beings are born entrepreneurs," led him to found Grameen (meaning "village") Bank in 1983. The bank offered microcredit loans to poor women and cooperative groups. Grameen Bank played a big role as a catalyst for microcredit's huge expansion. Although it was one way to get people out of poverty in its heyday, financial experts now see it through a different lens: to expand options for poor people by offering more reliable financial services. Extremely poor people need these services just like everyone else, and the availability of capital to deal with irregular and, at times, unpredictable incomes is a huge help to them.[228]

CHALLENGING RELIGIOUS SANCTIONS

The deliberate denial of women's financial rights is the primary cause of the perception that women are financially illiterate and therefore unable to manage money. This contributes to their lack of confidence, resulting in their abandonment of financial management, which then negatively impacts their long-term well-being.

Fearing that it will undermine traditional family structures, conservative clerics oppose a larger role for women in finance. However, early Muslim women who raised children, managed the household, and actively participated in the marketplace disprove this theory. It is false and grossly exaggerated that a Muslim woman who works outside the home neglects her responsibilities as mother and homemaker. I know scores of successful, observant Muslim women who manage an impeccable household, care for their husband, and raise educated, productive, Muslim children—all while earning a living. They reconcile their professional and familial obligations through sacrifice and conviction.

As an example, Malaysian women are keenly aware that in Islam earning a living has nothing to do with gender. Malaysia is an Islamic country where women are generally observant. It is home to female Shariah scholars who authorize businesses to designate themselves as Shariah-compliant. Malaysia's Central Bank governor is a woman devoted to fostering the growth of Islamic finance, and Malaysia's Islamic institutions also feature women in executive positions. Fouzia Amanullah is the world's first female chief executive officer of an Islamic bank. Her tenure as CEO is possibly the longest tenure held by a woman CEO of an Islamic bank, not just in Malaysia, but throughout the world. But she remains an inconspicuous woman leader in the global Islamic financial services industry due to her focus on the job alone.[229]

According to Ibn al-Qayyim al-Jawziyyah, a jurist from the thirteenth century, there is no Shariah restriction preventing women from playing important roles in the development of Islamic finance at all levels. Likewise, many of Aisha's Shariah rulings are implemented into contemporary Islamic finance.[230]

Consider also the example of Sarah Al-Suhaimi, who chairs Saudi Arabia's stock exchange (*Tadawul*), with a market capitalization of $2.9 billion. This is over 1,400 years after Khadijah managed the largest trading business in Mecca. Al-Suhaimi's appointment and reappointment as chair in 2017 and 2020, respectively, demonstrate her business acumen. In 2014, she also became the first woman to head a Saudi investment bank, and she currently serves as the CEO of NCB Capital, the world's largest Shariah-compliant asset manager with over $50 billion in assets under management. Despite these strides in Islamic finance in the Gulf region, the under representation of women in leadership roles, reflects misconceptions and age-old prejudices.[231]

#20 | TO OWN PROPERTY

Shabana's forced marriage to an abusive older man was arranged by her family. Her brother forbade her from returning to the family house when she sought to escape from her husband and reclaim the property she had received from her father. Her brother told her she had no claim to their father's estate since he had not made a will. This is a common story among Indian Muslim women, where an overwhelming majority of 82 percent do not own property, and those who obtained it got it through their husbands rather than through inheritance, according to research conducted in 2015 by Bharatiya Muslim Mahila Andolan.

Before Islam, except for affluent women, most women in Arabia had no property rights. The Quran elevated the status of women by allowing them to buy, manage, and sell property and commodities regardless of their marital status: *"He has also caused you to take over their lands, homes, and wealth as well as lands you have not yet set foot on"* (Q 33:27).

Land is the earliest and most accessible source of wealth, as it is the source of trees, grain, pasturage, and water springs. It encompasses everything that humans can labor on, including oceans, rivers, minerals, and springs.[232] *"As for the earth, He spread it out as well, bringing forth its water and its pastures"* (Q 79:30-31).

According to Mariam M. Salasal, author of "The Concept of Land Ownership," land is a gift from God that should be used to its maximum potential, as stated in the Quran. Water, air, and sunshine are all God's property; in fact, everything in the universe, even the soil on which we stand, belongs to God: *"[T]o him belongs whatever's in the heavens and the earth..."* (Q 16:52). No one can claim absolute ownership over land, nor can they damage it, because "all land is ultimately held by God."[233]

Salasal states that land and property ownership are legally guaranteed to both men and women, so they can contribute to the prosperity of future generations and make the most of these privileges. *"He is the One Who smoothed out the earth for you, so move about it in its regions and eat from His provisions" (Q 67:15).*

Land ownership brings direct economic advantages by enabling people to apply their skills for productivity and products and wealth accumulation. This ownership generates income through food production, benefitting both humans and animals. It establishes financial stability, promotes a culture of long-term investments, and fosters collaboration among individuals and groups.[234] *"Let people then consider their food, how We pour down rain in abundance and meticulously split the earth open 'for sprouts,' causing grain to grow in it, as well as grapes and greens, and olives and date palm trees, and dense orchards and fruits and fodder—all as 'a means of' sustenance for you and your animals" (Q 80:24-32).*

EXAMPLES FROM THE PROPHET

The Quran empowers women with property rights, allowing them to purchase, manage, sell, mortgage, lease, borrow, lend, and execute legal contracts. *"There is a share for men and a share for women from what is left by parents and those nearest related, whether the property is small or large—a legal share" (Q 4:7).*

According to Miriam Salasal, ownership entails the right of free and exclusive use, modification, disposal, or destruction of the owned object. As ownership is a social institution, the right to ownership entails both advantages and disadvantages. Among the benefits are the enjoyment of profits, the freedom of the user, the right to file legal claims, and the right to be free of interference. These benefits must be earned by also attending to duties, liabilities, and disabilities.

During the Prophet's time, women inherited and owned property. On one occasion, two married women asked the Prophet if it was permissible for their husbands to be beneficiaries of their *zakat* (charity). "Yes," said the Prophet. *Zakat* is a duty and a consequence of ownership. Another time the Prophet was asked by a Meccan woman if her maternal aunt who was divorced was allowed to harvest the dates on her land. She complained that she was reprimanded for venturing out during the *idda* period. The Prophet replied, "Of course, she may pick dates from her palm trees, as she may give charity or perform an act of kindness."[235] The Prophet supported her right to provide for herself and use her wealth to benefit others.

According to Asghar Ali Engineer, a woman's right to own property is so absolute that even if she is rich she is under no obligation to spend anything from her property to support herself and her children. (64)

As illustrated here, humans believe they have the sole right to own, control, and decide the fate of their possession. Ibn Ashur relates a story from the Quran about the people of Madyan who felt so entitled to their wealth that they were shocked when Prophet Shu'ayb warned them about their unfair financial transactions. (281) *"Oh, my people! [D]o not defraud people of their property" (Q 11:85)*. They were astonished that he was attempting to put restrictions on their economic dealings, so they mocked him and rejected his appeal, saying, *"'O Shu'ayb! Does your prayer command you that we should abandon what our forefathers worshipped or give up managing our wealth as we please?" (Q 11:87)* (281)

WOMEN'S HISTORICAL ACQUISITION AND MANAGEMENT OF PROPERTY

Islamic law favors the equitable position of independent and separate contractual capacities of both husband and wife, allowing a woman to voluntarily enter or terminate a contract with her husband. Based on this, Ibn Masud, a companion of the Prophet, entered into a sale agreement with his wife Zaynab, who stipulated that if her husband (the buyer) decides to sell the item in the future, she will be the preferred buyer. The deal was presented to Caliph Umar bin Al-Khattab, who approved it without hesitation.[236]

The patterns of property endowments among Mumluk males (1250–1517 CE), as described by Leila Ahmed, show that fathers had deep bonds of affection with their daughters, sisters, and wives. Men often created *waqf* endowments for their female relatives and named them administrators without interference from husbands or male relatives. Their property and any income derived from it were solely for them. No one was permitted to sell, rent, or use a woman's property without her permission. If they did, they would be prosecuted in court. Al Masuna Tatarkhan's father appointed her administrator of an estate that included several hundred *fedans* of agricultural land, six townhouses, numerous stores, and other rental properties in Cairo. The fact that both Zaynab and Al Masuna were designated to receive and manage property suggests that men viewed them as capable of managing the responsibility. (106)

In the meantime, Ottoman women were active in the purchase, sale, and licensing of real estate, which provided them a substantial source of financial security. Asli Sancar mentions that in the seventeenth century, one-third of women in Bursa, Turkey, possessed their homes, according to state records. The court records of Kayseri reveal that "women of Kayseri accumulate an extraordinary amount of land and property in the city." For example, at least 40 percent of 1,602 land and property transfers involved at least one woman. (165)

Two more extraordinary medieval Muslim women stand out as brilliant examples of female agency and competence in property ownership and development. Despite living in separate eras and countries, Valide Sultan Bezm-I Alem Sultan and Mughal Princess Jahanara both left a lasting legacy via their property development.

Sancar describes Valide Sultan Bezm-I Alem Sultan, mother of Sultan Abdulmecid and wife of Mahmud II, who had an interest in architecture, and embarked on ambitious construction projects, such as the establishment of the Gureba Hospital in 1843, which provided care and support to the ill and poor. Another noteworthy gift was the founding of what is now known as Istanbul Girls High School, which she not only built in 1850, but where hundreds of books were left to improve the learning environment. Her architectural efforts did not stop there. She exhibited her devotion to infrastructure development by building the Galata Bridge in 1845, which provided a key link between different regions of the city. Her legacy lasted well beyond her death, as her burial place is in the tomb of her husband, Sultan Mahmud II, a tribute to her deep influence on the empire. (114)

In a different era and area, seventeenth-century Mughal Princess Jahanara had enormous authority in the Mughal court and used her position to build close relationships with other nations. Her vision and architectural aptitude allowed her to make a substantial contribution to the appearance of Shahjahanabad, the historical name of Delhi. Her imagination inspired her to commission the construction of five out of eighteen structures, all of which were designed by women. She built a beautiful *caravanserai*, or travel lodge, for tourists and traders and designed the main road in the walled city of Old Delhi, Chandni Chowk, which remains today.

These Muslim women each demonstrated an ability to acquire and manage property, showing their competence in developing, designing, and constructing. We honor the crucial role they played in shaping the history of Islamic civilization.

MISAPPROPRIATED GUIDANCE

Despite this legacy, the property rights of women are frequently violated. As we've seen, women's property is frequently registered under a man's name—her father, husband, or brother—making it more challenging for women to obtain legal ownership. This stems from the erroneous belief that men are the caretakers of women, which results in women being denied the right to own and use their property as they please. And, too often in Muslim cultures, it is thought to be shameful for females to obtain property, because their brothers have a greater financial responsibility to maintain the household. All of this is contrary to the Quran, which prohibits the exploitation and/or illegal hoarding of another person's property: *"Do not consume one another's wealth unjustly, nor deliberately bribe authorities in order to devour a portion of others property, knowing that it is a sin" (Q 2:188).*

During his farewell sermon, Prophet Mohammed emphasized: "Your lives and properties are forbidden to one another till you meet your lord on the day of resurrection." He strictly forbade the unjust acquisition of another person's property, arguing that it was a form of oppression, and equated the sanctity of human life with property ownership: "No doubt, your blood, and your properties are sacred to one another like the sanctity of this day of yours, in this month (*Dhul al-Hijjah*) of yours, in this town (*Makkah*) of yours."[237]

BLESSINGS AND RESPONSIBILITIES OF OWNERSHIP

According to Mariam Salsala, another aspect that Islam rejects is the monopolization of a gift bestowed by God. A gift must not be concentrated in the hands of a few. Unequal wealth distribution and accumulation by a small segment of Muslims is strictly forbidden.

The purpose of Shariah, according to Muhammad Ibn Ashur is to regulate property ownership to ensure its just distribution in the community as much as possible and to provide all the necessary means for its growth. The Quran mandates formal obligations and documentation to acquire wealth and property transparently and to avoid damage and disputes. (277) *"O believers! Do not devour one another's wealth illegally, but rather trade by mutual consent" (Q 4:29).*

Ibn Ashur shows why Shariah protects a person's wealth and private property. The advantages and usefulness of private property contribute to the public welfare. If women were denied the right to own property, they would be unable to contribute to the well-being of their community through the acquisition and expenditure of wealth. The owner has the right to use one's property so long as it does not harm, impede, or threaten the broader interests of society. The Quran states, *"Do not entrust the incapable 'among your dependents' with your wealth which God has made a means of support for you—but feed and clothe them from it and speak to them kindly" (Q 4:5).* The state has the authority to take receivership of the property if the owner is incapable of managing it, provided the owner is compensated fairly.

Maulana Muhammad Ali describes that ownership is gender-neutral, which includes all sorts of contractual ability. To protect the squandering of a gift from God the owner must be mature, and property must not be entrusted to the weak-minded or simpletons, even if they are lawful owners: *"Test the competence of the orphans until they reach marriageable age. Then if you feel they are capable of sound judgment, return their property to them" (Q 4:6).*

SuFaha are individuals who are intellectually deficient, have limited comprehension, or require assistance from others, according to the Quran. The community or state is urged not to grant *SuFaha* ownership because "their property" cannot function as a "means of support for them." Nevertheless, they are still to be supported by the property's revenues. Some scholars have incorrectly applied the term *SuFaha* to women. Ibn Jarir rejects the notion that women are *SuFaha*. It is incorrect to assume women are weak, deficient, and incapable of managing property.[238] The myth that women are immature or deficient, *SuFaha*, ignores the immense contribution made by Muslim women throughout history to own, manage, build, and sell properties all throughout the world.

I am a living example of the numerous advantages of property ownership. Owning a portfolio of rental properties has been a game changer for me because it generates consistent monthly cash flow that supports my livelihood and allows me to contribute to causes I care about and volunteer for. Property ownership provides considerable opportunity for many Muslim women to earn a living and achieve financial independence. It helps to maintain economic stability. Furthermore, as assets, property appreciates over time, bolstering long-term prosperity—which women need, just as do men. This makes it easier to secure loans and finance, expand a business, and contribute to an equal allocation of power within the family, allowing women to make important decisions about home, family, and the future.

Furthermore, owning a property raises a person's social standing and recognition within the family and community—which women need. This improved status can lead to increased confidence, allowing women to take on bigger challenges in other areas. The benefits of property ownership go well beyond monetary gain, improving lives and promoting equality and elevating the status of women around the world.

HIDDEN BARRIERS TO WOMEN'S OWNERSHIP

Over the centuries the privilege of women to property ownership has diminished rather than expanded. The manipulation of the Quran by those in authority has exacerbated this situation, leading to institutional dissonance. The root of the problem rests in laws that deny women property rights, a problem that is pronounced in countries like Pakistan, where remnants of colonial laws still predominate. The synthesis of Islamic and British law by male legislators has perpetuated the denial of property rights for women.

During the Ottoman and Mamluk eras, women asserted their property rights in court. In many modern legal systems, however, women's property rights are not sufficiently protected. In Iran, for example, the law may protect women's rights, but its enforcement is often lax, and discriminatory conditions persist due to the influence of tradition and social norms. Even though there are no legal restrictions on women's land ownership, the number of women landowners remains very low.

The Property Rights Index demonstrates that promoting women's economic activity, particularly their property rights, can result in tremendous economic growth. Considering this, Muslim nations must align their laws with the Quran's injunctions. When women have access to capital based on their assets, this will encourage them to establish their own businesses and enhance the lives of their families, particularly their children.

In 2020, Saudi Arabia took the leadership in this area. The Real Estate Development Fund (REDF) in Saudi Arabia has made mortgage loans available to 73,000 Saudi women, enabling them to realize their dream of property ownership. REDF's general supervisor Mansour bin Madhi has stated that the fund's strategy has always included allowing Saudi women to purchase their own home. This is because women make up half of Saudi society and are essential to rapid growth.[239]

EXAMPLE OF A UAE REAL ESTATE COMPANY EXECUTIVE

In 2014, Khadija Meziane El Otmani cofounded Driven Holiday Homes in the United Arab Emirates. She notes that, at first, she only recruited women since it was hard to find men who were willing to be supervised by women. "I felt that, especially in real estate, you needed to have a strong personality; you needed to be a hustler," she says. "Despite the fact that my family history is Arab, and my religion is Islam, I still had this bias."

Initially, she recognized those qualities most in the women she interviewed. Over time, her opinion evolved, and now the company has gender parity. But she continues to prioritize the needs of women in all aspects of her business. She reserved a section of an office for children and their parents to hang out and complete schoolwork throughout the day. She planned for the room to double as a nursing area for mothers employed there. However, because of the rapid expansion of her firm, her space was quickly appropriated for corporate use. Despite all this, a nursery is still at the top of her priority list.[240]

PART V

THE RIGHT TO YOUR LIFE

• • • • • • • • •

A woman has the right to move freely to advance her personal position and the social, political, and religious advancement of her community. Without social or legal coercion, she may express modesty through inner qualities and culturally acceptable outward expressions. She must be protected from intimate partner abuse and all forms of violence that endanger her life and the well-being of her family. Her body may not be mutilated, which would prevent her from exercising her conjugal rights. She has the right to live in peace and must never be coerced into nonconsensual sex; even within a marriage, she must not be stigmatized for sexual offenses committed against her, and she must never be compelled to marry a rapist. She must be protected from acts of human trafficking that violate her bodily autonomy and dignity and undermine the moral fabric of society. As a child bearer, she must receive prenatal care without stigma and have access to excellent hygiene to promote physical sanitation and spiritual purity.

These objectives aim to preserve not only the sanctity of life but also of the body:

- Human life, safety, and security are essential, or *daruriyyat*.
- Personal health, access to healthcare, and freedom of social mobility and expression are necessary, or *hajiyyat*.
- Having adequate rest, enjoyment, and recreation is complementary, or *tahsiniyyat*.

#21 | TO FREEDOM OF MOVEMENT

My father traveled to Kargil, Kashmir, to find out why the newly built girls' school had minimal enrollment. At midnight on his first night, he was awakened by quiet whispers outside his window. He saw ladies and girls carrying clothes to a drying line. Why would these women dry their clothes at night? "Out here, women's and girls' faces cannot be seen during the day," his host said when he inquired. Papa was confused. "Why are young girls subject to this rule?" he asked. His host continued shaking his head. "Unfortunately, every girl and woman in Kargil is required to observe strict *purdah*, a religious law that prevents them from leaving their home, isolating them from society as a whole. My father immediately understood why Shia girls were not in school.

In Islam, a woman is a legal person, spiritual being, social person, responsible agent, free citizen, and God's servant. She has the right to move freely to pursue her interests and utilize her skills in all spheres of human endeavour.[241] *"Indeed, we have honored the children of Adam, carried them on land and sea, granted them good and lawful provisions, and privileged them far above many of Our creatures" (Q 17:70)*.

In 622 CE, the Prophet's migration from Mecca to Medina was crucial for the survival of early Muslims. Many of the Prophet's followers were women. They put their lives at risk to help establish the community of believers. Without their husbands or families, they travelled long distances to pledge allegiance (*bayah*), to their new spiritual leader, the Prophet *(Q 2:218)*. Their participation in the Hijrah strengthened the followers as they traveled to transmit knowledge and aid in the moral and religious development of new Muslims. In collaboration with men, they were able to build a thriving community in Medina.

When Umm Salama, the Prophet's wife, complained to him that the Quran mentions men's participation in the Hijrah migration but never women. In response, a verse was revealed to demonstrate that

God equally values the devotion and dedication of women to his cause: *"Those who have believed, emigrated and strived in the cause of God, with their wealth and their lives are greater in rank in the sight of God, It is they who will triumph" (Q 9:20).*

Mahnaz Afkhami states that women pledged their *bayah* to the Prophet, at the first and second Aqabah Conference (Bayat al-Aqaba al Awla wa'l-Thaniyya), which is believed to have been the foundation of the Islamic state in Yatrib (Medina). (61) A group of Muslim women, including a young woman named Um Kulthum bint Uqba bin Abu Muait traveled to meet the Prophet. When Um Kulthum's family requested that the Prophet return her to them, he refused to break her resolve, as she had traveled a considerable distance. He acknowledged her determination and allowed her to remain.[242]

EARLY MUSLIM WOMEN CIRCULATING IN SOCIETY

Early Muslim women were not confined to the home, according to Amira Abou-Taleb; they advanced society by freely moving and engaging in political, social, and religious activities. Male-female interaction was so common in Mecca that it once spared the Prophet's life. Raqiqa bint Abu Sayfi forewarned the Prophet that the Quraysh planned to assassinate him one night, which allowed the Prophet to evade the attempt. While the Prophet fled, Ali ibn Abi Talib slept in his place, thereby sparing his life. (195)

On another occasion, when the Prophet was secretly preaching, Sumayyah bint Khayyat, an imposing Yemeni enslaved woman, answered his call. She began publicly spreading the Prophet's message, urging women not to tolerate female infanticide and encouraging enslaved individuals to think for themselves. Her message, which incited defiance among the slaves, infuriated her master, Ammar, who was enraged by her disobedience and tortured her. One day while he was berating her while staring down at her bound body, she responded, "[Y]ou cannot control my mind and my heart, which belonged to me and my creator, as does my body." He seized a spear and plunged it with such force that it pierced her heart. Summaya thus achieved the distinction of being Islam's first martyr!

In response to Sumayyah's martyrdom, the Prophet received this Revelation: *"Never say that those martyred in the cause of God are dead—in fact, they are alive! But you do not perceive it" (Q 2:154).* Jebara describes how with these words the Prophet invoked the words *akhira,* (afterlife) suggesting that, though people like Sumaya may die, their investment would yield a valuable return. The true benefit of one's deeds may emerge only many years later, or after death. (139)

Many other women joined the Prophet's movement, among them Barakah bint Tha'alaba, also known as Umm Ayman, who was his one constant companion since birth and throughout his entire life. She helped the vulnerable orphan make sense of the tragedies in his life and taught him to persevere despite the bleak odds. Imam Al-Halbi, in his As-Sirat-ul-Halabiyyah, notes that "Um Ayman [Barakah] was a crucial eyewitness"—a woman present throughout the Prophet's life, including the scenes of his birth and death. Barakah would be just one of many strong female mentors and supporters who propelled the future prophet.[243]

There was also Nusayba bint al-Harith, known sometimes as Umm Atiyya, a jurist who fought alongside the Prophet in numerous battles. Also, during times of war, skilled nurse Rufaidah bint Sa'ad established the first makeshift clinic to treat the wounded. Khawla bint al-Azwar and Nusayba bint Kaab al-Ansariyyah were renowned for their excellent fighting skills—both took part in fighting alongside men.

The list of courageous women goes on. Umm' Umarah devoted herself to the Prophet. She participated in seven battles. She would remain in the men's compound to prepare their meals, heal their wounds, and care for the sick. The Prophet hailed her, saying, "She fought on every front, was present everywhere, at the mosque, on the battlefield. She was always present when duty demanded."[244]

THE PARADOX OF PROTECTION THROUGH CONFINEMENT

Years later, jurists who, apparently concerned for the safety of women, developed rulings restricting their mobility. These new laws required women travelers to be accompanied by a *mahram* (near male relative). And as this practice gained traction and became the norm, it reversed longstanding traditions of women being completely engaged to being viewed as defenseless beings needing male protection.[245]

According to Asma Lamrabet, women are frequently framed as fragile and vulnerable, which perpetuates the notion that they require a *mahram* outside the home. She says it is quite common to find books that compare a Muslim woman to a pearl, or a gem in a jewelry box, or a flower that must be protected, defended, and saved from an eternal external enemy, which Quran does not mention. Even if she is sealed up or imprisoned, it is always supposedly for her own good.

Hoda El-Saadi states that some jurists who portrayed women as treacherous and dangerous needed to control them to safeguard society from the temptations they posed. They limited their interactions with men in public spaces and set conditions for women's presence in the public sphere: women were only permitted to walk the streets early in the morning at dawn or late at night, when darkness concealed them. (265)

Khaled Abou El Fadl explains how the notion of *fitnah* and temptation resulted in the exclusion of women from society; the men who place these restrictions on women rely on the dubious logic that women should pay the price for men's impious failures. To prevent *fitnah*, women's education, mobility, safety, and religious freedom are sacrificed. Under the guise of *fitnah*, women are banned from driving, working, serving in the military, or appearing in public life.

Those who restrict women from leaving their homes without a *mahram* use this verse: *"Settle in your homes, and do not display yourselves as women did in the days of 'pre-Islamic' ignorance" (Q 33:33)*. But this passage does not apply to all women; it solely relates to the Prophet's wives, and the Quran explicitly states that "the wives are not like any other woman."[246]

Barbara Stowasser describes how the directive of "Stay in your houses" for the wives came to have broader meaning such as (1) strutting, prance; (2) flirting, coquettishness; or (3) embellishment, the showing of the refinery, the flaunting of bodily charms, as was practiced by women before Abraham's prophethood. Domesticity was defined as the core of female righteousness, the crucial criterion of a Muslim woman's true citizenship in her faith community. (98)

THE FIRST CIVIL WAR WAGED BY AISHA

Amira Abou-Taleb describes how the biographer Ibn Sa'd (d. 845 CE) omitted information from text depicting the Prophet's wives as having strong individual traits and being publicly engaged. He excluded Aisha's camel battle from his seventeen-page account of her, focusing instead on her regrets and shortcomings. (201) Many men who restrict women's mobility today have been influenced by male scholars' bias against women's participation in public and political events. The historical and contemporary significance of Aisha's public engagement compels us to consider Aisha's story not from reports written about her but from the accounts of her lived experience.

In "Aisha's Corrective of the Companions," Sofia Abdur Rehman describes how Aisha is a historical figure, a signifier for the ideal Muslim woman, meaning that her story is not only told by the events of what occurred in her life and how she responded to each, but it is also influenced by the external needs those stories could fulfill in developing a narrative for Muslim women seeking a model of Muslimah piety. In her life experiences, however, she occasionally exhibits traits and behaviors she is not intended to model.

As the most prominent wife of the Prophet, she did not always publicly confine herself to her home; when falsely accused of adultery, she was vulnerable, yet was a paragon of composure and strength. She left her husband's home and maintained her innocence for which she was exonerated through divine intervention. When political issues arose between Uthman and his people, she held him to account with authority. She was a dutiful person, not a rebellious one, yet she raised an army against Caliph Ali. She did not oppose male authority, yet her home was a center for gathering those who were disgruntled by Uthman's caliphate.

In retaliation for Caliph Ali's alleged failure to avenge the murder of Caliph Uthman, Aisha left the private, internal, domestic sphere of the home and entered the public/political sphere, organizing a military campaign against him. She made all strategic and crucial decisions regarding recruitment of soldiers. She spent the entire day of the battle alternating between reciting the Quran and poetry to bolster the morale of her soldiers and encourage them to continue fighting. When she lost the battle, she took her defeat gracefully. Despite this, her political and military legacy has continued to be the subject of contentious debate throughout the history of the development of Islam, focusing squarely on her gender.

Sophia Abdur Rehman describes how these incidents reveal Aisha's strength, independence, autonomy, unwavering faith, sense of justice, participation in public life, and the merging of the public and domestic spheres. Even though the battle ended in a disaster, her willingness to take risks while placing her own life in danger would have been sufficient for men in a similar situation to be hailed as heroes. Unfortunately, her voice got drowned out by the potent assertion of the ideal devout Muslim woman that Aisha is perceived to represent and the politically contradictory arguments of the Sunni-Shia divide.[247]

RESTRICTING LONG DISTANCE TRAVEL

During my April 2022 trip to Afghanistan, I was disappointed to discover that the Taliban had issued a fresh decree prohibiting women from leaving their homes without a *mahram*. This disrupted the careers and livelihoods of millions of Afghan women from all social classes. Up until the Taliban takeover of the country, for instance, it was common for women to work and attend school and university. When I asked a group of women why they adhered to this decree, they cited Aisha's failed attempt and the need to observe a hadith.

So, I researched the hadith, which states, "It is not lawful for a believing woman to undertake a journey extending over a day and a night except when there is a *mahram* with her."[248] In another hadith, the Prophet said, "A woman should not travel for more than three days except with a Mahram."[249] This refers to the duration of the journey, not the distance traveled. A woman should have a *mahram* to guarantee her safety, not to confine her to her household, as advised by the Prophet. It was clear that the safety of women was the primary concern, as they would face many dangers if they traveled on camels or horses across deserts and roads. It was normal for travelers, in previous centuries, both male and female, to be plundered by outlaws or harassed by men with ill intentions.

I contacted Dr. Basma Abdelgafar, an eminent Shariah scholar, to provide an explanation of the hadith. She stated that it had a specific context, and the Prophet said that the journey should not take more than three days. Scholars calculated a journey lasting a day and a night which would encompass a minimum distance of seventy-five kilometers.

Other scholars, according to Dr. Abdelgafar, permit a woman to travel without a *mahram* if she is safe during her journey. She could travel in a group, similar to the Hajj in Saudi Arabia. Al-Hassan Al-Basri, Al-Awza'i, Ibn Hazm, and the Shi'i school hold this view. She also cited a hadith by Adi ibn Hatem AL-Tai that is routinely ignored by scholars, in which the Prophet predicted that one day a woman would travel alone on her camel from Hira (in Iraq) to Mecca to perform Hajj with no one protecting her. Adi, upon hearing the hadith, remarked, "I lived until I have witnessed that."[250] In addition, she stated that some Hanbali scholars, such as Ibn Muflih and Ibn Taymiyyah, asserted that a woman could perform Hajj or travel for lawful purposes on her own if she was secure.[251]

The hadith used by the Taliban to restrict women's movement in Afghanistan today is intended for lengthy journeys, not city travel. When I asked a Taliban member what they had done for the Afghan people, they replied, "Afghans can now travel from Kabul to Kandahar without fear because their safety is guaranteed." I responded, "Since your takeover, you have ensured the safety of all Afghans, which means Afghan women can travel freely to fulfill their responsibilities and meet their daily needs without fear." I got a nod and a grin.

OTHER HISTORICAL RESTRICTIONS

From the ninth century to the seventeenth, visiting gravesites was popular among Muslims, requiring women's prolonged absences from home and high levels of public visibility. When certain scholars in Egypt complained about their inability to exert control over these activities, they forbade women from visiting graveyards and shrines.[252]

The most common argument in support of such religious laws is that women are too emotional and are prone to uncontrollable sobbing at the death of a loved one. It is true that the Prophet wished to eliminate the pre-Islamic practice in which grieving women would excessively lament, weep, or strike themselves. Consequently, he prohibited the practice of mourning at burials and even visiting graves.[253] But when he was moved by his own experience of visiting his mother's grave, he changed his stance, saying, "I requested God for permission to visit my mother's grave, and when he granted me permission, I tell you, visit graves, for it makes you mindful of death."[254]

The general rule for legal commands is that they apply equally to both genders. Even though this hadith is addressed to all his followers, there were differing opinions among scholars regarding the presence of women at burials. In the forty-five-volume *al-Mawsu'a al-Fiqhiyya*, published by the Kuwaiti Ministry of Endowments, the views of differing scholars are presented. The Hanafis prohibitively discourage it; the Shafis moderately discourage it; the Malikis permit it where there is no fear of *fitna*; and the Hanbalis moderately discourage it. Therefore, prohibiting women from attending burials is a minority view. Even Aisha clarified what the Prophet meant: he never said that God would punish the believer because of the weeping (of any one of the members of his family) but said that God would increase the punishment of the unbeliever because of the weeping of his family over him. She concluded that the Quran is enough for you when it states: *"No soul burdened with sin will bear the burden of another" (Q 6:164).*[255]

These restrictions are so ingrained that women living in the West are routinely excluded from public religious activities and rituals. Sarah, a New York-based attorney, encountered deep trauma at her mother's burial, which was organized by a local mosque. As Sarah approached the cemetery, she observed that none of the community's women were present at the funeral. When her mother's corpse was about to be lowered into the grave, she stepped forward with her sons to get a last glimpse of her mother.

An unknown Muslim man shoved Sarah and the boys aside with force. Sarah exclaimed, "That is MY mother!" The individual stood in front of the grave with his arms crossed, obstructing their view. Gibran, the nine-year-old son of Sarah, rapidly formed an opinion regarding Islam: "Mom, Islam is very sexist." Sarah worried for her son, immediately brought Gibran to speak to me. After listening and taking in the surroundings, Gibran realized that his first impression was based on a single unpleasant experience, which did not reflect the Islam practiced by billions worldwide.

PIONEERING WOMEN

While it is true that women's mobility is still restricted in some societies, it is essential to demonstrate that Islam does not support these restrictions. In the annals of Islamic history, there were women who left an indelible mark through their courage and tenacity. They demonstrate that a woman's place is not simply in the home or alongside a *mahram but in every sphere of society.*

Mernissi provides an account of Sukayna bint-al-Husayn, (b. 671 CE) a member of the ahl al-Bayt. Sukayna, great-granddaughter of the Prophet, endured numerous tribulations following the tragic martyrdom of her father, Hussain, and her husband in Karbala. She did not, however, allow her losses to dampen her spirits. The most powerful men debated with her; Caliphs and princes proposed marriage to her, which she disdained for political reasons. Nevertheless, she ended up marrying five or six husbands. When the grandson of Uthman bin Affan, Zayd bint Umar, proposed marriage to her, Sukayna accepted the proposal, stipulating three conditions: she would not obey her husband, she would do as she pleased, and a monogamous marriage. She challenged the prevalent norms with her demand and continued meetings with poets, attending meetings of the Qurashi tribal councils, the equivalent of today's democratic municipal councils. She exemplified the spirit of an independent woman. (192)

Centuries later, Lalla Aicha bint Ali was forced to abandon Spain with her family as a child during a period in which Muslims were compelled to convert to Catholicism. Aicha settled in Morocco and married the Tetouan governor. After his death, she assumed his responsibilities and was given the title Sayyida al-Hurra, or "free and independent noblewoman." However, Aicha's ambitions extended beyond the position of governor. Eventually, she expanded her power, took to the seas, and became one of the most powerful pirates in the Mediterranean. She seized a large number of Spanish and Portuguese captives and used them as leverage against those who persecuted Muslims.[256]

In the meantime, Queen Amina of Zaria became a legend in northern Nigeria. Amina, renowned for her military acumen and strategic ingenuity, led the expansion of Zazzau beyond its borders. Her military victories resulted in the construction of fortified walls known as ganuwar "Amina's wall," which protected the city from ruthless enemies. Amina's success as a conqueror led to widespread recognition; she was considered as capable as a man in terms of competence and political acumen.

Another formidable historical figure was Chand Bibi, the "Invincible Lady of Ahmadnagar." After marrying the Sultan of Bejapur, Ali Adil Shah, Chand Bibi's advice on governance and military affairs proved invaluable. Her influence drew the ire of males who resented her authority, which ultimately led to her husband's death. She departed Bejapur and moved to her brother's capital of Ahmadnagar. In 1594, following his death, she defended Ahmadnagar against the Mughals. Chand Bibi withstood gunfire and stone attacks while wearing a *burqa*.

She displayed unwavering courage by spending the entire night repairing a fissure in the city's walls. Her bravery and will prevented the Mughals from capturing Ahmadnagar.

THE TREND OF EMPOWERED WOMEN

Mobility and autonomy are interconnected. Restricting women's movements has personal and societal effects. It perpetuates gender stereotypes and makes women more vulnerable to abuse as they become dependent on male family members for all decision-making. Seclusion at home isolates women from community, prevents them from earning a living, and keeps them from participating in religious services and social activities.

As evidenced by the profiles of early Muslim women, an honorable woman is one whose actions benefit both herself and her community. Freedom of movement is essential for the pursuit of knowledge, participation in civic life, and fulfillment of religious duties. Before 2021, a higher percentage of Afghan women served in parliament and law enforcement than did women in the United States. But currently, Afghan women are subject to severe restrictions on freedom of movement, employment, education, and recreation, limiting quality of life and ambition to pursue other life objectives. If they cannot access religious and public spaces such as *madrasas*, mosques, universities, hospitals, and voting stations, they cannot positively impact themselves or their society.

Muslim women over the last 1,400 years have played a crucial role in the evolution of their communities, influencing Islamic ideas, practices, and movements, yet their contributions are frequently overlooked.[257] As we review the *fiqh* literature of the past, we see many incoherent legal positions that prevent women from having equal access to spiritual spaces for fear of *fitnah*, despite the fact that women interact with the opposite sex working on farms, in the office, at shopping malls, marketplaces, going to cinema, attending universities, joining social gatherings like weddings, and so on. Most of these spaces are not segregated, and *fitnah* is most likely to occur in spaces when God-consciousness is at its lowest.

Today, scores of women are contributing to the productivity, prosperity, and economic development of their nations despite these obstacles. They have excelled in a variety of fields, such as navigating aircraft across continents, serving as astronauts on space exploration missions, and leading nations; however, this would not be feasible if they remained secluded in the inner sanctum of their homes.

We require a balanced *fiqh* that allows both men and women to participate in spiritual, social, and political activities while maintaining a modest Islamic ethos, so that spiritual deeds denied to women do not negatively affect the rest of their lives. We must not restrict spiritual and personal development—we must foster it.

Consider Yassmin Abdel-Magied in Britain, who has a peculiar and singular ambition: to become the first female Muslim Formula One racing driver. "Everyone thought it was a passing phase," she says with a chuckle. But that is not the case. Six years ago, while watching a movie, Yassmin became obsessed with fast vehicles, and she hasn't ceased fantasizing about them ever since. She prefers Ferraris, but any muscle car will suffice. For example, the Corvette Sting Ray from the 1960s. Abdel-Magied exclaims, "It's fantastic!" She acknowledges that people are sometimes startled to hear this kind of bravado from a conservatively dressed Muslim woman who immigrated from Sudan with her parents as an infant and attended a Brisbane Islamic school during her formative years. However, Abdel-Magied appears to enjoy defying stereotypes. She is clearly a Muslim woman on the move.[258]

#22 | TO EXPRESSION OF MODESTY

In September 2022 there was a global outcry when twenty-two-year-old Mahsa Amini, a Kurdish Iranian woman, was detained by Iran's morality police on accusations of wearing *hijab* improperly. While in captivity, she was beaten by the police and suffered head injuries resulting in her senseless death on September 16, 2022. This sparked outrage among women, igniting widespread demonstrations across Iran and around the world. Younger women born after the revolution, who had been indoctrinated from childhood to accept *hijab* as a supreme Islamic value, pushed back. Some were seen burning their *hijabs* and cutting their hair as resistance against the regime's "best *hijab* policy." Amini's death resulted in forty-one protestors and security personnel dying, yet the regime has failed to produce any Islamic juridical arguments in defense of the policy for enforcing morality.

The Quran ranks modesty alongside the virtues of truthfulness, charity, prayer, and fasting. Although the Quran instructs believers to cover their private parts with clothing, it emphasizes that righteousness is the best garment. *"O children of Adam! We have provided for you clothing to cover your nakedness as an adornment. However, the best clothing is righteousness"* (Q 7:26).

The term for modesty is *hayaa*, derived from the word for life, *hayat*, and signifies a virtuous way of being, respecting both oneself and others. Having *hayaa* promotes decency and opposes self-objectification. *Hayaa* is both internal and external; inward modesty entails avoiding traits and qualities that displease God, while outward modesty involves behaving courteously, speaking respectfully, and involves not revealing oneself to illicit sexual advances.

According to Asma Barlas, the Quran does not indicate that the body is sinful, but it does establish that private parts are designed to arouse desire, and hence God emphasizes the significance of covering them to avoid unwanted sexual advances. (45) But it gives no description of private parts or "nakedness" that Adam and Eve covered with leaves: *"[T]heir nakedness was exposed to them, prompting them to cover themselves with leaves from paradise" (Q 7:20).*

This divergence in viewpoints regarding the definition of a person's private parts or erogenous zones is shaped by the cultural, customary, and normative practices unique to each society. Among more conservative scholars, there exists a notion designating a women's entire body as the private part, *awrah*, likening it to a vulnerable space, like a house without walls, which is vulnerable to theft. They advocate for full coverage and a detailed dress code for the entire body, excluding the face and limbs or feet. Other scholars advocate for custom and culture in defining the appropriate coverage for men and women. Rather than prescribing a specific dress code, they emphasize generalized modesty, leaving room for individuals to draw upon their culture and personal conscience to decide.

EMBRACING MODESTY AND GAZING WITH HUMILITY

In pre-Islamic Arabia, women did not dress appropriately; they wore scant clothing, flaunted their ornaments, and some were sexually harassed by men when they left their homes. When Muslim women were harassed by men, they complained to the Prophet and God revealed this command to women to adopt new social norms that stop men from accosting women: *"O Prophet! Ask your wives, daughters, and the 'believing' women to draw their cloaks (jilbab) over their bodies. In this way, it is more likely that they will be recognized as virtuous and not harassed" (Q 33:59).*

In his book, *Hijab or Niqab: An Islamic Critique of the Face Veil*, Syed Mutawalli Ad-Darsh states that the Quran sought to remedy this social malady by warning people that a new decency standard with a distinct code of conduct in public life was now in full force. A concealed woman could be identified as a virtuous woman and not molested because they would never mistakenly be identified as "available."[259]

The Prophet promoted the new modesty norm: "Every religion has an innate character, and the character of Islam is modesty."[260] Another verse detailed the framework of modesty with both genders lowering their gaze, women not attracting attention by displaying their adornments and covering their body and their bosom: *"Tell the believing men* to lower their gaze and guard their chastity, and not to reveal their adornments, except what normally appears. Let them draw their veils over their chest, and not reveal their hidden ornaments except to their husbands, fathers, sons. Let them not stomp their feet, drawing attention to their hidden ornaments" (Q 24:31).

After this Revelation, it became forbidden for men and women to look at the other with passion or desire. This is demonstrated by the Prophet when he was riding and a handsome man, Al-Fadl Ibn Abbas, was behind him. On their way, they encountered a beautiful woman from the tribe of Khatham. Al-Fadl kept staring at her, captivated by her beauty. The Prophet kept averting his face away, fearing seduction would develop between two young people.

Ibn al-Kattan, a Hadith scholar (d. 1231 CE), said that it is permissible to look when there is no fear of seduction or desire. Other scholars state that if the social morality of a country has advanced to the point where women leaving their homes are not teased or harassed, the initial reason for requiring women to wear a long outer garment dissipates. (89)

The mention of "adornment" in verse 24:31 is in a specific historical context of women of ill repute wearing ankle bracelets that chimed as they walked. This was apparently a form of advertising for their services. As Medina was rife with prostitution, the Quran cautioned women not to flaunt themselves and be misconstrued for adulterous behavior. Over time, the "adornments" have been described differently. Some Quran commentaries state that an adornment is hair, body shape, and underclothes, while "hidden adornments" are hair, arms, and legs. Still other scholars say it is the beauty of the body, and al-Razi (b. 865 CE) refers to it exclusively as external ornaments, citing the last part of the verse, "Let them not stomp their feet, drawing attention to their hidden adornments."

Whether or not this report is historical, the reference to leg-stomping and not wearing revealing ornaments is intended to teach modesty and not attract unwanted attention. Jasser Auda cites this verse, "*O Children of Adam! take your adornments at every mosque*" (Q 7:31), as a reminder to Muslims that arriving at the mosque dressed appropriately is also a directive, highlighting the importance of intention: to draw closer to God, not to man. (88)

Some scholars view applying perfume in public as a form of adornment as it can be an aphrodisiac. The Prophet taught his sister-in-law Asma how to perform ablution and apply musk to smell good. But he cautioned her against wearing excessive amounts, as it could attract the attention of men and arouse desires through the fragrance. (88)

The meaning of "except what normally appears," in 24:31 according to Ibn Kathir and Ibn Masud it means clothes, which women might be wearing. Ibn Umar says it means face, hands, and rings; and Ibn Abbas says it could mean eye paint, signets, or hand paint.

FORBIDDEN DRESS: UNDERSTANDING SARTORIAL DETAILS

Women are commanded to use their *khimar* to conceal their chests (*juyub*): "[L]et them draw their veils over their chests, and not reveal their hidden ornaments, except to their husbands, fathers, sons" (Q 24:31). Sarah Mainuddin, author of *Demystifying the Niqab*, states that during the time of the Prophet women wore an ornamental piece of cloth that trailed down the back of their heads, and their tunics were open, sometimes exposing their bust. The word *khimar* can refer to a variety of cloth worn on the head or neck, such as a woman's shirt, blouse, shawl, or a man's turban, or other clothing.[261]

Scholars who believe that a women should cover their body, head, and hair interpret that the *khimar*, which needed to cover the bust, was presumably used as a head covering during that time. To understand this, it is essential to comprehend what a *khimar* is and what was it intended to cover. An American Muslim woman consulted an eminent jurist, Khaled Abou El Fadl, for further clarification on this topic. He responded with "Fatwa: On Hijab (the Hair-Covering of Women)," in which he sought to clarify that both schools of thought—the one that views *khimar* as covering the face, and the other which says *khimar* covers the hair and not the face—are ahistorical because they assume the existence of an unproven historical practice. There is no evidence that the *khimar* in pre-Islamic Hijaz concealed the face or hair. In Q 24:31 Muslim women were commanded to draw a piece of cloth (*khimar*) over the bosom (*juyub*), but whether the cloth also covered the hair or face is unknown. Anything further would necessitate extensive research into the social practices of *khimar* attire at the time of the Revelation. Abou El Fadl explains in his *fatwa* the relationship between *khimar* and adultery (*zina*), stating that modesty requires not displaying *zina* (i.e. immodest dress or behaviour that goes against the Islamic principles of modesty and decency) in front of people with permissible relationships, such as a husband, father, son, and that the *khimar* should cover the bosom.

Abou El Fadl also states that the historical practice of the first generation of Muslims was considerably more nuanced than what contemporary writers presume it to be. There are reports of women in the Hijaz, shortly after the death of the Prophet, not covering their hair in public. Sakinah bint al-Usayn bin 'Al, a member of the Ahl-ul Bayt and the Prophet's great-granddaughter, invented a hairdo or style known as al-ṭurrah al-Sukayniyyah (Sukaynah-style curls) that she wore in public. She refused to cover her hair and is reported to have been imitated by the noble women of the Hijaz. On the other hand, some women, such as Khawlah bint al-Azwar, one of the greatest warriors, fought against the Byzantines and rescued her brother from their armies while wearing a face veil. The Byzantine emperor even offered to marry her.[262]

Ziba Mir-Hosseini, author of "Hijab and Choice: Between Politics and Theology," explains that the *fiqh* texts that establish rulings (*ahkam*), or what we can term "positive law," contain no explicit rulings on women's dress or on how women should appear in public. They do not use the term *hijab* and instead use the term for covering (*sitr*) to discuss the issue of dress for both men and women, and only in two contexts: rulings for covering the body during prayers, and rulings that govern a man's "gaze" at a woman before marriage.[263]

Ayatollah Morteza Montazeri stated that hair covering is not obligatory (*vajeb*), but rather is recommended (*mostahah*), since the Quranic verses and traditions do not imply obligation but rather recommendation. He provided several arguments for his view, among which is the obligation for men and women to cover the *awrah*. However, since there is no consensus among jurists regarding what constitutes *awrah* in women, or whether it encompasses her hair, neither definition can be definitively determined.

THE SANCTITY OF PRIVATE PARTS

One hadith cited over five verses (33:53, 7:46, 19:16, 41:5, 42:51) to promote a form of dress that exposes a woman's hands, face, and feet is the story of the Prophet's sister-in-law, Asma, who inadvertently wore a see-through dress in front of the Prophet. Instead of reprimanding her, he told her, "O Asma, when a woman reaches the age of menstruation, it does not suit her that she displays her parts of the body except this and this, and he pointed to her face and hands."[264]

According to Khaled Abou El Fadel, this hadith has been the subject of substantial debate; at the very least, its chain of transmission is problematic. How can working women conceal their faces or wrists without difficulty? According to him, how can women cover their faces or hands without hardship while working? Her face, hair, and hands are not *awrah*. Her feet are not *awrah*, especially for poorer women who cannot afford to cover their feet with shoes or socks. Working women were not required to cover their hair or face if wearing a veil stopped them from earning a wage or if wearing a veil while working could cause harm to them. Given these factors, the early scholars disagreed with the rest.

ORNAMENTATION OR SELF-OBJECTIFICATION

In *verse 33:33*, Quran commands the Prophet's wives to *"Settle in your homes, and do not display yourself (tabarruj) as women did in the days of pre-Islamic ignorance."* Mahnaz Afkhami cites a prominent scholar Nazira Zin al-Din, who states that when God ordered the wives to observe hijab for special reasons related to the Prophet's household, God, as if fearing that Muslim women might imitate the wives, stressed *"O wives of the Prophet! you are not like any other women"* (Q 33:32)—thus, according to Nazira Zin al-Din it is clear that God did not want us to measure ourselves against the wives of the Prophet and wear hijabs like them. There is no ambiguity whatsoever regarding this verse. (72)

Barbara Stowasser describes how this verse directed at the wives got applied to all women and how *tabarruj* was expanded to a woman's public display of her physical self, including her unrestricted gait and wearing revealing garments that displayed physical features, ornaments, and cosmetics, among other things. Today, *tabarruj* includes everything from uncovered hair to elaborate salon-style hairstyles, hairpieces, and wigs; facial foundation, powder, blush, lip color, and mascara; manicures and enamel. It also includes all Western apparel in general, specifically if it is haute couture or aims to be fashionable in the Western sense. While the exact definition of *tabarruj* has evolved over time, its condemnation by custodians of communal morality has always included the Quranic reference that it is un-Islamic, a matter of *jahiliyyah (33:33)*, and therefore a threat to Islamic society. (98)

HIJAB INSTILS GOOD MALE MANNERS

Although the word *hijab* is commonly referred to as a women's headscarf, in none of the verses below does the word indicate clothing—a veil, scarf, headdress, or any other form of dress for women. *Hijab* is mentioned seven times in the Quran, twice as *hijaban* and five times as *hijab*, where it is described as a screen, covering, partition, division, mantle, curtain, drape or divide, a barrier: *"There will be a barrier between Paradise and Hell" (Q 7:46); "Maryam withdrew herself, [S]creening herself from them" (Q 19:17);* and *"[T]here is a barrier between us and you" (Q 41:5).*

Fatima Mernissi gives a detailed explanation of the *hijab* verse, *"[A]sk them from behind the barrier,"* (Q 7:46) revealed in 627 CE on the Prophet's wedding night to Zaynab. It was late at night and some tactless male guests were engrossed in conversation. The Prophet was a public figure, an arbitrator of conflict who was accustomed to tolerating crude, boorish men. However, he was at a loss for what to do in this case. The Quran, which was anchored in the Prophet's and his community's everyday lives, often had a response to a given situation.

This incident was seen by Anas ibn Malik. He added that when the three men departed, just as the Prophet entered his chamber, he drew a curtain between himself and Anas to safeguard his privacy, and this verse was revealed to him: *"[B]ut if you are invited, then enter 'on time.' Once you have eaten, then go on your way, and do not stay for casual talk. Such behavior is truly annoying to the Prophet, yet he is too shy to ask you to leave...and when you believers ask his wives for something, ask them from behind a barrier. This is purer for your hearts and theirs. And it is not right for you to annoy the Messenger of God, nor ever marry his wives after him. This would certainly be a major offense in the sight of God" (Q 33:53).*

Mernissi states that the verse instructs men to speak with the Prophet's wives from behind a screen, or *hijab*. This may have occurred because some men inappropriately saw a wife. She emphasizes the significance of the verse containing God's prohibition on Muslim men marrying the Prophet's surviving wives and criticizes Muslims for not concentrating on men's bad behavior and instead interpreting the verse as referring to a woman's headdress. (85–88)

MODESTY, COVERING, AND PROTECTION

Mernissi describes how the notion of modesty in Islam has elicited differing perspectives in the modern era. In the same way that sin is significant in the Christian context, and credit is significant in capitalist societies, understanding the implications of the *hijab* is essential in Islam. But the concept of modesty is devalued when it is reduced to a piece of fabric imposed by men on women. By recognizing the Quran's refusal to objectify women from its inception, we can better comprehend its twenty-first-century revival. (95)

Some women see this resurgence to safeguard their autonomy and avoid objectification. Authorities use veiling to resolve political issues and shield women from western influence, while others use it as a protest to reclaim their religious identity, whereas mandating the veil raises concerns about religious liberty and transforms women's bodies into community symbols. Ziba Mir-Hosseini explores the various meanings and symbolism surrounding the practice of head covering, also known as *hijab*, in the broader social context. Let's embark on an exploration of *hijab* and veiling, considering their many dimensions and perspectives. (198–203)

AS PROTECTION

While some argue that *hijab* confines women, the ultimate purpose of *hijab* is to let women participate in society rather than restrict them. According to Ayatollah Mortaza Motahari, the concept of *hijab* as protection grants women agency and authority that clerical discourse had previously denied them. This authority, however, is a double-edged sword in that it not only throws the weight of society's moral and sexual purity on women by compelling them to wear the *hijab*, but it also renders any other manner of attire a provocation.

AS SYMBOL OF PROTEST

The *hijab* controversy sparks debate, particularly in areas where it is enforced, restricted, or denied. In Iran, *hijab* evolved from a marker of tradition into a symbol of protest when women revolted against fifty years of Western colonization culture, which they claimed was plotting to change them into pseudo-Westerners. This symbol of defiance became an emblem of the revolution, and the *chador* became a marker of Islamic identity and a flag for the revolution. The Islamic republic considered the *chador* "the best hijab" and made it compulsory, and public appearances without it is a moral violation punishable by up to seventy-four lashes. The *chador* was defended so fiercely that it became a cornerstone of the new republic and a red line no one dared cross—until Mahsa Amini's death in 2021.

AS IMPOSITION/LEGISLATION

For almost a century since the formation of the secular Turkish republic, religious women in Türkiye fought for the right to wear *hijab* in universities and state institutions. They succeeded after they backed a religious party that promised to abolish the prohibition on headscarves in colleges, offices, and government organizations. They protested on the streets, voted to secure their right to practice their faith freely.

In Afghanistan, on the other hand, there has been a rise in enforcement, causing concern for personal freedom and the impact on women's lives. The Taliban have imposed the *hijab* on all women going out in the public and the "best hijab" is a *burka*. By doing so, these men exhibit a deep mistrust towards their closest female relatives, constantly harboring suspicions about their mothers, daughters, sisters, and wives—and living in constant fear of potential betrayal.

AS PERSONAL CHOICE

In the West, *hijab* is not enforced by anyone, yet many choose to wear it to express self-control, power, and agency. It is worn to defy discrimination and to assert religious identity. Some rebel against state policies, asserting a position that challenges the marginalization of women, while others act defiantly against racism, ignorance, or oppression. All do so with fortitude and conviction.

Muslim women are more likely than men to experience anti-Muslim violence in public. Even though scholars have issued *fatwas* stating that if Muslim women feared harassment, or lost employment opportunities, they were obligated to save their lives and ensure their livelihood by removing their *hijab*. Still, Muslim women remain resolute in their commitment to their Muslim identity, unwilling to compromise their cherished values.

ETHICAL NOT CRIMINAL

When a state or local government mandates the *hijab*, it fails to distinguish between a religious sin and a legal crime. The imposition of the *hijab* as a legal mandate conflates violation of religious teaching with violation of the law. According to Mohsin Kadivar, religious texts do not mandate any form of attire or covering for women; therefore, the issue of *hijab* comes under ethical, not legal, matters. It should be up to Muslim women to choose the form and extent of their coverage in accordance with their religious beliefs, morals, and commitment.

A *hijab* cannot be imposed on believers because it falls under religious freedom: *"Let there be no compulsion in religion" (Q 2:256)*. Since *hijab* and Quranic injunctions regarding women come under the category of social norms (*ahkam-eejtema'i*), they are subject to change based on societal shifts and the status of women. Jurists engaged in *fiqh* can adapt to the changes by developing rulings that align with the new circumstances.

NIQAB: A CULTURAL EXPRESSION

The *niqab* remains a flashpoint, particularly in the West since it is an excellent symbol for Islamophobes. Women who wear a face veil, or *niqab*, conceal their faces but leave their eyes visible. Because the face is the portion of the body by which a person can be most easily recognized, it is mandatory that faces not be concealed during the Hajj or prayer, two important pillars of Islam. Muhammad Al-Ghazali states that people who say that wearing *niqab* is necessary for women's reform are deceiving God and His Prophet. The truth is that if wearing the *hijab*, *niqab*, or any other covering was a clear directive in the Quran, scholars would not have compromised on such a command, and its practice would not be subject to multiple interpretations, as it is with alcohol and pork.[265]

HIJAB AND INDIVIDUAL PIETY

In the last few decades, what women wear has become the core issue of debates on Islam, and central to Muslim identity in both the East and the West. However, a woman's piety or commitment to Islam can never be measured by yards of fabric. The unrelenting discourse that focuses only on Muslim women's head coverings gives an oversimplified version of Islam's teachings. The politicization of the veil in the modern era, has become the marker of a "good" woman for Muslims but a "bad" woman for westerners. Some women end up reducing the core of their demands to only this act which, due to its constant repetition, loses credibility and becomes an empty slogan. They place the importance of "Muslimness" upon what a woman wears, regardless of whether said woman follows any tenets of Islam.

This verse allows women over the age of marriage to discard their outer clothing: *"As for the elderly women past the age of marriage, there is no blame on them if they take off their 'outer garments' without revealing their adornments, but it is better for them if they avoid this altogether" (Q 24:60)*. This indicates that forms of modest dress do not determine a woman's piety; in reality, it is about shielding women from unwelcome sexual advances, which older women are presumably immune to. But piety for women of any age is determined not by outward appearances, but by their inner character and intentions. Piety resides in a woman's spirit, and her commitment to modesty and dignity.

When I was a young teen in Kashmir, my young male cousin was standing with a disapproving expression on his face, demanding that I cover my hair. Why was he trying to impose his will on me? He was adamant that no one should see me without a veil. When I asked what he would do if I didn't comply, his answer sent chills down my spine. He threatened to throw acid in my face before others did. This is when I grasped the magnitude of the issue. It wasn't just about my hair; it was a fight for my independence. I stood my ground and roared back, knowing full well that the elders of the family had my back.

Decades later, in New York, a beautiful Muslim brother approached me after *Jummah* with a plea. "Sister Daisy, if only you wore a *hijab* you would be a perfect model for all women, and everyone would know you," he said. My heart swelled up with emotion as I felt a genuine desire on his part to encourage me on my spiritual voyage. He meant for me to become a more recognizable leader, to be on stage at Muslim conferences, to be respected by other religious leaders.

We sat down and he respectfully listened as I agreed with him that my spiritual path had been fraught with barriers. I reminded him that my relationship with God is between us and is defined by prayers, fasting, charity, and in my commitment to do good. I said I find fortitude and solace without the symbolism of a headscarf. Then I asked him if he thought I was less righteous because I did not cover my hair.

Even though he apologized profusely for his intrusion, I realized this well-meaning, genuinely spiritual brother had come to put my faith to the test. In my two interactions, I discovered that actions are determined by their intention. The demand to cover was intended to subjugate, in the first case, and to give me more authority in the second.

With sadness, I have observed the occasional judgment and criticism that many women like me receive from fellow Muslims and Muslim leaders. It is important to remember that we are not the final arbiters of one another's beliefs. Only God, in His infinite wisdom, is aware of what resides within our souls, minds, and hearts. Our strength is derived from our unity, not from our division. It is truly wise not to assess a woman's devotion solely by her clothing, but rather, to appreciate her for the nobility of her character, her service to humanity, and her agency. As expressed in the Quran, *"[T]he best attire is righteousness" (7:26)*. We must task ourselves with creating an environment that overflows with respect, in which every individual is accepted, embraced, and cherished.

ONE WOMAN CREATES BURKINI SO WOMEN OF FAITH CAN SWIM

Aheda Zanetti, a Libyan-Australian designer, watched her young niece play her first game of netball. Her niece, she thought, looked like a tomato because she wore her uniform on top of her Islamic dress.

So Aheda invented a solution, a *hijood*—a breathable and easy-to-put-on garment that would cover the head and allow modest Muslim women to play sports easily. Then she read that Muslim women were wading into the water wearing *burqas* and so she created the "burkini," a swimwear style for Muslim women who could participate in activities at a level they had never expected. She even helped Surf Life Saving Australia find female Muslim lifeguards, and then designed outfits to meet the requirement of a lifeguard.

Soon her creation attracted women of other faiths: Jews, Hindus, Christians, Mormons, and women with body issues. Her customers—who wish to conceal their body and enjoy swimming—are pleased that they can now swim with their children in public. The burkini is a global sensation which has created a lot of confidence among women of faith traditionally marginalized by the swimwear industry.

#23 | TO FREEDOM FROM DOMESTIC VIOLENCE

A South Asian man in England traveled to Pakistan with his mother to find a wife and chose Nasreen. After marrying Nasreen they moved to London, where she knew no one. She discovered her husband had no intention of living with her as his wife. He married her to look after his mother and house and expected her to obey him and his family. He began beating her, and the abuse worsened as time passed. Nasreen was a virtual prisoner. When he punched her, she had to undergo surgery. She attempted suicide but survived. When she tried to flee the house, he dragged her back by her hair. When a neighbor saw the abuse, the police intervened, and the husband was found guilty of domestic abuse and imprisoned. Nasreen had to start her life all over again, all by herself.

In light of Nasreen's traumatic experience, the Quran's teachings provide a stark contrast to the depravity she endured. The Quran not only extols the virtues of marriage but also directs individuals toward the principles of mutual respect and regard. It explicitly prohibits forms of verbal abuse, such as tormenting and nicknaming: *"Do not taunt one another among yourselves, nor call one another by nicknames. It is an evil thing to be called by a bad name after faith! And whoever does not repent, it is they who are the true wrongdoers"* (Q 49:11). Even during the divorce process, the Quran sets out a framework for the dignified dissolution of the marriage, emphasizing the need to protect the well-being and honor of all parties involved. *"When you divorce women, [D]o not retain them only to harm them or to take advantage of them"* (Q 2:231).

Muslims who condone domestic violence point to verse 4:34, that tells men to reconcile differences with women, but which some misinterpret as a license to beat their wives: *"Men are caretakers [qiwama] of women, as men have been provisioned by God over* women and tasked with supporting them financially. And righteous women [qanitat] are devoutly obedient and, when alone, protective of what God has entrusted them with. And if you sense ill conduct from your women, [nushuz], advice 'first,' if they still persist, do not share their beds, but if they still persist, then discipline [daraba] them gently" (Q 4:34).

FAMILY IS A MINIATURE COMMUNITY

The common misunderstanding of this verse is that a husband has authority over his wife because he is responsible for her. A righteous wife must be obedient to her husband. If she stands up to her husband, she is deemed disobedient. To discipline her, the husband must first speak to her, and if she does not respond, he must leave her bed; if she continues to resist, he must strike her. Abdul Hamid A. AbuSulayman, author of *Marital Discord*, explains that this interpretation of Q 4:34 had led to the exploitation of women by husbands and in-laws who believe their actions are justified. They take liberties in disciplining, which may involve reprimanding, humiliating, or subjugating the wife, inducing fear among other members and children. If a wife is financially insecure, she may be compelled to endure abuse, and if she lacks family support, she may feel trapped and obligated to remain in the marriage against her will.[266]

To refute the prevalent notion that the Quran condones wife-beating, and to stop this cycle of violence, it is imperative to examine and analyze this verse in its entirety. For starters, we will determine the meaning of *qiwama*, which means to stand up to responsibility: Do men have authority over women, and if so, how? Then, we will examine the definition of *qanitat*, a pious woman, who is expected to be obedient to God or to man. Then we will look at *nushuz*—does it mean to resist? And finally, we will provide a list of opinions on *daraba*: does this mean strike or beat a wife to resolve marital conflict? And if not, what can best lead to reconciliation in a marriage?

QIWAMA: THE CARETAKER OF WOMEN?

The word *qawwamun* is translated in many ways: "caretakers of women," "protectors of women," "supporters of wives," and "in charge of women." Men are *qawwamun* because they spend their wealth or resources to support and provide for their spouses and family. Kecia Ali states that if men no longer support women, then they lose their resultant authority. Thus, in a family where both husband and wife contribute to the household expenses, the husband would not be the wife's *qawwam*. (153)

Asma Lamrabet says that in the context of Q 4:34, *qawwamun* means "a provider or supporter," which has erroneously been translated as "superiority." Scholars influenced by the misogynist sociocultural context go as far as to compare the institution of marriage to a prison where the man is the absolute master, and the woman is entirely subordinate to his power, like a prisoner. (124)

Azizah al-Hibri considers men's *qiwama* over women only conditional in certain instances: (1) God endowed a man with an ability (in a particular circumstance) that a particular woman lacks, and (2) that man is "maintaining that particular woman." In this case, men's *qiwama* is not a privilege, but rather a *taklif* (burden/responsibility), particularly when women are financially dependent and live sheltered lives. A man is therefore responsible for supporting such women by providing them with "guidance and advice in those areas where he is more qualified or experienced."[267]

In her book, *Rebellious Wives, Neglectful Husbands*, Hadia Mubarak shows how scholars' interpretations of *qiwama* are conditional and align with the Quranic verse that does not prefer men to women and that one's superiority is determined by their level of God-consciousness (taqwa). "The nobler among you in the sight of God is the more righteous [muttaqi] among you" (Q 49:13).

She describes the opinion of Abdu Abdullah Muhammad al-Qurtubi (d. 1273 CE) who said, "Whenever a man is unable to provide for his wife financially, he is no longer *qawwam* over his wife. If he is no longer *qawwam* upon her, then she has the right to annul the marriage contract (in court)." Similarly, Tunisian philosopher Ibn-Ashur (1973) views *qiwama* as men's functional duty, not as a kind of ontological supremacy. He views *qiwama* as men's duty to protect, defend, and provide for women and makes no value judgment about women who work outside the house. He says men's financial maintenance of women has been established for generations, which is why the verse puts the verb in the past tense, "and due to what they spent of their wealth."

Al-Tabari (d. 923 CE) defined *qiwama* as legal rights exchange. Mens's *qiwama* was "premised on the material preference men had been granted." He considered *qiwama* contingent on a socioeconomic phenomenon rather than some inherent quality of man or woman per se." Men are granted *qiwama* over their wives' affairs in return for providing women with the following legal rights: (1) Paying a dower to their wives, (2) providing financial maintenance, and (3) fulfilling women's essential roles.[268]

As stated by Asma Barlas, the term "maintainer of the family/spouse" is not gender specific. In modern terms, the breadwinner is more of a job description than a gendered role. (58). Khadijah, the wealthy wife of the Prophet, provided for her husband, children, relatives, and the earliest believers. We would never argue, based on this logic, that Khadijah is superior to her husband and children, and that those she supported owed her obedience. *Qiwama* is the duty that God imposes on all men to tend to the needs of women, as exemplified by the Prophet, who cared for his wives after the death of Khadijah without ever abusing, hurting, controlling, or asking for their obedience.[269]

QANITAT: THE OBEDIENCE ISSUE

Kecia Ali defines *qanitat* as the feminine plural of *qanit*, which signifies a person who is subservient, obedient, or differential—a person who demonstrates *qunut*. In this context, medieval commentators often equate *qunut* with a woman's obedience to her husband. However, the term *qanit* is only used for obedience to God and God's messenger elsewhere in the Quran. Abdullah Yusuf Ali's translation renders the term as "devoutly obedient" and applies it to both men and women in Q 33:35, which includes devoutly obedient men *(qanitin)* and women *(qanat)* on the list of those whom God will reward. The term *qanit* also describes exceptional figures such as Maryam and Abraham in the Quran. Thus, there is no reason to believe that the term in 4:34 refers to anything other than the obedience and devotion of women to God. (153-54).

According to Amina Wadud, the Quran never orders a woman to obey her husband. It never states that obedience to a husband is a characteristic of "better women," nor is it a prerequisite for a woman to join the Islamic community. (77) *"Perhaps, if he were to divorce you all, his Lord would replace you with better wives who are 'submissive to God,' faithful to him, devout repent, dedicated to worship and fasting- previously married or virgins" (Q 66:5).*

NUSHUZ: STANDING UP

The word *nushuz* means "to stand up" from a seated or sleeping position in order to leave. This is how it is consistently used in other parts of the Quran in verses 58:11 and 2:259. So, in the context of Q 4:34, *nushuz* must mean to resist, get up, and leave the marriage. In contemporary usage, a "nashiz wife" has left her marital home and is living elsewhere but is not yet divorced. *Nushuz* can also be associated with the husband. *"If a woman fears indifference or neglect from her husband" (Q 4:128)*. Yet, interestingly, *nushuz* is never understood as "disobedience" by the husband; instead, interpretations often change when applied to a man versus a woman.[270] But if *nushuz* is interpreted as disobedient, then it must apply to both cases, a disobedient wife and a disobedient husband. Would Muslim men be willing to say that they are "disobedient" to their wives?[271]

Mohamad Jebara explains that the term *nushuz* literally describes the protruding fangs of an antagonized snake secreting venom, which implies it is not a female characteristic, or permanent state of being, but a situation that arises from time to time in reaction to a threat. *Nushuz* in Q 4:128 and 4:34 references women and men, which means the situation refers to either or both parties in the marriage, which can be remedied with the correct intervention. The word refers to a toxic atmosphere in any male-female relationship, specifically the behavior of the parties involved.[272]

Asma Barlas points out that the Quran clearly states that men can be guilty of *nushuz* too. *Q 4:128* refers to wives fearing their husbands' *nushuz*: *"If a wife fears indifference of neglect from her husband."* If we read the word as disloyalty and ill-conduct on the wife's part toward the husband, we must also read it as disloyalty and ill-conduct on the husband's part toward his wife. (219)

Mubarak explains how the phrase, "those women whose *nushuz* you fear" in the Quran casts *nushuz* as an object of perception or speculation, creating a distance between the subject of woman and the action of *nushuz*. Premodern scholars defined women's *nushuz* as defiance and disobedience in four ways: (1) Spousal disobedience, (2) refusal to have sex, (3) rising above one's husband, and (4) hatred toward him. Similarly, men's *nushuz* was interpreted as hatred, cruelty, or sexual abandonment of women. But why did some scholars link refusal to have sex with defiance and disobedience? They understood *nushuz* to imply a woman reneging on her wifely duties, namely engaging in sexual relations with her husband. Ironically, neither the Quran nor the Prophetic tradition ever suggests disciplinary consequences for a wife who rejects her husband's sexual advances. (123-124)

She describes how Al-Tabari argues that it's ironic that the Quran says a wife should be sexually abandoned if she won't sleep with her husband. Scholars tend to agree that a *nashiz* wife who doesn't like her husband will be happy if he stops being sexually intimate with her. If a wife's *nushuz* means she is cheating on her husband, the husband's withdrawal serves as a protest until she ceases. Most scholars also argue that men must exhaust the first step before moving on to the second and then to the third. (123-124)

DARABA: STRIKE LIGHTLY

Though the majority of classical scholars have interpreted *daraba* to mean "beat," it has twenty-five different meanings; "beat" or "chastise" are two of them, another one is to "go or turn away" or "move about," and "travel through" (as in *verses 2:273, 3:156, 5:106,* and *73:20*). In verses 28:15, 38:41 it means "beat or stomp." The d-r-b root of *daraba* carries at least seventeen distinct connotations, including "strike" *(Q 26:63)*, "hold up as an example" *(Q 43:57)*, "travel through" *(Q 4:101)*, and "cover" *(Q 3:112)*, just to name a few. At the same time, no other verses support the "beating" interpretation of 4:34, and there are other verses that support the "distancing" or "going away from" meaning.[273]

Translating *daraba* as "beat" the wife in the context of fixing deteriorating matrimonial relations produces a contradiction between Quranic verses when comparing 4:34 to those on divorce that offer a picture of noncoercion in marriage, even while the marriage is being dissolved. This contradiction does not arise if 4:34 is translated as "go away from."

Asma Barlas questions whether the word *daraba* refers to striking, even symbolically. She cites Rafi Ullah Shahab's book *Muslim Women in Political Power*, in which he says *daraba* also means "to prevent." The verse tells husbands to "leave [the wives] alone in their beds and prevent them from going outside of houses." In support of his reading, he points out that verse Q 4:15 provides similar treatment of lewd wives. (217).

In Q 38:44, Prophet Job is commanded to take some grass and strike it. Author Leena Ali discovered translations that have inserted either the words "your wife" or "her" into verse 38:44 after the word "strike," as in: "And take a bunch of grass in your hand and strike [your wife/her] with it, and do not break your oath"—in stark contrast to the original, which many popular translations have as: *"And take a bunch of grass in your hand and strike with it, and do not break your oath. Truly We found him steadfast—an excellent servant, ever turning (to God)" (Q 38:44).*[274]

SOLVING FAMILY PROBLEMS WITH COMPASSION AND WISDOM

The Sunnah of the Prophet Muhammad reflects his interpretation of the Quran, which contradicts the meaning of *daraba* as "beat." The Prophet said, "God does not bestow mercy on someone who does not show mercy to others."[275] Anas ibn Malik, a Prophet companion, remarked, "I have never seen anyone more kind to one's family than Muhammad." If the Prophet Muhammad had understood verse 4:34 to require physical discipline, he would have used it; instead, he said, "A believing man should not hate a believing woman; if he dislikes one of her characteristics, he will be pleased with another."[276]

According to Abdul Hamid AbuSulayman, when the Prophet experienced conflict with his wives—particularly during the tense period when they demanded a higher standard of living that he could not afford—he resorted to seclusion (*al-mashrabah*) for a month and followed this command: *"O Prophet! Say to your wives, 'if you desire the life of this world and its luxury, then come, I will give you a suitable compensation for divorce and let you go graciously" (Q 33:28-29).* He gave his wives the option of accepting the standard of living he could afford, remaining together, or releasing the marriage contract and separating with dignity. (20)

His habit of "separating" himself from the conflict by "leaving" his home and withdrawing into seclusion gave everyone time to calm down. He knew instinctively that it was wrong to injure another person. As described in *Q 16:126: "If you retaliate, then let it be equivalent to what you have suffered."* This was disclosed prior to Q 4:34; he understood that retribution is reciprocal.

According to Abu Sulayman, 4:34 is a command to reconcile in a dignified manner, without coercion or intimidation, since each spouse has the right to dissolve the marriage. It establishes a three-step procedure for preventing injury and reducing violence. Early jurists, who generally interpreted *daraba* to imply strike, also limited the verse's application. Most of them viewed beating as only marginally permissible or symbolic. Some have suggested using a toothbrush or a folded handkerchief for pounding. If we adopt Ibn Abbas's interpretation of this verb as a few strokes or taps with a *siwak* or similar object, such as a toothbrush or pencil, then this meaning clearly does not include punishment, injury, or suffering. (10) Still, according to Hadia Mubarak, allowing a husband to symbolically hit his wife with a *siwak* or handkerchief is problematic for a number of reasons, including the inherent authority it confers on the husband over a wife's body, and the loophole it leaves for justifying violence against a spouse, a practice that Prophet Muhammad personally shunned and discouraged.[277]

Some early jurists restricted the scope of spousal violence to a remarkable degree. Ibn Rushd, a theologian, insisted that "even a man who caught his wife in bed with another man could either forgive or divorce her, but nothing beyond that."[278] Abdul Hamid AbuSulayman concludes that "moving away" or "distance himself from her" is the right interpretation. Both are more compatible with the Quran than their association with physical injury, psychological pain, and disgrace. The latter does not result in a dignified marital relationship or promote human dignity, nor does it create affection and compassion, which are the foundations of a lasting marriage—especially considering the present era's values, prospects, and views. (16)

A LANDMARK TRANSLATION AND INTERPRETATION

I recall the first time I encountered verse 4:34. In 2006, I organized a WISE conference for 200 Muslim women leaders at which Laleh Bakhtiar, a renowned Iranian American scholar and author of dozens of books on spirituality, disclosed that while translating 4:34 into English, she discovered it had been misinterpreted for more than 1,400 years.

In her research she found that the word *daraba*, which is used for "to beat," has many meanings, including "to leave" or "to go away." So, Laleh sought the opinion of about thirty scholars—imams, sheikhs, ayatollahs—and asked about the Prophet actions.

They said the Prophet emphasized nonviolence; he commended those who treated their wives with kindness: "The most perfect of the believers in faith is the best of them in moral excellence, and the best of you are the kindest to their wives."[279] He also ordered Muslim men to "Never beat God's handmaidens."[280] They all agreed that the Prophet was a walking Quran and he never hit his wives, and when he was agitated, he would leave his home. So, Laleh said, the meaning of this word was not "to beat" but "to go away."

The women in the room broke out in loud applause, cheering, and whistling. There were cries of "Domestic violence and beating women to death has been done in the name of an error of interpretation!" At that moment, it became clear that women needed to be involved in interpreting the scriptural text, as evidenced by Laleh's following groundbreaking translation in *The Sublime Quran* published in 2009:

> Men are supporters [*qiwama*] of wives because God has given some of them an advantage over others and because they have "spent" of their wealth. So, the ones in accord with morality [*qanitat*] are those who are morally obligated and the ones who guard the unseen of what God has kept safe. And those whose resistance [*nushuz*] you fear, then admonish them and abandon them in their sleeping places and go away [*daraba*] from them.[281]

Today, at least seven English translations on islamawakened.org website show similar translations from the following authors: Safi Kaskas ("then depart away from them"); Shabbir Ahmed ("and keep admonishing them with examples so that they stop rebelling"); The Clear Quran ("then discipline them gently"); Dr. Tahir-ul-Qadri ("turn away from them, striking a temporary parting"); Imam W. D. Mohammed Community ("and separate from them"); and Dr. Kamal Omar ("then bring forward to them").

In 2010, a Polish American Muslim woman brought a custody case against her husband, a Muslim doctor from India. She claimed he hit her for "disobedience" and withheld household allowance, depleting her savings before marriage. She avoided going to the police to protect her husband's medical license, as she financially depended on him. She took her husband to court to fight for sole custody of her four children. In court, the husband brought a Quran which translated *daraba* to mean "scourge" to justify his actions under American religious freedom law. However, his wife presented a Bakhtiar translation to mean "go away from them." The judge used Laleh's translation to disprove his religious freedom argument and *The Sublime Quran* interpretation was sufficient evidence for the wife to win the child custody case!

#24 | TO SAFEGUARD AGAINST FGM

Nawal El Saadawi, an Egyptian novelist, was subjected to female genital mutilation (FGM) at six years of age. She did not allow this to define her. Instead, she trained as a psychiatrist and a university lecturer. Tackling women's issues in Egypt, particularly FGM, El Saadawi's outspoken views led to her being charged with crimes against the state. She was jailed for three months. She used the time in jail to write a memoir. She wrote on rolls of toilet paper using an eyebrow pencil smuggled in. Drawing from her own experience with FGM, and as a doctor witnessing the terrible physical damage women endured, she campaigned for fifty years for the practice to be banned. A ban was finally instituted in Egypt in 2008. Still, El Saadawi asserts that the practice "still happens—it is even increasing."[282]

Islam recognizes that everyone has ownership rights over their body, and they act as stewards over it. Therefore, no one is permitted to harm, injure, violate, or alter the body of another individual without their consent, unless for medical reasons.

FGM is not a religious practice, it is cultural norm which predates Islam and Christianity. The origins of the practice are unknown, but evidence from mummies suggests that it originated in Pharaonic Egypt. FGM is practiced overtly in twenty-nine African nations and in secret in parts of the Middle East, Asia, Europe, and Australia, as well as the United States.[283] FGM is practiced by people of many ethnicities and religious groups, including Christians, Jews, Muslims, and adherents to traditional African religions. Over 200 million women have been afflicted by FGM in some form, and three million girls are at risk each year.[284] Most girls are subjected to FGM between the ages of four and ten, before they reach puberty.

PURIFICATION AND MALE GRATIFICATION

FGM is a risky procedure that involves cutting and/or removing all or part of a girl's external genitalia. Practitioners believe that removing or inhibiting the growth of the clitoris will render the girl pure, protect her virginity, and prevent promiscuity because no man will be able to seduce her. According to Ellen Gruenbaum, the motives are largely moral and sexual in nature, while some people find it aesthetically pleasing. They support the ritual as a type of purification which they tie to her sexuality. This rite of passage increases a girl's marriageability when she enters womanhood.

Sexual misconduct is forbidden for both sexes in Islam, and it is wrong to use the prevention of sexual misconduct or the maintaining of virginity as justification for FGM. Haifa Jawad explains that the real reason for continuing the practice is to gratify the man or make him happy. This is especially true for infibulation, in which it is believed that by narrowing the vaginal entrance, the husband will experience the maximum sexual gratification, which will result in winning him over. (57)

In certain Muslim contexts, female virginity and chastity are valued more than women's and girls' complete humanity. Kecia Ali says female experiences are diverse, multiple, plural— neither static nor universal. Yet, female bodies and sexuality are subject to greater scrutiny and surveillance than male bodies and male sexuality. (143)

UNMASKING THE FALLACIES

In 2008, my organization was requested to help prevent FGM among Muslims. I wanted to better understand, for instance, why FGM continued in Egypt despite being banned, so I consulted a local Egyptian non-governmental organization that specializes in FGM. I wanted to learn if fathers were perpetuating this harmful custom. Our research revealed that they were not; rather, the grandmother most often served as the family's enforcer. Girls were being cut by midwives and barbers since, due to the illegality of FGM, the practice had gone underground.

It was also at this time that I had the pleasure of meeting Dr. Adriana Kaplan-Marcusán in Madrid, Spain. She lived in The Gambia and had previously used scientific evidence against FGM in her advocacy efforts. She confessed that religious leaders are the only ones who can persuade their followers to abandon FGM, since they are the ones who justified the practice in the first place. She requested that WISE's

Global Muslim Women's Shura Council publish a position paper refuting FGM from an Islamic perspective. So, the Shura Council spent six months compiling material before publishing a paper in 2009 in which they concluded that FGM is un-Islamic.

The Council began by using the Quran to support arguments against FGM. There is no command in the Quran regarding FGM, and custom is not an acceptable justification, as those who blindly follow harmful traditions are condemned: *"[F]ollow, what God has revealed. They reply, 'No! We only follow what we found our forefathers practicing.' Would they still do so, even if their forefathers had absolutely no understanding or guidance?" (Q 2:170)*

The health, justice, and compassion messages of the Quran contradict any cultural practice that results in bodily harm. The holy scriptures state that humans are created "in the best form" *(Q 95:4)* and condemn actions that negatively impact the human body: *"[D]o not let your own hands throw you into destruction" (Q 2:195)*.

THE TRUTH ABOUT WEAK HADITH

The Prophet stated, "There should be neither harming nor reciprocating harm."[285] He explicitly instructed spouses to maintain sexual relations and affirmed that sex must be for the pleasure of the couple. The removal of a woman's vital organ that generates pleasure denies her the conjugal right to experience sexual pleasure and climax.

There is no evidence that any female members of the Prophet's household underwent clitoral hoodectomy or labiaplasty, the two most common practices of FGM. In contrast, Al-Hassan, and Al-Hussein, his two grandsons, were circumcised. Still, the promoters of FGM cite an unreliable hadith narrated by Um Atiyyat al-Ansariyyah, who claimed that the Prophet told a woman who performed circumcision in Medina, "Do not cut too severely, as that is better for a woman and more desirable for a husband."[286] This hadith is missing a link in the chain of transmitters and is considered "weak" (*mursal*) and unreliable.

Sayyid Sabiq, author of *Fiqh-us-Sunnah*, debunked the authenticity of this hadith based on the fact that it appears in only one of the six compilations generally recognized as authentic. Indeed, all hadiths pertaining to FGM have been deemed unreliable by past and present scholars. Even so, if we were to assume that the hadith was indeed acceptable, Kecia Ali still asserts that it does not convey an obligation; rather, it recommends moderation of an existing practice, not the imposition of something new.[287]

The International Islamic Center for Population Studies and Research at Al-Azhar University issued the following statement: "The use of the term 'Sunnah Circumcision' is nothing but a form of deception intended to misguide people and give the impression that the practice is Islamic."[288]

ABSENCE OF SCHOLARLY CONSENSUS AND VARIED FATWAS

Except for one, there is no scholarly consensus (*ijma*) among classical legal (*fiqh*) schools regarding FGM.[289] Unlike other Sunni schools, the Shafis believed that female and male circumcision is obligatory.[290] However, it is likely that the scholars who deemed this practice permissible were unaware of its harmful effects, as Islamic law permits permissibility only for cultural practices that do not hurt an individual or society.

FGM has never been a unified practice in Muslim communities. It may be performed in some Muslim countries and communities, but the extent of the incision varies even among these communities. Had female genital mutilation been as closely connected to Islam as male circumcision, the extent of cutting would have been clearly defined by jurists, and the practice would have been as equally widespread as male circumcision.

In recent years, with the expansion of scientific and medical knowledge regarding the detrimental effects of FGM on children, women, and families, eminent scholars have begun to reach a consensus. In 2009, Egypt's Dar Al-Ifta, the international leader in Islamic legal research, issued a *fatwa* condemning "female circumcision" as a harmful cultural practice, declaring, "Anyone familiar with the reality of the situation cannot speak against its prohibition."

MALE AND FEMALE CIRCUMCISION: AN INCONGRUOUS COMPARISON

Some argue that FGM is the same as male circumcision, and is therefore required by Islam. They cite the Islamic legal tradition of analogy (*qiyas*). But FGM is in stark contrast to male circumcision, as FGM frequently involves the removal, modification, or cutting of functional organs. Dr.

Suad Saleh of Al-Azhar University says FGM does not resemble male circumcision so much as it does the pre-Islamic practice of burying girls alive.[291]

There are established medical benefits to male circumcision, but no advantages have been reported for FGM. The American Academy of Pediatrics found substantial evidence that male circumcision, (removal of foreskin) reduces the risk of HIV infection, sexually transmitted infections (STIs), genital herpes, and genital ulceration. There are also benefits for female partners of circumcised men; the risk of HR-HPV for female partners was reduced by 28 percent, the risk of bacterial vaginosis was reduced by 40 percent, and the risk of trichomoniasis was reduced by 48 percent.[292]

Opponents of male circumcision assert that it is similar to FGM because it is not performed with boys' consent. They advocate delaying male circumcision until a child is eighteen years old. If parents' beliefs prohibit circumcision, those are valid reasons; however, an argument based on consent is weak—as compared to FGM performed on girls—because parents routinely act in their child's best interest, and FGM is not in their interest. Parents also provide consent for many preventive procedures such as immunization, including hepatitis B vaccination, without the child's consultation.

MEDICALIZATION AND ITS DETRIMENTAL EFFECTS

There is no evidence that risks associated with FGM are reduced or that there are fewer long-term complications when performed by healthcare professionals, so the Shura Council members took a strong stance against the "medicalization" of FGM, which is carried out by healthcare workers in nonclinical settings.[293] Kecia Ali notes, for example, in Indonesia neonatal female circumcision performed in hospitals by medical professional involves a cutting implement instead of a ritual scraping or pricking, making the procedure a severe operation. Having doctors perform the procedure is thought to legitimize the practice. (141)

According to the six objectives of Shari'a which include the protection and promotion of religion, life, mind, family, wealth, and dignity, FGM violates at least five of these objectives:

1. Protection of life (*al-nafs*): FGM harms infants, girls, and women, endangering their lives and the lives of their future children. Females

who undergo FGM are considerably more likely to die during childbirth or give birth to a stillborn child. In fact, regions where FGM is practiced have the highest rates of maternal and infant mortality in the world.

2. Protection of mind (al-'aql): FGM prevents the normal development of girls' minds, leading to psychological and psychiatric issues, undermining their mental and psychosexual health, and causing psychosis and trauma.

3. Protection of the family (al-nasl): The Quran emphasizes sexuality within marriage and encourages mutual delight during sexual relations: *"It has been made permissible for you to be intimate with your wives during the nights proceeding the fast"* (Q 2:187). FGM prevents family cohesion by denying the fulfillment of mutually pleasurable conjugal relations. A woman who has undergone FGM may be at a higher risk of contracting sexually transmitted diseases, infertility, and even divorce. She may experience discomfort during sexual activity, and infections can cause hemorrhage, cysts, and incontinence.

4. Protection of dignity (al-'ird): Female genital mutilation compromises a woman's dignity by condemning her to a life of repeated infections, intimate scarring, and disfigured genitalia, thereby denying her the divine right to live a life of dignity.

5. Protection of religion (al-din): The sutures and scars produced by FGM make it impossible for the cut female to attain ritual purity (tahara), thereby denying her the right to worship freely. The Prophet stated, "There are two blessings that many people are deceived into losing: health and free time."[294] Women's health problems prevent women from enjoying these two blessings.

PRAGMATIC ENGAGEMENT AND ENLIGHTED IMAMS

With the position paper on FGM in hand, WISE recruited an Egyptian partner to identify FGM practitioners in Egypt to end the practice. We began with barbers. We discovered that they were often performing procedures to supplement their meager income. We financed new barbershops with adjustable modern chairs, television, basins with flowing water, blow dryers, and Hollywood-lit mirrors. Villagers admired these modernized shops, and their businesses increased as a result. Newly confident, barbers were prepared to sign a contract promising to end the practices of FGM. They also gave us the names of other practitioners, whom we approached with the same message and plan for their businesses: a convenience store, a tuk-tuk service, and a chicken shop.

While in Cairo, I asked a prominent imam if he had witnessed the negative effects of FGM. He stated that FGM is underlying every sexual difficulty a couple comes to discuss. He was so convinced that he added, "Let me be very clear: FGM is not a Muslim practice." When I asked him if he was willing to become our champion and make these statements public, he said, "Of course. My religious obligation is to prevent this harmful act. It has caused long-term damage to many families; regrettably, some have broken up because of it."

A month later, I met Aisha, a midwife practitioner who had stopped performing FGM in exchange for an investment in a new chicken store. In her shop, a small black-and-white television flickered on a metal cart beside a wall of chickens clucking in cages. When I thanked Aisha, she hugged me. "Now I sleep soundly at night, I don't hear the screams of girls. Now, I have everything I could wish for. I'm not harming anyone—and because I have a steady income, I have peace of mind." Aisha handed me a chicken, "Or-Gan-Nic!" as she gave it to me as a present, I just wondered how I would get a live chicken through customs. I looked at Aisha as she stood at her organic chicken business, flanked by her two young male assistants underneath a sign that read WISE.

Dr. Adriana Kaplan Marcusán, who had originally persuaded me to publish the FGM position paper, used it to educate imams in Africa. She remarked, "The rigorous and pedagogical document on FGM from WISE has been disseminated at all of my conferences, workshops, and classes, allowing us to obtain our first *fatwa*." In 2008, she presented the results to a group of thirty-four Muslim scholars and clerics from West Africa. As they read the compelling arguments presented by the Shura Council against FGM, they said to Adriana, "Today, we're issuing a *fatwa* against this practice. We should ban this practice forever."

In February 2018, Adriana invited me to an international conference in The Gambia to commemorate the United Nations' International Day of Zero Tolerance for Female Genital Mutilation, where I met the past vice president of The Gambia, Fatoumata Jallow Tambajang, who thanked me for publishing the FGM position papers, stating that this was the "missing piece of the puzzle" that convinced their imams to declare FGM un-Islamic. The Gambia outlawed the practice in 2018, and since then, prominent scholars including Sheikh Sayyid Sabiq,

Sheik Mohammad Arafa, Sheikh Shaltoot, Sheikh Abubakar Aljazaairy, Dr. Suad Saleh, and Dr. Selim al-Awwa have followed suit.

ONE MORE EXAMPLE OF FGM REEDUCATION

Mariya Taher was raised in the Dawoodi Bohra community in the US, a Shia Islamic sect with Indian roots. At the age of seven, she was circumcised. Taher did not challenge the practice because she believed that *khatna*, as it is known in the Dawoodi Bohra community, was obligatory for girls. But later, as she learned more about FGM and recognized it as a form of gender-based violence, she pursued a thesis entitled "Understanding the Continuation of Female Genital Cutting in the United States Amongst the Dawoodi Bohra Community."

After the publication of her thesis, Taher gained a reputation as an authority on FGM in Asian and American contexts. She utilized the power of storytelling to promote the cultural abandonment of FGM not only in the Bohra community, but in all populations where FGM is practiced. In 2015, she cofounded Sahiyo, a nonprofit organization dedicated to assisting survivors. The petition she helped initiate on Change.org received over 300,000 signatures, which helped enact a law in Massachusetts to protect all girls from FGM. Tahir also aided in the formation of the Connecticut Coalition to end FGM, and now she functions as a consultant for the implementation of community-based direct services for survivors of FGM. There is still much work to do!

SELF-EXPRESSION THROUGH BODY MODIFICATION

There is one additional matter that merits consideration. I am frequently asked about the legal ramifications of body-altering and cosmetic procedures, a subject that is rarely discussed openly. This void in discourse prompts many to question whether Islam prohibits body-beautification measures in the same manner as Female Genital Mutilation (FGM).

It is essential to note that Islamic teachings do not inherently prohibit the adornment of the body, so long as such adornments are not for vain purposes. To illustrate, there are numerous instances of individuals undergoing a spectrum of interventions in response to illness, ranging from the removal of tonsils and the replacement of kidneys to organ transplants, ear and nostril piercings, hair transplants, mole removals, hair dying, and even body tattoos.

Let us just focus on tattoos since they are gaining popularity among athletes and young people. Most scholars consider tattoos to be mutilation ("altering God's creation") because they are formed by bursting pigment. They prohibit tattoos on the grounds that they conceal the natural body and are a form of deception. Others maintain that a tattoo hinders proper ablution and invalidates prayer, but since the tattoo is under the epidermis and does not prohibit water from reaching the skin, this argument is unconvincing.[295] Some scholars cite a hadith that states, "The Prophet cursed the one who does tattoos and the one who has a tattoo done."[296] The precise motive behind the Prophet's disdain for tattoos is unclear. It is plausible that he banned tattoos because of their association with superstitious beliefs and idol worship. The Prophet was committed to uniting tribes and forging bonds of brotherhood among believers. He probably viewed these tribal insignia as factors that divided people. In fact, Bedouin Arabs have used tattoos with crescents, stars, and other geometric designs as a means of tribal and spiritual identification for centuries. These identifiers are generally accepted, whereas modern tattoos are not.

It is my belief that the underlying intent behind the tattoo serves as the distinguishing factor between the two, as I experienced firsthand in 2022 when I presented my dissertation on women's rights at The New Seminary. My colleague, a non-Muslim professor, presented her dissertation, which included a tracing of her personal, spiritual journey. She explained how she wandered through woods and forests seeking greater meaning in life. On the final leg of her winding trip, she had a stunning epiphany: Nothing happens without God's will. "Only if God wills it!" she said emphatically. "Just to remind me," she said, while raising her arm, "I had these words tattooed on my wrist." It astounded and touched me to see in Arabic script "Inshallah" (God willing). Could a tattoo that encourages reliance on God (*tawwakul*) and confidence in his infinite power, displease God? When Muslims are unsure of a thing, they typically proclaim, "Only God knows!" *Allah hu Alam.*

#25 | TO PROTECTION FROM RAPE, SEXUAL ASSAULT, AND ADULTERY

In 2002, Mukhtar Mai described how, on the dictates of village elders, she was gang-raped and humiliated in front of her community and—when the case received international publicity—the world. Mai spoke up, pursued a case against her assailants, and transformed her tragedy into a mission, even though local customs would have expected her to commit suicide after being violated. She established a high school for girls as well as crisis control centers and clinics for both boys and girls in her village. Her organization, Mukhtar Mai Women's Welfare Organization, provides victims of violence with shelter and legal assistance. "Our only hope is to fight for justice and end oppression through education," is her credo. "Ignorance is a crime, apathy is a crime, and silence regarding a crime is a crime."

In the context of her work, the principles outlined in Islam become a pivotal part of the narrative. Islam strictly forbids rape, recognizing it as a heinous crime where victims are coerced into sexual acts against their will, often under the threat of death.[297] The Quran forbids forced, coerced, or involuntary sexual behavior, emphasizing the sanctity of personal autonomy. Further, men are prohibited from engaging in exploitative trade of women's sexual activities and encourages marriage as a means to prevent the sexual exploitation of women. (Q 4:25)

A TOOL OF CONTROL, FEAR, AND DOMINATION

Rape is a demonstration of dominance to keep women in their place and a weapon to control their bodies. It is also a public example aimed at instilling fear in all women, forcing them to submit to a male power structure and adhere to cultural norms.

According to Mahnaz Afkhami, rape has long been used as a tool for retribution and persecution. For instance, men avenge themselves by raping the mothers, spouses, daughters, and sisters of their rivals to resolve disputes. To show society final retribution, women are occasionally gang-raped and exhibited. (168-69). In Iraq, rape was employed as a strategy to recruit fighters and intimidate civilian populations. The terrorist group, Daesh, raped Yazidi women and girls and used it as a marketing tool to recruit young soldiers drawn to power and control. Rape was also a distinguishing feature of Boko Haram's terror in Nigeria. Militants there abducted 7,000 schoolgirls, many of whom were raped and forced to marry their rapist.[298]

According to Asifa Quraishi, the word *hiraba* (which encompasses rape as terrorism) literally means "forcibly taking," and when elaborated further, means "any type of forcible assault upon the people involving some sort of taking of property." Under *hiraba*, rape is a violent crime that uses sexual coercion as a weapon. Forcibly taking a victim's property (her sexual autonomy) is considered a theft of her dignity and autonomy over her body. Ibn Arabi classified rape as "*Hiraba* with the private parts," and much worse than "*Hiraba* with money." He said, "Anyone would prefer to be subjected to the latter over the former."

Islamic law assigns possession rights to each part of a person's body and a compensation right for any unlawful damage to any of those parts. Major schools of law state that whenever a woman is raped or subject to any form of sexual assault, she is entitled to full financial compensation for the injury caused by the attack. In accordance with Islamic jurisprudence, damage to sexual organs entitles the victim to compensation. Quraishi states, "In its law of wounds, *jirah* Islamic jurisprudence provides an avenue for civil redress for a rape survivor." (131-132)

PROTECTING AGAINST SEXUAL COERCION

According to the Quran, *"[I]t is not permissible for you to inherit women against their will" (Q 4:19)*. This verse came in response to a Madinan woman whose stepson claimed to inherit her upon the death of her husband. Before this verse was revealed, male relatives could marry a widow after her husband's death, prevent her from remarrying, exploit her sexually, and retain her inheritance.

Those who believe sex can be coerced with a wife frequently cite verse 2:222, which was disclosed in response to a question about when and how men could have sex with their wives. God permits sexual activity at any time, except during woman's menstrual cycle. *"[S]o, keep away* and do not have intercourse with your wives during their monthly cycles until they are purified. When they purify themselves, you may approach them in the manner specified by God" (Q 2:222). Most commentators emphatically say that this verse does not refer to when or how or at whose behest intercourse takes place.

Another frequently cited verse which needs clarity because the english translation does not reflect the intended meaning in the Quran is, "Your wives are like farmland (harth) for you, so approach them 'consensually' as you please" (Q 2:223).

As an example, Mustafa Khattab describes harth to mean "farmland"—meaning the husband being like the farmer, the wife like productive land, and children like seeds—a metaphor for fertility and growth. (19) Yusuf Ali's translation says, "Your wives are a 'tilth' unto you, so approach your tilth when and how you will."

Asma Barlas explains that if tilth is what is prepared for cultivation, then the spouse performs no discernible role in this preparation. Through presumably self-conscious ritual bathing, it is the wife who prepares herself for his approach. Moreover, if male dominance in marital intimacy is not divinely ordained, then 2:223 does not entitle a man to intimacy without his wife's consent. It describes approaching "consensually," after she has bathed and is ready for him, and the symbolism of *tilth* refers to procreation. (188) This verse speaks of approaching martial intimacy within the bounds of what is permissible. Lily Munir, an Indonesian academic describes this metaphor in Carla Powers' book: "Soil must be prepared for the seed; it must be watered, made soft, smooth, and ready." (168)

Asma Barlas says it is inaccurate to link the word *harth* with the idea that women are sexual property, given that the Quran never refers to a human being, including a slave, as another's property. The term *harth* (gain)*"Whoever desires the harvest (gain) of the Hereafter, we will increase his harvest (gain). And whoever desires only the harvest (gain) of this world, We will give them some of it, but they will have no share in the Hereafter"(Q 42:20)* refers to anything that humans benefit from, and that they sow in "this world" and harvest in "this world" or the next, does not exist as land or property in another verse.

THE TERM "MARITAL RAPE"

In "Islamic Perspective on Marital Rape," a study by Muhammad E. Susila, he explains that, since rape is viewed as a sexual transgression, and marriage is a union for socially sanctioned sex, the term "marital rape" is controversial and causes confusion. Many Muslims find it difficult to believe that a Muslim marriage could contain a rape. The wife is protected from being such a victim, since "marital rape" is identical to any other kind of rape—that is, forcible unwelcome sexual contact—with the exception that it occurs between married people.[299]

Prophet Muhammad tells husbands to treat their wives with compassion—*muasharah bil maaruf*—which includes respecting the wife's requirements and willingness to be sexually approached. Yet, some Muslims believe that a husband has the right to impose himself on his wife whenever he desires and without her permission. Likewise, a wife who is not in an optimal physical state may refuse sexual relations for various reasons, such as exhaustion or lack of desire. Despite this, if a husband demands intercourse from his wife and she refuses, and if he is using force and the threat of physical violence, that is rape.

Those who deny the existence of marital rape presume that the husband is the dominant partner and has the right to use his wife's body for his gratification; they mention verse 2:223. Once married, a woman has no right to deny sex with her spouse (because he has the right to enforce his conjugal rights at will), according to their theory. This allows the husband permission for sexual access and a "license to rape."

Yet, as we've seen, according to the Quran, spouses have the right to procreate, plan their families, and enjoy sexual gratification. Forced sex yields the opposite results, including: long-term trauma, resentment, and pain.

Susila explains that compared to sexual assaults committed by strangers or acquaintances, women are less likely to report sexual assaults perpetrated by their husbands. This is possibly why rape laws rarely apply to married women. In contrast, laws that grant absolute immunity to the spouse in relation to his wife are founded solely on their marital status. In Indonesia, for example, one third of women have experienced rape, sexual assault, or partner-related violence. In 2017, the largest gathering of female Muslim clerics in the world issued a *fatwa* declaring marital rape *haram*, or forbidden, under Islamic law, urging the government to make it illegal.[300]

PROSECUTION OF ADULTERY VERSUS RAPE

The Quran forbids unlawful extramarital sex and warns against the perils of adultery: *"Do not go near adultery. It is truly a shameful deed and an evil way" (Q 17:32)*. Because of its corrupting effect on family and society, adultery (*zina*) is regarded as an immoral offense. Adulterers betray the spouse and children, cause the collapse of the family, and create a negative impact on their social standing. They are decried by family and community as untrustworthy. Imam Ibn Al-Qayyim, a medieval theologian, said that you will never find an adulterer or fornicator who is pious, keeps his promises, speaks the truth, or maintains friendships; he will be characterized by lies, deception, betrayal, accepting prohibitions, and not being mindful of God.[301]

According to Islamic law, adultery is prosecuted as a crime if the act becomes a matter of "public indecency." This means a consensual sex act is performed so openly that four people can witness it without intruding on the person's privacy. If the couple is accused and four credible witnesses can prove the actual offense (witness the penetration), then the offense is prosecuted as a crime, with punishment specified in the Quran: *"As for female and male fornicators, give each of them one hundred lashes and do not let pity for them make you lenient in enforcing the law of God" (Q 24:2)*.

It is important to make a distinction between adultery and rape, as they are opposites. Adultery is consensual and illicit extramarital sex, whereas rape is coerced sex. The rape victim is grossly harmed by placing sexual violence in the same category as sexual acts of consent.[302]

Even though rape is nonconsensual, far too frequently women have been held accountable for the violence perpetrated against them against their will. Rape is determined not by whether the victim consented, but by the accused's intent, their actions, expert testimony, and physical evidence—including medical observations and forensic DNA.

Asifa Quraishi mentions scholars' views asserting that pregnancy does not amount to proof of illicit relations in cases where an unmarried woman, not claiming rape, is involved. She argues that linking adultery with pregnancy is problematic because the shift in burden of proof is even more patently unfair when the pregnant women is a victim of rape. This unfairness is not supported by the spirit of the Quran verses, which insists that no presumptions be made about women's sexual activity without four witnesses to the act. (115)

As with adultery, to establish rape as a crime, Islamic law requires that the judge be presented with four witnesses. But asking a rape victim to produce four witnesses is a farce and deception, as most assaults are not committed in public and it is nearly impossible to locate even one witness, let alone four. Further complicating matters, rape and sexual assault survivors frequently remain silent and do not seek help out of fear of ostracization by their community, further hostility from their rapist, or the failure of the justice system.

But the shame associated with rape should rest solely on the shoulders of the perpetrators, their enablers, and their defenders. Rape stigmatization is cultural and has no roots in Islam. Victims of rape must not be shunned due to their victimization. In contrast, the perpetrator should be punished by every means at our disposal, while the victim should receive the necessary physical, mental, and emotional rehabilitation support.

FEMALE SEXUAL ASSAULT OFFENDERS

The majority of sexual assaults are committed by men, making a female offender an anomaly. However, the Quran does provide a detailed account of a woman sexual assaulter to illustrate the injury that results from false accusation, abuse of power, failure of a political authority to enforce the law, and finally—redemption. This story does not imply that women are seductresses, but it highlights the plight of a victim grappling with the effects of injustice.

In a chapter entitled "Yusuf/Joseph," the Quran describes Zuleykha, the influential wife of the governor in whose household Yusuf serves as a servant. Zuleykha develops an affection for Joseph and is overcome with desire for him even though he is socially disadvantaged. When Zuleykha attempts to seduce him, he refuses, to her surprise. As he attempts to flee, she rips his shirt from behind and then accuses him of dishonorable intent when she sees her husband at the door. Joseph immediately protests his innocence, saying, "She was the one who attempted to seduce me." Her husband calls a household witness who provides a plausible statement: *"If his shirt is torn from the front, then she is telling the truth and he is liar. But if it is torn from the back, she has lied, and he is truthful"* (Q 12:26-27).

Despite Joseph's innocence being proven, the governor throws him in jail to stop the gossip. *"And so, it occurred to those in charge, despite seeing all the proofs of innocence that he should be imprisoned for a while"* (Q 12:35). For years in jail, Joseph waits for Zuleikha's public confession while he gains a reputation for dream interpretation. One day, he interprets a dream for the king that contains a significant warning, and so the king summons him. Joseph is then released after Zuleikha admits to his innocence. She then seeks forgiveness and redemption from God.

Celene Ibrahim explains how this narrative illuminates the dynamics of sex, political power, coercion, testimony, and the pursuit of justice. God views the punishment of a victim (Joseph) as an injustice, as revealed by the story's lessons. Despite physical evidence proving his innocence, political authorities failed to subject him to justice. Significantly, the story highlights the propensity of the powerful to exert control over the vulnerable and to conceal potential scandals and controversies. It depicts the role of enablers in sexual coercion and dominance, as opposed to those who seek the truth with honorable intentions and integrity. (35)

Sexual assault, in all of its forms, is a deliberate method of controlling others. Victims know 93 percent of their offenders, who are most often friends, neighbors, instructors, family, or lovers. They typically use their charisma and trustworthiness to silence their victims. Some assaulters lavish victims with gifts and praise to build their trust before the abuse occurs. Others may use authority to control those they victimize. They may threaten victims' careers, livelihoods, immigration status, or safety to gain control.

The sad reality is that victims of sexual assault always have an uphill battle. They are mocked and derided in many ways. Some are not believed and are unjustly accused of having a prior sexual experience; and if they are Muslim women, as nonvirgins their marital prospects vanish. Some are accused of inviting the assault, especially if their dress or appearance is immodest. Even *hijab*- and *abaya*-wearing women describe being sexually assaulted, harassed in public transportation, the workplace, and even during Hajj.

MUSLIM #METOO

Acts of aggression against women are not necessarily sexual, and they are often expressions of power and control. Sexual assault or coercion against women sometimes exerts comparable influence over another person—whether in the mosque, Hollywood, or Hajj. The #MeToo movement touched all corners of business, religion, media, sports, politics, academia, and culture in America. As expected, reports of abuse and exploitation have surfaced from within the Muslim community in the US and abroad.

One Pakistani woman reported sexual harassment during the Hajj to Mecca on Facebook. And then the #MosqueMeToo campaign began when an Egyptian-American activist named Mona Eltahawy recounted her story of abuse as a teenager.

More cases surface in the public eye every week. Muslim women continue to report stories of inappropriate sexual experiences within their communities and sacred spaces—environments meant to nurture spiritual growth. This has provoked responses ranging from supportive sisterhood to rage and even disbelief. Even Muslim women are deeply divided, and many find themselves torn between centuries of tradition, modern social pressures, and their beliefs.[303]

Silence is not spiritual in the face of these crimes. The #MeToo movement has identified church and synagogue spiritual leaders, and Muslim leaders as well. We are not exempt from "spiritual" abuse either, which is defined as the use of religion to manipulate, control, and intimidate under the guise of spiritual claims or religious principles. Included in this is the use of religion for sexual favors or financial gain. With phrases such as "it is better to remain silent because others will destroy your reputation" or "this family is strong; you'll make it through," many victims are encouraged to remain silent, be patient, and persevere. Even though these messages may be good coping mechanisms, they may cause more injury and impede seeking healing and justice.

Most often, Muslim leaders accused of sexual assault did well during the #MeToo movement. It was deemed detrimental to Muslims to expose their dirty laundry so that they were not called out publicly. Typically, victims of public figures remain mute to avoid accusations of slander or having ulterior motives, such as seeking revenge, gaining financial gain, or pursuing fame. But the Quran tells Muslims to be for truth: *"O [b]elievers! Be mindful of God and be with the truthful" (Q 9:119).*

Due to the trust people place in religious leaders, they should be held to a higher moral standard. However, as humans, they are capable of perpetrating transgressions and crimes, including sexual assault. As the Quran states: *"Blame is only on those who wrong people" (Q 42:42).* Thus, leaders who are sexual predators must seek absolution from the victim and face the consequences of their actions.

There are numerous options available for victims. Specifically, they can pursue justice or choose to be courageous and forgive their aggressor. Again, only the victim can determine how, when, and which option to exercise.

The Prophet was known to defend victims, not perpetrators, and stated that concealing or facilitating a crime is unjust: "Say the truth even though it is bitter."[304] Sexual assault is not a minor error or oversight. It is an oppressive deed. Still, he implored people not to condemn others for life, but to be lenient and, when necessary, be flexible, allowing those who made an error to change. He said to help those who commit oppression by stopping them.[305]

However, the concept of forgiveness—*"And whoever endures patiently and forgives surely this is a resolve to aspire to" (Q 42:43)*—and the idea of "taking the higher ground" should not be manipulated to silence victims and protect the accused. Some may choose to uphold their privacy by not going public, and others will maintain the confidentiality of a person who discloses sexual matters to them.

It is unmistakably evident that victims of any form of sexual assault must never be blamed or shamed for the coercive actions of other people because the Quran gives victims the right to fully pursue justice: *"There is no blame on those who enforce justice after being wronged" (Q 42:41)*. The victim's emotions and the ensuing trauma must be adequately processed, including financial compensation for the harm they caused, and every effort must be made to restore their self-esteem and make them feel whole, safe, and trusted.

For example, after escaping an abusive marriage, Sidra Humayun resolved to fight sexual assault against women in her native Pakistan. Her nonprofit organization, War Against Rape, provides victims with therapy, legal representation, social support, and medical care. She works to ensure that the criminal justice and medical systems effectively respond to the victims' complex requirements.

Just recently, a fourteen-year-old Pakistani girl who had been raped by her father's cousin had the courage to report the crime to the police. She had to undergo a traumatic and invasive "virginity test" to ascertain if she had a sexual history. Bear in mind that only 3–5 percent of sexual assault allegations are false, while 95 percent or more are true. Practices such as virginity tests deny victims the justice they deserve.

Sidra characterizes these ordeals this way: "I count this as another rape in itself, and most victims I have worked with have spoken of being traumatized by it." Despite threats, Sidra continues to volunteer her time to help vulnerable women and girls get access to services that would otherwise be unavailable to them.

#26 | TO SAFEGUARD AGAINST CHILD AND HUMAN TRAFFICKING

Luiza relocated from Uzbekistan to Kyrgyzstan at the age of twenty-two in search of employment. When she arrived in Bishkek for a position as a waitress, her prospective employers took her passport and detained her against her will. Along with other individuals, she was compelled to perform sex labor in Dubai after being trafficked there. According to Luiza, she became a sex slave. After enduring a year and a half of torment she allowed herself to be captured by the police and served a year in prison.[306]

The Quran in condemnation of such injustices perpetrated by evildoers, prohibits human trafficking, particularly commercial exploitation of women and children forced into providing services for the financial gain of others, described as follows: *"Warn them 'O Prophet' of the approaching Day when the hearts will jump into the throats, suppressing distress. The wrongdoers will have neither a close friend nor intercessor to be heard"* (Q 40:18).

Islam prohibits violating a person's fundamental rights. It opposes inhumane, degrading, and humiliating treatment, such as kidnapping, sexual servitude, and recruitment of minors into the military. Transporting individuals against their will for sex work, forced labor, or organ transplant is contrary to Islamic teachings and is universally condemned as a form of modern slavery. Prophet Muhammad forewarned his community, "There are three categories of people against whom I shall myself be a plaintiff on the Day of Judgement. Of these three, one is he who enslaves a free man, then sells him and eats this money."[307]

THE DARK JOURNEY OF TRAFFICKED SOULS

The Quran commands people to promote the good and forbid the bad. It emphasizes the right of the persecuted individual to seek refuge elsewhere, just as the Prophet did when he fled persecution in Mecca and found sanctuary in Yatrib: *"God has certainly turned in mercy to the Prophet as well as the Emigrants and the Helpers who stood by him in the time of hardship, after the hearts of a group of them had almost faltered"* (Q 9:117).

According to the Quran, displaced people are entitled to humane treatment: *"Those who believed, emigrated, and strived with their wealth and lives in the cause of God, as well as those who gave them shelter and help—they are truly guardians of one another"* (Q 8:72-75). As many human trafficking victims frequently face retaliation at the hands of their traffickers in their home countries, the countries of destination should offer refuge to victims rescued on their soil, in accordance with the Prophet's words: "Whoever relieves the suffering of another believer, God will relieve his suffering on the Day of Judgment."[308]

In addition to praising those who safeguard refugees, the Quran commands Muslims to treat victims of injustice with dignity and respect as well as to provide them with assistance and protection. Due to factors such as poverty, unequal access to opportunities as well as precarious conditions—women, refugees, migrants, displaced people, children, and runaways are at a greater risk for human trafficking.

There are also subtle factors which sometimes convince people that crimes perpetuated most often against women are less important to address. For example, the insistence that women belong in the private sphere of the home leads to the conclusion that women are somehow less valuable; they do not contribute to formal employment and do not generate financial benefits; perhaps their rights are less important than the rights of men. The perception of their lower status and worth makes them all the more susceptible to trafficking.

In conflict zones with limited economic opportunities, women and girls who flee or emigrate in search of better economic prospects frequently fall victim to human traffickers who exploit them for financial gain and force them to perform sex work against their will. The Quran cautions against sexual exploitation: *"Do not force your 'slave' girls into prostitution for your own worldly gains while they wish to remain chaste"* (Q 24:33). As sexual exploitation for profit is prohibited, the Prophet forbade taking the earnings of a soothsayer and the money earned by prostitution.[309]

EDUCATING COMMUNITIES

As a natural result of the parent-child bond, parents are entrusted with the responsibility to safeguard their child's physiological, emotional, and spiritual rights. Children must be protected from conditions that could force them to abandon their homes and make them susceptible to human traffickers.

Child selling is a form of trafficking in which parents or relatives give up their children in exchange for money, goods, or other benefits. This can be motivated by a variety of factors: poverty, conflict, and the vulnerability of family members. Typically, this occurs when a family is in financial need or believes that their child would have a better life elsewhere.

Child trafficking had become widespread in Afghanistan, a country plagued by decades of conflict and political instability. Parents rationalize their actions as the lesser of two evils, wishing to rescue the entire family at the price of one child. To save money, some families resort to selling off a girl, which often results in her being enslaved for the rest of her life.

According to Al-Azhar University of Cairo, the concept of child protection cannot be realized without combating all forms of abuse, violence, and exploitation that threaten children or deprive them of their fundamental rights. These include parental care, education, healthcare, the enjoyment of recreation and sports, and freedom of expression and thought.[310]

THE EFFECTS OF CHILD TRAFFICKING

Human and child trafficking are flagrant violations of all human rights, as they violate all six objectives of Shariah: family life, intellect, wealth, religion, and dignity. Child trafficking undermines the sanctity of family institutions and unravels the family.

Children who have been trafficked may lose or be unable to trace their ancestry or even their most fundamental cultural traditions. When a child is removed from a family, the essential bonds of affection and communication for the development of healthy relationships are disrupted. Their right to be raised by their mother and other biological family members is violated. They grow up with severe separation trauma and frequently endure humiliation in the society to which they are transported. These manipulations severely impair an ability to later find a suitable spouse, marry, and raise a family of their own.

As a result of oppression and injustice, the life of a child who has been trafficked is misappropriated, and their life quality is severely degraded. They suffer bodily harm as they lack adequate food, clothing, and sufficient shelter to protect them against harsh elements. When children are forced to work, they have no time to rest, play, or engage in activities necessary for their healthy development as children and adolescents.

A trafficked child is compelled to forego education and remain illiterate, and is denied free rational thought, all of which hinder intellectual development, another basic Islamic right. Through knowledge, a child learns responsibility for their actions, and denial of education prevents them from realizing this potential. Trafficked children may experience a loss of psychological security because of exposure to intoxicants and narcotics, causing irreparable damage as they are indoctrinated with sectarian rhetoric and coerced into joining militant groups.

Trafficked children are denied wealth and inheritance and forced to live in abject poverty. As victims of forced labor, they are denied fair wages and a safe working environment. When young boys are sold into culturally exploitative sexual servitude, they receive meager wages in exchange for their labor, blood, and dignity. Some boys are forced to dress as girls and perform immoral and degrading acts for the sexual amusement of affluent and powerful men.[311] These actions have no justification, and the Quran threatens to punish those who devour orphans' money: *"Indeed, those who unjustly consume orphans' wealth [in fact] consume nothing but fire into their bellies. And they will be burned in a blazing Hell!"* (Q 4:10).

Learning religion from their parents helps children build their character, deepen their faith, and understand their religious rights and obligations. When a child is denied the opportunity to learn about morals and ethics that form the foundation of faith, their impressionable brains are quickly perverted by exposure to lawlessness and immorality.

Trafficked children are denied their God-given dignity. They are housed in filthy, unhygienic conditions, in large groupings, with no right to privacy or autonomy; they are treated like livestock. This prevents them from conversing privately with family, hindering their mental and emotional development. The child's self-esteem is irreparably damaged by this abusive treatment.[312]

HUMAN TRAFFICKING AND SLAVERY IDENTICAL

At the age of nine, the Prophet discovered that his beloved surrogate mother, Barakah, was enslaved. Mohamad Jebara describes that he was so revolted by the idea of slavery that he decided to stand on the steps of the Kaaba declaring, "I hereby declare Barakah to be free like the wind." Some in the crowd snickered, while Barakah wept with joy. Though she was now free to return home, she remained by his side until his death. (48)

When he married Khadijah, he began to sow the seeds of emancipation in her mind and they showed care for enslaved household members, which was unheard of in Meccan culture. When he watched a master viciously flogging his enslaved worker one day, he immediately offered the owner double the man's worth and bought his freedom. When he discovered that most of his slaves had previously been free and had been enslaved as children, that they had been subjected to the agony of kidnapping and dehumanization, and that they had free minds hidden within their imprisoned bodies, he restored their dignity by encouraging them to voice their opinions.

This couple understood that publicly liberating slaves would cause an outcry and enrage masters who relied on slave labor for a living. As a result, they held a secret ceremony in Khadijah's warehouse, where Khadijah formally released them, declaring, "You are now all free, like the birds of the sky and the wind." When the Prophet began preaching his message, many slaves followed him, infuriating the Meccan elites. His message was incomprehensible: Their slaves were equal to them and deserved to be recognized as human beings.

The Prophet no longer felt safe in public, so he retreated to a cave outside of town where Bilal, an enslaved African, was grazing his master's sheep. When the Prophet saw Bilal, he encouraged him to sit next to him. This astonished Bilal since it was the first time he had been treated as a free man; Bilal became a Muslim without hesitation. Later, his master tied and dragged him across Mecca before whipping him senseless; despite his inability to speak, Bilal uttered mournfully, "God is One! Just One!"

Grieved by the unimaginable torture that Bilal endured, the Prophet exhausted his resources, asking Abu Bakr to buy the tortured Bilal out of slavery. This first effort led to the emancipation of many slaves. The Prophet appointed Bilal as the first *mu'adhin*, or caller to prayer, and gave him the title *Sayyid al-Mu'adhin*, or Master of the Callers to Prayer.

The high bar set by the Prophet was followed by his companions, who freed tens of thousands of slaves of their own volition. A verse revealed early in the Prophet's career instructed Muslims that the first step in the journey towards God is through freeing slaves: *"And what will make you realize what 'attempting' the challenging path is? It is to free a slave, or to give food in times of famine to an orphan relative"* (Q 90:12).

Khadijah and Abu Bakr, both wealthy people, became almost penniless through buying slaves their freedom. For them, liberating slaves was not merely one specific good deed, but one of the ultimate means of attaining spiritual excellence. In fact, scores of former slaves were drawn to Islam by the Prophet's antislavery movement and the Quran's central theme of human equality: *"O humanity! Indeed, we created you from a male and a female and made you into peoples and tribes so that you may [get to] know one another. Surely the most noble of you in the sight of God is the most righteous among you"* (Q 49:13).

REVIVAL OF SLAVERY IN OUR DAY

Nowhere in the Quran is it permissible for a Muslim to enslave another person and no verse in the Quran commands that the practice be continued or reinstated. God commanded Muslims to obey the Prophet, who was a fierce opponent of slavery: *"[S]hould you disagree on anything, then refer it to God and His Messenger if you 'truly' believe in God and the Last Day. This is the best and fairest resolution"* (Q 4:59). In addition, numerous verses in the Quran refer to the emancipation of slaves, such as, *"The penalty for a broken oath is to feed ten people from what you normally feed your own family, or to clothe them, or free a bondsperson"* (Q 5:89).

The Prophet despised slavery but was unable to completely eradicate it, and in his final address he underlined the benefits of releasing people from bondage: "Whoever frees a Muslim slave, God will save all the parts of his body from the [Hell] Fire as he has freed the body parts of the slave."[313]

Despite this example and Quranic passages, in recent years both

Daesh and Boko Haram interpreted the mere mention of slavery in the Quran with approval and encouragement, ignoring the verses that clearly call for its elimination. To justify abduction, imprisonment, and trafficking of women and children, they cited *verse 4:25: "But if you cannot afford to marry a free believing women, then let him marry a believing bond[s]woman possessed by one of them, so, marry them with the permission of their owners, giving them their dowry in fairness."* The term "believing bond[s]woman" referred to a "temporary" institution of servitude that existed at the time and was permitted only in early Islamic society. In contrast, the verse was intended to send a potent message to new Muslims: 1) Do not be humiliated to marry a bondswoman because you all belong to the same human family; and 2) set an example by marrying and emancipating a slave woman.

Based on Islam's emphasis on establishing an egalitarian society and the Prophet's movement for the emancipation of captives, Muslims must be at the forefront of speaking out against all forms of slavery and raising their voices above groups like Daesh, Boko Haram, and human and child traffickers. *"[S]o do not let your desires cause you to deviate from injustice" (Q 4:135).*

Nazira Zin al-Din, provides a higher perspective, comparing the suppression of women to the subjugation of nations and the deprivation of their citizens' freedom. She claims that no slave has ever excelled prior to gaining his freedom, as the injustice he faces saps his mental power and precludes its effects from appearing.[314]

Islam accords special protection to women and children, and failing to protect them is a sin because whoever neglects an obligation is legally liable for its consequences. Thus, the Prophet assigned every person a role: "Each of you is a caretaker and responsible for those under his care."[315] Parents, guardians, and governments have a responsibility to ensure that a female child (as much as a male child) is secure and nurtured until she becomes an adult, a moral and productive member of society.

The Prophet emphasized the protection of the vulnerable and came to break the chains of bondage. Once unshackled, formerly enslaved men and women restored their inner self and leaped forward to establish a global movement of believers without precedent. Today, we must follow the Prophet's example and join forces to combat modern human trafficking networks. Only by embracing our shared responsibility and eradicating stigma will we be able to liberate all forms of enslaved people, and bask in freedom's embrace.

There is still much work to be done, but many are taking up the cause. Take Gulnara Karakulova, for example, who has fought to help Kazakhstan's women, particularly those who have been victims of human trafficking. In 2002 she founded a safe house for survivors of domestic abuse and human trafficking, which is currently available to anybody in need. This refuge offers a secure place for women to reside while they seek medical, legal, and mental health services. The National Commission for Family and Women of the president of the Republic of Kazakhstan honored her with a diploma for her participation in this essential work. Karakulova also wrote a book, *Help for Human Trafficking Victims: Legal Considerations*, and is a patron of an orphanage in the village of Sairam in South Kazakhstan. Gulnara's work has become a source of empowerment for others, a rallying cry that echoed through legislative corridors and community gatherings alike.

#27 | TO HEALTH AND HYGIENE

More than sixty female interns and guests passed through the security checkpoint at the Kandahar provincial governor's office with only one female security officer responsible for vetting the visitors. The regional director of women's affairs in Kandahar noted that the officer appeared fragile, and on the verge of collapsing. The regional director offered the screener water, which the screener declined. "Why?" asked the regional director.

"Because if I drink water, I'll need to use the restroom, and there are no female toilets," the screener explained. The regional administrator was stunned. The screener concluded, "It's true. There is a restroom with a lock that I can use, but a man with a large key ring must be summoned. It takes him a long time to arrive. He jangles all the keys to alert everyone that I must use the toilet. It is extremely humiliating. I do not drink during the day because of this."

In Islam, cleanliness is a valued aspect of a believer's life. The Quran considers ritual purity akin to holiness and emphasizes hygiene as part of outward and inward purity. *"He loves those who keep themselves pure and clean" (Q 2:222)*.

Moreover, the Quran suggests that the body's condition affects the condition of the spirit. It is essential to be always clean—focus on a daily ritual purity (*taharah*), prior to prayer (*salah*).[316] To purify oneself, one must perform ablution, *wudu*, or under certain conditions, a full bath, *ghusl*. *"[W]hen you rise up for prayer, wash your faces and your hands up to the elbows, wipe your heads, and wash your feet to the ankles. And if you are in state of full impurity, then take a full bath" (Q 5:6)*. It is not God's will to burden people, so if water is not available or people are traveling, then a dry ablution, called *tayammum*, is permitted.

The Prophet proclaimed, "Cleanliness is one-half of faith."[317] He emphasized that the requirement for hygiene should not impede the integrity of faith and taught women how to clean themselves during menstruation so that they could remain spiritually active. To maintain hygiene and fulfill religious commitments women need access to water and bathrooms. Lack of public restrooms makes it difficult for women to prepare their minds, bodies, and spirits for the various forms of worship.

TIDINESS AND GROOMING

Muslims are instructed to maintain a healthy balance between physical, mental, and spiritual life. Besides hand washing and bathing, Muslims are told to wear clean clothes. *"Arise and warn all. Revere your Lord alone. Purify your garments" (Q 74:1-4).*

The Prophet instructed Muslims to maintain a respectable appearance through grooming and to be civically responsible by keeping streets and public spaces clean. He said, "Removing dangerous objects from the road is a charitable act,"[318] and in another passage, "Keep your saddles and clothing clean. Be remarkable in the sight of the people." On another occasion he stated, "Don't ever come with your hair and beard disheveled like the devil." And in another, "Had I not been afraid of overburdening my community, I would have ordered them to brush their teeth before every prayer."[319]

OUR MEDICAL HERITAGE

Also, according to the Quran, there is no ailment for which God has not created a treatment. *"And He alone heals me when I am sick" (Q 26:80).* The Quran motivated early Muslim physicians to develop cures for sicknesses. *Bimaristans* (from the Persian words *bimar*, meaning "sick person," and *stan*, meaning "place") were established in the ninth century to satisfy the moral responsibility to heal everyone. Male or female, civilian or military, adult or minor, wealthy or poor, Muslim or non-Muslim, these hospitals and hospices were open to anyone regardless of socioeconomic status.

Sadly, many Muslims are unaware of this immense medical heritage: Muslim scientists made major discoveries. Born in Raz, Iran, Muhammad Ibn Zakariya Al-Razi (864–932 CE), for example, was a renowned physician. He was the first physician to describe how to differentiate between measles and smallpox, as well as the first to write about specific treatments and discover that fever is a defense mechanism.[320]

Ibn Sina (980 CE), a Persian physician of the eleventh century known in the West as Avicenna, was Europe's foremost authority on medical matters for several centuries. In his five-volume work, *The Canon of Medicine*, he devised a system of medical care in which physical and psychological factors, medication regimens, and nutrition were combined to provide patients with a holistic treatment. According to Ibn Sina, health education begins in the embryonic period; therefore, pregnant and nursing mothers must care for their health to assure the health of their infants. Additionally, he stressed the importance of health education and care for all Muslims, including women at all stages of life.

Ibn Sina emphasized that it is a duty of mothers to teach their children how to care for their bodies and satisfy their physical needs. His innovative religious and scientific approach to achieving inner peace and well-being contributed to the development of psychological concepts as well.[321] His five-volume encyclopedia became the cornerstone of Western medical education between the thirteenth and seventeenth centuries. In it, he argued that disease is transmitted through microscopic, imperceptible particles. He suggested isolating for forty days (*arba iniya*) to prevent the spread of the disease. As a result, during the Black Plague of the 1300s, anchored merchant ships from Venice were quarantined for forty days. The Venetians called it *quarantina*.

During the 2020–23 pandemic, it became evident that the concept of quarantine to control the spread of disease originated in 1025, when Ibn Sina published his first works. Ibn Sina adhered to the Prophet's explicit instructions regarding contagious diseases and protective measures: "One should flee the leper as one would a lion." Concerning isolation, he advised, "Do not place a sick patient with a healthy person." To maintain a safe distance, he advised, "When interacting with someone who has a contagious disease, there should be a spear's length between you and that person." He suggested a quarantine to prevent the spread of a pandemic: "If you hear of an outbreak of plague in a country, do not enter it; if the plague breaks out in a location while you are there, do not leave."[322]

When the Covid-19 virus first emerged, Dr. Ozlem Türeci, a Turkish German Muslim woman and cofounder of BioNTech, understood the urgency of developing a vaccine to prevent it from spreading. Under her direction, BioNTech and Pfizer collaborated on a vaccination that was 90 percent efficacious. Two billion vaccinations administered by 2021 saved millions of lives. Dr. Ozlem Türeci and her husband were named "People of the Year 2020" for "one of the greatest medical breakthroughs of our time."

UNEARTHING THE LEGACY OF MEDIEVAL MEDICINE WOMEN

Muslim women in the medical professions and arts are nothing new. Quran and Hadith are replete with references to hygiene and healthcare, and medieval females played pivotal roles in society as both medical practitioners and patients.

In their paper on "Muslim Women Healers," Nada Darwish and Alan Weber chronicle medieval Muslim women. Ottoman Egypt (1299-1922 CE) saw women serving as physicians, surgeons, midwives, visiting their patients' homes, and at times running their own shops. Female patients believed women had a greater understanding of uterine disease and other female-related ailments than men. However, female physicians did not provide care strictly for women. One sixteenth century chronicle refers to a Turkish female physician who was respected by both male and female patients and praised for her talent in treating women with hysteria.

Also notable, the daughter of Sari Eldin al-Saigh held a medical managerial position as a woman physician. She was so competent that she became president of her physician guild and succeeded her father as chief physician of the al-Mansuri hospital, which was built in 1284 CE. Women healers had titles such as female manager (*hastalar kethüdası kadın*), female assistant (*hastalar kethüdasının cariyesi*), female physician (*hekim kadın*), and mistress of the sick (*hastalar ustası hanım ana*). Women served the imperial family, cared for the sick as nurses, provided medical consultation and treatment for both genders, and were highly skilled surgeons.

Sufi Sheikhas were even more prominent than their male counterparts as physicians and geomancers. The majority of clientele of popular female healers were other women who utilized folk medicine. In addition to preventing illnesses such as plague, they also sought solutions for private worries. Among them were barrenness, infertility, childbirth, and infant mortality, all of which jeopardized their marriages, social and economic prestige, and even their lives.[323]

DISTINCTIVE ASPECTS OF WOMEN'S HEALTH

A variety of biological, physiological, and social factors differentiate women's health needs from those of men. Women's health considerations are unique and include menstruation, contraception, pregnancy, childbirth, and menopause. For gynecological conditions such as menstrual disorders, ovarian cysts, uterine fibroids, and breast health, they also require specialized care. Throughout their lifetimes, women's bodies undergo significant hormonal fluctuations, including hormonal disorders that can have a negative impact on fertility. They are more likely to develop breast cancer than men, and are also susceptible to ovarian, cervical, and uterine cancers, among others. Certain women experience mood disorders such as premenstrual syndrome (PMS), perinatal depression, and postpartum depression. Some women may have body image issues and experience social pressure as a result.

The Quran emphasizes health and well-being as a blessing. The Prophet considered illness a test, "Do not curse the fever, for verily it forgives sins as a fire gets rid of impurities in iron."[324] Illness and disease are viewed as suffering endured by believers as a means of spiritual purification when religious transgressions manifest as illnesses, or as a means of elevating the devotee. In underserved communities, where nurses and midwives fill the vacuum left by the absence of healthcare providers, women's health concerns are frequently misdiagnosed. In addition, women's decisions to seek medical care are influenced by cultural and religious norms, such as misconstrued beliefs about fatalism and predestination.

Even though the Prophet preached the importance of obtaining medical advice—"Utilize medical treatment, for God has not created a disease without a remedy, with the exception of one disease, old age"[325]—still, some Muslims believe illness is part of God's will and that seeking treatment will go against God's plan. This claim is refuted by Imam Ghazali, who viewed providing healthcare as a communal obligation (*fard kifaya*).[326] Women have a fundamental right to healthcare, and those with the resources and talent to provide it, have an obligation to do so.

FACTORS BEHIND WOMEN'S HEALTHCARE DENIAL

Social stigmas and cultural barriers often hinder women's access to healthcare, especially when sexual and reproductive health topics are seen as taboo or highly sensitive. Specific medical treatments may even be subject to legal and policy restrictions, thus affecting women's freedom to make healthcare decisions. Furthermore, issues such as gender segregation and preference, modesty observance, lack of knowledge, and dogmatic attitudes inhibit women's autonomy and access to comprehensive healthcare.

In some conservative societies, privacy concerns are of the utmost importance, and healthcare facilities are gender-segregated. This separation can restrict women's access to adequate care. Those who insist on female doctors stigmatize medical care provided by male physicians to female patients, again causing women to be hesitant. And due to a shortage of women doctors, women are deprived of essential reproductive and gynecological services that are unique to their gender.

Some Muslims adhere to strict modesty practices that involve family members in their medical care, causing women to be reluctant to discuss confidential concerns with male doctors. When a husband accompanies a wife, for instance, the patient and practitioner may feel uncomfortable if the woman refuses to remove her garments. If she is unable to disclose her body for a thorough examination, her diagnosis and treatment will be inadequate.

For example, Dr. Hanan Gewefal had noted the absence of breast cancer screening facilities in Egypt as a cause of breast cancer-related deaths. She founded the Women and Fetal Imaging Clinic to spearhead efforts to elevate community-wide awareness of breast cancer. Women are now able to learn about early detection techniques and obtain free mammograms and screenings at the facility. Dr. Hanan's efforts alone have saved countless Egyptian women's lives.

MISPLACED OBSERVANCE HARMING WOMEN AND CHILDREN

According to the Quran, women who are pregnant, lactating, or menstruating are exempt from fasting during Ramadan. Muslims can make up the fast by feeding the poor or fasting later. Despite this provision, some pregnant women fast out of religious conviction or social pressure. They are unaware of the detrimental effects that starvation can have on both mother and fetus. Additionally, a fasting person is uncertain if they can receive medications or undergo procedures such as injections, blood tests, medications absorbed through the skin, gargling without ingesting, vaccinations, ear and nasal drops, suppositories, pessaries, and inhaled medications. Although they can, differing scholarly opinions frequently obfuscate the issue, causing widespread confusion regarding the importance of healthcare while being observant.[327]

Incorrect religious beliefs and dogmas also overshadow the priorities and ethics of public health. In the case of eradicating polio through vaccination, for example, Pakistan came under intensified scrutiny when pockets of resistant populations refused the shot. They were influenced by *fatwas*, which they acknowledge as authoritative, and which prohibited vaccinations. But vaccination continues to be the most effective public health intervention for reducing diseases such as polio and measles, as well as infant mortality rates. The refusal to vaccinate children subjects mothers and families to a lifetime of caregiving. In fact, those who issued such edicts contradict the consensus of Muslim jurists worldwide that "vaccinations are obligatory."

Furthermore, when it is regarded through a strictly religious lens, mental health is almost always overlooked. Some believe that Muslims who practice Islam correctly cannot succumb to depression. Others believe that bipolar depression is caused by *jinn* possession, which can only be treated by exorcism. By failing to recognize mental illness as a treatable condition, they deny patients access to treatment, placing undue stress on the family, particularly mother and siblings who are encumbered with emotional regret, exhaustion, and financial difficulties.

For these reasons, Dr. Farha Abbasi, a psychiatrist and the managing editor of the *Journal of Muslim Mental Health*, has come forward to promote integration, not isolation, among American Muslims. She instructs medical students on how to treat Muslim patients in a culturally sensitive manner. She organizes an annual conference on Muslim mental health to proactively address the obstacles that stigmatize and suppress mental health.

MOTHER-CENTRIC BIRTHING

Nearly 90 percent of Muslim women experience childbirth. Prior to the twentieth century, most of them labored at home. In some cultures, women gave birth in the woodlands. Farmers continue to give birth amid orchards, paddies, and tea plantations. In a chapter titled "Maryam," the Quran describes an extraordinary birth in the woods when, pregnant with Jesus, Mary's labor pain forces her to retreat into a remote area where she embraces the trunk of a palm tree. In the throes of labor, she cries out in anguish, *"I wish I had died before this, and I was a thing long forgotten!" (Q. 19:22-24).* Throughout the millennia, women in labor have felt similar emotions as they endured labor pains.

In the age-old profession of midwifery (*tabiba*)—women delivered babies and provided advice on women-focused health issues. Ibn Khaldun regarded midwifery as one of the most noble professions because midwives were trained in childbirth and had more knowledge of children's illnesses than men.[328] Midwives are one of many ways that Muslim civilizations over the centuries have focused on women's needs in healthcare.

Asli Sancar describes how the Ottoman Royal Court lavished the new mother with beautiful ceremonies. To facilitate her delivery, a chair with a high back and arms was carved. A skilled midwife would then assist in childbirth. Mothers would recite the *Shahada* to the newborn, while the father would recite the Call to Prayer in the infant's ear and repeat its name three times. Lohusa, a new mother, reclined on a settee with a Quran in an embroidered bag hanging at its head to ward off evil. She remained for forty days to heal her internal organs. On the fortieth day, an opulent public celebration with entertainment and refreshments was held, during which she was plastered with healing honey, ointments, and various aromatic condiments to strengthen and recover her body. (73)

This tradition has been replaced by obstetrics, derived from the Latin word for "observant," which means literally "one who watches and observes." Notice how this is both similar and different from the historical "patient observation" role of male doctors. One theory has it that King Henry VIII of sixteenth-century England was responsible for altering how women gave birth because he enjoyed witnessing childbirth and invited male physicians to observe the delivery with him. Over time, they began delivering babies, and now most urban women today give birth with the assistance of an obstetrician in a hospital.

Obstetricians are trained to manage pregnancies and make crucial decisions for the best possible outcome for mother and child. Nevertheless, some obstetricians recommend "cleaner," expensive, and often superfluous C-sections, resulting in their financial gain at the expense of the best practices and needs of women. Twenty years ago, C-sections were common in Iran, with unethical doctors frequently forcing them on women. Women were convinced that they were overweight/out of shape/angular for a typical delivery forcing C-sections upon them.[329] Alaa, from Egypt, was advised to undergo a C-section without being informed of the potential risks. No one described the technique, leaving her powerless, humiliated, and without physical autonomy.[330] Women should not be compelled to abandon their childbearing plans for non-medical reasons. Natural birth has numerous advantages for both mother and infant, whereas C-sections carry greater risks and require a prolonged recovery period. In a society influenced by remorse, body shaming, and excessive reverence for doctors, women's birthing choices and medical care may get buried.

But there is nothing more wonderous than seeing a mother give birth to her child—a moment that contains the promise of not only a new life, but the capacity to transform family, community, and society. As we rejoice in the beauty of childbirth, let us also endeavor to ensure that every woman's pregnancy, as well as her pre- and post-delivery journey, is characterized by compassion, care, and respect for the decisions she makes. This will help to secure a more promising future for generations to come.

A PAKISTANI DIGITAL DOCTOR WHO SAVES LIVES

Pregnancy should be a joyful time for women and their families, but Dr. Sara Khurrum was forced to choose between her radiology job and having a child. Her story is consistent with the experience of female physicians in Pakistan. She faced challenges early in her profession, including a pregnancy that nearly ended her career.

That's when she started doctHERs, an organization that uses technology to link millions of underserved patients with female doctors. Nurses and paramedics use aided video consultations to offer patients a full, diagnostic medical checkup and prescribe medicine digitally. This digital doctor tackles gender barrier by delivering vital clinical treatment that is socially relevant and culturally acceptable.[331]

PART VI

THE RIGHT TO YOUR DIGNITY

. . . .

God is the origin of human dignity, as God breathed his spirit into the human body. This dignity allows a woman to assume divine trust. The dignity of a woman is found in her being honored and respected for her own sake.

As a bearer of dignity, every woman is endowed with rationality to make choices and distinguish between good and evil. Women have the right to live free of unlawful aggression that violates their dignity. They have the right to maintain their reputations and must never be the victim of false accusations or character assassination. And women must be allowed to defend transgressions that inhibit their ability to live a life of self-worth and self-respect.

The objective of promoting and protecting human dignity and honor is the right of every person to be valued without conditions:

- All people must be protected against false accusation, defamation of reputation, and disrespect.
- Many jurists consider the basic human dignity to be the basis for human rights, pointing to the verse in the Quran that exhorts us to cooperate with one another in goodness and righteousness, and not to cooperate in sin and aggression (Q 5:2).
- Hence, human rights are fundamentally essential, or *daruriyyat*.

#28 | TO FULFILL BEING A TRUSTEE OF GOD ON EARTH

In the tradition of the Prophet, God—Creator of the heavens and the earth—announced, "I was a hidden treasure; when I wished to be discovered, I brought into being the whole creation." God created the universe for divine self-discovery. And just as God created humans for him to be known, humans create the consciousness of God within them so that they can be known. Therefore, self-discovery is not only the path that leads to God's discovery; it is no less true that God's discovery leads to greater self-discovery.[332]

Human creation begins with Adam and Eve—known as *Hawwa* in Arabic, described in the Quran this way: "*[A]nd He originated the creation of humankind from clay. Then He made his descendants from an extract of humble fluid*" (Q 32:7-8). Then a "mate" was created with Adam, from the same essence and soul: "*He is the one who created you from a single soul, then made from it its spouse, so he may find comfort in her*" (Q 7:189).

When God completed Adam's creation from clay, he breathed his Divine Spirit into his earthly form. From the perspective of divinity, humans are the earthly receptacle, container, and repository of Divine Spirit (*ruh*), a unique, highly exalted trust (*amanah*), and a divine mandate being bestowed upon them. Our exaltedness lies in our spirituality, not in our physiology. The former makes us God's trustee and servant. As such, an exalted form of creation, humans are the most elevated form of creation.

God declared to the angels, "*[I] am going to place a successive 'human' authority on earth*" (Q 2:30). Then when the angels, who were shocked and worried, told God they feared humans would shed blood and cause corruption because humans contained such conflicting forces within them, God added, "*[I] know what you do not know*" (Q 2:30).

The entirety of creation shuddered and refused God's offer of vice-regency, except for humanity, which accepted it. *"[W]e offered the trust to the heavens and the earth and the mountains, but they all declined to bear it, being fearful of it. But humanity assumed it, 'for' they are truly wrongful 'to themselves' and ignorant of the consequences"* (Q 33:72). God is aware that, unlike other species, humans will continue to be in constant want and will exploit the earth's resources, yet God accepted their willingness to serve as his trustees: *"[W]e have created humankind in 'constant' struggle. Do they think that no one has power over them? [D]o they think that no one sees them? Have We not given them two eyes, a tongue, and two lips and shown them the two ways 'of right and wrong'?"* (Q 90:4). God wishes humans would instead choose the arduous path of righteousness.

Khalifa is the name given in the Quran to a trustee of God. A trustee is granted worldly entitlements, endowed by the Creator with specific divine attributes, appointed to act in accordance with God's covenant and rewarded for their good deeds. *"Then We made you successors in the land to see how you would act"* (Q 10:14). *Khalifa* also means "those who come after," and the majority of scholars concur that it pertains directly to the succession of the four "rightly guided caliphs," namely Abu Bakr, Umar, Uthman, and Ali. After the Prophet's death, each was proclaimed his successor through *shura* consultation. Under the first caliph, Abu Bakr, the first Caliphate was established as a civic state based on and governed by the principles of the Quran and the example of the Prophet.[333]

THE UNIVERSE SERVES HUMANS TO SERVE GOD

Being a *khalifa* of God is a blessing and a privilege, but it also requires attention, since God constantly tests their righteousness. *"He is the One Who has placed you as successors on earth and elevated some of you in rank over others, so He may test you with what He has given you"* (Q 6:165).

All men and women bear the obligation of *khilafat*. The Quran refers to men and women's personal relationship with the Creator as *istikhlaf*, which translates as God's privilege extended to humans. This honor symbolizes one of the most prestigious assignments bestowed: the establishment of human civilization on earth. The guiding concept of *hisbah*, which means the promotion of good and the prevention of evil, guides God's trustees. God expects humans to do good works for other humans, and each person will be judged according to their deeds in the world to come. The just will be rewarded, while the unjust will be punished.[334]

According to Nimat Hafez Barazangi, author of *Vicegerency and Gender Justice in Islam*, to properly carry out its obligations a *khalifa* must provide justice, freedom, and equality. They must possess knowledge in all aspects of life and have complete autonomy as individuals, regardless of gender. A person performs their job as God's trustee in two ways: by involving all members in public and domestic matters, and by protecting both domains of life from immoral exposure.[335] The creation of humankind and the appointment of human beings as *al-Khalifa* is made possible by entrusting humans with this divine intent (the moral law). This act is based on a higher level of moral action, namely, the freedom to choose whether or not to fulfill God's will.

KHALIFA TO HUMANKIND

The *Khilafah* is entrusted to all of humanity, not just Muslims. The Quran does not affirm any racial or gender-based differences in the endowment of intellect, ethics, talents, or anything else required to carry out the responsibility, which is consistent with God's absolute transcendence and absolute justice, which are maintained throughout the Quran.[336]

But even though men and women have an equal responsibility to serve God and humanity, some Muslims believe men have a greater claim to vice-regency than women, whose stewardship should be limited to family life. To counter this perception, Asma Barlas argues that the idea of vice-regency is independent of gender, and while it is a relational term, it does not imply that humans are vice-regents over one another. They are vice-regents on earth. The Quran does not support those who misrepresent God as male and male sovereignty as coextensive with God. This inaccuracy stems from a tendency to anthropomorphize God (with human characteristics), and from misunderstanding the theme of vice-regency. (111)

Some Muslim men limit women's participation because they believe that as God's vice-regents they have dominion over women. They quote these two verses: *"[M]en have a degree 'of responsibility' above them (women)" (Q 2:228)*, and *"Men are caretakers of women, as men have been provisioned by God over women and tasked with supporting them financially" (Q 4:34)*. But Amina Wadud, in *Windows of Faith*, defines males as having an advantage over women only in the matter of their physical strength. As far as men being women's protectors, maintainers, and guardians, she says the Quran and Hadith do not have such demeaning notions about women's obligation to fulfill their trusteeship on earth for the sake of God: "A blatant violation of this trusteeship has resulted from the silencing and prohibiting the female voice, the only legitimate articulation of female experiences." (3–21)

According to Nimat Barazangi, the notion that women require consistent male protection leads to the belief that women are incapable of functioning independently in public life, despite what is taught in the Quran and exemplified by the life of the Prophet Muhammad.[337] If women were not intended to participate in public life, the Quran would not have granted her civil rights such as inheritance, disposal of her wealth, and voting (*baya*)—among others. Some incorrectly contend that the confined woman is still fulfilling her role as vice-regent because the men in her life participate in the public sphere on her behalf. But this forcible assumption of female responsibility is condemned by the Quran, which emphasizes the personal character of responsibility and forbids all vicarious responsibility.

Nimat Barazangi states that when men subsume the public responsibilities of women under the guise of protection, it results in a forced dependence on men, diminishes women's agency, and impedes their relationship with and accountability to God. This practice deprives women of their humanity and their capacity to make and bear the consequences of their decisions. This is why education is compulsory for all Muslims, as it helps a person to be intellectually and spiritually autonomous, capable of actively discharging their obligations as a *khalifa*, and only then can they pursue the path toward attaining societal responsibility.

Basma Abdelgafar offers a deeper perspective, claiming that it is not *khilafah* per se that is essential here, but the reality that every human being is endowed with light. The real "right" is the ability to distinguish between good and evil on a fundamental level and to accept revelation brought by messengers. There is no difference between men and women in this regard, which is why we are guardians of each other. Truth is not subject to a gender monopoly.[338]

Abdelgafar provides a subtle analysis and some cautionary words to explain how following God's guidance does not equate to representing him: "Only He represents Himself. For example, the most elevated of humanity, namely, the prophets and messengers, are never referred to as representatives of God. The understanding that any person can be God's Khalifa simply by being placed on this earth has caused too much damage with men bestowing on themselves too much power and, God forbid, Divinity."[339]

The world saw an egregious example of this when Daesh, aka ISIS, co-opted the name *khalifa* and declared the establishment of their Caliphate as "the abandoned responsibility of the era." This Caliphate broke all of the Quran's precepts, prohibiting millions of Muslims from seeing a potential future based on fundamental ideals of peace, freedom, and human dignity.[340] In contrast, Abdelgafar reminds us that our claim to truth, peace, love, and justice is not representative of God, but rather as followers of His guidance and grace, as human beings with a right to discern truths: "We are all guests on this earth, here for a short time and then gone. But our duties and custodianship are serious commitments."[341]

STEWARDS OF THE ENVIRONMENT

God created human nature with exquisite proportions and instilled us with its essence. Through a journey of self-discovery in God, the spirit within us motivates us to attain a heightened awareness of God.

Salma Arastu is a California artist who uses her art to convey something of the Islamic ideal: the beauty of God, devotion to the Creator, and respect for nature. She felt a deep concern for the degradation of the environment and assumed her role as steward with conviction. "Our delicate, diverse, and vibrant world makes me wonder how lucky we are, how we belong, and why we should care about our extended family," she says.[342]

Arastu explains that as a *khalifa* she wanted to signal the stern warnings from the Quran combined with an urgent appeal to humans to live a balanced life without excess or deficiency, where each species depends on the other, making life on earth prosperous. Salma collaborated with author Basma Abdelgafar to publish a book, *Through Our Earth: Embracing All Communities*.

Abdelgafar reminds us that in Arabic, the word "earth" is a "she"—a feminine form. The earth is not an "it." She reminds us that the earth is God's creation—beautiful, decorated, autonomous, and yielding only to His commands. As stewards, we are commanded to take care of her, respect and protect her from vice and destruction. The responsibility and blessing of *khilafat* make it incumbent upon all men and women to protect the vulnerable, ensure the welfare of others, and see to the well-being of God's creation, including flora and fauna.

#29 | TO FREEDOM FROM GOSSIP, SLANDER, LIBEL, DEFAMATION, AND TO PRIVACY

As an increasing number of Iraqi women enter politics, smear campaigns against them on social media have increased. Faryal Al-Kaabi, an expert on women's issues, asserts that political opponents will often fabricate and spread fraudulent allegations about prominent women in an attempt to discredit them. Sometimes women withdraw their candidacies due to false allegations made on social media. Many women in the public eye fear that they and their families will be targeted.[343]

Islam explicitly condemns disseminating falsehoods, slander, and false accusations. The Quran compares backbiting and slander to the morally repugnant act of cannibalism, emphasizing the immorality of these behaviors: *"O [b]elievers! Avoid many suspicions for indeed, some suspicions are sinful. And do not spy, nor backbite one another. Would any of you like to eat the flesh of their dead brother? You would despise that!" (Q 49:12)*

Recognizing the inherent human tendency to indulge in idle gossip, the Quran acknowledges that individuals will be held accountable for their actions, even those that appear to be inconsequential: *"Do not follow what you have no sure knowledge of. Indeed, all will be called to account for their hearing, sight, and intellect" (Q 17:36)*. The Quran also warns against gossip, citing its corrosive effects on relationships, damaging friendships, causing suspicion within families, ruining professional reputations, and spreading distrust among people. Notably, those who refrain from idle gossip are praised, and the Quran encourages responding to falsehood with compassion. Muslims must take the higher road, promote understanding and discourage the spread of rumors. Faced with slander, the Quran suggests disengagement: *"When they hear slanderous talk, they turn away from it, saying, 'We are* accountable for our deeds and you for yours. Peace, is our only response to you. We want nothing to do with those who act ignorantly'" (Q 28:55).

The Prophet's teachings emphasize the significance of choosing one's words carefully. When someone has committed a wrongdoing, the emphasis should be on cultivating understanding rather than dwelling on the negative. The Prophet's advice is clear: "Let the one who believes in God and the Hereafter utter good words or let him be silent."[344] When prompted to define gossip, the Prophet responded succinctly: saying something about your brother that he dislikes.[345] If the information is false, the Prophet emphasized, it goes beyond backbiting and becomes slander: "If what you say is true, then you have backbitten about him, and if it is false, then you have slandered him."[346]

SLANDER, METAPHOR, AND UNCERTAIN ACCUSATIONS

Islam vehemently condemns hearsay, slander, and libel because it recognizes the harm they can cause. No one may infringe upon a person's right to public dignity because God equates a person's reputation with their physical safety. The Prophet reminded his people, "Everything of a Muslim is forbidden for another Muslim: his blood, wealth, and reputation."[347]

The intent of slander and libel is to destroy a life through character assassination, and both are major sins. Slander is communicated verbally, whereas libel is committed in writing. Both are described under the umbrella term *qadhf*, which means to "throw" words of abuse at another person. It encompasses all forms of abusive speech, such as slander, libel, insults, and obscenities.[348]

Qadhf is also defined more narrowly as making an explicit accusation of adultery against another person, such as when one says, "You adulterer," or "You fornicator." If this accusation is unverified, the Quran prescribes a mandatory punishment for slander. Slander is *al-Qadhf bil-Kinayah*, which refers to using a lesser accusation with derogatory terms such as "bastard, lecher, womanizer, or whore." As it is not an explicit accusation of infidelity, there is no prescribed punishment in the Quran. However, it is vile enough that a person may bring the matter before a judge.

God consistently condemns crimes of slander and demonstrates how dangerous it can be, even and especially when directed toward women: "*Surely, those who accuse chaste, unsuspecting believing women* are cursed in this life and the Hereafter. And they will suffer a tremendous punishment" (Q 24:23).

The first instance of slander in Islam occurred when Aisha and the Prophet were on a journey with a caravan. Aisha dropped a valuable necklace and when the caravan stopped, she went in search of it. The caravan continued its journey unaware that she had been left behind. Aisha waited for the Prophet's return, knowing that he would eventually come for her. But it was Safwan bin Al-Mu'attil As-Sulami Adh-Dhakw-ani who found her and brought her home, and when people saw her alone with Safwan, rumors spread that she had strayed from the caravan to commit adultery.

Despite her parents' doubts, she moved to their house while maintaining her innocence. During a month of agony, she became physically unwell upon learning that the Prophet was under pressure to divorce her, and although he was silent, he was not treating her with the same compassion as before. Celene Ibrahim describes God's response to the anguish, despair, and suffering of an innocent woman as follows: "Aisha acts with discretion when she finds herself alone with an unrelated young man, is accused of infidelity by her people, and the Quran itself testifies to her innocence." (34-35) God revealed a verse, sending a stern warning to slanderers that their horrific actions will not go unpunished: "[T]hose who came up with that 'outrageous' slander are a group of you. Do not think this is bad for you. Rather it is good for you. They will be punished, each according to their share of the sin. As for their mastermind, he will suffer a tremendous punishment. If only the believing men and women had thought well of one another, when you heard this rumor and said, 'this is clearly an outrageous slander,' why did you not produce four witnesses? Now, since they have failed to produce four witnesses, they are truly liars in the sight of God" (Q 24:11-13). This verse chastises men who unjustly accuse women of slander without presenting witnesses and reminds people to act in the face of such lies.

Prophet Muhammad compared slandering a chaste woman to the seven sins that damn a person to hell: "Associating anything with God, magic, killing of one whom God has declared inviolate without a just cause, consuming orphan's property, and consuming of usury, turning back when the army advances, and slandering chaste women who are believers, but unwary."[349]

As witnessed by Aisha's ordeal, slander can cause irreparable harm to a person's reputation and their ability to experience trust of family members, peers, and community members. Asifa Quraishi states that Muslims are prohibited from speculating about the sexual behavior of others. Except when leveling formal charges, no one has the right to cast doubt on a woman's character unless there is specific, credible evidence that her behavior violates public decency. The Quran says the perpetrators of this "outrageous" slander will be punished proportionally to their guilt. *"Indeed, those who love to see indecency spread among the believers will suffer a painful punishment in this life and Hereafter" (Q 24:19).*

The Quran's response to any indication of a woman's sexual impropriety is to walk away. Leave her alone. Leave her dignity intact. A woman's honor is not a tool; it is her inalienable right. Quraishi explains that in the absence of such direct evidence, those who make such accusations are subject to physical punishment for slander. (113–114)

CHARACTER AND REPUTATION

Defamation, the act of damaging a person's reputation, is another culpable offense. The Prophet regarded personal slights and defaming someone based on their actions, character, or appearance to be unsavory and inexcusable. He reprimanded Umar bin Khattab for accusing Hatib ibn Abi Balta'a of hypocrisy. When Aisha made fun of his other wife, Safiyya, for being short, he told her, "You've said something that, if mixed with the oceans, would permeate them entirely."[350] And when Abu Dharr insulted Bilal by saying, "You son of a black woman," the Prophet responded, "You are a man who possesses pre-Islamic ignorance."[351]

Jurists consider curses and personal defamation to be offenses punishable at the discretion of the judge. Ibn Humam al-Hanafi (1388–1457 CE) stated that a discretionary punishment becomes obligatory when a Muslim is slandered with phrases such as "You sinner, you *kafir*, you vile person, you thief," and similar phrases meant to harm him and disparage his name. Hashiyat Qalyubi, a scholar of the Maliki school, viewed ridicule as a similar offense and used the example of Umar to support the application of discretionary punishments for ridicule, vindictiveness, and defamation. Imam Malik stated in the Al-Mudawwanah Al-Kubra, a compendium of legal opinions, that some people are known for their evil. Because of this, such people should receive a severe punishment.[352]

RIGHT TO PRIVACY AND DATA PROTECTION

Islam guarantees and reveres privacy; a person's privacy must not be invaded without permission or made public without their consent. No one can intrude on someone's privacy without legal due process, and government surveillance or arbitrary inquiries are only allowed when sufficient evidence of an offense exists.

For example, one reason for requesting permission before entering a home is to prevent people from even glancing inside. *"[D]o not enter houses other than your own until you have asked permission and greeted its occupants.... If you find no one at home, do not enter it until you have been given permission. And if you are asked to leave, then leave" (Q 24:27-29)*. On certain occasions, the Prophet stood to the side of a door waiting, because some residences lacked curtains on the door itself. He even forbade his followers from unexpectedly entering their own homes without prior notification. The purpose was to ensure that the occupants of the house were aware of someone's arrival so that no one would encounter a female family member in a state in which they would prefer not to be seen.[353]

In Mariam Sherwani's article, "The Right to Privacy under International and Islamic Law," she explains how Islam reveres the confidentiality of data as well. The Prophet stated that whoever looks at his brother's letter without his permission looks into a fire. Consequently, unauthorized access to private documents, letters, communications, and emails is expressly prohibited. The violation of a person's privacy can result in the disclosure of their secrets, which, once in the hands of their adversaries, can have severe repercussions: *"And do not spy, nor backbite one other" (Q 49:12)*.

Breaching people's privacy causes mutual distrust and suspicion among people, Sherwani states. The Prophet said that if you search for people's faults, it will nearly corrupt them. By inference, intruding into somebody's private life, property, house communication, and messages cannot be justified in any case, even by people in positions of power. (36)

MUSLIMS DEFAMING MUSLIM WOMEN

A rumor persisted in Iraq during the time of the Prophet that a man's prayer would be invalidated if an animal or woman walked in front of him while he was praying. In addition to equating women with lesser creatures, they also created an animal taboo that had no foundation in the Quran or Hadith. So, when Aisha, the Prophet's wife, heard these allegations, she said, "Listen, Iraqis! You believe that a man's prayer is disrupted when a donkey, a dog, a woman, and a cat pass in front of him while he is praying. You have equated us, women, with them. Push away whoever comes in front of you as much as possible for you. For nothing cuts the prayer. You have compared women to...animals!"[354]

Shamefully, not much has changed today, as many Muslims defame other Muslims, and women are increasingly the targets. In certain countries, there are Muslims posing as self-appointed "God squads" tasked with regulating the religiosity of women. In Sarah Mainuddin's book, interviewees who wear the *niqab* share stories of women being denied agency within their communities. In her journal, one woman writes: "I first interacted with the *haram* police when I began using social media. After one of my TikTok videos went viral, my comment section and direct messages were abruptly inundated with hurtful comments. I was astounded by the contemptuous manner in which they addressed me, a Muslim and a newcomer to Islam. Some individuals hesitate to convert to Islam because they are terrified of being evaluated by Muslims. Using their authority, the self-appointed *haram* police frequently slander other Muslims via social media and word of mouth. Not caring, publicly shaming someone, and gossiping is a cardinal sin in Islam."

A *hijabi* herself, Sarah Mainuddin says that an older woman once berated her after the *salat* for her wrist showing while she was praying at the mosque. This is the reality of both covered and uncovered women who are routinely subjected to slander online and offline: they are spurned by their own people. Those who don't cover are told they are not devout enough and are damned to hell, and *niqabis* are told they are not representing Islam.

SLANDERING ISLAM

Nothing had prepared me for the wholesale slandering of Islam that took place several years ago in the US and other countries. In 2009, eight years after the 9/11 attacks, I was interviewed by Laura Ingraham on *The O'Reilly Factor* on Fox News. I talked about an Islamic Cultural Center in lower Manhattan named Cordoba House, a first of its kind center of learning, arts, education, devotion, and achievement. The goal was to create a vibrant Muslim community center similar to a

Jewish Community Center or a YMCA in a city that boasts of being the Mecca of the Muslim community. I explained how it would bring much needed revival and healing to the devastated neighborhood in lower Manhattan.

Ingram had no problem with any of it. But in January 2010, after the *New York Times* wrote an article about it, opposition groups seized the opportunity to defame Islam. Soon, the building of Cordoba House ignited a furor demonstrated by a prominently featured headline about the "13-story Ground Zero mosque." A local newspaper then jumped on the bandwagon with an editorial piece headlined, "Mosque Madness at Ground Zero." Opposition groups branded it a "Ground Zero mosque" and a "mosquezilla." This unleashed a tidal wave of Islamophobia: hatred, fear, prejudice, hostility, and discriminatory practices toward Muslims, leading to a widespread slandering. A group named Stop Islamization of America began with a full-scale hate initiative. Suddenly, the far-right media portrayed me as an extremist, claiming that I was constructing a victory mosque at Ground Zero and harboring secret plans to create a caliphate and institute Shariah law in the United States.

ABC and CNN anchor Christiane Amanpour persuaded me to participate in a debate titled, "Should Americans Fear Islam?" I entered the green room and introduced myself to Rev. Franklin Graham, the renowned evangelical preacher. Graham stated with sanctimonious pride, to my astonishment, "I want you to know that I do not believe in Islam! I do not believe a single word. I adore Muslims, but your religion is not authentic." I was stunned and appalled by his claim to be a Christian. I looked him in the eye and said, "I attended a Catholic school for eleven years and have recited the Lord's Prayer more than three thousand times." I went on, "Jesus is this close to my heart," pointing to my chest, "and your statements do not match the teachings of the Jesus I know." He was flummoxed when he heard a Muslim woman talk about her love for Jesus, so much so that he stood speechless.

Vitriol and slander went rampant on social media and through the mail in those weeks and months. Nothing could have prepared me for the frightening misspelled letters dripping with sadistic, obscenely sexualized, and scatological fury. The envelopes were addressed to DAISY (THE CLOSET TERRORIST) KHAN. One read, "THE MUSLIMS PLAN IS NOT TO COEXIST BUT TO CONVERT + TAKE OVER!" The standard boilerplate seemed to be the use of ALL CAPS on the envelope.

Obviously, people were confusing our objectives with those of al-Qaeda, and other people were simply not thinking at all. One letter, simply signed as from an "American Soldier" stated, "Muslims are a threat to Western Civilization, and mosques are an insult to the American people. Even if such a monstrosity were constructed, it would be destroyed by dutiful American people. Islam is an evil religion that should be wiped from the face of the earth!" It had an image of a mushroom cloud and the phrase "Back Off!" Was this meant to convey that Muslims pose a nuclear threat to the United States, or that the US poses a nuclear threat to Muslims? Either way, it wasn't good.[355]

ISLAMOPHOBIA WORLDWIDE

These threats, this hate, and this slander affect both women and men. Every human being—as the Quran makes plain—is to be free from this oppression.

With the widespread defamation of Muslim women—intolerance, extremism, chauvinism, misogyny, and xenophobia attained a new peak in 2022. Ismat Ara, an Indian journalist, reported being targeted by the app Bulli Bai, which refers to Muslim women in a derogatory manner. The application distributed images of her and dozens of other Muslim women for "auction." Their images were used without permission to create an open-source application on the GitHub platform. "It was violent, threatening, and meant to instill fear and shame in my mind," Ara explained, "as well as the minds of all women who are being targeted in this sexist manner." Eventually, a twenty-one-year-old man and a woman were apprehended, and GitHub blocked the user who created the app.[356]

The internet is a powerful tool that influences user behavior, and it often includes the use of intimidation and harassment and the prejudice that seeks to defame women through speech. And slandering Muslim women must be condemned, both by Muslim men and by the people of other religious traditions (or none) who stand against Islamophobia of all kinds.

There has long been a Western fascination with "the harem," which "though often voyeuristic, placed a high premium on renditions of the segregated world into which Western men were not permitted."[357] Susan Carland, in her book *Fighting Islam*, states that this goes back to the Victorian era, when Western Christendom championed a puritanical, chaste view of Christian women that they projected onto Muslim women, who were seen as harem-bound temptresses and lascivious dancers. The veil that Muslim women wore was regarded as a method of seduction rather than modesty, and the harem—as a hotbed of unbridled sexuality.

This fascination with harems created a lucrative market for Western-authored "harem" accounts, even though the harem was always a private space within a household where women were segregated. As these began to appear, Zeyneb Hanoum (1883–1923 CE), an Ottoman Turkish woman, criticized non-Muslim accounts of harem life emerging for Western audiences. She proclaimed that nine out of ten books on the harem should be destroyed because they were so erroneous. In turn, she wrote her account of living within a harem to redress the inaccuracy and imbalance.[358]

This deep-seeded mischaracterization of Muslim women creates a stereotype that still exists today, that all Muslim women are subjugated, subservient, and confined to harem-like lives. Look around and you will see how often a subjugated Muslim woman is depicted as wearing a headscarf, whereas the militant Muslim woman is a *jihadi* bride wearing a *hijab* and carrying a gun!

FALSE IDEOLOGY IN THE LIGHT OF DAY

Depictions of Muslim men as violent and misogynistic serve as propaganda in which Islam is portrayed as an ideological adversary of the secular West. Showcasing Muslim women as invisible or tempting beings, does the same. But Islamophobia is merely an expedient scapegoat for society's ills. There are many problems we must fix, and we must look at them honestly and confront them directly.

False propaganda against women disregards the autonomy, independence, and diversity of their lives. Muslim women who have experienced cultural aggression, ethnic slander, harassment, bullying, and body shaming are intimately acquainted with the damage that Islamophobes aim to cause. Many online platforms allow Muslims and non-Muslims to defame and slander without repercussions. Let us keep reminding them all how the Quran forbids spreading false rumors, engaging in slander, and backbiting—all sins that are converging when the Prophet warns in his farewell sermon: Your lives, wealth, and dignity are sacred between you, like the sacredness of this day, this month, and this land.[359]

Together, we can create an environment in which a person's dignity is honored, reputation safeguarded, gossip silenced, and slander refuted. Our words have the power to either harm or heal, so let us be mindful of our words. As Sufi sages say, "The tongue only says what is in the heart."

A UK GROUP MONITORING HATE

Let me share with you one more example of hope in a world where people hide behind the anonymity of the web blogs and forums to send hate messages to Muslims online. Tell MAMA (which stands for "Measuring Anti-Muslim Attacks") was founded in 2012 in the United Kingdom to track the increase in anti-Muslim hate crimes. It is led by Imam Atta OBE.

The bulk of the 548 incidences of anti-Muslim harassment recorded by MAMA in 2015 took place online.[360] In addition, almost 20 percent of service users said they had experienced anti-Muslim hatred in person many times, with Muslim women more likely to be victims than men. Attackers were predominantly white men, and victims tended to be dressed in traditional garb at the time of attack. More than 20,000 people have been helped by MAMA, and more than 16,000 cases of anti-Muslim hatred have been handled. They make sure people get help through the justice system with lobbying, advocacy, signposting, and counseling. They work through spikes of anti-Muslim hatred and engage with politicians to grasp the evolving vocabulary of surging anti-Muslim hate.

#30 | TO SAFEGUARD HONOR

Khadija was betrothed to her cousin but fell in love with her neighbor, who wanted to marry her. The village gossiped when they eloped to avoid a forced marriage, forcing her family to move. But then her uncle recruited relatives to scour every road and bus stop for the two of them. Once they were caught, Khadija was imprisoned until the boy's family arrived to protect him. Her sister Kulsoom cried for her "sinner" sister. Three men—her uncle and two others—escorted Khadija out from the home to reclaim their honor. They showed Khadija an empty grave at a cemetery. She saw no weapons. Her bold stare, assertive tone, and upright stance unnerved the three men, so they choked her to death. Buried her. For love. Honor killed her at age fourteen. Grief killed Khadija's mother. Their acts killed her father. The murder on that day led to the death and destruction of an entire family. It left no room for honor.[361]

The Quran strictly prohibits all forms of murder without due legal process. It considers taking a human life to be a grievous violation and accentuates the gravity of this sin by prescribing a punishment for murder: *"And whoever kills a believer intentionally their reward will be hell—where they will stay indefinitely. God will be displeased with them, condemn them, and will prepare for them a tremendous punishment"* (Q 4:93).

Importantly, the Quran contains no verses that sanction killing in the name of honor. In contrast, the Quran condemns and illustrates the immorality of honor murders. Those who accuse honorable women of slander to justify their actions are criminalized: *"Those who accuse chaste women of adultery, and fail [to] produce four witnesses, give them eighty lashes each"* (Q 24:4).

The explicit position against honor killing is derived from Prophet Muhammad's edicts. Once, a man approached the Prophet and asked him whether a man who discovered his wife with another man should murder her and then be killed in return (given that killing without evidence makes the killer culpable for homicide). Prophet Muhammad was angered by this offensive question and refused to respond. But the man repeated his question, this time in public. At this juncture, God revealed this verse which recommends spouses follow a procedure of mutual condemnation to avoid punishment: *"And those who accuse their wives of adultery but have no witnesses except themselves, the accuser must testify, swearing four times by God that he is telling the truth and a fifth oath that God must condemn him if he is lying. For her to be spared the punishment, she must swear four times by God that he is lying, and a fifth oath that God may be displeased with her if he is telling the truth" (Q 24:6–9).* The Prophet advised the couple to adhere to the principles enumerated in the Quran, and the couple chose to divorce; therefore, no one was required to sacrifice themselves to safeguard "honor."[362]

ISLAMIC LAW'S FIRM PROHIBITION

Honor killings are unequivocally condemned by Islamic law, which views them as a violation of Islamic principles and teachings. Among these fundamental principles are the sanctity of life, equality, justice, consent, and the prohibition of vigilantism. Islam upholds the principles of human dignity and rights for all individuals, regardless of gender or social standing. Under Shariah law, killing a woman for adultery or any other sexual/romantic act constitutes murder (Q. 5:32) and should be treated as such, regardless of motive.

It is crucial to distinguish cultural practices from religious doctrines and to acknowledge that honor killings committed in the name of custom are not sanctioned by Islam.

Jonathan Brown states that in the modern era many of the most eminent Muslim scholars of all sects and backgrounds, including the Sunnis Yūsuf al-Qaraḍāwī and ʿAbdallāh al-Ghumārī (d. 1993 CE), and the late Shiite scholar Muḥammad Ḥusayn Faḍlāllāh (d. 2010 CE), have declared honor killing totally impermissible in Islam.[363] Yemeni scholar al-Shawkānī (d. 1834 CE) also wrote that men who murder women for supposed slights of honor are liable to be executed.

In societies where honor killings occur, women are considered the vanguard of morality and maintainers of dignity. It is argued that the collective family honor is more critical than an individual's dignity; thus, they believe that managing a woman's reputation is a social necessity. All of this is based on the belief that a woman belongs to a man. If she causes shame to her family through unchaste behavior, this shame can only be removed by killing her.

The concept of honor (*izzat*) is inextricably linked to the sense that males have a natural right to possess and control women. Mahnaz Afkhami explains that the objectification of a woman's honor is equated to men's possession of gold and land. For example, women, gold, and land are said to be the most coveted commodities in places such as remote provinces of Pakistan, where honor killings still take place. These three commodities are the root of all conflict. It follows logically, then, that women cannot possess honor in the same manner as men, given that they are themselves objects of honor. Thus, women lose their sense of individuality in the community; they are reduced to manipulable possessions. Raping a woman robs a man of his most prized possession. Once a man's honor is violated, he is expected to pursue vengeance. As for the raped woman, no one cares or dares to care. She does not exist as an individual. (169)

COLONIAL ROOTS OF SOME HONOR CRIME RULES

Honor killings persist in some Muslim nations due to prevailing rules imposed by British and French colonizers. Honor killings were legally unknown in India and Pakistan until the British started overturning Shariah court sentences of the death penalty for homicide on the basis of "provocation."[364] The Ottoman Criminal Code of 1858, which was constructed from the French Code of 1832, reproduced the wholesale honor-killings clause, which served as the foundation for laws relating to honor killings found in Arab nations' penal codes, creating a parallel value system that in action is not Islamic.

According to Fadia Faqir, in nations such as Jordan, the penal code allowing honor killing in certain circumstances can be traced back to the 1810 French penal code, article 324: "The protection of honor now takes precedence over Islamic teachings [and] societal and political structures conspire to form a parallel value system that is stronger than the Islamic religion."[365]

Honor murders (they are not simply killings, but murders) continue to occur in modern communities and are part of a larger problem of gender-based violence, particularly violence against women. This violence is common in communities that otherwise differ greatly in terms of race, religion, and class, and many of the world's legal systems have failed to punish it. "In Europe, honor killings are called 'crimes of passion,' but they are identical," Sumbul Ali-Karamali adds. Muslims are connected with honor killings, whereas non-Muslims are associated with crimes of passion. This is crucial since, in polls of French, British, and German respondents, some of the same persons who deemed "honor killings" morally objectionable also judged "crimes of passion" morally acceptable! (171)

Islam does not sanction any form of a targeted killing. The Quran says, *"[W]hoever, takes a life—unless as a punishment for murder or mischief in the land—it will be as if they have killed all of humanity and whoever saves a life, it will be as if they saved all of humanity" (Q 5:32)*. Individuals, families, and communities are fractured by targeted killings, and when a woman is targeted, not only is her life taken from her but everything else as well.

In some war-torn and conflict-ridden Muslim nations, there are also premeditated murders of rights advocates, civil servants, and media figures, the majority of whom are also women. The purpose of these attacks is to send a chilling message to their rank and file. Others are silenced in public spheres because they fear retribution, harassment, intimidation, or censorship because of the murders. The forced silence has catastrophic effects on the health of the community, the family, and faith. Because these crimes involve the unjustified taking of human life, they are in opposition to the Shariah's objectives of life, family, intellect, and wealth. When a woman is killed, not only is her life cut short, but so are the lives of her offspring and the elderly members of her family. Instability is fueled by threats, dread, and anxiety, resulting in mental distress and a lifetime of trauma.

Moreover, when a primary provider passes away—these are sometimes women—dependents are left without financial support and unable to accumulate wealth.[366] This is one of the effects that never gets talked about.

A PAKISTANI WITNESS WHO DISMANTLED THE SYSTEM

Take for example, Khalida Brohi, 16, who set out to alter the system when her cousin was murdered in the name of honor. Khalida began the Wake-Up Campaign in 2008 to highlight honor killings. After being accused of promoting western culture in an honorable society, she fled the village.

When Khalida fell in love with David, an Italian American, she was aware that their families' prejudices and preconceptions would be tough to overcome. They won their parents over after a two-year campaign of lengthy chats over cups of chai.

Khalida founded Sughar Empowerment Society and The Chai Spot to empower women economically after marrying. The Chai Spot, a social venture promotes peace between East and West, works with women in 12 Sindh and Baluchistan communities. Modern fashions with antique needlework are skillfully made by these women. The Chai spot has become a thriving hub of change-related debate and connection in New York City.

APOSTASY-RELATED VIOLENCE

Muslims around the world, including women who experience Islam to be an oppressive state system, are sometimes renouncing their faith publicly. Using social media, some proclaim their atheism, while others convert to other religions. If they are deemed a political liability, they are charged with apostasy or treason and either imprisoned or murdered by enraged masses.

But, the Quran emphasizes free will and individual responsibility for one's beliefs and actions: *"Had your Lord so willed, 'O Prophet,' all people on earth would have certainly believed, every single one of them! Would you then force people to become believers?" (Q 10:99)*. Respect for differences among believers is emphasized, as is the fact that the decision to pursue the correct path ultimately rests with every individual: *"You have your Way, and I have my Way" (Q 109:6)*.

The Quran also makes it plain that the Prophet was not appointed as a guardian or overseer of the actions and decisions of people. He was sent to convey the message and guide people along the correct path through his example: *"[K]now that We have not sent you 'O Prophet' as a keeper over them" (Q 4:80)*. The Quran promotes tolerance and respect for diverse religious practices and beliefs. Muslims who disagree are instructed to embrace one another's perspectives, recognizing that people may follow different paths. *"Surely, this is a reminder. So let whoever wills take the Right Way to their Lord" (Q 76:29)*.

To completely comprehend apostasy as an act of leaving the faith, according to Jonathan Brown, we must examine the Prophet's attitude toward apostates within his own ranks. Ibn al-all (d. 1103 CE), a Cordoba scholar, said that when the Prophet's companion Ubaydallh bin Jahsh left Islam to convert to Christianity while the Muslims were seeking refuge in Ethiopia, the Prophet did not punish him. The Treaty of Ḥudaybiyya, which the Prophet concluded with the Quraysh, stated that if anyone decided to leave the Muslim community in Medina, no harm would befall them. There was no mention of a punishment for apostasy. A man who had come to the Prophet the previous day to swear allegiance to Islam wished to be released from his oath; the Prophet granted his request. Imam al-Shāfi'i himself notes how, during the Prophet's time in Medina, "Some people believed and then apostatized. Then they again took on the outer trappings of faith. But the Prophet did not kill them."[367]

Brown continues to explain how the early caliphs also followed the Prophet's example. When six men from the Bakr bin Wā'il tribe apostatized during a campaign in southern Iran, the leaders of the army killed them. When the Caliph Umar was informed of this, he upbraided the commanders. Had he been making the decision, the caliph explained, he would have offered the men "a way back in from the door they took out," or he would have put them in prison. Similarly, when Umayyad Caliph 'Umar bin 'Abd al-'Azīz (d. 720 CE) was told that a group of recent converts to Islam in northern Iraq had apostatized, he allowed them to revert to their previous status as a protected non-Muslim minority.

Brown explains that Muslim scholars distinguish between treason, which is a punishable act, and apostasy, which is not a punishable one. To begin, scholars disagreed on whether a Muslim who has rejected their faith should be given the chance to repent. Three Sunni schools required that they be given a chance, and the Hanafi agreed too. Most scholars agreed that they should be allowed to recant since the Prophet mentioned giving apostates a chance to change their minds, which Caliph Umar did. Most legal scholars agreed on three days or three chances, although Ibn Ḥanbal (d. 855 CE) and Abu Ḥanīfa (d. 767 CE) agreed on a month for the accused to repent. According to Ibn Ḥazm (d. 1064 CE), the apostate should be questioned if they desire to recant forever. Brown highlights a case of Malaysia, where apostasy can result in 180 days of rehabilitative detention. In the state of Negeri Sembilan, they take a different approach. They require permission for Muslims to leave Islam. Only after being interviewed to establish their sincerity and advised to the contrary, can individuals apostatize.

When I hear of individuals being accused of apostasy, I am immediately transported to a time when Salman Rushdie was issued a *fatwa* for writing his novel, *The Satanic Verses*. As I was unfamiliar with my religion at the time, I did not comprehend the author's intent or the social implications of his book. I was unable to distinguish between faith and fanaticism due to my confusion over how fanatics had co-opted my religion. As a Muslim, I was no longer able to maintain neutrality, and I progressively lost my faith and walked away from Islam. Yet I gained the ability to discern my own path, and gradually, by divine decree and as if by osmosis, I found an American shaykh who had converted to Islam and immersed myself in the teachings.

When I read this verse of the Quran, I realized that there is a risk of falling back into disbelief: *"Indeed, those who believed then disbelieved, then believed and again disbelieved- only increasing in disbelief, God will neither forgive them nor guide them to the Right Way" (Q 4:137)*. I began to fear that, given the propensity of humans to question, investigate, confirm, or reject faith, I would fall into this category. So, I asked the shaykh how I could ensure that I would never fall back. He smiled and said, "Once the heart goes into prostration [*sajdah*], it never rises from it. Let your heart go into *sajdah* first."

Eventually, I began studying the Quran, which became the means by which I drew closer to God. And watching the divine plan unfold showed me how to lead a successful life. I often wonder what would have happened if I had lived in a country where I would have been judged, ostracized, accused of apostasy, imprisoned, or even executed. What would society have gained if I had been killed? What would my obituary say? How would my family heal from the traumatic event? Surely, I never could have become who I am today.

I am reminded of all the times I was forced to step up and undertake greater responsibility. Who would have filled the vacuum when the Muslim community was so fragmented and there was a call for Muslims to speak out because our silence was considered complicity? Who would present a nuanced view of Islam and Muslim women? If not me, then who? Would my death have helped the world, or the Muslim community?

I follow the Prophet because he is the greatest guide. He was a man of peace who advocated against violence in all circumstances, guaranteeing the safety and security of all Muslims. He knew the Quran emphasizes forgiveness (3:134) and respects the sanctity of human life. No matter how great a crime, the Prophet encouraged everyone to find peaceful solutions and seek humane and fair treatment. He inspired a movement that would transform nearly one-quarter of the world's population. It is his example and the Quran's injunctions toward peace that Muslims must follow. Communities must engage in a discourse in which attitudes towards family honor can be transformed, and protecting a person's life, rather than taking it, should be the focus of our honor.

RESOURCES | TOOLKIT AND PUBLIC AWARENESS

Through this work, I seek not only to inspire change but to propel Muslim women toward a brighter, more equitable future. I have developed educational tools, intensive training, social media engagement, and online platforms to increase public awareness. I have done my part, and now I hope that you will do yours.

In addition to my global network of female activists, I intend to form circles of female leaders who will be taught and accredited as Islamic authority on women's rights. Armed with conviction and credentials, they can reach and teach other women and girls in their networks.

I am certain that arming women with knowledge of Islamic legal and ethical traditions will enable them to defend their rights and break away from cultural norms, which are often conflated with Islam. We can bridge the age gap and foster a supportive family atmosphere by educating young Muslims on how to express their rights.

I want to bring to your attention a companion tool my friend Ayse Kadayifci-Orellana, PhD, developed: *Islam and Negotiation: Action Guide for Women*. This tool combines negotiation skills with Islamic sources of peacebuilding, conflict resolution and mediation. It will help Muslim peace activists to organize, strategize and negotiate their rights within their respective countries and communities. This tool that bridges tradition and progression, will ensure Muslim women are not just participants but are skilled at sitting at any negotiation table.

Remember that our work is just beginning, by collaborating, we can take crucial steps toward dismantling long-held stereotypes and misconceptions regarding Muslim women. Finally, we can witness a future in which Muslim women not only survive but thrive—into a future in which their rights are no longer a question but an undeniable truth.

TOOLKIT FOR YOUR USE

To facilitate accessibility, WISE organization website will feature a new Knowledge Center where the 30 Rights of Muslim Women resources can be downloaded. Visit www.wisemuslimwomen.org. You will also find there:

1. ***Six Key "Takeaways" for Each of the 30 Rights***: A summary of the key aspects concerning each right.
2. ***Lesson Plans and Reflections***: To assist students in comprehending and internalizing the significance of these rights.
3. ***Thirty Ways Prophet Muhammad Empowered Women***: Examples of how the Prophet advanced women rights.
4. ***Thirty Ways Women Supported the Prophet***: Describes women's contributions to and support of the Prophet's mission.
5. ***Fifteen Medieval Muslim Women You Must Know***: Important Muslim women from history, highlighting their experiences and achievements.
6. ***Training for 30 Rights through Webinars***: Video resources.
7. ***The "Global Declaration of Muslim Women's Rights"***: To make the 30 Rights actionable with politicians and legislators and to serve as an example of how faith-based activism can influence public engagement in our century.
8. ***Smartphone App for the 30 Rights***: Allow individuals to obtain information about the 30 Rights from their smartphones.
9. ***Podcast Series***: Using a streaming service to discuss the 30 Rights and highlight Magnificent Muslim Women of the past and present.

For book readings, speaking engagements, queries or feedback contact me at www.daisykhan.com. To request training and webinars email info@wisemuslimwomen.org or call 551-312-5578.

ACKNOWLEDGMENTS

This book is dedicated to women advocates around the world. A deep gratitude goes to WISE's Muslim Women Shura Council, whose position papers laid this book's foundation. They are Margot Badran, Ziba Mir Hosseini, Asma Asfarruddin, Ivana Hrdlickova, Afra Jalabi, Farheen Kapra, Fatima Sadiqi, Homayra Ziad, Nevin Reda, Laisa Alamia, Sumbul Ali-Karamali, Fatma Hyder, Samah Helmy, Zlakha Ahmed, Santanina Rasul, Sheeba Aslam Fehmi, Laila al-Zwaini, Gonca Aydin, Ayesha S. Chaudhry, Jamila Afghani, Moliah Hashim and late Laleh Bakhtiar.

Muslim women scholars whose works have significantly contributed to my understanding of this subject deserve special recognition. They are Leila Ahmed, Amina Wadud, Asma Barlas, Fatima Mernissi, Asma Lamrabet, Nevin Reda, Yasmin Amin, Gisela Webb, Haifaa A. Jawad, Mehnaz Afkhami, Barbara Freyer Stowasser, Kecia Ali, Ingrid Mattson, Azizah al Hibri, Asifa Quraishi, Myriam Francois-Cerrah, Hadia Mubarak, Amira Abou Taleb, Celene Ibrahim, Nimat Barazangi, Riffat Hassan, Aisha Musa, Zahra Ayubi, and Shahla Haeri.

I deeply appreciate Dr. Basma Abdelgafar for spending hours providing valuable input. I am indebted to Dr. Aisha Musa, who responded with short notice to ensure the accuracy of Hadith references. To Rahat Kurd for shaping the narrative early on, to my writer friend Rafique for prodding me to make the book accessible to a lay audience. To Monkfish, Paul Cohen and Jon Sweeney for believing in the book and bringing it into the world. To Colin Rolfe's mastery in laying out the book.

This herculean task would be impossible without Sarah McCrumb, who has conscientiously edited and researched for two years. My thanks go to my interns Leena Khan, Aidan Salamone, Sean Bandfield, Katie Hammond, Ayan Ali, Marissa Meyer, Saima Choudhury, Olivia Lapine, Mishal Haq, Merna Aboul-Ezz, Zoha Malik, Liane Jammalova, Amina Sarfraz, Siena Wigert, Grace Samaritano, Liz Walker, Yeatasmin

Shiropa, Madelyn Starr, Amina Belchec, Allison Roberts, and Razan Elzubair. I am grateful to Feyza Oytan for designing a cover that showcases Muslim women as they truly appear around the world: vibrant, confident, and energetic.

The book would not have been possible without the grants provided by many supporters. I am grateful to Cynda Collins Arsenault, John F. Fetzer Institute, William and Mary Greve Foundation, Dr. Arfa and Faroque Khan, Sara Abassi, Osmani Family Foundation, Saya Foundation, Stanley & Marion Bergman Family Charitable Foundation, Fareed & Laura Siddiq, Mamak Shahbazi, Khadija Mustafa, Sophia Said, Sally Kitch, Mumtaz Mir, Nazir and Halima Khan, Abid Khan, Musarat Shareeff, Zahid & Muzzamil Khan, Insha & Azeem Malik, Maria & Shamim Malik, Omar & Amina Shareeff, Nazim & Husnara Sayed, Sana & Imran Arain, Nida & Omer Zuberi, Lina Salhi, Ayesha Gilani Taylor, Maryam Khabeer Kaye, Hind Jarrah, Mary McClymont, Marisa Barthel, Kevin James, Dana Khuthaila, Gina Safdar, Yasmeen Butt, Azam Sher, Fozia Qureshi, Havva Idriss, Hind Kamal Ahmed Khogali, Sumbul Karamali, Mino Akhtar, Moina Noor, Muzaffar Chishti, Ruth Messinger, Khatijah Barday Wood, Abdullah Dar, Tamam Khan, Saima Ahmed, Junaid Chida, Tita Beal, Kate Wetstone, and many others whose support was vital to the completion of this book. I appreciate them all.

NOTES

1. Muhammad Abdul-Rauf, *The Islamic View of Women and the Family*, 3rd ed. (Alexandria, VA: Al-Saadawi, 1995).

#1. TO CIVIC/POLITICAL LEADERSHIP

2. Barbara Freyer Stowasser, *Women in the Qur'an, Traditions, and Interpretation* (New York: Oxford University Press, 1996), 66.
3. Nevin Reda and Asma Afsaruddin, "Reading the Quran through a Gendered, Egalitarian Lens," in *Islamic Interpretive Tradition and Gender Justice: Processes of Canonization, Subversion, and Change*, ed. Yasmin Amin (Montreal: McGill-Queen's University Press, 2020), 100-26.
4. sister-hood staff, "Sitt Al-Mulk 970-1023," *sister-hood* [online], January 30, 2019.
5. Farhad Daftary, "Sayyida Hurra: The Isma'ili Sulayhid Queen of Yemen Farhad Daftary," Medievalists.net, n.d., accessed June 7, 2023.
6. David E. Jones, *Women Warriors: A History* (Washington, DC: Brassey's, 2005), 42-43; N. Jayapalan, *History of India: From 1773 to Lord Minto, Including Constitutional Development* (New Delhi: Atlantic, 2001), 10-11.
7. Bouthaina Shaaban, "The Muted Voices of Women Interpreters," in *Faith and Freedom: Women's Human Rights in the Muslim World*, ed. Mahnaz Afkhami (Syracuse: Syracuse University Press, 1995).
8. Asli Sancar, *Ottoman Women, Myth and Reality* (Somerset, NJ: Light, 2007), 101-105.
9. Amira Abou-Taleb, "Constructing the Image of the Model Muslim Woman," in *Islamic Interpretive Tradition and Gender Justice*, 199.
10. Muhammad Abdul-Rauf, *The Islamic View of Women and Family*, 3rd ed. (Alexandria, VA: Al-Saadawi, 1995), 114.
11. Leila Ahmed, *Women and Gender in Islam* (New Haven: Yale University Press, 1992), 84.
12. Amina Wadud, *Qur'an and Women: Rereading the Sacred Text from a Woman's Perspective* (New York: Oxford University Press, 1999), 71-73.
13. Bukhari 7099, Book 92, Hadith 50, Sunnah.com [website]. Translation varies slightly.
14. Mohammad Fadel, "Is Historicism a Viable Strategy for Islamic Legal Reform? The Case of 'Never Shall a Folk Prosper Who Have Appointed a Woman to Rule Them,'" *Islamic Law and Society* (2011): 131-76.
15. Bukhari 1462, Book 24, Hadith 64.

#2. TO SECULAR EDUCATION

16. Mohamad Jebara, *Muhammad, the World-Changer: An Intimate Portrait* (New York: St. Martin's Essentials, 2021), 135.

17 Amjad M. Hussain, *A Social History of Education in the Muslim World* (London: Ta-Ha Publishers, 2011) 26.
18 "*Allah, Quran, Knowledge and 'The Surrender,*'" Chapter 6, Islamic Governance [website] n.d., accessed July 26, 2023.
19 Hadith 2687 in Jami'at Tirmidhi Sunnah.com [website]. Translation varies slightly.
20 Tirmidhi 4977 and Baihaqi Hadith of at-Tirmidhi on the authority of Sa'id ibn Al-'as.
21 Sajid Ullah Sheikh and Muhammad Abid Ali, "Al-Ghazali's Aims and Objectives of Islamic Education," *Journal of Education and Educational Development* (Institute of Business Management, Pakistan) 6, no. 1 (June 2019).
22 Haifaa Jawad, *The Rights of Women in Islam: An Authentic Approach* (Basingstoke, UK: Palgrave, 2001).
23 "*Women's Day*," 1001 Inventions [website], n.d., accessed June 7, 2023.
24 Asli Sancar, *Ottoman Women, Myth and Reality* (Somerset, NJ: Light, 2007). Mohammad Saiful, "Importance of Girls' Education as Right: A Legal Study from Islamic Approach," *Beijing Law Review* 7 (2016): 1–11.
25 Anas bin Malik, Jami' at-Tirmidhi 2647, Sunnah.com [website], n.d. Translation varies slightly.
26 M. Basheer Ahmed, MD, ed., *The Rise and Fall of Muslim Civilization: Hope for the Future* (Frisco, TX: Mary Ethel Eckard, 2022).
27 "The Women who founded the world's first university," The startup/Medium [website], n.d., accessed July 10, 2023.
28 Hadith 2244, Ibn Majah, Sunnah.com [website].

#3. TO CAREER PURSUIT

29 Jebara, *Muhammad, the World-Changer*.
30 "The Deaths of Khadija and Abu Talib—A.D. 619," Restatement of History of Islam and Muslims, Al-Islam [website] n.d., accessed June 7, 2023.
31 Sunan an-Nasa'i 2584, Sunnah.com [website].
32 Jami' at-Tirmidhi 1358, Book 15, Hadith 38.
33 Muslim 2452, Sunnah.com [website].
34 Maulana Wahiduddin Khan, *The Moral Vision* (New Delhi: Goodword Books, 1999)
35 Heather Shaw, "The Powerful Woman Who Helped Prophet Muhammad in Hijrah," AboutIslam [website], August 18, 2020.
36 Maria Zain, "Lady Maimunah: A Woman of High Morals," AboutIslam [website], October 27, 2021.
37 Sunan Abi Dawud 2578, Book 15, Hadith 102.
38 "Muslim Women: Past and Present," Women's Islamic Initiative in Spirituality and Equality (WISE) [website], n.d., accessed June 7, 2023.
39 Azizah Al-Hibri, "An Introduction to Muslim Women's Rights," in *Windows of Faith: Muslim Women Scholar-Activists in North America*, ed. Gisela Webb (Syracuse: Syracuse University Press, 2000), 63.
40 Hoda El-Saadi, "Fiqh Rulings and Gendering the Public Space: The Discrepancy between Written Formality and Daily Reality," in *Islamic Interpretive Tradition*

and Gender Justice, eds. Nevin Reda and Amin Yasmin (Montreal: McGill-Queen's University Press, 2020), 271.

#4. TO FREEDOM OF SPEECH AND EXPRESSION

41 Bukhari, Book 68:32.

42 Asma Lamrabet, *Women in the Qur'an: An Emancipatory Reading* (New York: Kube, 2016), 138.

43 Mohja Kahf, "Braiding the Stories," in *Windows of Faith: Muslim Women Scholar-Activists in North America*, ed. Gisela Webb (Syracuse: Syracuse University Press, 2000), 157.

44 Leila Ahmed, *Women and Gender in Islam*.

45 Tabari, vol. 19, p. 189, Archive.org [website].

46 "Al-Khansā'," Encyclopædia Britannica [website], n.d., accessed June 7, 2023.

47 "Sunday Classics: Al Khansa, the 'Greatest among Those with Breasts' (& Testicles, Too)," *Arablit & Arablit Quarterly*, n.d., accessed June 7, 2023.

48 Pitamber Kaushik, "Lal Ded: The 14th Century Mystic Poet of Kashmir," Feminism In India [website], May 7, 2019.

49 Khaled Abou El Fadl, *Speaking in God's Name: Islamic Law, Authority, and Women*, (Oxford: Oneworld, 2001), 18.

50 Mariam Fam and Aysha Khan, "Amid Debate, Women Lift Their Voices with Muslim Sacred Text," AP, February 16, 2022.

51 Dilshad Ali, ed., "Ustadha Maryam Amir's Qariah App Is Giving Space & Validation to Women Quran Reciters," The Haute Take (blog), [website], April 9, 2022.

52 Aisha Y. Musa, "Freedom of Conscience," *Journal of Islamic and Muslim Studies*, Indiana University Press, May 2019.

53 Mohammad Hashim Kamali, *Freedom of Expression in Islam* (Cambridge, UK: Islamic Texts Society, 1997), 92.

54 Riyad as-Salihin 184, Introduction, Hadith 184.

55 Noor Asma Said and Wan Mohd Khairul Firdaus Wan Khairuldin, "Freedom of Speech in Islam and Its Connection with Street Demonstrations," *International Journal of Academic Research in Business and Social Sciences* 7, no. 4 (2017).

#5. TO TESTIMONY AND WITNESS

56 Muslim 2577a, Book 45, Hadith 70 Sunnah.com [website] Translation varies slightly.

57 Mustafa Khattab, *The Clear Quran* (Lombard, IL: Book of Signs Foundation, 2016), 26.

58 Mohammad Fadel, *Two Women, One Man: Knowledge, Power, and Gender in Medieval Sunni Legal Thought* (New York: Cambridge University Press, 1997), 192.

59 Asma Barlas, *Believing Women in Islam* (Austin: University of Texas Press, 2002, rev. 2019), 64.

60 "The Testimony of Women in Islam," Dar Al-Ifta [website], n.d., accessed July 25, 2023.

61 Asifa Quraishi, "Her Honor: An Islamic Critique of the Rape Laws of Pakistan from a

Woman-Sensitive Perspective," in *Windows of Faith: Muslim Women Scholar-Activists in North America*, ed. Gisela Webb (Syracuse: Syracuse University Press, 2000), 123–24.

62 Bukhari 2052, Book 34, Hadith 6.
63 Jennifer Heath, *The Scimitar and the Veil: Extraordinary Women of Islam* (Mahwah, NJ: Hidden Spring, 2004), 140–44.
64 "Khutbah Hajjatul Wida" (The Farewell Sermon).

#6. TO RELIGIOUS AND SPIRITUAL LEADERSHIP

65 Seyyed Hossein Nasr, *The Study Quran* (New York: HarperOne, 2015).
66 Simonetta Calderini, *Women as Imams: Classical Islamic Sources and Modern Debates on Leading Prayer* (London: I. B. Tauris, 2022).
67 Muslim 672a, Sunnah.com [website], n.d. Translation varies slightly.
68 Abu Mas'ud al-Ansari, Book 4, Hadith 1420.
69 Jasser Auda, *Reclaiming the Mosque: The Role of Women in Islam's House of Worship* (Swansea, UK: Claritas Books 2017), 113.
70 Nevin Reda, "The Islamic Basis for Female-Led Prayer," Islamic Research Foundation International [website], n.d., accessed June 7, 2023.
71 Mohamed Jebara, "The (Downplayed) Story of Female Scholars, Teachers and Leaders in Islam: The vibrant history of successful Muslim women has been disregarded and dismissed by conservative groups like the Taliban," New Lines Magazine, newlinesmag.com, [website], June 3, 2022.
72 Maria Jaschok and Jingjun Shui, *The History of Women's Mosques in Chinese Islam: A Mosque of Their Own* (Richmond, UK: Curzon Press, 2000), 166.
73 Calderini, *Women as Imams*.
74 Jeff Chu and Nadia Musafa, "Her Turn to Pray," *TIME Magazine*, March 28, 2005.
75 "Woman Acting as Imam in Prayer," IslamOnline [website], October 12, 2021.
76 Camille Adams Helminski, *Women of Sufism: A Hidden Treasure* (Boston, Shambhala, 2003).
77 "Biography," Cemalnur Sargut [website], n.d., accessed June 7, 2023.
78 Yigal Schleifer, "In Turkey, Muslim Women Gain Expanded Religious Authority," *Christian Science Monitor*, April 27, 2005.
79 "Meet Egypt's First Female Islamic Wedding Officiant," Cairo Scene [website], March 30, 2018.
80 Bukhari, Al-Adab al-Mufrad, Sunanh.com [website].
81 Khaled Abou El Fadl, "Fatwa: On Women Leading Prayer," The Search for Beauty: On Beauty and Reason in Islam [website], April 5, 2010.

#7. TO BE JURISTS AND INTERPRETERS OF ISLAMIC TEXTS

82 Ziba Mir-Hosseini, "The Construction of Gender in Islamic Legal Thought and Strategies for Reform," *Hawwa: Journal of Women of the Middle East and the Islamic World* 1, no. 1 (2003): 1–28.

NOTES   313

83   Muslim 1827 Sunnah.com [website] Translation varies slightly.
84   Fatima Mernissi, *The Veil and The Male Elite: A Feminist Interpretation of Women's Rights in Islam*, trans. Mary Jo Lakeland (New York: Basic Books, 1992), 77–78.
85   Aisha Geissinger, "Female Figures, Marginality, and Qur'anic Exegesis in Ibn al-Jawzi's Sifat al-Safwa" in *Islamic Interpretive Tradition and Gender Justice*, ed. Nevin Reda (McGill-Queen's University Press, 2020), 157.
86   Carla Power, *If the Oceans Were Ink: An Unlikely Friendship and a Journey to the Heart of the Quran* (New York: Holt, 2015), 128–133.
87   Leila Ahmed, *Women and Gender in Islam*.
88   Recep Senturk, "A Blueprint for the Muftya Project," [unpublished], 2009.
89   Rasha Elass, "Women Muftis by the End of 2010," The National News, [website], n.d., accessed September 13, 2010.
90   A. Morrow and Khaled Moussa al-Omrani, "Egypt: Female Judge Appointments Stir Controversy," *Inter Press Service*, April 16, 2007.
91   Monique Cardinal, "Why Aren't Women Shariah Court Judges? The Case of Syria," *Islamic Law and Society* 17, no. 2 (2010): 185–214.
92   Nimat Hafez Barazangi, *Woman's Identity and Rethinking the Hadith* (New York: Routledge, 2016).
93   "Confronting Patriarchy and Advocating for the Rights of Muslim Women in Uganda," Equitas [website], 2020.
94   Liz Gooch, "The Female Face of Islamic Law in Malaysia," *Al Jazeera*, August 16, 2017.

#8. TO GAIN SPIRITUAL KNOWLEDGE

95   "Afghanistan Taliban Girls' Education," *AP News* [website], n.d., accessed July 13, 2023.
96   Ibn Majah 243, Sunanh.com [website].
97   "Importance of Girls' Education as Right: A Legal Study from Islamic Approach," Mohammad Saiful Islam, International Islamic University Chittagong, Bangladesh, *Beijing Law Review* 7, no. 1 (March 2016).
98   "Islam: History of Islamic Education, Aims, and Objectives of Islamic Education," StateUniversity.com Education Encyclopedia, n.d., accessed June 7, 2023.
99   Sajid Ullah Sheikh and Muhammad Abid Ali, "Al-Ghazali's Aims and Objectives of Islamic Education."
100 Nabia Abbott, "Women and the State in Early Islam," *Journal of Near Eastern Studies* 1, no. 1 (1942): 106–26.
101 Sahih Muslim, Book 3, Hadith 649.
102 Ingrid Mattson, *The Story of the Quran* (Hoboken, NJ: John Wiley and Sons, 2013), 89.
103 "Women Scholars of Hadith: Part 2," IslamOnline [website], n.d., accessed June 7, 2023.
104 "Subj: Zaynab al-Ghazali," Jannah.Org [website], n.d., accessed June 7, 2023.
105 "Scholarship and Philanthropy: Visiting the Life of Nafisa Al-Tahira bint Al-Hassan," TMWT: The Muslim Women Times [website], n.d., accessed June 7, 2023.

106 Barbara Daly Metcalf, *Perfecting Women* (Berkeley: University of California Press, 1990), 295.
107 "Subj: Zaynab al-Ghazali."
108 Amira El-Azhary Sonbol, *Beyond the Exotic: Women's Histories in Islamic Societies* (Syracuse: Syracuse University Press, 2005), 297–300.
109 "Education in Muslim Areas," Facts and Details [website], n.d., accessed June 7, 2023.
110 Bukhari 5027, Sunnah.com [website]. Translation varies slightly.
111 Musharraf Hussain, *Seven Steps to Spiritual Intelligence* (New York: Kube, 2014), 35.
112 Sahih al-Bukhari, 1423.
113 *Farid ad-Din 'Attar's Memorial of God's Friends: Lives and Sayings of Sufis*, trans. Paul Losensky, (Mahwah, NJ: Paulist Press, 2009), 104.
114 Muslim 91a, Sunnah.com [website]. Translation varies slightly.
115 Nasa'i 1015, Sunnah.com [website].
116 John Renard, *Seven Doors to Islam: Spirituality and the Religious Life of Muslims* (Berkeley: University of California Press, 1996).
117 Anadolu Agency, "41-Year-Old Calligrapher Trains Aspiring Women," Daily Sabah [website], January 5, 2018.

#9. TO ACCESS RELIGIOUS SPACES

118 Abu Dawud 570, Sunnah.com [website].
119 Hafsa Lodi, "Mosques have become 'boys' Clubs,' despite what Islam really says," *Independent*, April 12, 2022.
120 Muslim 442c. Sunnah.com [website].
121 Marion Holmes Katz, *Women in the Mosque: A History of Legal Thought and Social Practice* (New York: Columbia University Press, 2021) 134.
122 Maria Jaschok and Jingjun Shui, *The History of Women's Mosques in Chinese Islam: A Mosque of Their Own* (London: Routledge, 2015).
123 Tafsīr al-Qurṭubī 14:244.
124 Amina Wadud, *Inside the Gender Jihad: Women's Reform in Islam* (Oxford: Oneworld, 2008), 175.
125 Daisy Khan, *Born with Wings: The Spiritual Journey of a Modern Muslim Woman* (New York: Penguin Random House, 2018), 264.
126 Harriet Sherwood, "Women Lead Friday Prayers at Denmark's First Female-Run Mosque," *Guardian*, August 26, 2016.
127 Description of Our Services, The Women's Mosque of America, [website], n.d., accessed June 7, 2023.
128 "A Place to Organize," Qal'bu Maryam Women's Justice Center [website], n.d., accessed June 7, 2023.
129 "Our Herstory," Women's Mosque of Canada [website], n.d., accessed June 7, 2023.

#10. TO MARRIAGE

130 Bukhari 5063.
131 Amira El-Azhary Sonbol, "A History of Marriage Contracts in Egypt," in *The Islamic*

132. *Marriage Contract: Case Studies in Islamic Family Law*, eds. Asifa Quraishi and Frank E. Vogel (Cambridge, MA: Harvard University Press, 2008), 87–122.
132. Waqar Akbar Cheema, "The Age of Khadija at the Time of Her Marriage with the Prophet," Islamic Center for Research and Academics (ICRAA) [website], March 17, 2016.
133. "Famous Women in Islam: Khadijah (RA)," Hadithoftheday.com [website], November 7, 2019.
134. "Khadija the Woman to Whom God Sent Greetings," Last Prophet [website], n.d., downloaded July 7 and 12, 2023.
135. Muhammad Ali, *The Religion of Islam: A Comprehensive Discussion*, 6th ed. (Chelsea, MI: Book Crafters, 1990).
136. Muslims For Progressive Values, "Can Muslim Women Marry Non-Muslim Men?" YouTube video, August 23, 2012.
137. Aisha Musa, "Freedom of Conscience in the Qur'an and Hadith," *Journal of Islamic and Muslim Studies* 4, no. 1: 132.
138. Aisha Musa, *Freedom of Conscience in the Qur'an and Hadith*.
139. John L. Esposito, "How Is Islam Similar to Christianity and Judaism?" IslamiCity [website], December 23, 2021.
140. Sunan Ibn Majah 1856, Book 9, Hadith 12, Vol. 3, Book 9, Hadith 1856.
141. Sunan al-Tirmidhī 2517.

#11. TO BE FREE OF FORCED MARRIAGE

142. Bulugh al-Maram, Book 8, Hadith 18.
143. "A Woman's Right to Choose Her Husband," Egypt's Dar Al-Ifta [website], n.d., accessed June 7, 2023.
144. Hena Zuberi, "Arranged Marriage Is Not Forced Marriage," Muslim Matters.org, [website], n.d., accessed, July 23, 2023.
145. Asma Lamrabet, "Do Muslim Women Have the Right to Contract Their Own Marriage in the Absence of a Guardian or Wali?" Asma-Lamrabet.com [website], November 2016.
146. Maha Akeel and Abeer Mishkhas, "Women Welcome Grand Mufti's Ruling on Forced Marriages," *Arab News*, April 13, 2005.
147. "Muslim Girl Can Declare Marriage 'Null and Void' If Forced," *Outlook*, (OutlookIndia.com), February 17, 2002.
148. "Taliban Chief Bans Forced Marriage of Women in Afghanistan," *AP News*, December 3, 2021.

#12. TO MATURELY CHOOSE MARRIAGE

149. Ahmad Kazemi Moussavi, *Guide to Equality in the Family in the Maghreb* (Syracuse: Syracuse University Press, 2005), 35.
150. Dr. Wan Azhar bin Wan Ahmad, "Child Marriage In Islam: A Myth?" IKIM Government (Institute of Islamic Understanding Maylaysia) [website], n.d., accessed July 21, 2023.
151. Asma Malik and Maria Hanif, "A nine-year-old is a child, not a bride and needs to be in school," *Gulfnews* (GN Media), May 31, 2012.
152. Bukhari 5138, Book 67, Hadith 74.

153. Asghar Ali Engineer, *The Rights of Women in Islam* (New York: St. Martin's Press, 1992), 110–11.
154. Ibn Rushd, *The Distinguished Jurist's Primer: A Translation of Bidayat Al-Mujtahid*, vol. 2 (Reading, UK: Garnet, 1996), 3.
155. "How Come You Allow Little Girls to Get Married? Child Marriage in Yemen," Human Rights Watch [website], December 8, 2011.
156. Ikram Hawramani, "A Hadith Scholar Presents New Evidence that Aisha was Near 18 the Day of Her Marriage to the Prophet Muhammad," Ikram Hawramani's Website, November 4, 2018.
157. Yasmin Amin, "Revisiting the Issue of Minor Marriages," in *Islamic Interpretive Tradition*, 318–19.
158. Bukhari 5081, Book 67, Hadith 19.
159. Hawramani, "A Hadith Scholar."
160. Yasmin Amin, "Revisiting the Issue of Minor Marriages."
161. Hadith 4:131, narrated by Anas.
162. "What Was the Age Difference between Hazrat Muhammad SAW and Hazrat Aisha RA?" Quora [website], n.d., accessed June 7, 2023.
163. Maya Brown, "She was forced to wed at 13: Now she's helped make child marriage illegal in N.Y.," NBCNews.com [website], n.d., accessed, July 2023.

#13. TO ACCEPT OR REFUSE A POLYGAMOUS MARRIAGE

164. Bukhari 5230, Book 67, Hadith 163.
165. Kaukab Siddique, *Liberation of Women Thru Islam* (Kingsville, MD: American Society for Education and Religion, 1990), 69–70.
166. Debra Majeed, *Polygyny: What It Means When African American Muslim Women Share Their Husbands* (Gainesville: University Press of Florida, 2015).
167. Muhammad Aqeel Khan and Hidayat Ur Rehman, (Department of Law, Abdul Wali Khan University), "Polygamy in Islam: A Critical Analysis," *Journal of Applied Environmental and Biological Sciences* (TextRoad.com) 6, no. 10 (August 29, 2016): 138–41. Accessed September, 12, 2023.
168. Ibrahim Malabari, "The Prophet's Marriages" in *WISE Up: Knowledge Ends Extremism*, ed. Daisy Khan (New York: Women's Islamic Initiative in Spirituality & Equality, 2017), 122.
169. Kecia Ali, *Sexual Ethics and Islam: Feminist Reflections on Qur'an, Hadith, and Jurisprudence* (Oxford: Oneworld Publications, 2006).
170. Damien Carrick, "What It's Like to Be in a Polygamous Marriage? Muslim Malaysians Share Their Stories," ABC (Australian Broadcasting Corporation), February 14, 2020.
171. "'Marriage without Strings': Saudi Confronts Rise of 'Misyar,'" *Times of India*, July 4, 2021.
172. Ibn Majah, Book 10, Hadith 3.

#14. TO DIVORCE

173. Nawal El Saadawi, "Woman and Islam," *Women's Studies International Forum* 5, no. 2 (1982): 194–96.
174. Hadia Mubarak, "Classical Qur'anic Exegesis and Women," in *The Routledge Handbook*

of *Islam and Gender*, ed. Justin Howe (London: Routledge, 2020), 72.
175   Wael B. Hallaq, *An Introduction to Islamic Law* (New York: Cambridge University Press, 2011), 65.
176   L. Clarke and P. Cross, "Custody and Child Support" in *Muslim and Canadian Family Laws: A Comparative Primer* (Toronto: Canadian Council of Muslim Women, 2006), 66-73, ccmw.com/publications [website].

#15. TO FAMILY PLANNING AND REPRODUCTIVE JUSTICE

177   Sarah Elshamy, "The Rights of Children Over Parents: Part 1," Al Jummah [website], April 11, 2023.
178   Huda, "What Are the Islamic Views on Breastfeeding?" Learn Religions [website], June 25, 2019.
179   Nurul Hariah Astuti and Ony Linda, "Sexual and Reproductive Rights in Islamic Perspective and Kemuhammadiyahan," in Proceedings of the 1st International Conference on Social Determinants of Health (December 19, 2018).
180   Riyad as-Salihin 120.
181   Bukhari 5199, Sunnah.com [website]. Translation varies slightly.
182   Muslim 1440c, Sunnah.com [website].
183   Farzaneh Roudi-Fahimi, "Islam and Family Planning," Population Reference Bureau/Middle East and North Africa Policy Briefs Program, [website], 2004.
184   Astuti and Linda, "Sexual and Reproductive Rights in Islamic Perspective.
185   Usama Hasan, *Abortion, Stages of the Embryo, and the Beginning of Life* (Beruit: Dar al-Basha ir al-Islamiyyah, 2005), 428-51.
186   Rafaqat Rashid, "When Does Ensoulment Occur in the Human Foetus?" Islam and Science, Human Embryological Development, and Abortion, pt. 1 (Al Balagh Academy Publication Paper, 2020), 6-8.
187   Rashad Ali, "How Islam Settled Roe v. Wade." *New Lines Magazine*, newlines.com [website], May 20, 2022.
188   Sa'diyya Shaikh, "Family Planning, Contraception and Abortion in Islam: Undertaking Khilafah," in *Sacred Rights: The Case for Contraception and Abortion in World Religions*, ed. Daniel Maguire (New York: Oxford University Press, 2003), 105-19.
189   Rashad Ali, "How Islam Settled Roe v. Wade."
190   Dr. Omar Suleiman, "Islam and the Abortion Debate," Yaqeen Institute [website], March 20, 2017, updated September 20, 2022.
191   Fatima A. Husain, "Reproductive Issues from the Islamic Perspective," *Human Fertility* 3, no. 2 (2000): 124-28.

#16. TO CARE FOR ORPHANS THROUGH ADOPTION

192   Jamila Bargach, *Orphans of Islam: Family, Abandonment, and Secret Adoption in Morocco* (Lanham, MD: Rowman & Littlefield, 2002), 27.
193   Bukhari 6005, Sunnah.com [website].
194   Muslim Women's Shura Council, "Adoption and the Care of Orphan Children," wisemuslimwomen.org [website]," accessed, July 17, 2023.

195. "ISS/IRC Fact Sheet No. 50: Specific Case Kafalah," Save the Children Child Rights Resource Centre, 2007, International Reference Centre for the Rights of Children Deprived of their Family (IRC), [website].
196. Elizabeth Hormann, *Breastfeeding an Adopted Baby and Relactation* (Schaumburg, IL: La Leche League International, 2006).

#17. TO MOTHERHOOD AND WOMANHOOD

197. "Afghanistan: Voices of Mothers," Action Against Hunger [website], February 23, 2022.
198. Aliah Schleifer, *Mary the Blessed Virgin of Islam* (Louisville, KY: Fons Vitae, 1997), 46–52.
199. Celene Ibrahim, *Women and Gender in the Qur'an* (New York: Oxford University Press, 2020), 85.
200. Nabeela Jamil, "Was Rabi'a Basri—the Single Most Influential Sufi Woman—a Feminist?" Feminism In India [website], October 10, 2018.
201. Shabda Kahn, Faisal Muqaddam, Bilal Hyde, Wali Ali Meyer, *The 99 Beautiful Names of Allah: Physicians of the Heart Wafiza Card Set* (San Rafael, CA: Mandala, 2022).
202. Seyyed Hossein Nasr, *The Study Quran: A New Translation and Commentary* (New York: HarperOne, 2005), 189.
203. Muslim 2753c, Sunnah.com [website].
204. Bukhari 5971, Sunnah.com [website].
205. Bukhari 5971, Sunnah.com [website].
206. Nasa'i 3104, Sunnah.com [website].
207. Ziauddin Sardar, *Reading the Qur'an: The Contemporary Relevance of the Sacred Text of Islam* (New York: Oxford University Press, 2017), 3.
208. Emily Goodhue, *The Role of Mothers in Muslim Families in Ouakam Dakar: Navigating Traditional Gender Roles in a Modern Context*, St. Olaf College, School for International Training, Independent Study Project (ISP) Collection (2012), accessed July 13, 2023.
209. Goodhue, *The Role of Mothers*, 19–20.
210. "'Leaning In' While Wearing a Niqab," The World from PRX, March 19, 2014.

#18. TO INHERITANCE

211. Muhammad Abdul-Rauf, *Inheritance in Islam: All That We Have to Know About Inheritance* (Alexandria, VA: Al-Saadawi, 2000), 147.
212. Aisha B. Lemu and Fatima Heeren, *Women in Islam* (London: Islamic Foundation, 1978), 23.
213. Fariba Zarinebaf-Shahr, "Women, Law, and Imperial Justice in Ottoman Istanbul in the Late Seventeenth Century" in *Women, the Family, and Divorce Laws in Islamic History*, ed. Amira El Azhary Sonbol (Syracuse: Syracuse University Press, 1996), 89.
214. "Zubaida Trail, Located in Saudi Arabia's Qassim Region," Arab News, January 11, 2020.
215. Sara Bardhan, "Jahanara Begum Defied All Stereotypes of Being a Mughal Princess," New Age Islam [website], June 1, 2018.

NOTES

[216] Zainab Chaudhry, "The Myth of Misogyny: A Reanalysis of Women's Inheritance in Islamic Law," *Albany Law Review* 61, no. 2 (1997).

#19. TO FINANCIAL INDEPENDENCE AND EQUAL PAY

[217] Sahih Muslim 1627a, Book 25, Hadith 1.
[218] Bukhari 2270, Sunnah.com [website].
[219] Nasa'i 2533, Sunnah.com [website].
[220] Ibn Majah 2443, Sunnah.com [website].
[221] Rashed Hasan, *Free to Choose: Volume 2 of Removing the Middleman*, (Alexandria, VA: Rashed Hasan, 2017), 48.
[222] Nasa'i 3651, Sunnah.com [website].
[223] *Journal of Wealth Management and Financial Planning*, vol. 2, Malaysian Financial Planning Council, June 2015.
[224] Sumbul Ali-Karamali, *Demystifying Shariah: What It Is, How It Works, and Why It's Not Taking over Our Country* (Boston: Beacon Press, 2020), 62.
[225] Ibn Majah 2760, Sunnah.com [website].
[226] "Fair and Just Financial Rights Upon Divorce," Musawah Policy Brief #05, 2021, Musawah.org [website] accessed September 15, 2022.
[227] Dar Al-Ifta Misriyyah, "Fatawa—A Wife's Financial Independence," dar-alifta.org [website], n.d., accessed July 19, 2023.
[228] Stephanie Wykstra, "Microcredit Was a Hugely Hyped Solution to Global Poverty: What Happened?" Vox, January 15, 2019.
[229] Humayon Dar, "Top 10 Women in Islamic Banking and Finance," LinkedIn, February 15, 2017.
[230] Shaheen Pasha, "Could Women Play a Bigger Role in Islamic Finance?" *Reuters*, September 29, 2010.
[231] "Most Powerful Women International: Sarah Al-Suhaimi," *Fortune* [website], n.d., accessed June 7, 2023.

#20. TO OWN PROPERTY

[232] Muhammad Al-Tahir ibn Ashur, *Ibn Ashur: Treatise on Maqasid al-Shari'ah*, trans. Mohamed El-Tahir El-Mesawi (Herndon, VA: The International Institute of Islamic Thought, 2006), 283.
[233] Siti Mariam Malinumbay S. Salasal, "The Concept of Land Ownership: Islamic Perspective," *Buletin Geoinformasi* 2, no. 2 (1998): 285–304.
[234] Azhar Aslam and Shaista Kazmi, "Muslim Women and Property Rights," *Economic Affairs*, Institute of Economic Affairs (July 16, 2009): 1887, 1015.
[235] Sahih Muslim Book 18, Hadith 69.
[236] Abdul-Razzaq Alaro, "An Appraisal of Women's Proprietary Rights under Islamic Law of Transactions," *University of Maiduguri Law Journal* 13 (2015).
[237] "The Last Sermon of Prophet Muhammad," Intl' Islamic University Malaysia, 11um.edu.my [website]. Accessing this website caused a security warning.
[238] Abdul-Razzaq A. Alaro, "An Appraisal of Women's Proprietary Rights Under Islamic

Law of Transactions," *University of Maiduguri Law Journal* 13, (2015): 70–80.
239 "Saudi fund helps more than 73,000 women to own homes," *Arab News*, December 6, 2020.
240 Kelsey Warner and Lukman Hajje, "Why Female Real Estate Entrepreneurs Thrive in the UAE," *Khaleej Times*, March 7, 2018.

#21. TO FREEDOM OF MOVEMENT

241 Muhammad Abdul-Rauf, *Inheritance in Islam*.
242 "Umm Kulthum bint Uqba," IDEALMuslimah [website], n.d., accessed June 7, 2023.
243 "Barakah bint Tha'alaba (Umm Ayman)," Women's Islamic Initiative in Spirituality and Equality (WISE) [website], n.d., accessed June 7, 2023.
244 Sahih Bukhari Book 67, Hadith 115.
245 Lamrabet, *Women in The Qur'an*, 138.
246 Abou El Fadl, *Speaking in God's Name*, 235.
247 Sofia Abdur Rehman, "Ā'isha's Corrective of the Companions," PhD Diss., The University of Leeds School of Philosophy, Religion and the History of Science School of Languages, Cultures and Societies, October 2019.
248 Muslim 1339c, 15, Hadith 472.
249 Bukhari 1087, Book 18, Hadith 8.
250 Jami` at-Tirmidhi 2953b, Book 47, Hadith 5.
251 Fatawa Ibn Taymiyyah 5/381.
252 Taleb, "Constructing the Image of the Model Muslim Woman," 270.
253 Muslim Volume 2, Book 23, Number 368.
254 Muslim 976b, Book 11: Hadith 135, Sunnah.com [website]. Translation varies slightly.
255 Muslim 928b, 927i, 929b: Book 11, Hadith 28
256 Mahnaz Afkhami, *Faith and Freedom: Women's Human Rights in the Muslim World* (Syracuse, NY: Syracuse University Press, 1995), 62.
257 Muhammad Upal Afzal and Carole M. Cusack, *Handbook of Islamic Sects and Movements* (Leiden: Brill, 2021).
258 Daniel Flitton, "Fired up to be the first female, Muslim F1 driver," *Sydney Morning Herald*, January 3, 2011.

#22. TO EXPRESSION OF MODESTY

259 Syed Mutawalli Ad-Darsh, *Hijab or Niqab: An Islamic Critique of the Face Veil*, (Kuala Lumpur, Maylasia: Islamic Book Trust, 1997).
260 Al-Muwatta, Hadith 47.9.
261 Sarah Mainuddin, *Demystifying the Niqab: A History of The Face Veil, The Laws Against It, and Why It Is Important* (self-published, 2021).
262 Kahled Abou El Fadl, "Fatwa: On Hijab (the Hair-Covering of Women) Updated," The Search for Beauty: On beauty and reason in Islam, searchforbeauty.org [website], January 2, 2016.
263 Ziba Mir-Hosseini, "Hijab and Choice: Between Politics and Theology," in *Innovation*

in Islam: Traditions and Contributions, ed. Mehran Kamrava (Berkeley, CA: University of California Press, 2011), 191.

264 Sunan Abi Dawud, 4104 Book 34 Hadith 85 [website Sunnah.com].

265 Shaaban, "The Muted Voices of Women Interpreters."

#23. TO FREEDOM FROM DOMESTIC VIOLENCE

266 AbdulHamid A. AbuSulayman, *Marital Discord: Recapturing Human Dignity Through the Higher Objectives of Islamic Law*, new rev. ed., Occasional Papers Series II (London: International Institute of Islamic Thought, 2008), 20-21.

267 Nurhannah Binte Irwan, "Qiwama and Gender (in) Justice," (blog), pergas.org [website], November 14, 2018.

268 Hadia Mubarak, *Rebellious Wives, Neglectful Husbands: Controversies in Modern Qur'anic Commentaries* (New York: Oxford University Press, 2022), 128.

269 "Islam Promotes Justice & Healthy Relationships," Peaceful Families Project [website], n.d., accessed June 7, 2023.

270 Global Muslim Women's Shura Council, "Domestic Violence: Jihad Against Violence," Wisemuslimwomen.com (WISE) [website], 2017.

271 Laleh Bakhtiar, "The Sublime Quran: The Misinterpretation of Chapter 4 Verse 34," *European Journal of Women's Studies* 18, no. 4 (2011): 431-39.

272 Mohamed Jebara, "The (Downplayed) Story of Female Scholars, Teachers and Leaders in Islam: The vibrant history of successful Muslim women has been disregarded and dismissed by conservative groups like the Taliban," *New Lines Magazine*, newlinesmag.com, [website], June 3, 2022.

273 Global Muslim Women's Shura Council, "Domestic Violence," accessed September 15, 2022

274 Leena El-Ali, *No Truth Without Beauty: God, the Qur'an, and Women's Rights* (Basingstoke, UK: Palgrave Macmillan, 2021), 269.

275 Sahih al-Bukhari 7376.

276 Sahih Muslim, 1468 b, Book 17, Hadith 81, Sunnah.com [website].

277 Hadia Mubarak, "Intersections: Modernity, Gender, and Qur'anic Exegesis," (PhD Diss., Georgetown University, 2014), 70.

278 Global Muslim Women's Shura Council, "Domestic Violence."

279 Jami` at-Tirmidhi, 1162.

280 Sunan Abi Dawud 2146, [Sunnah.com].

281 Bakhtiar, "The Sublime Quran."

#24. TO SAFEGUARD AGAINST FGM

282 Homa Khaleeli, "Nawal El Saadawi: Egypt's Radical Feminist," *Guardian*, April 15, 2010.

283 Susan Costello, "Female Genital Mutilation/Cutting: Risk Management and Strategies for Social Workers and Health Care Professionals," *Risk Management and Healthcare Policy* 8 (2015): 225-33.

284 "Female Genital Mutilation (FGM) Frequently Asked Questions," United Nations

285. Population Fund [website], February 2022, accessed June 7, 2023.
286. Sunan Ibn Majah 2340, Book 13, Hadith 33.
287. Sunan Abi Dawud 5271.
288. Kecia Ali, *Sexual Ethics and Islam*, 135.
289. G. I. Serour, "Ethical Issues in Human Reproduction: Islamic Perspectives," *Gynecological Endocrinology: The Official Journal of the International Society of Gynecological Endocrinology* 29, no. 11 (2013): 951.
290. Global Muslim Women's Shura Council, "Female Genital Mutilation," Wisemuslimwomen.com [website], 2009, accessed July 14, 2023.
291. Kecia Ali, *Sexual Ethics and Islam*.
292. Serour, "Ethical Issues in Human Reproduction."
293. Aaron A. R. Tobian and Ronald H. Gray, "The Medical Benefits of Male Circumcision," *JAMA* 306, no. 13 (2011): 1479–80.
294. Global Muslim Women's Shura Council, "Female Genital Mutilation."
295. Bukhari 6412 Sunnah.com [website].
296. Huda, "Are Muslims Allowed to Get Tattoos?" Learn Religions [website], September 30, 2018 (updated).
297. Muhammad Noor, "Is Tattoo Haram In Islam? (Answered With Proof)," Halal or Haram Guide [website], n.d., accessed June 7, 2023.

#25. TO PROTECTION FROM RAPE, SEXUAL ASSAULT, AND ADULTERY

297. "Rape," Dictionary.com, n.d., accessed June 7, 2023.
298. Dionne Searcey, "They Fled Boko Haram, Only to Be Raped by Nigeria's Security Forces," *New York Times*, December 8, 2017.
299. Muhammad E. Susila, "Islamic Perspective on Marital Rape," *Journal Media Hukum* (2013): 317–32.
300. Eleanor Ross, "World's Largest Gathering of Female Muslim Clerics Issue Fatwa Against Marital Rape, Child Marriage," *Newsweek*, April 28, 2017.
301. "Fornication and Adultery: Major Sins in Islam," islamweb.net [website], July 4, 2019.
302. "Heart: Facts About Sexual Violence Within Muslim Communities," heartwomenandgirls.org [website], n.d.
303. Daisy Khan, "The #MosqueMeToo Movement," *Wall Street Journal*, June 28, 2018.
304. Bulugh al-Maram 7:132 Sunnah.com [website].
305. "Heart: Facts About Sexual Violence Within Muslim Communities."

#26. TO SAFEGUARD AGAINST CHILD AND HUMAN TRAFFICKING

306. "In the Words of Luiza Karimova: 'We Were Sex Slaves,'" UN Women, Africa. unwomen.org [website], February 17, 2017.
307. Sahih al-Bukhari and Ibn Majjah.
308. Abu Amina Elias, "Hadith on Brotherhood: Allah helps him as long as he helps his brother," Daily Hadith Online: The Teachings of Prophet Muhammad, abusaminaelias.com [website], January 15, 2012.
309. UNODC, *Combating Trafficking*, 25.

NOTES

310 Al-Azar University and UNICEF, *Children in Islam: Their Care Upbringing, and Protection* (Cairo, Egypt: Al-Azhar University, 2005), 1.
311 RFE/RL, "US Adds Afghanistan To List Of Worst Human Traffickers Over Child Sexual Slavery, Child Soldiers," RadioFreeEurope/RadioLiberty, June 25, 2020.
312 "Psychosocial Development," Lifespan Development [website], n.d., accessed June 7, 2023.
313 Sahih al-Bukhari 2517, Book 49, Hadith 1.
314 Afkhami, *Faith and Freedom*.
315 Ṣaḥīḥ al-Bukhari 7138, Ṣaḥīḥ Muslim 1829.

#27. TO HEALTH AND HYGIENE

316 Javaria Akbar, "A Muslim's Guide to Anal Hygiene," Vice Media Group, vice.com [website], December 11, 2014.
317 Sahih Muslim 223, Book 2, Hadith 1. Translation varies slightly.
318 Ṣaḥīḥ Muslim 2618.
319 1. Abu Dawud, 2. Al-Tirmidhi, 3. Bukhari.
320 M. Basheer Ahmed, *The Rise and Fall of Muslim Civilization*, 42.
321 Mohadeseh Borhani Nejad, Mohammad Rashidi, and Mohammad Mehdi Oloumi, "Avicenna's Educational Views with Emphasis on the Education of Hygiene and Wellness," *International Journal of Health Policy and Management* 1, no. 3 (2013): 201–5.
322 Sahih Bukhari 5728, Sunnah.com [website].
323 Nada Darwish and Alan S. Weber, "Muslim women healers of the medieval and early modern ottoman empire," hekint.org [website], accessed September 12, 2023.
324 Hadith, Muslim 2575.
325 Abu Dawud 29.1.
326 H. A. Hellyer, ed. "The Islamic tradition and the human rights discourse," Atlantic Council, September 5, 2018, 3, atlanticcouncil.org [website].
327 "Islamic beliefs affecting healthcare." Queensland Health Multicultural Clinic. Health.qld.gov.au [website].
328 Sherry Sayed Gadelrab, "Medical Healers in Ottoman Egypt, 1517–1805," *Medical History* 54, no. 3 (2010): 365–86.
329 Azadeh Moaveni, *Honeymoon in Tehran: Two Years of Love and Danger in Iran*, Kindle ed. (New York: Random House, 209), 223.
330 Bahira Amin, "Egypt's Poor Treatment of Pregnant Women: High cesarean rate is but one symptom of the routine mistreatment of mothers-to-be," *New Lines Magazine*, April 21, 2022.
331 Cynthia Charchi, "The Story of DoctHERS," Center for Health Market Innovations [website], March 28, 2016.

#28. TO FULFILL BEING A TRUSTEE OF GOD ON EARTH

332 Imam Feisal Abdul Rauf, "Asceticism in Islam," *Cross Currents* 57, no. 4 (2008): 593.
333 Dr. Wael Azmeh, Dr. Saeed Albezreh, Daisy Khan *WISE Up: Knowledge Ends Extremism*,

(New York: Women's Islamic Initiative in Spirituality and Equality, 2017).

334 Mustafa Akyol, *Islam Without Extremes: A Muslim Case for Liberty* (New York: W. W. Norton, 2011), 50.

335 Nimat Hafez Barazangi, "Vicegerency and Gender Justice in Islam," in *Islamic Identity and the Struggle for Justice*, eds. Nimat Hafez Barazangi, M. Raquibuz Zaman, and Omar Afzal (Gainesville, FL: University Press of Florida, 1996), 77–94.

336 Maysam J. Al-Faruqi, "Women's Self-Identity in the Qur'an and Islamic Law," in *Windows of Faith: Muslim Women Scholar-Activists in North America*, ed. Gisela Webb (Syracuse, NY: Syracuse University Press, 2000), 79.

337 Nimat Hafez Barazangi, "Muslim Women's Islamic Higher Learning as a Human Right," in *Windows of Faith*.

338 Sheikh Mohammad Abdullah Draz, *Morality in the Qur'an: The Greater Good of Humanity*, ed. Basma I. Abdelgafar, Ph.D. (Kuala Lumpur: Islamic Book Trust, 2018).

339 Abdelgafar, ed., in M. A. Draz, *Morality in the Qur'an*.

340 Daisy Khan, exec. ed., *WISE Up: Knowledge Ends Extremism* (New York: Women's Islamic Initiative in Spirituality and Equality, 2017), 220–22.).

341 Abdelgafar, ed., in M.A. Draz, *Morality in the Qur'an*.

342 Salma Arastu, *Our Earth: Embracing All Communities* (self-published, 2020).

#29. TO FREEDOM FROM GOSSIP, SLANDER, LIBEL, DEFAMATION, AND TO PRIVACY

343 Manar Al-Zubaidi, "For a Safe Participation in the Polls, This Is How the Fears of Iraqi Women Candidates for the Early Elections Are Dispelled," *Al-Jazeera*, July 6, 2021.

344 Sahih Bukhari 6136, Book 78, Hadith 163.

345 Abu Dawud 6874, Sunnah.com [website].

346 "Hadith: Do You Know What Backbiting Is?" HadeethEnc.com, n.d., accessed June 7, 2023.

347 Shirazi 5.

348 David L. Hudson Jr., "Libel and Slander," *The First Amendment Encyclopedia* [website], May 14, 2020.

349 Sahih Muslim 89, Book 1, Hadith 168, Sunnah.com [website]. Translation varies slightly.

350 Jami` at-Tirmidhi 2502, Book 37, Sunnah.com [website]. Translation varies slightly.

351 Sahih al-Bukhari 30.

352 Joe Bradford, "To Make A Fair Show In the Flesh: Defamation under Islamic Law & the Dangers of Ambiguity," joebradford.net [website], September 27, 2017.

353 Mariam Sherwani, "The Right to Privacy under International and Islamic Law: A Comparative Legal Analysis," *Kardana Journal for Social Sciences and Humanities* 1 (2018): 36.

354 Susan Carland, *Fighting Hislam: Women, Faith and Sexism* [Kindle ed.] (Melbourne: Melbourne University Press, 2017), 16–17.

355 Daisy Khan, *Born with Wings: The Spiritual Journey of a Modern Muslim Woman* (New York: Random House, 2018).

[356] Rajendra Jadhav, "Indian police make first arrest in alleged online abuse of Muslim women," *Reuters*, January 4, 2022.
[357] Reina Lewis and Nancy Micklewright, *Gender, Modernity, and Liberty: Middle Eastern and Western Women's Writings; A Critical Sourcebook* (London: I. B. Tauris, 2006).
[358] Zeyneb Hanoum, *A Turkish Woman's European Impressions*, trans. Reina Lewis (Piscataway, NJ: Gorgias Press, 2005).
[359] Ṣaḥīḥ al-Bukhari 67, Book 3, Hadith 9, Sunnah.com.
[360] Imran Awan, *Islamophobia in Cyberspace: Hate Crimes Go Viral* (London: Routledge, 2020).

#30. TO SAFEGUARD HONOR

[361] Khalida Brohi, *I Should Have Honor: A Memoir of Hope and Pride in Pakistan* (New York: Random House, 2018).
[362] L. Clarke and P. Cross, *Muslim and Canadian Family Laws: A Comparative Primer* (Toronto: Canadian Council of Muslim Women, 2006), 54, ccmw.com [website], accessed September 1, 2022.
[363] Dr. Jonathan Brown, "Islam is not the Cause of Honor Killings: It's Part of the Solution," Yaqeen Institute for Islamic Research [website], October 25, 2016 (updated October 22, 2020).
[364] Tahir H. Wasti, "The Law of Honour-Killing: A British Innovation in the Criminal Law of the Indian Subcontinent," Al-Mahdi Institute [research seminar], n.d., based on journal article by Tahir H. Wasti in *South Asian Studies: A Research Journal of South Asian Studies* 25, no. 2 (2010): 361–411.
[365] Fadia Faqir, "Intrafamily Femicide in Defence of Honour: The Case of Jordan," *Third World Quarterly* 22, no. 1 (2001): 75.
[366] Global Muslim Women's Shura Council, "Jihad Against Violence, Muslim Women's Struggle for Peace," 2017, wisemuslimwomen.org [website], accessed September, 2021
[367] Dr. Jonathan Brown, "The Issue of Apostasy in Islam," Yaqeen Institute for Islamic Research [website], July 5, 2017, (updated October 21, 2020).

Dr. Daisy Khan is an award-winning speaker, author, and activist known for founding the Women's Islamic Initiative in Spirituality and Equality (WISE), a global network promoting peace, gender equality, and human dignity. With over two decades of grassroots involvement in combating anti-Muslim bias, she is a thought leader on Muslim women's rights and Islam in America. Dr. Khan is a bridge builder, producing interfaith programs and specializing in DEI focused on Anti-bias and Islamophobia training.

She founded the first global Muslim women's Shura Council, focusing on publishing position papers on women's issues. To counter Islamophobia, she authored *WISE Up: Knowledge Ends Extremism* and her memoir, *Born with Wings*, depicts her journey as a modern Muslim woman leader.

Dr. Khan is a prolific speaker, lecturing at prestigious institutions and appearing on major media outlets like CNN, BBC, and PBS, and is featured in documentaries and publications like the *Wall Street Journal*, *Newsweek*, *Guardian*, *New York Times*, *Elle*, and many others.

She has received over twenty awards, including the Eleanor Roosevelt Human Rights Award and recognition as one of "21 Women of the 21st Century." Khan was mentioned in *TIME Magazine*'s "100 Most Influential People" and in *Huffington Post* as, "Top Ten Women Faith Leaders, "

Born in Kashmir, she dedicated twenty-five years to architectural design before committing to full-time community service and positive change globally.

www.daisykhan.com

www.ingramcontent.com/pod-product-compliance
Lightning Source LLC
Chambersburg PA
CBHW020636230426
43665CB00008B/196